THE MONARCHY AND THE CONSTITUTION

The Monarchy and the Constitution

VERNON BOGDANOR

CLARENDON PRESS · OXFORD

Oxford University Press, Great Clarendon Street, Oxford OX2 6DP

Oxford New York
Athens Auckland Bangkok Bogota Bombay
Buenos Aires Calcutta Cape Town Dar es Salaam
Delhi Florence Hong Kong Istanbul Karachi
Kuala Lumpur Madras Madrid Melbourne
Mexico City Nairobi Paris Singapore
Taipei Tokyo Toronto Warsaw
and associated companies in
Berlin Ibadan

Oxford is a trade mark of Oxford University Press

Published in the United States by
Oxford University Press Inc., New York

First published 1995
First issued as paperback 1997

British Library Cataloguing in Publication Data
Data available

Library of Congress Cataloging in Publication Data
Data available
ISBN 0–19–827769–5
ISBN 0–19–829334–8 (Pbk)

Printed in Great Britain
on acid-free paper by
Biddles Ltd.,
Guildford and King's Lynn

321.87/

For Judy, Paul, and Adam,
with thanks

PREFACE

The Monarchy and the Constitution seeks to answer the question: 'How does monarchy function in a modern democracy?' The British Constitution is, as Dicey noticed, a 'historic' constitution, the product not of design but of spontaneous development. Of all our institutions, the monarchy is perhaps the one that lies most deeply rooted in our history. Understanding of constitutional monarchy must begin, therefore, with an account of its development through the centuries.

Constitutional monarchy is a monarchy regulated by rules. These rules are of two types. There are, first, rules regulating the sovereign in his or her *personal* capacity—rules regulating *who* shall exercise authority. Secondly, there are rules regulating the sovereign in his or her *constitutional* capacity, as head of state, in relation both to the *executive*—the appointment of a prime minister—and to the *legislature*—the granting or refusal of a dissolution of parliament. These are rules regulating *how* the royal authority should be exercised. Analysis of these rules shows that the personal prerogatives of the sovereign remain very much alive and could again become of importance in a constitutional crisis. Three such constitutional crises are analysed—the conflict over the House of Lords in 1910, the Home Rule crisis of 1914, and the abdication in 1936.

One of the main reasons why the sovereign has rarely been called upon to exercise his or her powers in Britain in the twentieth century is that the two-party system and an electoral system which generally yields a clear majority for one party have made royal intervention unnecessary. But the two-party system is contingent and not inherent in the constitution. In the case of a hung parliament, the sovereign might well have to adopt a more active role; and hung parliaments could become frequent were Britain to adopt proportional representation, a change that is by no means inconceivable.

In addition to appointing a prime minister and dissolving parliament, the sovereign holds two further roles of constitutional significance, roles which can be understood only in the light of history—Supreme Governor of the Church of England and Head of the Commonwealth.

The concluding chapter offers some reflections on the future of constitutional monarchy in Britain, reinforcing what is the central theme of *The Monarchy and the Constitution*—that, under late-twentieth-century conditions, constitutional monarchy, far from being incompatible with democratic government, serves, by giving it legitimacy, both to stabilize and to sustain it.

ACKNOWLEDGEMENTS

I should like to acknowledge the gracious permission of Her Majesty the Queen for allowing me the privilege of using the Royal Archives at Windsor Castle, and for granting me permission to quote from papers in the Archives. I owe an enormous debt of gratitude to Oliver Everett, Librarian, Windsor Castle, and Lady de Bellaigue, the Registrar, for giving me the benefit of their deep knowledge of the history of the monarchy. Pamela Clark, the Deputy Registrar, was kind enough to send me detailed notes on an earlier draft of this book and has saved me from numerous errors and misinterpretations.

I am grateful, also, to Lady Avon and the Avon Trustees for allowing me to quote from the Avon Papers at Birmingham University Library, and to Ben Benedikz, formerly librarian in charge of the special collections at the Library, for many kindnesses. I should also like to thank Melanie Barber for guiding me through the intricacies of Lambeth Palace Library.

I should like to thank Andrew Macdonald of the Public Record Office for sharing with me his unrivalled knowledge of the PRO, and for drawing my attention to files which I would otherwise have missed; Professor Peter Hennessy, with characteristic generosity, has made a number of very helpful suggestions concerning the PRO, even though our views on the monarchy are not quite the same. I should also like to thank Anthony Bevins of the *Observer*, the Honourable Lady Johnston, Professor Ian Machin, Alex May, and Hugo Vickers for generously sending me helpful material; and I am grateful to Frances Adamson of the Australian High Commission in London, who went out of her way to supply me with material about the republican debate in Australia as well as reading and commenting on an earlier draft of Chapter 10 on the Commonwealth.

The chaplain of Brasenose, Revd Dr Grayson Carter, has not only read and commented on the chapter on the Church, but also allowed me free rein of his vast library of works on ecclesiastical history, and introduced me to the intricacies of this subject.

Lord Holme of Cheltenham, formerly Director of the

Constitutional Reform Centre, has generously allowed me to include parts of a pamphlet, 'No Overall Majority: Forming a Government in a Multi-Party Parliament', which I wrote for the Centre in 1986, in Chapter 6 of the book.

Jessica Douglas-Home kindly allowed me to look at an unpublished manuscript on the monarchy by her late husband, Charles, which I hope will in due course be published.

The late Frances Donaldson was kind enough to show me the notes she had made for her biography of Edward VIII, which has always seemed to me one of the best books ever written on the monarchy. I am very grateful to her for her encouragement and I am only sorry that she did not survive to see my own book.

I owe thanks to the following for reading and commenting on either the whole or parts of the manuscript—Dr John Blair, Michael Brock, Dr David Butler, the Rt Hon. Sir Zelman Cowen, the Revd Professor Peter Hinchliffe, Dr Harry Judge, Janet Lewis-Jones, Dr Paul Langford, the Hon. Sir Gavin Lightman, Don Markwell, Dr Geoffrey Marshall, the Hon. Sir Humphrey Maud, Professor Robert O'Neill, the Rt Revd Lord Runcie, Dr E. A. Smith, Michael Steed, and the Very Revd James Weatherhead. They have all improved the text to its great benefit but none of them is to be implicated in my arguments, still less in my errors.

I am grateful also to Tim Barton and Hilary Walford of Oxford University Press for the patience and skill with which they have handled the manuscript; and to Jane Shafto and Pat Spight for their efficient secretarial help.

The Principal and Fellows of Brasenose have provided both intellectual stimulus and warm friendship over many years and I count myself fortunate in being a member of so uniquely enlightened a society.

But my greatest debt is to my wife and to my two sons, Paul and Adam, not only for putting up with my long absences at the word processor, but also for encouraging me throughout.

Vernon Bogdanor

Brasenose College, Oxford
April 1995

CONTENTS

——◼◆◼——

 1. The Evolution of Constitutional Monarchy   1
 2. The Basic Constitutional Rules: The Rules of Succession   42
 3. The Basic Constitutional Rules: Influence and the
    Prerogative   61
 4. The Appointment of a Prime Minister   84
 5. Three Constitutional Crises   113
 6. Hung Parliaments and Proportional Representation   145
 7. The Financing of the Monarchy   183
 8. The Sovereign's Private Secretary   197
 9. The Sovereign and the Church   215
10. The Sovereign and the Commonwealth   240
11. The Future of Constitutional Monarchy   298

Appendices
 1. Sovereigns since Henry VIII   310
 2. British prime ministers since 1782   311
 3. Private secretaries since 1870   313
 4. Member states of the Commonwealth, 1995   314
 5. Some constitutional episodes involving the use of royal
    power since 1900   316

Select Bibliography   318
Index   323

1

The Evolution of Constitutional Monarchy

——◆◆◆——

A monarchy in the strict sense of the term is a state ruled by a single absolute hereditary ruler. A constitutional monarchy, however, is a state headed by a sovereign who rules according to the constitution. Such a constitution may be 'written' and codified, as indeed it is in the vast majority of the constitutional monarchies of the modern world. But Britain is one of only two constitutional monarchies—the other is New Zealand—where the constitution remains 'unwritten' and uncodified.

The term 'constitutional monarchy' seems first to have been used by a French writer, W. Dupré, who wrote in 1801 of 'La monarchie constitutionnelle' and 'Un roi constitutionnel'. In a modern constitutional monarchy, the constitution, whether codified or not, permits the sovereign to perform only a very small number of public acts without the sanction of his or her ministers. Thus today a constitutional monarchy is also a *limited* monarchy: the constitution does not allow the sovereign actually to govern. Macaulay was one of the first, perhaps the very first, to notice this modern meaning of 'constitutional monarchy' when he wrote in 1855 in his *History of England*: 'According to the pure idea of constitutional royalty, the prince reigns, and does not govern; and constitutional royalty, as it now exists in England, comes nearer than in any other country to the pure idea.'[1] A constitutional monarchy, then, can be defined as a state which is headed by a sovereign who reigns but does not rule.

Until the First World War, monarchy was by far the prevalent form of government. Indeed, in 1914 there were only three republican governments in Europe—France, Portugal (whose sovereign had been deposed as recently as 1910), and Switzerland. Not every

[1] Macaulay, *History of England* (1849–61), IV. xvii. 10.

monarchy was constitutional, however. Constitutional monarchy was restricted to Britain, Italy, the Scandinavian monarchies—Denmark, Norway, and Sweden—and the Low Countries—Belgium, Luxembourg, and the Netherlands. Of the three great continental empires, Austria–Hungary might just have been called a constitutional state, but Germany was doubtfully constitutional, and Tsarist Russia certainly was not; nor were the monarchies of the smaller states of Central Europe.

Today, by contrast, although the majority of states in Europe are republics, all of the monarchies which have survived are without doubt constitutional monarchies. Seven European states apart from Britain are monarchies—the three Scandinavian countries, the Low Countries, and Spain (where the monarchy was restored in 1975 after the death of General Franco). These states are amongst the most stable and prosperous in the modern world, and, with the exception of Spain, their history has been one of evolution rather than radical change. The survival of monarchy may indeed be said to symbolize this process of evolutionary change.

II

Of the European monarchies, the British is by far the oldest, except perhaps for that of Denmark. Queen Elizabeth can trace her descent back to Egbert, King of Wessex, in the ninth century; and, except for the brief Cromwellian interregnum between 1649 and 1660, the descendants of Egbert have reigned continuously in Britain for nearly twelve hundred years. It is indeed the remarkable dynastic continuity of the British monarchy which differentiates it from its continental counterparts, and forms perhaps its most striking characteristic.

From very early times, there were attempts to ensure that the sovereign governed, not solely according to his or her own wishes, but according to law. Succession to the throne required more than simply a claim based upon descent. In Anglo-Saxon times it was accepted that a new sovereign had to belong to the royal house, but actual succession depended on the outcome of complex dynastic loyalties and feuds. The succession to the throne would be determined by the leading territorial magnates who comprised the Witan—the council of the sovereign's advisers—which had the power to depose a sovereign who proved inadequate. One can perhaps perceive, in these arrangements, the germs of contractual monarchy bound by statute, which the monarchy was to become after 1689. The sovereign was conceived of as being responsible to the community which the Witan was supposed to represent.

The early Norman kings went through a form of election or 'recognition' by the Witan's successor, the *Commune Concilium*. Obedience was granted in exchange for royal protection. Both William the Conqueror in his coronation oath and Henry I in his coronation charter in 1100 promised to observe the laws of Edward the Confessor, and their subjects in return promised to be faithful. In practice, however, the Norman monarchy tended to absolutism.[2]

The real beginning of the idea of constitutional monarchy dates from Magna Carta in 1215, for the terms of Magna Carta are more precise than the promises of the coronation oath. Magna Carta has been described indeed as a 'first attempt to express in exact legal terms some of the leading ideas of constitutional government'.[3] It consisted of a preamble and sixty-three clauses, the most influential of which concern the freedom of the Church, the redress of feudal grievances concerning land, the need to consult before new taxation is imposed, regulation of the machinery of justice to ensure that justice is available to all, and the need to control the behaviour of royal officials. Perhaps the most important clause was clause 39, which declared that no one could be imprisoned without due process of law.[4]

The significance of Magna Carta, however, lies less in its specific provisions than in the two fundamental principles which it implied. The first principle required the sovereign to rule according to law and to make himself or herself accountable for the way in which he or she ruled. Magna Carta was indeed the first formal document to insist that the sovereign was as much under the rule of law as his or her subjects. The second fundamental principle was that the rights of individuals took precedence over the personal wishes of the sovereign.

[2] Sir William Anson, *The Law and Custom of the Constitution*, ii. *The Crown*, 4th edn., ed. A. Berriedale Keith (Oxford University Press, 1935), pt. I, p. 23.

[3] W. S. Holdsworth, *A History of English Law* (3rd edn., Methuen, 1923), i. 216.

[4] The text of Magna Carta can most conveniently be found in J. C. Holt, *Magna Carta* (Cambridge University Press, 1965), 317 ff. Four original copies of the charter remain extant—two of them are in the British Museum, the third is in Lincoln Castle, and the fourth in Salisbury Cathedral. See also Geoffrey Hindley, *The Book of Magna Carta* (Constable, 1990), and Anne Pallister, *Magna Carta: The Heritage of Liberty* (Oxford University Press, 1971).

Magna Carta not only implied fundamental principles. It also, for the first time, devised means to ensure that the principles were observed. The charter was drawn up by the barons and accepted by King John, at Runnymede, on 19 June 1215, under threat of civil war. Clause 61 of Magna Carta established a council of twenty-five barons who were to ensure that the sovereign observed the charter, and the barons were to have the right of waging war on him if he did not. Magna Carta thus had something of the character of a treaty, under which the king would be granted allegiance by his subjects only in return for recognizing reciprocal duties towards them. Moreover, Magna Carta showed that there was a politically active class developing in England, based primarily upon the barons, but extending to the knights and the gentry. This was of considerable significance for the growth of representative government, and indeed parliament first met during the reign of Edward I (1272–1307).

So fundamental has Magna Carta been to the English self-image that, even though hardly anything of it survives on the statute book, the great nineteenth-century medieval historian Stubbs declared that 'the whole of the constitutional history of England' was but a 'commentary' upon it.[5]

Although the principles embodied in Magna Carta were in no way entrenched but declaratory, and were often to be repudiated in later centuries, they none the less echo through the ages. They were heard in the great constitutional battles of the seventeenth century, when Magna Carta was used by parliamentarians as a weapon against the divine-right theory of the Stuart kings. The jurist Sir Edward Coke, for example, based the Petition of Right of 1628, which proposed further to limit the royal prerogative, upon the principles enshrined in Magna Carta, which was, he claimed, 'declaratory of the principal grounds of the fundamental laws of England'. Magna Carta thus acquired a symbolic significance, enabling reformers to declare that it was they who were the genuine conservatives since they were acting in conformity with long-established principles, and that it was the Stuart kings who, in seeking to undermine these principles, were the real radicals. This, of course, is a familiar motif in Britain's constitutional history.

---

[5] Cited in J. C. Holt, *Magna Carta and Mediaeval Government* (Hambledon Press, 1985), 291.

III

The principles of Magna Carta were elaborated in the Glorious Revolution of 1689, an essentially pragmatic adjustment of the relationship between the sovereign and parliament. The Glorious Revolution achieved two things. First, it changed the line of succession to the throne, showing that parliament could alter the title to the throne in case of royal misgovernment. Secondly, through the Bill of Rights, the Glorious Revolution limited the power of the sovereign so as to prevent abuses of power such as had occurred during the reign of James II.

In contemporary usage, a Bill of Rights, as in the United States, is a code which seeks to limit the powers of government and parliament over the citizen. The Bill of Rights of 1689, however, was something quite different. It sought, not to limit the powers of government or parliament, but to limit the powers of the sovereign *vis-à-vis* parliament, and to establish a parliamentary monarchy.

In 1689 James II, having fled the country, was declared by a Convention Parliament, comprising the House of Commons and the House of Lords meeting together, to have 'abdicated'. The Convention Parliament, breaking with the doctrine of perpetuity by which the sovereign never dies, declared the throne to be vacant, and invited William of Orange and Mary to fill it as joint sovereigns. But William and Mary's claim to the throne could not be based solely on hereditary right, nor ought it, in the Convention's view, to be based solely on the right of conquest. Instead, William and Mary became sovereigns primarily in virtue of an Act of Parliament, although it could be argued that, if James II had abdicated and if, as was alleged, his son was illegitimate, then Mary was the next in line. Nevertheless, it appeared to many that a deliberate breach had been made in the order of succession so as to bring the monarchy once again under the rule of law, as Magna Carta had implied nearly five centuries earlier.

On 12 February 1689 the Convention Parliament drew up a Declaration of Rights, which was presented to William and Mary at a formal ceremony at which they were jointly offered the Crown. The Crown was admittedly not offered on *condition* that William and Mary accepted the Declaration, but the Declaration nevertheless served to remind the new joint sovereigns of the basis under which they were to rule; and, after accepting the Crown in the Banqueting House on 13 February 1689, William promised to fulfil its provisions and 'to preserve your religion, laws and liberties'.

The Bill of Rights is the final legislative form of the Declaration of Rights, and it received the Royal Assent on 16 December 1689.[6] It regulated the succession by making the exclusion of James II and his heirs general and excluding all Catholics and those married to Catholics from the throne. The Coronation Oath Act of 1689 had already required the sovereign to swear to maintain the Protestant religion.

The Bill of Rights linked succession to the throne with the preservation of popular rights and liberties, to be secured through parliament. It severely limited the powers of the sovereign, preventing him or her from suspending laws he or she disagreed with, or executing laws or raising taxation without the consent of parliament. The sovereign was deprived of his or her power to interfere with elections. He or she was also forbidden to interfere with the legal system by establishing personal courts or initiating arbitrary prosecutions. The Stuart kings had used this power for political ends. In the case of *Godden v. Hales*, 1686, for example, James II had dismissed no less than six judges, together with the solicitor-general, to secure the verdict that he wanted. The Act of Settlement in 1701 was to provide that judges should hold office during good behaviour, and could be dismissed only through an address by both Houses of Parliament. The effect of these fundamental provisions was to ensure that parliament was able to function without royal interference.

But the Bill of Rights also provided for guarantees against the abuses of power of which James II and previous Stuart kings had been accused. The sovereign was required to summon parliament regularly, a provision made more precise by the Triennial Act, 1694, requiring parliaments to be summoned at least once every three years. Freedom of speech and debate in parliament were guaranteed. The sovereign was forbidden to maintain a standing army in peacetime without the consent of parliament. Above all, the sovereign was

---

[6] In Scotland, a Claim of Right was passed with broadly equivalent constitutional consequences. The text of the Bill of Rights can most conveniently be found in E. N. Williams, *The Eighteenth Century: 1688–1815: Documents and Commentary* (Cambridge University Press, 1960), 26–33. See also W. A. Speck, *Reluctant Revolutionaries: Englishmen and the Revolution of 1688* (Oxford University Press, 1988).

made largely dependent on parliament for funds. During the reigns of the later Stuarts—Charles II and James II—between 1660 and 1688, the condition of the royal finances became such that sovereigns were able to avoid seeking parliamentary approval for their actions. Indeed, during the last four years of his reign, Charles II had been able to dispense with parliament altogether. Under the provisions of the Civil List Act of 1697, however, the sovereign was made dependent upon parliament for annual grants fixed at the beginning of each reign. During the reign of George II, a revival of trade increased the value of the duties granted on the hereditary revenues which the sovereign had been allowed to retain and threatened to make the sovereign as independent of parliament as Charles II had been. But, in 1760, George III voluntarily surrendered the bulk of the hereditary revenues and was forced to go back to parliament on more than one occasion, under humiliating circumstances. Under the principle requiring 'redress of grievances before supply', the right of MPs to withhold funds if the sovereign failed to comply with their wishes was to be explicitly recognized. The Bill of Rights, therefore, ensured that the sovereign would come to be financially dependent upon parliament.[7]

The Act of Settlement of 1701 gave further definition to the idea of constitutional monarchy. It provided for the succession to the throne as being with Princess Sophia, Electress of Hanover, granddaughter of James I, and her descendants, provided that they were Protestant. In fact, Sophia predeceased Queen Anne in 1714 by some eight weeks, and the throne passed to Sophia's son, the Elector of Hanover, who became George I, King of Britain. The Act of Settlement confirmed that no Catholic nor anyone married to a Catholic could succeed to the throne. It also required the sovereign to be in communion with the Church of England and to swear to maintain it. After the Treaty of Union between England and Scotland in 1707, the sovereign was required to swear to maintain the presbyterian Church of Scotland also.

The Act of Settlement was a further breach with the hereditary right of succession. In terms of hereditary right, there were over fifty descendants of the Stuart kings who had a better claim to the throne than George I. The Act of Settlement thus reinforced the

---

[7] On the financial arrangements, the fundamental works are C. D. Chandaman, *The English Public Revenue, 1660–1688* (Oxford University Press, 1975); and P. G. M. Dickson, *The Financial Revolution* (Oxford University Press, 1967).

fundamental constitutional rule established when William and Mary came to the throne, that parliament had the right both to determine the succession to the throne and also the conditions under which the Crown was to be held.[8]

This process of constitutional evolution from Magna Carta to the Bill of Rights and the Act of Settlement established the principle that in Britain the sovereign owed his or her position not only to hereditary right, but also to the consent of parliament, and that it could be taken away if he or she misgoverned. The implication of the 1689 settlement, enshrined in the coronation oath in which the sovereign promised to govern according to 'the statutes in parliament agreed upon, and the laws and customs of the same', is that the sovereign rules through the consent of parliament. Allegiance to the sovereign is not unconditional but dependent upon the sovereign's keeping to the terms of this oath. Thus the Glorious Revolution not merely altered the succession; it also fundamentally changed the basis on which the sovereign reigned. The sovereign was deprived of the ability to attack the position or the independence of parliament in the constitution. Since 1689, indeed, parliament has met every year and the monarchy has owed its title to parliament. Thus the new settlement made the monarchy into a parliamentary, and therefore constitutional monarchy. From 1689 onwards, the supreme power in the state no longer lay with the sovereign alone, but with the sovereign in parliament. It is perhaps for this reason that one authority regards 1689 as 'a watershed in the political and constitutional history of Eastern and Western Europe. It is the greatest in the sense of being the most effective, of the revolutions that occurred in early modern European history.'[9] In the mid-nineteenth century, Macaulay was to argue that 'It is because we had a preserving revolution in the seventeenth century that we have not had a destroying revolution in the nineteenth.'[10]

---

[8] The text of the Act of Settlement can most conveniently be found in Williams, *The Eighteenth Century*, 56–60.

[9] Lois G. Schwoerer, *The Declaration of Rights 1689* (Johns Hopkins University Press, Baltimore, 1981), 291.

[10] Cited in J. R. Western, *Monarchy and Revolution: The English State in the 1680s* (Blandford Press, 1972), 2.

IV

The 'preserving revolution' of the seventeenth century established the principle of the supremacy of parliament. But, under the eighteenth-century 'mixed constitution', power came in practice to be shared between the sovereign and parliament. 'Content with its practical assertion of the ultimate supremacy of Parliament, it left to the tact and self-interest of subsequent monarchs the avoidance of any constitutional deadlocks that might arise from unwise insistence on the letter of the prerogative.'[11] The precise balance of power depended upon the political vicissitudes of the day.

The sovereign still retained wide powers which could be exercised without parliamentary approval. He or she retained, in particular, the right to appoint and dismiss ministers and to determine general policy. Indeed, until the accession of George I in 1714, it could still be said that the sovereign governed the country, even though required to govern through ministers.[12]

The powers which the sovereign retained enabled him or her to exercise considerable, and sometimes a determining influence on policy. But these powers had to be exercised within a framework of constitutional rules, which precluded arbitrary government. The sovereign's powers depended upon getting a responsible minister to defend him or her in parliament. Within this framework, sovereigns still sought to secure governments which could carry out their policies, but they had to achieve this through methods of political management. They could no longer interfere with elections, but they could seek to influence them. Indeed, George III, seeking to build up a party of his own, became 'the first of the borough-mongering, electioneering gentlemen of England'.[13] Similarly, sovereigns could no longer ignore parliament, but they could seek to influence it. In the eighteenth century, they sought to manage parliament and elections through royal patronage, and parliamentary placemen, the 'King's Friends'. Until 1784, indeed, there were generally around 200 such

---

[11] John B. Owen, *The Rise of The Pelhams* (Methuen, 1957), 35.

[12] Anson, *Law and Customs*, 54: 'Then [before 1714] the King or Queen governed through ministers; now ministers govern through the instrumentality of the Crown.'

[13] L. B. Namier, *England in the Age of the American Revolution* (Macmillan, 1930), 4.

'King's Friends' in the House of Commons who could be relied upon to support whichever ministers the king appointed.[14]

A further factor conducive to royal power was that government was far less dominated by legislation than it has come to be in the nineteenth and twentieth centuries. Governments in the eighteenth century existed primarily to govern rather than to legislate.[15] As late as the 1830s, indeed, Lord Melbourne could tell the House of Lords that the making of laws was 'only a subsidiary and incidental duty of Parliament'.[16] Because legislation played a less important role in government than was later to be the case, George II, even more than George III, 'frequently, and often with impunity,—ignored or over-rode the advice of his ministers;—his was the dominant voice in the conduct of war and diplomacy'.[17]

But the Hanoverian kings, unlike their Stuart predecessors, had to operate through parliament. They had to persuade parliament. They could not, in the last resort, overcome it. It is this factor which distinguishes the constitutional monarchy in eighteenth-century Britain from the personal monarchy in eighteenth-century France before the revolution.[18]

During the period between the Glorious Revolution of 1689 and the Reform Act of 1832, the sovereign's powers were gradually diminished, despite a powerful rearguard action fought by George III; and by the time of the Reform Act, the sovereign's power to determine policy had effectively been reduced to influence. In the eighteenth century, anyone who sought to become a minister would benefit by enjoying the sovereign's support, but such support was becoming neither sufficient nor necessary. George II was unable to

[14] Betty Kemp, *King and Commons, 1660–1832* (Macmillan, 1957), 95. This book offers an excellent account of constitutional developments for the period with which it deals.

[15] Richard Pares, *King George III and the Politicians* (Oxford University Press, 1953), 195.

[16] E. L. Woodward, *The Age of Reform* (2nd edn., Oxford University Press, 1962), 99.

[17] John B. Owen, 'George II Reconsidered' in Anne Whiteman, J. S. Bromley, and P. G. M. Dickson (eds.), *Statesmen, Scholars and Merchants* (Oxford University Press, 1973), 133.

[18] This distinction in my view renders unsustainable the 'revisionist' view of the effects of 1689 put forward by Jonathan Clark in two stimulating books, *English Society, 1688–1832: Social Structure and Political Practice during the Ancien Regime* (Cambridge University Press, 1985), and *Revolution and Rebellion: State and Society in England in the Seventeenth and Eighteenth Centuries* (Cambridge University Press, 1986).

keep Walpole in office in 1742, nor Carteret in 1744. He succeeded admittedly in keeping the elder Pitt out of office for many years, and Pitt complained in 1754 that 'The weight of the irremovable royal displeasure is too heavy for any man to move under . . .'.[19] Yet, in 1756, the king was forced to accept him. Pitt certainly believed that, to remain in office, he needed royal support, which he did his best to cultivate. It was said, indeed, that he bowed so low in the closet that his hooked nose could be seen from behind his bowed legs.[20] The position of the prime minister, however, came gradually to rest not so much on royal support, as upon the support of the Commons; although, in the eighteenth century, 'The longest and most stable administrations—those of Walpole, Pelham, North, and the younger Pitt—were when the crown found a minister who could both serve its needs and command the Commons.'[21]

'Ministers', George II had complained as early as 1744, 'are the kings in this country.'[22] Yet, until the late eighteenth century, ministers were seen as no more than advisers to the sovereign. Their task was to proffer advice, and it was then for the sovereign to consider whether or not to accept that advice. Once the sovereign had made a decision, ministers were under a duty to comply, even if their advice had been rejected. During the first part of the reign of George III, from 1760 until 1783, a genuine constitutional conflict took place between this conception of the relationship between the king and his ministers, and the modern conception according to which the sovereign was required to accept the advice of ministers even if it was unpalatable. The conflict was resolved after the defeat of British troops at Yorktown in 1781 in the American War of Independence, when the king was compelled to accept the resignation of Lord North, and the appointment of the Marquess of Rockingham as his successor. Before accepting office, Rockingham in effect dictated terms to the king by insisting that he would no longer veto American independence. The king, who keenly felt 'the indignity offered to His Person', threatened abdication, but in the end gave way.[23]

Royal power, however, had by no means come to an end. In 1783

---

[19] Cited in John Cannon and Ralph Griffiths (eds.), *The Oxford Illustrated History of the British Monarchy* (Oxford University Press, 1988), 445.
[20] Ibid. 476.   [21] Ibid. 444.   [22] Cited in ibid. 473.
[23] Correspondence of George III, v. 393, cited in Conor Cruise O'Brien, *The Great Melody: A Thematic Biography of Edmund Burke* (Sinclair-Stevenson, 1992), 226. O'Brien gives a penetrating account of the constitutional crisis of 1782.

George III was able to secure the rejection of the India Bill, a measure which sought to reform the East India Company. The Bill was passed comfortably in the Commons by 229 votes to 120, and would, in the normal course of events, have passed in the Lords also, since the government enjoyed a majority in the upper house. Shortly before the second reading in the Lords, however, the king allowed it to be said 'that whoever voted for the India Bill was not only not his friend, but would be considered by him as an enemy',[24] even though the Bill was one that was being proposed by the king's own cabinet. Knowledge of the king's disapproval of the Bill was sufficient for it to be defeated in the Lords.

In 1783 George III followed his campaign against the India Bill by dismissing his government, the Fox–North coalition, and appointing the younger Pitt prime minister. Pitt lacked a majority in the Commons, but the king used his powers of patronage to whittle away the majority against his new prime minister. Despite lacking majority support, Pitt ruled for three months, until the majority against him had been reduced to one. The king then dissolved parliament. The power of the king's name, together with the use of royal influence, which did not exclude bribery, were deployed in Pitt's favour, but there is no doubt, despite the criticisms of Burke, that the unbribed portion of the electorate overwhelmingly supported George III against the Fox–North Coalition. Pitt proved victorious in the general election of 1784 and this seemed an electoral vindication of the course that the king had taken.

Pitt was now to find himself in a stronger position *vis-à-vis* the king than previous prime ministers. George III could not dismiss him as he had dismissed his predecessors, for fear that he would have once more to seek a Whig prime minister and find himself compelled to return to his *bête noire*, Charles James Fox. The degree of independence which Pitt enjoyed has caused one authority to regard him as the first modern prime minister, since he was the first effective head of an administration who was not under the control of the sovereign.[25] Nevertheless, when, in 1785, Pitt sought parliamentary reform, it was the king who in effect stopped it, just as he was later to prevent Catholic Emancipation. Government during this period can best be understood, then, not by analogy with modern concep-

[24] Correspondence of George III, v. 119, cited in O'Brien, *The Great Melody*, 330.
[25] O'Brien, *The Great Melody*, 242.

tions of cabinet government, but as a partnership between the king and a prime minister chosen by him, yet broadly accountable to parliament and to the electorate, both of which were nevertheless open to 'influence' by the king.

Even though the power of the sovereign was weakening after 1784, it still remained an important factor in political calculations. In 1801 George III declared that anyone who voted for Catholic Emancipation, a measure which the king believed would violate his coronation oath to maintain the Protestant religion, was his enemy. In consequence, Pitt insisted on resigning, although the king tried to dissuade him. In 1807 the king in effect dismissed Grenville's Ministry of All the Talents because it refused to accede to the royal request that it would never again propose Catholic Emancipation.

Once, however, it had become accepted that the prime minister owed his or her position, not only to royal favour but also to parliamentary approval, the sovereign's role came inevitably to be limited. The growth of 'connection' in the late eighteenth century—a 'connection' being a group of politicians acting together because animated by a similar set of ideas—circumscribed that influence even more severely. The one factor needed to transform the monarchy into a constitutional monarchy of the modern type was the development of a disciplined party system. In the eighteenth century the ties of 'connection' were far looser than those animating political parties today. But the idea of the legitimacy of opposition was gaining ground, although the phrase 'His Majesty's Opposition' was not actually employed until 1826; and when J. C. Hobhouse first used the words in the House of Commons in that year, it was to the accompaniment of laughter.[26] For much of the eighteenth century it had been regarded as factious to oppose the policy of the king's government; a responsible politician was one who assisted the king, rather than obstructing his advisers. The interests of the sovereign were those of the nation, and anyone who consistently opposed the sovereign rendered himself liable to the accusation of lack of patriotism.

During the eighteenth century, however, the working of monarchy came to be profoundly affected by the development of constitutional conventions, non-legal rules which, nevertheless, acquire a binding force. Conventions play an important part in all constitutions, but

[26] *Oxford English Dictionary*, 2nd edn., x. 869.

are perhaps particularly important in Britain, since the constitution remains uncodified. It may be argued, indeed, that constitutional monarchy became a reality as much through the development of conventions in the eighteenth century as through the seventeenth-century revolution and the enactments which followed it.

The most important of the conventions to develop in the eighteenth century was the principle of responsible government. From 1717 George I began to absent himself from cabinet meetings, his place being taken by the senior minister, who eventually came to be known as the prime minister. Since the time of George I, the sovereign has attended cabinet meetings only on a very small number of formal occasions, or to consider pardons, and since 1837 the sovereign has not attended cabinet at all. Thus the sovereign gradually came to play a smaller role in the general determination of policy.[27] A clear distinction was coming to be drawn between the head of state, the sovereign, and the head of government, the prime minister.

It followed that, if the sovereign was not primarily responsible for the determination of policy, he or she ought not to be held responsible for the outcome. As Palmerston was to put it in 1859:

The maxim of the British Constitution is that the Sovereign can do no wrong, but that does not mean that no wrong can be done by Royal authority; it means that if wrong be done, the public servant who advised the act, and not the Sovereign, must be held answerable for the wrongdoing.[28]

This principle is one of fundamental importance to the development of constitutional monarchy.

It was indeed precisely this principle which was at issue in 1807 when George III demanded pledges from the Whigs, before he would admit them to office, that they would not again bring forward the Catholic question. The Whigs took the view that such a request amounted to a violation of their oath as privy counsellors and contradicted the principle of ministerial responsibility. They conceded that the king had the right to choose his ministers, but contended that he had no right to restrict the advice which they might offer

---

[27] Similarly, in later years, responsible government came to be symbolized by the governor's ceasing to preside in cabinet. This occurred first in Canada in 1854 (Anson, *Law and Custom*, 53 n. 3).

[28] *The Letters of Queen Victoria*, 1st ser., ed. A. C. Benson and Viscount Esher, (John Murray, 1907), iii. 449.

him, for they would then not be wholly responsible for that advice, and this conflicted with the maxim that the king could do no wrong. Thus royal immunity depended upon ministerial responsibility. Ministers could not be called to account for advice if they had already pledged themselves to withhold advice in any area of policy. Although the king carried his point in 1807, never again did the sovereign successfully demand pledges from his ministers. Thus the power to determine policy could no longer be divided between the sovereign and the prime minister. The unrestricted power to give advice had to be in the hands of the government of the day; and the sovereign would have no option but to accept it.

V

In 1810 George III became incurably insane, and his son, the future George IV, became Prince Regent in the following year. The reign of George IV from 1820 to 1830 saw a further weakening of royal power. The growth of a strong Tory party, sustained by the House of Commons, which held office during most of the period of the Napoleonic wars, and then continuously until 1830, altered the conditions of political life and proved an important factor in further constraining the sovereign. George IV, unlike his father, was unable to prevent Catholic Emancipation, which was passed in 1829 against his wishes, and despite the king's threat of abdication. Earlier, in 1824, his only recourse against Canning's recognition of the South American republics of Buenos Aires, Mexico, and Colombia had been to refuse to read the royal speech announcing this step, pleading that he was suffering from gout and had lost his false teeth.[29]

Thus the sovereign was no longer in a position to overcome a determined government. One of the factors causing this change was the rising power of the press and of pressure groups, themselves the product of a newly articulate public opinion which was shaping political issues so that the country was gradually coming to be divided between reformers and conservatives.[30] The passage of Catholic Emancipation in 1829 marks an important watershed in the evolution of constitutional monarchy, by which the sovereign was ceasing to be an independent power in the realm.

[29] Woodward, *The Age of Reform*, 211.
[30] Owen, 'George II Reconsidered', 133.

The conflict between reformers and conservatives came to a head in November 1830, when the prime minister, the Duke of Wellington, declared in the House of Lords against parliamentary reform, a declaration which led to the defeat and resignation of his government. The fact that Wellington retained the support of his sovereign could not save him in the face of a hostile parliamentary majority and he was replaced by the Whig leader, Earl Grey. In April 1831 the new king was forced to grant a dissolution to Grey, so that the government could seek a mandate for parliamentary reform. In 1832 the king had to promise to create peers to overcome the opposition of the House of Lords to the Reform Bill, and he pressed Tory peers to abandon their hostility to the Bill, even though he was himself a very half-hearted reformer.

The 1832 Reform Act seemed to have made parliament the indisputable victor in its conflict with the king. Yet the triumph of parliament was to be short lived, for parliament itself was, even before the reign of Queen Victoria had ended, ultimately to be deposed by a new force unleashed by the Reform Act—the modern organized political party, which, under a democratic system, becomes the final arbiter of who is to govern and what broad lines of policy that government must follow.

VI

The Reform Act of 1832 had fundamental consequences for the evolution of constitutional monarchy. It both abolished rotten and nomination boroughs, and expanded and rationalized the franchise. It stimulated the growth of new electoral organization which could reach out to the new voters. It also stimulated the development of the modern party system.

During the nineteenth century, these two interconnected factors—the expansion of the franchise and the development of organized political parties—were to limit, not the power of the sovereign (that had already been almost wholly undermined before the Reform Act), but his or her influence. As long as parliament was composed of groups and factions, the sovereign could safely manœuvre amongst the various combinations. But, in expanding the electorate, the Reform Act put a premium on party organization and a united appeal to the country. Indeed, the first modern party programme was put forward within two years of the Act, in 1834, when Peel, in his Tamworth Manifesto, abjured reaction, accepted parliamentary reform, and committed the Conservatives to a policy of cautious and moderate progress.

With the rise of party, the sovereign's room for manœuvre came to be severely limited. If a government was supported by a majority in the Commons and that majority remained disciplined, the sovereign would be unable to find an alternative administration. Therefore, he or she had no alternative but to accept the advice of ministers, however unpalatable that might be.

Moreover, the expansion of the electorate and the development of electoral organization made it more difficult for the sovereign to influence general elections. This meant that the sovereign could no longer manage the House of Commons through a party of 'the King's Friends'. As Sir Francis Burdett, a Radical MP, appreciated, 'by the Reform Bill he [i.e. the king] cannot in reality appoint his Ministers, as whoever he appoints must go to large bodies of constituents to be approved'.[31] A government appointed by the sovereign could no longer be sure of endorsement by the electorate. Moreover, since the sovereign was no longer able to influence the outcome of the election, a royal dissolution of parliament, such as George III had undertaken in 1784, would be a risky undertaking. By 1846, indeed, Queen Victoria told Lord John Russell that the sovereign's power of dissolution had become a weapon 'which ought not to be used except in extreme cases and with a certainty of success. To use this instrument and be defeated is a thing most lowering to the Crown and hurtful to the country.'[32]

Since the backing of the Crown was no longer a factor that would enable an administration to win a general election, the Reform Act drastically undermined the sovereign's power to appoint a prime minister, for, unless the prime minister enjoyed support in the country, he or she could not survive. This was shown in 1834, when William IV, following the precedent of 1783, dismissed the Whig prime minister, Lord Melbourne, and appointed a Conservative, Peel, as premier, even though Peel was in a minority in the

[31] Norman Gash, *Reaction and Reconstruction in English Politics, 1832–1852* (Oxford University Press, 1965), 3; chapter 1 of this book, entitled 'The End of the Hanoverian Monarchy', gives the best short picture of the consequences of the Reform Act for the monarchy.

[32] *Letters of Queen Victoria*, 1st ser., ii. 108.

Commons. Peel took office with some reluctance, but in the belief that, if he did not, his sovereign would be humiliated. He obtained a dissolution of parliament, and, in the Tamworth Manifesto, he declared that he 'had a firm belief that the people of this country will so far maintain the prerogative of the King, as to give the Ministers of his choice not an implicit confidence, but a fair trial'.[33]

The Conservatives, however, despite nearly doubling their representation and becoming the largest single party in the House, were still unable to carry the Commons. But, because he believed that the king's government was entitled to a fair trial in the new House, Peel nevertheless sought to continue in office. The king took the eighteenth-century view that 'the confidence, the countenance, and the support of the Sovereign are indispensable to the existence and the maintenance of the Government, so long as the Constitution of the country is monarchical'. The change of administration in 1834 was, he insisted, 'his own immediate and exclusive Act. He removed Ministers whom he considered no longer capable of carrying on the business of the country with advantage, and he called to his councils others whom he considered deserving of his confidence.' Thus any censure on the government 'would be a direct censure passed upon His Majesty's conduct, by a party avowing its determination to force itself upon him, and into his councils, in opposition to his declared principles and sentiments, his wishes and his conscience'. It was, he concluded, 'impossible that he can give his confidence to men so introduced to his councils'.[34] In obedience to the view which held that it was factious to oppose the king's government, the Whigs refrained from any direct vote of censure upon Peel's administration. Since the existence of disciplined blocs in the House of Commons was a new phenomenon, it was not yet appreciated that a parliamentary majority rather than the support of the sovereign was the key factor necessary for a government to remain in office. Yet, by clinging to office without the support of the Commons, Peel laid himself open to the quip that he had every virtue except resignation; and in April 1835 he was finally forced to resign, having been defeated six times within six weeks. William IV was then compelled

[33] Cited in K. B. Smellie, *A Hundred Years of Government* (2nd edn., Duckworth, 1950), 43.

[34] William IV to Peel, 22 Feb. 1835, cited in H. J. Hanham, *The Nineteenth Century Constitution: Documents and Commentary* (Cambridge University Press, 1969), 43–4.

again to accept the Whigs, even though he had declared that he could have no confidence in a Whig government. This was the last occasion on which the sovereign dismissed a government.

VII

When Queen Victoria acceded to the throne on the death of William IV in 1837, she, understandably, failed fully to appreciate the significance of the constitutional revolution that had almost wholly destroyed the power of the sovereign and was severely limiting its influence. She still hankered after the earlier world in which she had been brought up, in which the sovereign was an independent political power able to make and unmake ministries. She was not attuned—how could she have been—to the modern world in which the sovereign's role is one of constitutionally restricted influence rather than power. It is futile, however, to blame her for not acting by the precedents of George V, when the precedents she was familiar with were those of George III and George IV.

From the point of view of the constitutional historian, Queen Victoria's reign can be divided into four distinct phases. The first, which lasted from her accession in 1837 to her marriage to Prince Albert of Saxe-Coburg Gotha in 1840, was characterized by excessive reliance, due to inexperience, on her prime minister, Lord Melbourne. The second phase, which lasted from 1840 to the Prince Consort's death in 1861, was almost a joint monarchy, and was the period of greatest royal influence during the Victorian age. The third phase, lasting from 1861 to around 1876, was characterized by a withdrawal from public life and the beginnings of a republican campaign against the monarchy. The fourth phase, lasting until the queen's death in 1901, was characterized by renewed attempts to exercise royal influence, and blatant partisanship against the Liberal governments of the period and their leader, W. E. Gladstone.

At the beginning of her reign, the queen still regarded the government as *her* government and its ministers as *her* ministers. Her first prime minister was the Whig Lord Melbourne, to whom she grew greatly attached. When he resigned in 1839, she was forced to send for Peel, the Conservative leader. But she continued to seek the advice of the outgoing prime minister during the abortive negotiations for the formation of a Conservative government, and this gave rise to the 'Bedchamber incident': Peel sought, as a mark of confidence, that the queen remove those Ladies of the Bedchamber who were related to the outgoing Whig ministers. This the queen refused to do. Peel accordingly refused to take office, and the Whigs once again took up the reins of government.

The 'Bedchamber incident' led to much personal unpopularity for the new queen. 'It is', declared Greville, 'a high trial of our institutions when the caprice of a girl of nineteen can overturn a great ministerial combination.'[35] Following the incident, the royal toast was received in silence at Tory banquets, and, in her later years, the queen realized that she had made a mistake. Much later in her reign, she was to tell her private secretary that Melbourne had been 'an excellent man, but too much of a party man and made me a party Queen'.[36]

That Queen Victoria should have been 'a party Queen' accorded with the precedents governing the actions of the monarchy. During the eighteenth and nineteenth centuries, the political opinions of the sovereign were open and avowed. No one doubted, for example, that George III was a Tory; while, on the accession of Queen Victoria, Greville declared that 'No one can deny that [it] has given the Whig Government an advantage over the Tories. Hitherto the Government have been working against the stream, inasmuch as they had the influence of the Crown dead against them',[37] while the Duke of Wellington was to complain of 'being governed by a Sovereign who is the head of an adverse party'.[38] All the same, the 'Bedchamber incident' was to prove the last occasion on which a sovereign was able to frustrate the formation of a government to which she was politically opposed.

In 1840 the queen married Prince Albert of Saxe-Coburg Gotha, and this ended her emotional dependence upon Melbourne. Albert eased the transition to the Peel government after Melbourne was defeated in the general election of 1841. When Peel took office, the queen at first sought to continue her correspondence with her former prime minister, but Peel insisted that this come to an end, and

[35] Greville, *Diaries*, ed. Lytton Strachey and Roger Fulford (Macmillan, 1938), iv. 169, 12 May 1839.

[36] Giles St Aubyn, *Queen Victoria* (Sinclair-Stevenson, 1991), 115.

[37] Cited in Ivor Jennings, *Cabinet Government* (3rd edn., Cambridge University Press, 1959). 329 n.

[38] Cited in ibid. 330–1.

Albert supported Peel. The queen soon came to accept Peel on the same terms as Melbourne. From 1841 until the formation of Disraeli's second government in 1874, she assumed a position of broad neutrality between the parties. The sovereign began to work with, rather than against, the grain of politics, concerned to co-operate with and sustain her governments rather than frustrating or obstructing them.[39]

The Times described the general election of 1841 as a 'Triumph over the Influence of the Court'.[40] It was the first election which failed to return a government enjoying the favour of the sovereign. Before 1841, no prime minister appointed by the sovereign had lost a general election. The election of 1841, indeed, marked a fundamental change in the relationship between the sovereign and the electorate. Before that date, general elections had tended to *follow* changes of government, rather than preceding them, as is the case today. The purpose of a general election had been, as in 1784, to endorse the sovereign's choice of prime minister. It was, therefore, considered dishonourable for a prime minister to seek a dissolution unless there were a real prospect of increasing his strength, since the act of dissolution was considered the personal act of the sovereign and not of the government. Thus the Prince Consort's private secretary begged Melbourne in 1841 not to dissolve 'unless he thought there was some prospect of increasing his strength, and begged him to remember that what was done would not be considered the act of the Government but that of himself and the Queen, and that he individually would be held as the responsible person'.[41] Lord Brougham, a former lord chancellor, told Queen Victoria in 1841 that for a prime minister to seek a dissolution when the opposition might win would be 'perverting to the mere purposes of party the exercise of by far the most eminent of the Royal prerogatives'; while 'I pass over as wholly unworthy of notice the only other supposition which can with any decency be made . . . namely, that of a dissolution in entire ignorance of the national opinion and for the purpose of ascertaining to which side it inclines'.[42] Nevertheless, defeated on a no-confidence motion in the Commons, Melbourne dissolved in 1841 instead of resigning, thus exposing Queen Victoria to what she

---

[39] Gash, *Reaction and Reconstruction*, 29.

[40] Cited in E. T. Galpin, 'Social and Political Aspects of the British Monarchy', Cambridge M.Litt. thesis (1952), 21–2.

[41] *Letters of Queen Victoria*, 1st ser., i. 337.   [42] Ibid. i. 369.

thought of as a personal humiliation when Peel won the ensuing general election; and in 1846 the queen told Russell that 'she strongly feels that she made a mistake in allowing the Dissolution in 1841; the result has been a majority returned against her of nearly one hundred votes'.[43] Although the Conservatives won a majority, Melbourne decided to meet parliament, but resigned after being defeated on an amendment to the address.

This, then, was a further stage in the weakening of the power of the sovereign. In 1782, when George III had been compelled to accept Rockingham, it was clear that a determined parliamentary majority could force upon the sovereign a prime minister who lacked royal confidence. In 1830, when William IV could not save Wellington, it had become clear that royal confidence was of no avail when a prime minister had lost the confidence of the Commons. In 1841 it had become apparent that the confidence of the sovereign was of little use if a prime minister did not also enjoy the confidence of the electorate. Peel did not understand this development. As a man who still retained many of the instincts of an eighteenth-century man of government, he saw himself as the servant of the Crown, rather than of his party or of the people, a factor that led to his downfall in 1846 when he insisted upon repealing the Corn Laws in opposition to the instincts of the bulk of his party. Yet, had Peel's position been dependent upon royal confidence, he would never have become prime minister. It was the electorate and not his sovereign who had given him office in 1841.

The general election of 1841 did not, however, immediately set the pattern for the future. Between 1841 and 1868, every government fell, not through defeat at the polls, but through defeat in the Commons, defeat in a House which had been elected to support it. This was the result, not of royal intervention, but of the flux of parties which followed the repeal of the Corn Laws in 1846 and the split in the Conservative Party between the Peelites and the protectionists. The incipient two-party system of 1841 was broken up and replaced by a group system incapable of creating a stable majority. The absence of such a stable majority, although in no way due to royal action, gave the sovereign some room for manœuvre, and it was indeed during the middle years of her reign between 1846 and 1868 that Queen Victoria's influence was probably at its greatest.

[43] *Letters of Queen Victoria*, 1st ser., ii. 108.

Even during these years, however, her position was much weaker than George III's had been. Fox, having incurred the displeasure of George III in 1772, spent thirty-two of the remaining thirty-four years of his life in opposition. Palmerston, despite incurring the displeasure of the queen, who caused his resignation from the Foreign Office in 1851, nevertheless returned to government the following year, and was in power for all but two of the remaining fourteen years of his life, nine of them as prime minister.

VIII

Queen Victoria's non-partisanship during the middle period of her reign was in large part the result of the new political configuration following the Reform Act. But it was also due to the influence of Prince Albert who became Prince Consort in 1857, having been known unofficially by that title for many years previously. After the birth of their first child, in November 1840, the prince was given a key to government boxes and he became accustomed to attend audiences with the queen. He became, in Lord John Russell's words, 'an informal but potent member of all Cabinets'.[44]

Prince Albert was as devoted a partisan of Peel as the queen had been of Melbourne. He went so far as publicly to indicate his support for Peel by attending the House of Commons in February 1846, the first night of the debate on the repeal of the Corn Laws, and was duly rebuked by Lord George Bentinck, leader of the Protectionist wing of the Conservatives. But, after Peel's defeat in 1846, the prince ceased to be a party man. Indeed, it may be argued that Prince Albert's fundamental contribution to the development of constitutional monarchy was to insist that the Crown remain above party. It was he who, together with Queen Victoria, first began to adopt the methods that characterize the modern working of constitutional monarchy.

'The manner in which the Queen, in her own name, but under the influence of the Prince,' the diarist Greville reported Lord Clarendon as saying on 19 October 1857, when Albert was made Prince Consort,

[44] Cited in Robert Rhodes James, *Albert, Prince Consort* (Hamish Hamilton, 1983), 271.

exercised her functions was exceedingly good, and well became her position, and was exceedingly useful. She held each minister to the discharge of his duty and his responsibility to her, and constantly desired to be furnished with accurate and detailed information about all important matters, keeping a record of all the reports that were made to her, and constantly recurring to them . . . and again weeks or months afterwards referring to these returns and desiring to have everything relating to them explained and accounted for and so throughout every department. This is what none of her predecessors ever did, and is in fact the act of Albert, who is to all intents and purposes King, only acting entirely in her name. All his views and notions are those of a constitutional sovereign, and he fulfils the duties of one, and at the same time makes the Crown an entity and discharges the functions which properly belong to the Sovereign.[45]

Albert's 'views and notions' were not, however, despite Greville, 'those of a constitutional sovereign' in the modern sense. Albert took the view that the sovereign should remain detached from parties so as to be in a stronger position to influence policy, an influence which could be exerted all the more effectively because he or she was not partisan. He was considerably influenced in his view of the functions of monarchy by Baron Stockmar, who had previously been an adviser to the King of the Belgians. But Stockmar's grasp of the British Constitution was not wholly secure, being, in Gladstone's words, 'only an English top-dressing on a German soil'.[46]

In fact, Stockmar sought, through Albert, to introduce an ideology of monarchy into British life. The monarchy for him was an estate of the realm, since, unlike politicians, who were inevitably partisan, the monarch alone represented the state. Stockmar persuaded Albert that the sovereign could be a kind of umpire or arbiter who could use his or her powers in an independent manner for the good of the nation. The sovereign, then, could be the guide to the nation. He or she should, therefore, be neutral between parties, but only because that would enable him or her to exert more influence upon legislation, and increase the influence of the monarchy. Albert sought to *strengthen* the monarchy as a political factor in the realm. The prince believed that the sovereign was, as it were, a permanent prime minister, to whom the temporary head of the cabinet was required to appeal. He thought that the sovereign had a right to preside at every meeting of the cabinet, and even that a sagacious sov-

---

[45] Greville, *Diaries*, vii. 305, 19 Oct. 1857.
[46] W. E. Gladstone, *Gleanings of Past Years* (John Murray, 1879), ii. 84.

ereign should 'take his share in the preparatory arrangements of party organisation'.

Nowhere [Albert declared], does the Constitution demand an indifference on the part of the sovereign to the march of political events . . . Why are princes alone to be denied the credit of having political opinions based upon an anxiety for the national interests and honour of their country and the welfare of mankind? Are they not more independently placed than any other politician in the State? Are their interests not most intimately bound up with those of their country? Is the sovereign not the natural guardian of the honour of his country, is he not necessarily a politician?[47]

Albert believed that the monarchy's independent role was of particular importance in the field of foreign affairs, where he was a supporter of conservative and legitimist monarchies of the Continent against the liberal tendencies of the governments of the day. In 1843 Albert wrote to his cousin, Ferdinand, King of Portugal, without Peel's knowledge, revealing that he disagreed with the policies being pursued by his prime minister. He was later to brief newspapers and to plant articles in them in favour of Austrian rule in Poland and in Italy, a position which conflicted with the standpoint of the Whig governments of Lord John Russell and Lord Palmerston.

Albert's philosophy of monarchy was quite against the trends of the times, and could have led to serious difficulties with the queen's ministers. The main reason why the difficulties were so few is to be found in the flux of parties after 1846, which gave the queen and Prince Albert quite exceptional room for manœuvre, so that, after 1846, it became acceptable and even necessary for the sovereign to play an important role in the formation of governments. It was, in large part, through royal influence that the coalition government led by Lord Aberdeen came into existence in 1852, although this influence proved insufficient to maintain it in power after the disasters of the Crimean war. Royal influence was also to prove important in the formation of the next government in 1855, led by Palmerston, whose robust patriotism had partially overcome royal distrust, and it played its part also in the formation of Palmerston's second government in 1859.

It has been said that, in the late 1850s, 'To discuss the influence of the crown is to discuss the influence of the Prince.'[48] The Prince

[47] Cited in Rhodes James, *Albert, Prince Consort*, 218.

[48] C. H. Stuart, 'The Prince Consort and Ministerial Politics, 1856–9', in H. Trevor-Roper (ed.), *Essays in English History* (Macmillan, 1964), 69.

Consort's influence was generally employed in the direction of con-ciliation, and his last political initiative, in 1861, was to cause Palmerston to modify a harsh diplomatic note to the Northern states in the American civil war, whose tone might otherwise have led to a breach of diplomatic relations.

It was because of the flux of parties after 1846, rather than the Prince Consort's philosophy of monarchy, that the constitutional functions of monarchy were carried out so effectively during the Prince Consort's lifetime. Bagehot, writing in 1865, was to declare that 'it is only during the period of the present reign that in England the duties of a constitutional sovereign have ever been well per-formed'.[49] In 1858 Count Vitzthum, the Saxon Minister in London, summed up the role of the sovereign in the mid-Victorian Constitution:

What is called the British Constitution is like a whist party *à trois*. The dummy is public opinion. The House of Commons has now for many years been holding this dummy. The Crown and the House of Lords have, there-fore, been obliged to play against it . . . The House of Lords has lost many a trick. I must admit, however, that the Crown's hand has not been played so well for a long time as it has been of late years.[50]

On the Prince Consort's death in December 1861, Disraeli told Lord Stanley that he

had undoubtedly a fixed determination to increase the personal power of the Crown: had he lived to add to his great industry and talent the weight which age and long experience would have given in dealing with statesmen of his own standing, he might have made himself almost as powerful as the Prime Minister of the day.[51]

Disraeli also declared that 'If he had outlived some of our "old stagers", he would have given us, while retaining all our constitu-tional guarantees, the blessings of absolute government.'[52] What he may have meant by this delphic utterance was that the Prince Consort would have elevated the constitutional position of the sov-ereign, since, in Albert's view, only the sovereign could comprehend

[49] Walter Bagehot, *The English Constitution*, in *Collected Works*, ed. Norman St John-Stevas (The Economist, 1974), v. 258.

[50] Cited in Stuart, The Prince Consort', 269.

[51] *Disraeli, Derby and the Conservative Party: Journals and Memoirs of Edward Henry, Lord Stanley, 1849–1869*, ed. John Vincent (Harvester Press, 1978), 180–1.

[52] Robert Blake, *Disraeli* (Eyre & Spottiswoode, 1966), 431.

the true interests of his or her people and acquire a dispassionate view of the public good. It is unclear, however, how such a position would have proved compatible with the development of party government, and it was perhaps fortunate that the Prince Consort did not have to put his theories to the test in the late-Victorian period when politics was coming to be dominated by organized political parties. Indeed, Albert's conception of monarchy could have caused constitutional as well as political difficulties for the sovereign's relations with her ministers. The constitution makes no provision for a joint monarchy, since it is only the sovereign and not her consort who, being required to act on advice, is protected by the principle of ministerial responsibility to parliament.

From the 1870s, indeed, Victoria sought to resurrect the Prince Consort's notion of the sovereign as an independent power in politics, adopting, however, a far more partisan position than Albert would ever have allowed himself. The main significance of the queen's reign from 1861, however, was the failure of the attempt to make the monarchy an independent power in politics, for the growth of organized parties pushed the sovereign, somewhat against her will, above party.

The period of party flux came to an end in 1868, when, for the second time—1841 having been the first—a prime minister came to be designated through a general election. But in 1868, by contrast with 1841, Disraeli, having been defeated by Gladstone, resigned without bothering to meet parliament, thus acknowledging that it was public opinion and not the House of Commons which made and unmade governments. Thus the century-long conflict between the sovereign and parliament was finally resolved, not through the victory of either side to the conflict, but by the triumph of a new force, the force of public opinion making itself felt through party, a force which lay beyond the power of the sovereign to influence. It was now apparent that a government, even if it had the support of the House of Commons, had also to secure the support of the voters, and the sovereign could no longer influence the voters to return his or her preferred choice as prime minister. With public opinion now being the motive force of government, there was a fundamental change in the character of monarchy. The means by which the sovereign could exert influence came to change. It was not so much that the influence of the monarchy declined, but rather that it had to be exercised in a different manner, a manner that was both impartial and also private.

IX

These developments were, quite understandably, hidden both from the queen and from most of her ministers, who continued to act as if the old style of monarchy remained in place. The queen herself reacted to the death of the Prince Consort by withdrawing almost completely from public life and in the 1860s she came to be known as the 'Widow of Windsor'.

In the late 1860s and early 1870s there was a brief flurry of republicanism, a novel development in British politics. The Hanoverian monarchs had not been particularly respected, and yet, in the days before popular politics, there had been no organized movement against the monarchy. Moreover, republicanism amongst the working-class Chartist movement in the 1830s and 1840s had been comparatively muted. Chartist leaders called on the sovereign to dismiss ministers, but they did not call for the removal of the monarchy, which was seen as something separate from and even above the reactionary politicians who temporarily served it.

The seclusion of the queen after 1861 was a primary cause of republicanism in Britain. But republicanism was becoming an international phenomenon. After the abdication of Emperor Napoleon III in France in 1870, 'La Marseillaise' was sung in Trafalgar Square, and speakers looked forward to a 'Republic of England'. American influence was also strong amongst many on the Left. In 1871 a meeting of the London Republican Club was attended by 18,000 members, and the radical Charles Bradlaugh, later to achieve notoriety as the first avowed atheist to be returned to the Commons, published a republican pamphlet entitled 'Impeachment of the House of Brunswick'. The cause was taken up by the aristocratic radical Sir Charles Dilke, who, in a speech at Newcastle in November 1871, became the first Member of Parliament to declare himself a republican. He was in fact descended from no less than three men who had condemned Charles I to death.[53] Dilke was supported by his friend, the radical mayor of Birmingham, Joseph Chamberlain, who was to enter the Commons in 1876, and who told

---

[53] Peter Marsh, *Joseph Chamberlain: Entrepreneur in Politics* (Yale University Press, 1994), 115.

Dilke in 1871 that 'The Republic must come, and at the rate at which we are moving, it will come in our generation.'[54]

In November 1871, however, the Prince of Wales, the future Edward VII, was stricken with typhoid fever, and seemed, at one time, near to death. Upon his recovery, a thanksgiving service was held, in February 1872, at St Paul's, and this is generally held to mark the end of republican sentiment. In the following month, Dilke moved in the Commons a motion for an inquiry into the Civil List, but found himself supported by only two other MPs. The last republican conference was held at Birmingham in 1873, but Chamberlain did not come, and in 1874, as mayor, he received the Prince and Princess of Wales. In 1882 Dilke repudiated his early republicanism as 'opinions of political infancy'; and, since that date, there has never been any significant popular republican movement in Britain. The British Left, whether radical or socialist, has in general been as monarchist as the Conservative Party; and those on the Left who held republican sentiments have recognized that to attack the monarchy would alienate popular support. In 1933 Harold Laski, the socialist intellectual, who had criticized the role of George V during the 1931 crisis, confessed that the Labour Party could not hope to abolish the monarchy, since it was too popular. The best it could hope for was to demand that the throne be 'automatically neutral'.[55]

How strong was the republican movement in the 1860s? The positivist Frederic Harrison argued that

there is a very wide and deep republican feeling more or less definite and conscious. In London and the great cities the bulk of the working-classes are republican by conviction, unless where they are perfectly indifferent. There are a score of towns in the north and centre where the republican feeling is at fever-heat . . . Our whole cast of action and of life is now so essentially republican, that to any thoughtful mind hereditary monarchy as a principle can present itself only as a conspiracy or mummery.[56]

Yet, although it is impossible to gauge accurately the state of public opinion in Victorian times, it would be a mistake to deduce from the support given to leaders such as Bradlaugh and Dilke that the republican movement was a strong one. The objections of the public in the 1860s were perhaps not so much to monarchy as an

---

[54] Cited in Dorothy Thompson, *Queen Victoria: Gender and Power* (Virago, 1990), 104.
[55] Ibid. 125.   [56] Cited in Hanham, *The Nineteenth Century Constitution*, 35.

institution but to the fact that they never saw the monarch. Such popular criticism as there was directed itself not to the issue of extravagance, which Dilke highlighted, as to the absence of ceremony and colour associated with monarchy. Lord Halifax was probably nearer to the truth than Frederic Harrison when, in August 1871, he told the queen's private secretary, Henry Ponsonby, that 'the mass of the people expect a King or a Queen to look and play the part. They want to see a Crown and Sceptre and all that sort of thing. They want the gilding for their money.'[57] Paradoxically, the criticism was that there was too little monarchy, not too much. The monarchy, as both Bagehot and Disraeli were to appreciate, was becoming an emotional focus for the newly enfranchised masses. This meant that the ceremonial and symbolic functions were now part of its very essence. During her period of seclusion, the queen worked assiduously at her papers, and fulfilled all of her constitutional functions. But this mattered little to her subjects, many of whom, no doubt, were quite unaware of what these constitutional functions amounted to. What they missed was not the constitutional but the theatrical side of monarchy. 'To be invisible', wrote Bagehot, 'is to be forgotten . . . To be a symbol, and an effective symbol, you must be vividly and often seen.'[58] So it was that 'the Queen has done almost as much to injure the popularity of the monarchy by her long retirement from public life as the most unworthy of her predecessors did by his profligacy and frivolity'.[59]

X

The final phase of Queen Victoria's reign was marked by a strong anti-Liberal partisanship, which led her to undermine her Liberal governments and encourage her Conservative ones. Part of the reason for this partisanship was personal—the development of a close friendship with Disraeli and a bitter antagonism towards Gladstone. But the personal element in the queen's attitudes has probably been exaggerated. The queen was just as hostile to Gladstone's Liberal successor, Lord Rosebery, prime minister from 1894 to 1895, who was her own choice, as she had been to Gladstone; and she was as

[57] Arthur Ponsonby, *Henry Ponsonby, Queen Victoria's Private Secretary: His Life from his Letters* (Macmillan, 1943), 72.
[58] Bagehot, *Collected Works*, v. 419.   [59] Ibid. 431.

sympathetic to Lord Salisbury, Disraeli's successor as Conservative leader, as she had been to Disraeli himself.

Upon his appointment in 1870, the queen's private secretary, Sir Henry Ponsonby, noticed the strongly anti-Liberal orientation of the court. The queen's predilections towards the Conservatives were strengthened by Gladstone's approach, in opposition, to the Eastern Question in 1876. In attacking Disraeli's policy towards the Ottoman Empire, Gladstone was, in the queen's view, breaking the convention of bi-partisanship in foreign policy and undermining the national interest. Gladstone's general hostility to imperialism was seen by the queen as opposition to the extension of her own rule, and a willingness to surrender territory over which she reigned. But the queen was shocked as much by the methods which Gladstone employed in his attack on Disraeli's government, as by the attack itself. Gladstone was the first political leader to take his case to the people by conducting a popular agitation in the country, something that had previously been undertaken only by radicals outside the magic circle of those likely to be called to office.

In 1880, after the Liberal victory in the general election, the queen did not call upon Gladstone to form a government, but upon Lord Hartington, the Liberal leader in the Commons.[60] This was technically correct, but ignored the crucial political fact that Gladstone was responsible for the Liberal victory and that no Liberal government could be formed without him at its head. In December 1879 Lord Hartington had declared that 'There is not room for argument about the proposition that the man who leads the Liberal Party out of doors ought to lead it in Parliament. It is only fair to the Queen, to the country, to the party, that this should be acknowledged at once.'[61] It was understandable, however, that Queen Victoria should be slow to understand that the expansion of the franchise meant that what happened outside parliament was coming to determine what happened inside the Palace of Westminster and that the political centre of gravity was coming to be moved away from parliament to the platform. The growth of party was coming to deprive the sovereign of the power to choose the prime minister. This power would now be exercised by the party itself, as it was for the first time in 1880.

[60] Hartington, being the eldest son of a duke, enjoyed a courtesy title and so was not debarred from sitting in the Commons.

[61] Cited in Smellie, *A Hundred Years of Government*, 132.

During Gladstone's second ministry, the queen lost no opportunity of harassing or obstructing her government, and when, in 1885, Gladstone declared for Home Rule, a policy which the queen believed would lead to the break-up of her kingdom, her hostility knew no bounds. She intrigued, behind Gladstone's back, with Whig members of his party, to form a 'patriotic' coalition with the Conservatives which could defeat Home Rule and she informed opposition leaders of her conversations with her prime minister. By the end of her reign, the queen was, without question, a Conservative partisan.

Little of this was known, however, to the wider public, for there were only two occasions on which the queen's views were publicly announced. The first was in 1876, when Disraeli made it clear that it was the queen's wish that she be given the title Empress of India. The second was in 1885, after the murder of General Gordon in Khartoum, when the queen sent a telegram *en clair* to the government deploring its negligence. Gladstone's response to this telegram was to threaten resignation. If Gladstone had resigned, the queen's name would have been brought into politics and the monarchy threatened. But Gladstone, a strong monarchist, exercised considerable, perhaps superhuman restraint, in dealing with the queen's incessant harassment. It is due to him as much as to Disraeli that, until the publication of the third series of Queen Victoria's letters between 1930 and 1932, the general public had little idea of the extent of the queen's partisanship. So it was that, by the end of her reign, Victoria was seen by most of her subjects not as a fervent party politician but as Britain's first constitutional monarch.

XI

Paradoxically, however, the final period of Queen Victoria's reign, when she was at her most partisan, was also the period when she exercised the least influence. One of her most important personal prerogatives—the right to appoint the prime minister—had come to be severely circumscribed, while another—the right to veto the appointment of individual cabinet ministers—had been entirely extinguished. The reign of Queen Victoria also saw the end of the sovereign's supposed special responsibility for foreign affairs and the army, these areas of policy coming to fall under the general rules of ministerial responsibility and advice.

William IV, when he appointed Melbourne and Peel as prime ministers in 1834, was also appointing the leaders of the Whig and Tory parties. In the same way, Queen Victoria would make Salisbury in 1885 and Rosebery in 1894 the leaders of their respective parties. But, as we have seen, the expansion of the electorate and the growth of organized parties severely limited the sovereign's scope in appointing a prime minister. When, in 1880, Victoria tried to avoid appointing Gladstone, she was rebuffed, since it was clear that the Liberals would serve under no one else. The Liberal Party, or rather Liberal voters, insisted upon Gladstone.

The selection of Rosebery in 1894 seems at first sight a counter-example. The Queen did not consult the outgoing prime minister, Gladstone, who would have preferred Lord Spencer to have succeeded him, while the majority of Liberal MPs seem to have preferred Sir William Harcourt. The queen, however, was under no obligation to consult Gladstone, who was resigning because he had been repudiated by his cabinet on the issue of a reduction in naval expenditure. Gladstone had thus lost the authority which gave him the right to be consulted; and in any case Lord Spencer later declared that he would not have accepted appointment as premier. As for Harcourt, Liberal cabinet ministers would probably not have served under him, since they regarded him as an impossible colleague. Harcourt's biographer himself admits that 'Lord Rosebery was already emerging as the choice of the Cabinet'.[62] Had the Liberals seriously wished to serve under someone other than Rosebery, they could have acted as they undoubtedly would have done in 1880 had Hartington been nominated for the premiership; they could have refused to serve. In fact, however, the majority of the Liberal cabinet in 1894 seems definitely to have preferred Rosebery. Thus, 'the Queen was working with the grain of politics when she sent for Rosebery. She was exercising a casting vote rather than expressing a purely personal preference.'[63]

So, from having a fairly wide choice, the power of the sovereign in appointing a prime minister was coming to be severely restricted since the queen was required to choose the person who was most acceptable to the cabinet and whom the governing party also would accept. It was perhaps only a logical consequence that, rather than relying upon the sovereign to judge, perhaps inaccurately, the state

[62] A. G. Gardiner, *Life of Sir William Harcourt* (Constable, 1923), ii. 262.
[63] G. H. L. LeMay, *The Victorian Constitution* (Duckworth, 1979), 89.

of opinion, the parties would themselves elect their leader, so almost totally depriving the sovereign of the prerogative of choosing the prime minister.

During the latter part of Victoria's reign, the sovereign also lost the power to choose or to veto ministerial appointments against the wish of a determined premier and a united cabinet. The most that the queen could do was to ensure that ministers whom she disliked, such as Chamberlain, in his radical phase, and Dilke, were not given offices that brought them into personal contact with her. The only ministerial appointment which she successfully vetoed in the latter part of her reign was that of Henry Labouchere—a radical who had insulted the royal family—in 1892. But Labouchere had little popular following, and Gladstone was perhaps not too distressed at his exclusion. After the death of Queen Victoria in 1901, no sovereign was able to veto the appointment of a minister.

A wholly new conception of the monarchy was gradually coming into being during the latter part of Queen Victoria's reign. In place of power and partisanship, the sovereign was coming to be seen as above the political battle, so that his or her influence would be used, not for partisan purposes, but in a neutral and detached way. This subtle change in the evolution of monarchy was not generally understood during the Victorian era. Some believed that the decline of monarchical power would render the monarchy a cipher, a mere machine for undertaking various state acts, 'nothing but a mandarin figure which has to nod its head in assent, or shake it in denial, as his Minister pleases'.[64] In reality, however, during the Victorian era the monarchy, almost despite itself, was developing a new form of influence, one which relied for its efficacy on being exercised in private and in an entirely non-partisan way. It was, paradoxically, Gladstone, so often the victim of Queen Victoria's harassment, who was the first to have understood that there had been a 'subtle and silent, yet an almost entire transformation' in the role of the sovereign which 'may chiefly be perceived in a beneficial substitution of influence for power'; and that this influence conferred 'much benefit on the country without in the smallest degree relieving the advisers of the Crown from their undivided responsibility'.[65]

---

[64] Baron Stockmar to the Prince Consort, 1854, cited by Robert Blake, 'The Crown and Politics in the Twentieth Century', in Jeremy Murray-Brown (ed.), *The Monarchy and its Future* (Allen & Unwin, 1969), 11.

[65] Gladstone, *Gleanings*, i. 38, 41.

Queen Victoria was slow to appreciate, if she ever did, that the growth of party meant the inevitable limitation of her prerogative. In the future, it would only be when party lines became fluid, as in 1886, 1916, or 1931, or when it fell to the sovereign to choose a new prime minister in the absence of a party mechanism for selecting a leader, as in 1894 or 1923, or during a period of chronic constitutional crisis, such as occurred during the years 1910–14, that the sovereign would be able to exercise real power.

The monarchy, no longer encumbered by partisanship, could assume a new role as mediator between the parties during periods of acute political controversy, especially when this involved conflict between the House of Commons and the House of Lords. Victoria was the first sovereign to take this role seriously. In 1867 she sought to persuade the Conservatives not to oppose the Liberal Reform Bill, and then to persuade the Liberals to support the Conservative Bill. In 1869 and 1884–5 she mediated between the Liberal government and the Conservative opposition, dominant in the Lords, so as to prevent a clash between the two Houses. Edward VII was to attempt to mediate in the crises caused by the House of Lords' rejection of the Education Bill of 1906 and Lloyd George's 'People's Budget' of 1909. George V, in 1914, on Irish Home Rule, in 1915, over conscription, and in 1916 and 1931, when coalition governments were formed, held inter-party conferences at Buckingham Palace in an attempt to resolve differences. This use of the sovereign's symbolic powers to mediate presupposed that the head of state was politically neutral and above party.

The new role of the sovereign, then, depended upon influence rather than power. But the extent of the influence which the sovereign could exert would depend upon his or her assiduity in studying and understanding government policy. In this respect, Queen Victoria set to her successors an example of massive conscientiousness. It was, she declared, her 'great aim to follow the Prince's plan, which was to sign nothing until he had read it and made notes upon what he signed'.[66] It was not easy, however, for the sovereign to keep himself or herself informed before the formation of the Cabinet Secretariat in 1916, which instituted regular procedures for circulating the sovereign with cabinet papers. The extent to which sovereigns were informed before 1916 depended largely on the industry of the

[66] W. L. Arnstein, 'The Queen Opens Parliament: The Disinvention of Tradition', *Historical Research*, 63 (1990), 192.

prime minister and ministers concerned with particular proposals. Before 1916 there was no published cabinet agenda, and the sovereign would not know what was going to be discussed unless the prime minister provided the information and ministers circulated the relevant memoranda. It was the custom, however, after every cabinet meeting, for the prime minister to send the sovereign a letter telling him or her what the cabinet had discussed and what decisions had been made. This was indeed the only record extant of cabinet decisions and, on occasion, the letter from the prime minister was perfunctory. An extreme example was the report which Sir Henry Campbell-Bannerman, the Liberal prime minister, sent to Edward VII in November 1906, which stated merely that 'the Cabinet met to-day and was entirely engaged with arrangements of public business necessary for the conclusion of the session'.[67] In November 1907 Lord Knollys, the king's private secretary, wrote that Campbell-Bannerman's perfunctory reports of cabinet meetings were 'really making an absolute fool of the King'.[68] However, one reason why ministers took little trouble to keep Edward VII informed was that they knew that Edward VII was far less assiduous, and less interested in domestic politics, than Queen Victoria had been. For the sovereign to be able to exercise influence, therefore, the prime requirement was coming to be an unremitting dedication to work—work which could not be delegated.

As well as dedicating herself to work, Queen Victoria also proved herself a striking exemplar of the domestic virtues. This enabled the monarchy to become a moral force in Victorian society. 'The exaltation of Royalty is possible', Albert had told Stockmar in January 1846, 'only through the personal character of the Sovereign.'[69]

It was during Queen Victoria's reign that the monarchy first attained the prestige which it still enjoys today. Victoria's predecessors had been little respected and their private lives had been scandalous. Her three immediate predecessors, George III, George IV, and William IV, had been described as an imbecile, a profligate, and a buffoon. In 1830 *The Times* obituary of George IV declared that 'there never was an individual less regretted by his fellow creatures than this deceased King', and Sir Robert Peel declared that the monarchy had become so unpopular that only a miracle could save

[67] Philip Magnus, *King Edward the Seventh* (John Murray, 1964), 355.
[68] Ibid. 282.   [69] Rhodes James, *Albert, Prince Consort*, 268.

it.[70] The best *The Times* could say of William IV at his death in 1837 was that he had done no harm. 'It is no exaggeration to say that the accession of the Princess Victoria reinstated the English monarchy in the affections of the people. George IV had made the Throne unpopular; William IV had restored its popularity, but not its dignity.'[71] When Victoria ascended the throne, the status of the monarchy was low and its future uncertain. By the time of her death in 1901, it had reached a pinnacle of respect, and the institution of monarchy had assumed the basic form which it retains today.

Far from weakening the authority of the Crown, then, the transformation from power to influence served to increase it. The sovereign came to be seen as head of the nation as well as head of state.[72] 'I have always felt', Lord Salisbury declared, 'that when I knew what the Queen thought I knew pretty certainly what view her subjects would take, and especially the middle class of her subjects.'[73] Monarchy thus acquired a massive emotional significance in the new age of popular government. This fundamental change was first noticed by two men of genius, one the most brilliant journalist of the age, Walter Bagehot, the other its most imaginative politician, Benjamin Disraeli. In contrast to the Prince Consort's conception of a politically active monarchy, a presidential monarchy, they understood that the sovereign could prove a beneficent influence only in so far as he or she abstained entirely from seeking to rule. Only then could the head of the state become the head of the nation.

As Bagehot had foreseen, the magic of monarchy, its 'dignified' element, was dependent upon the withering-away of its 'efficient' functions, of its prerogatives, of its power. David Cannadine has shown that many of the ceremonies which are thought of as being hallowed by time immemorial were in fact developed during the Victorian era. In his view they were consciously created to attach popular sentiments to the monarchy.[74] It would, however, be a mistake to regard this development as a conscious 'invention of tradition'. Under a system of popular government, towards which Britain

---

[70] Cited in St Aubyn, *Queen Victoria*, 62.

[71] *The Letters of Queen Victoria*, 1st ser., i. 26.

[72] This distinction is well drawn in Antony Jay, *Elizabeth R* (BBC Books, 1992).

[73] Elizabeth Longford, *Victoria RI* (Weidenfeld & Nicolson, 1964), 567.

[74] See e.g. David Cannadine, 'The Context, Performance and Meaning of Ritual: The British Monarchy and the "Invention of Tradition", 1820–1977', in Eric Hobsbawm and Terence Ranger (eds.), *The Invention of Tradition* (Cambridge University Press, 1983), 101–64.

was evolving, popular attachment to the monarchy developed in a natural way and this attachment is not to be explained through metaphors of contrivance and invention, for it lies at a far deeper, and perhaps subconscious level. 'The tendency of advanced civilisation', Disraeli makes his philosopher hero, Sidonia, remark in his novel, *Coningsby*, published in 1845, 'is in truth to pure Monarchy'.[75] Monarchy, Disraeli appreciated, far from being an institution of merely historic significance, was in fact a form of government profoundly attuned to a system of popular rule since it satisfied deep-seated and widespread popular needs, needs perhaps imperfectly articulated and perhaps impossible to articulate with any degree of clarity, but none the less real for that. An élite system of government might not need the emotional sustenance which monarchy could provide. A popular system of government, however, undoubtedly did. It is not accidental, then, that Disraeli, the ideologist of party, the first politician to appreciate the centrality of party to parliamentary government—'I say it is utterly impossible to carry on your Parliamentary Constitution except by political parties'[76]— was also the ideologist of constitutional monarchy, appreciating that the development of party was changing the functions of monarchy while in no way lessening its importance. He it was who discerned the new relationships between Crown and Party, the new realities which, 'once shaped, were soon to be mistaken for primordial elements of the British Constitution'.[77]

This emotional attachment to monarchy was strengthened, as Disraeli had foreseen, by the growth of imperialism. At the beginning of Victoria's reign, the empire was in disarray. Canada was in a state of rebellion, while India was governed by a private company. The general belief was that the colonies were, in an era of free trade, merely an unwanted expense for the mother country, and that they would, in due course, detach themselves from her. 'Colonies', the French economist Turgot had declared in the eighteenth century, 'are like fruits which cling to the tree only till they ripen.'[78] In consequence, however, of the Durham Report of 1839, Canada, and

---

[75] *Coningsby*, pt. V, ch. 8.

[76] Cited in L. B. Namier, 'Monarchy and the Party System', Romanes Lecture 1952, in *Personalities and Powers* (Hamish Hamilton, 1955), 18.

[77] Ibid.

[78] Nicholas Mansergh, *The Commonwealth Experience* (Weidenfeld & Nicolson, 1969), 42.

later the other colonies of settlement, acquired a system of responsible self-government which was to prove perfectly compatible with retention of the imperial tie.

During the latter part of Victoria's reign, imperialism became a popular force, and the Royal Titles Act of 1876, by which the queen added the title 'Empress of India' to her existing title 'Queen of Great Britain and Ireland', linked the monarchy to this rising force. But it was the colonies of settlement which led the way in terms of constitutional evolution. This increased the importance of the monarchy as a personal link between the colonies and the 'mother country'. The queen was the head of what seemed to many to be a 'Greater Britain', the title of a book published by Dilke, a radical imperialist, in 1868. The Crown was to become the emblem of empire, and Edward VII was the first king to be proclaimed Emperor of India and ruler 'of the British Dominions beyond the seas'.[79] Writing to Edward VII in February 1901, shortly after the death of Queen Victoria, A. J. Balfour, the leader of the House of Commons, stressed this new function of monarchy.

The King [he wrote] 'is no longer merely King of Great Britain and Ireland and of a few dependencies whose whole value consisted in ministering to the wealth and security of Great Britain and Ireland. He is now the greatest constitutional bond uniting together in a single Empire communities of free men separated by half the circumference of the Globe. All the patriotic sentiment which makes such an Empire possible centres in him or centres chiefly in him; and everything which emphasises his personality to our kinsmen across the seas must be a gain to the Monarchy and the Empire.[80]

'During the latter half of Queen Victoria's reign,' Balfour declared in 1909, 'and more than ever now, Great Britain means the British Empire. Our people overseas do not care a rush for Asquith and me. They hardly know our names. For them the symbol of the Empire is the King.'[81] This new conception of the relationship of the sovereign to the colonies of settlement overseas was one which was to continue beyond the end of empire even to the present day, when the

---

[79] Although, paradoxically, Edward VII rarely used the style 'Edward R and I' in protest at the fact that Queen Victoria had not consulted him before adopting the title 'Empress of India'.

[80] Harold Nicolson, *King George V: His Life and Reign* (Constable, 1952), 67.

[81] *Journals and Letters of Reginald, Viscount Esher*, ed. Maurice V. Brett and Oliver, Viscount Esher (Nicholson & Watson, 1934–8), ii. 421.

sovereign has become Head of the Commonwealth, the only link between fifty-one otherwise quite disparate countries.

But how was it that constitutional monarchy took such strong root in Britain? The main developments in Victoria's reign which transformed the nature of the monarchy—the expansion of the franchise, the development of party, and of responsible government, both in Britain and in the colonies of settlement—were the product of the spread of liberal ideas. Victoria was profoundly sceptical of the spread of liberalism and downright hostile to democratic rule. 'She *cannot*', she told W. E. Forster in 1880, 'and will not be the Queen of a *democratic monarchy*.'[82] Yet, paradoxically, the prestige of the monarchy at the end of her reign stemmed from its association with parliamentary government, from the idea of an executive responsible to a parliament which was elected by popular vote. It was this which, at the end of the nineteenth century, distinguished Britain and the colonies of settlement from the great empires of the Continent—Austria-Hungary, Germany, and Russia. Indeed, it was only because Britain already enjoyed liberal institutions that they could be exported to the colonies of settlement. Only after Britain itself enjoyed responsible government would it be possible to create a government elsewhere based on the same principle; and it was responsible government which made Dominion status possible.

The association of the monarchy with liberalism enhanced it as an institution, since at that time liberalism was seen as the ideology of human progress. It is a paradox, however, that the development of modern constitutional monarchy came about as a result of political forces with which Victoria herself barely sympathized. She devoted much of the latter part of her reign trying to stem the tide of that very parliamentary liberalism which was modernizing the monarchy. So it was that modern constitutional monarchy came about much against the will of the queen who was Britain's first constitutional monarch.[83]

During the Victorian era, constitutional monarchy achieved its modern form. The sovereigns who succeeded Victoria all sought to reign according to the fundamental precepts of constitutional monarchy as laid down by Bagehot—for the writings of Bagehot

[82] *The Letters of Queen Victoria*, 2nd ser., ed. G. E. Buckle (John Murray, 1926–8), iii. 166.
[83] Cf. A. J. P. Taylor, 'Queen Victoria and the Constitution', in *Essays in English History* (Penguin, 1976), 66.

were to attain canonical status. It is known, indeed, that George V, George VI, Elizabeth II, and the Prince of Wales have all studied *The English Constitution*. Since Victoria the changes in the role of the monarchy have been changes in degree and not in kind. There have been no fundamental alterations to the monarchical model as it had evolved by the end of Victoria's reign.

The remainder of this book, therefore, is devoted to describing and analysing this model and how it has actually operated in the country which gave birth to the notion of constitutional monarchy.

2

The Basic Constitutional Rules: The Rules of Succession

I

Monarchy is, of its essence, a hereditary institution. Since it depends on the right of hereditary succession, rather than election or appointment, it is of prime importance that there be clear and unambiguous rules regulating the succession to the throne so that there can be no dispute as to who should succeed. In Britain, the rules regulating the succession are of two kinds: the non-statutory rules governing hereditary succession, and statutory rules laying down certain conditions which the holder of the throne must meet.

Hereditary succession is not by itself an unambiguous criterion. There are indeed three possible arrangements for hereditary succession. The first regulates the succession by means of the so-called Salic law, which entirely excludes females from the succession. This rule governed succession to the French monarchy, so that there were never any queens of France, except, of course, for queen consorts. The second rule provides that the right of succession passes to the eldest child of the sovereign, regardless of gender, females enjoying the same right of succession as males. This rule has been in force in Sweden since 1979.

The third alternative, which regulates the succession in Britain, provides that, under the common law, the Crown descends on the same basis as the inheritance of land. This means that male heirs take precedence over female, with children representing their deceased ancestors; and, under the rule of primogeniture, the older son precedes the younger. It is thus in general only a male who, in Britain, can be heir apparent. If the heir to the throne is female, she can only be heir presumptive rather than heir apparent, for her claim can always be defeated by the birth of a son to the sovereign who would then become heir apparent. Thus Princess Elizabeth was never heir apparent, since it was always possible that George VI might have had male issue.

Descent, however, as we have seen, is only one—albeit, under modern conditions, the most important—of the bases of succession. The great constitutional struggles of the seventeenth century, which culminated in the passage of the Bill of Rights of 1689 and the Act of Settlement of 1701, confirmed that the succession could be regulated by parliament.

In 1688–9 parliament asserted its right, first, in effect, to depose the sovereign for misgovernment, secondly, to determine the course of succession, and, thirdly, to lay down, in the Bill of Rights, pointers as to how the new sovereign was expected to act.

There is also, in the coronation ceremony, a reminiscence of a third element in the succession to the throne, the elective element, which was, as we have seen, of importance in Anglo-Saxon times. The coronation ceremony begins with the Recognition, the presentation of the sovereign by the Archbishop of Canterbury to those assembled, symbolizing the formal acceptance of the new sovereign by the people, 'a reminder of the old elective character of kingship'.[1] This third element is now of purely symbolic significance.

The statutory elements in the monarchy, however, remain of considerable importance. There are at present four statutory conditions which the sovereign must meet.

First, the sovereign must declare, at the first day of the meeting of the first parliament after her accession, or at the coronation, whichever occurs first, that he or she is a faithful Protestant, a requirement first laid down in 1688 and now regulated by the Accession Declaration Act, 1910. Elizabeth II made this declaration on opening the first parliament of her reign, on 4 November 1952. The declaration is necessary to meet the requirement of the Act of Settlement that no Roman Catholic can inherit the throne.

Secondly, the sovereign must, under the Coronation Oath Act, 1689, the Act of Settlement, and the Accession Declaration Act, 1910, take an oath at his or her coronation in a form prescribed by statute. The precise form of the oath has been varied on a number of occasions since 1689, but at her coronation in 1953 Elizabeth II promised to govern the peoples of all her realms, possessions, and

[1] A. Berriedale Keith, *The King and the Imperial Crown: The Powers and Duties of His Majesty* (Longmans Green, 1936), 21.

territories according to their respective laws and customs and to temper justice with mercy; to maintain the Protestant reformed religion *in the United Kingdom*; and to maintain and to preserve the settlement of the Church of England, and its doctrine, worship, discipline, and government *in England*.

Thirdly, the sovereign must promise, in accordance with the 25th Article of the Acts of Union with Scotland of 1706, to maintain the presbyterian Church of Scotland. This oath is normally taken on accession to the throne.

Fourthly, the sovereign must, under the Act of Settlement, be in communion with the Church of England, of which he or she is the Supreme Governor (see Chapter 9). There is, however, no statutory requirement that the sovereign actually be a *member* of the Church of England, and indeed, since the Act of Settlement, two sovereigns—George I and George II—have been German Lutherans. The presumption today, however, is that the sovereign is in fact a member of the Church of England.

Parliament retains the right to alter the succession, and it has in fact done so twice since 1689. The first occasion was in 1701, when the Act of Settlement provided that the succession should lie with Sophia, Electress of Hanover, and her heirs being Protestant, a breach, as we have seen, in the hereditary line of succession. The second occasion was in 1936, following the abdication. Legislation was then required, since neither the Bill of Rights nor the Act of Settlement had made provision for a voluntary abdication, for which indeed there was no precedent in English history. Since the title to the throne is parliamentary, it follows that an abdication and the installation of a successor, whether or not that successor is to be the next in line to the throne, requires legislation.[2]

The Declaration of Abdication Act, 1936, had four legal consequences. First, it gave statutory effect to the Instrument of Abdication which Edward VIII had signed; secondly, it provided that the next in line to the throne, the Duke of York, who was to take the title of George VI, should succeed; thirdly, it barred any possible future claim to the throne by Edward VIII or his descendants; and, fourthly, it declared that the Royal Marriages Act of 1772, which requires all descendants of George II other than the sov-

[2] R. T. E. Latham, 'Constitutional and Legal Aspects of the Abdication of King Edward VIII', in W. K. Hancock, *Survey of British Commonwealth Affairs*, i. *Problems of Nationality 1918–1936* (Oxford University Press, 1937), app., 616.

ereign, and the issue of princesses who marry into foreign families, to obtain the permission of the sovereign before contracting a valid marriage, should not apply to Edward VIII or his descendants.

The provisions of this Act were required, by convention, first laid down in 1930 and confirmed in the preamble to the Statute of Westminster, 1931, to be given the consent of the other members of the Commonwealth. Since today the sovereign is also the sovereign of fifteen other Commonwealth countries, there must be a common rule of succession, and it would be unconstitutional, although not illegal, for the British government unilaterally to alter the rule of succession.

The succession can, however, be altered *only* by Act of Parliament. In 1994 the Labour MP Tony Benn, a republican, wrote to the Lord President of the Council, Tony Newton, declaring that, upon the summoning of the Privy Council to proclaim a new sovereign, following the demise of Elizabeth II, he would express his opposition to the proclamation. Newton, however, replied that the heir apparent—the Prince of Wales—'would succeed immediately and automatically to the Throne on the death of the Sovereign', the right of succession being set out in the Act of Settlement and alterable only by parliament. Thus the registering of an objection at the meeting of the Privy Council to proclaim the new sovereign would have no legal effect.[3]

II

In terms of common-law doctrine, the sovereign never dies, but is immediately succeeded by his or her successor. This means that provision must be made for occasions when the sovereign is a minor, defined as being under the age of 18, or is incapable of carrying out monarchical functions. Until 1937 no permanent statutory provision had been made. The reason for this, no doubt, was that no minor had succeeded to the throne since the accession of the 9-year-old Edward VI in 1547, although Queen Victoria succeeded to the throne just twenty-seven days after reaching her eighteenth birthday. There has been only one case of complete incapacity in modern

[3] The correspondence between Benn and Newton can be found in Peter Hennessy's lecture, 'The Monarchy: Britain as "Disguised Republic"?' fo. 28, in his series 'In the Steps of Walter Bagehot: A Constitutional Health-Check', to be published by Cassell.

times, the insanity of George III in 1810. In the following year, the Prince of Wales took over the royal functions as Prince Regent.

On previous occasions when a minor had succeeded to the throne, *ad hoc* arrangements had been made. Either a council of government was established, or a regent appointed, a person invested with the royal authority and generally known as 'Protector'. In the case of Edward VI, statutory provision was made for the Duke of Somerset to act as Protector. On other occasions, *ad hoc* provisions were made for regencies, in case of the death of the sovereign before his or her successor came of age, by Henry VIII in 1536, by George II in 1751, by William IV in 1830, by Victoria in 1840, when Prince Albert was designated Regent, and by George V in 1910, when Queen Mary was designated Regent. In the case of the incapacity of George III, a Regency Act was passed in 1811 designating the Prince of Wales as Regent.

In cases of temporary incapacity, or when the sovereign was absent from Britain, the custom developed in the early part of the twentieth century of appointing a Council of State, comprising both royal personages and leading dignitaries such as the prime minister, the lord chancellor, and the Archbishop of Canterbury, to carry out the royal functions.

But these *ad hoc* arrangements were unsatisfactory. In the past they had led to unseemly struggles for power between rival claimants for the regency; while, in the case of the incapacity of the sovereign, it might be difficult if not impossible to secure the Royal Assent to a Bill appointing a Regent. Indeed, in 1788, when George III became temporarily insane, the Regency Bill became the subject of a political squabble between Pitt and Fox; and it was passed by means of a legal fiction, by which the Royal Assent was assumed to have been given. In the event, George III recovered before the Regency came into effect; nevertheless the dangers were clear. Nor was there any guarantee that a sovereign who was temporarily incapable would be able to take the necessary steps. Fortunately, George V, at the onset of his serious illness in 1928, was able to sign the proclamation constituting a Council of State; but in 1936 the sovereign had to subject himself to the indignity of signing the proclamation on his deathbed, something which he found great difficulty in doing.[4]

When George VI acceded to the throne in 1936, the next in line

---

[4] Harold Nicolson, *King George V: His Life and Reign* (Constable, 1952), 530–1.

to the throne, Princess Elizabeth, was a minor, aged 10. In a message to parliament in which he referred to 'the uncertainty of human life', the king therefore proposed that some permanent statutory provision be made; and effect was given to the king's wishes in the Regency Act of 1937.

This Act provided for four possible contingencies: the minority of the sovereign, the permanent incapacity of the sovereign, the temporary incapacity of the sovereign, and the absence of the sovereign from the United Kingdom. In the case of the first two contingencies, provision was made for a Regency; in the case of the second two, provision was made for the establishment of a Council of State.

The permanent incapacity of the sovereign would need to be certified by at least three out of five people—the sovereign's next of kin, the Lord Chancellor, the Speaker of the House of Commons, the Lord Chief Justice, and the Master of the Rolls. In 1937 it was proposed that the Regent be the person next in line to the throne who had reached the age of 21. The Regent would carry out all the royal functions, except that he or she could not assent to a Bill altering the order of succession to throne, nor could he or she alter the provisions of the Acts of Union with Scotland guaranteeing the Protestant religion and Scotland's system of presbyterian church government.

In the case of temporary incapacity or absence from the United Kingdom, a Council of State would be established. This would comprise the spouse of the sovereign and the four persons next in the line of succession to the throne who had reached the age of 21. The Counsellors are, however, constitutionally equal, and the heir to the throne has no precedence amongst them. Two of these five would be needed for a quorum. By contrast with the Council of State established by George V in 1928, in future a Council of State would include only royal personages, for in 1928 the Irish Free State had objected, as a member of the Commonwealth, to the inclusion in the Council of State of members of the British government, since it gave the impression that the British government could act as intermediary between the sovereign and other nations of the Commonwealth. As a result, during the illness of George V, only royal personages signed documents relating to the Irish Free State; and at the Imperial Conference of 1930 it was agreed that only members of the royal family should be eligible to be Counsellors of State.

The intention of the framers of the 1937 Act had been to lay down general provisions which could apply to all circumstances and obviate the need for *ad hoc* provision. This aim was not achieved, and the 1937 Act has already been twice amended, in 1943 and 1953. In 1943 provision was made for Princess Elizabeth, the heir to the throne, to become a Counsellor of State at the age of 18, in 1944. It was manifestly absurd that the Princess could succeed to the throne at the age of 18, but was deemed, before 1943, ineligible to assume the less onerous duties of a Counsellor of State until the age of 21. The provisions for the appointment of Counsellors of State were also made less rigid in 1943, by allowing any person eligible to be a Counsellor of State who happened to be outside the United Kingdom to be exempt from the need to serve.

In 1953 a third Regency Act was passed, at the request of the queen, further amending the provisions laid down in 1937. The first *ad hoc* amendment was that, were a Regency to be needed before Prince Charles came of age in 1966, the Regent should be, not Princess Margaret, the next in line to the throne, but Prince Philip, for, were the queen to die before the heir to the throne came of age, Prince Philip would naturally become the guardian of his son. It would be anomalous that he ought not also to be the Regent. The second *ad hoc* alteration was to allow Queen Elizabeth, the Queen Mother, to remain as a Counsellor of State, even though not otherwise eligible, thus bringing the number of Counsellors to six. This alteration, too, was seen as being in accord with sentiment and common sense.

Nevertheless, the *ad hoc* departures from the general provisions of 1937 were not without their dangers. In particular, the provision by which the Regent should be 'the best person' rather than the person next in line of succession could be criticized as, in certain circumstances, laying the monarchy open to controversy. While there can be no dispute about who is next in the line of succession, there can easily be an argument about who is best qualified to act as Regent. It may not be possible to legislate in advance, as was attempted in 1937, to meet all possible circumstances. Indeed, it may be argued that the very attempt to legislate for all foreseeable circumstances was bound to result in flaws. If that is so, then it might be right for the sovereign to enjoy within certain defined limits a degree of choice over the person who, besides being Regent, will also be guardian of the infant heir. That would require statutory provision to allow the sovereign to nominate from a class of persons to be defined in the statute, but limited to members of the royal family, the person to be Regent and guardian on the demise of the Crown.[5]

Two further constitutional points should be noted with regard to the Regency Acts. The first is that a Council of State cannot dissolve parliament, except upon the express instructions of the sovereign— given in 1951, when George VI was too ill to issue the Proclamation of Dissolution himself—nor create peerages, nor give the Royal Assent to any matter for which provision is made in the Act of Settlement, nor to any alteration in the Royal Style and Titles; nor can it have any functions with regard to the other realms of which the sovereign is head of state. The reason for this restriction is of significance.

The reason is that, according to Sir Edward Ford, a former assistant private secretary to Elizabeth II, it is a

misconception that the Counsellors of State have any power of constitutional decision. They clearly have not. They are in fact—if one may say it without disrespect to their persons—merely a piece of constitutional machinery—the nearest thing to a human rubber stamp that has perhaps yet been devised. And to make sure of this, it has been provided that even in the limited sphere in which they have power to act, they can never act singly but must do so by at least two of their number. The most obvious example of the royal prerogative, the granting of a dissolution of Parliament, is specifically excluded from their functions. So (I would be prepared to argue) are any other decisions on matters which the Sovereign has the right to question.

The Counsellors of State, therefore, are nothing 'other than the instrument by which the Sovereign's will is proclaimed during her absence or indisposition'.[6] For this reason it is absurd to ask what procedure should be followed should the Counsellors of State disagree. Since they have no decision-making power, the question cannot arise.

The second feature of significance concerning both the Regency and the Council of State is that, although agreed by the other Commonwealth governments in 1953, they apply only to Britain and not to any other Commonwealth country of which the sovereign is the head of state. It is for the other Commonwealth countries to make such provision for the minority or incapacity of the sovereign

[5] Memo. by Sir Maurice Hankey to J. A. N. Barlow, 12 Jan. 1934, Public Record Office (PRO) CAB 21/3727.
[6] Sir Edward Ford to Sir David Pitblado, 16 Feb. 1954, PRO PREM 11/751.

as they might think suitable. In fact, however, the problem does not arise in the same form in any other Commonwealth country of which the sovereign is the head of state, for the functions of the sovereign in those countries are normally undertaken by a governor-general. Thus the question of a Regency is irrelevant, since the governor-general will never be a minor; and, since the governor-general is appointed for a limited period, there can be no question of permanent incapacity. In the case of temporary incapacity, provision is generally made for the Chief Justice or some other dignitary to assume his or her functions. Thus the arrangements for the Regency and for the Council of State apply only to Britain. The monarchy is related to Britain in a special way not replicated in the other Commonwealth nations which acknowledge the king or queen as their head of state, in that it is only in Britain that the sovereign exercises his or her functions directly. Formal notice, however, would be given to the other Commonwealth countries of which the sovereign was head of state, were a Regency ever to come into effect, and to other members of the Commonwealth, by courtesy, in virtue of the fact that the sovereign is Head of the Commonwealth.

There is, however, a gap in the provisions made for the exercise of the royal prerogative with respect to those members of the Commonwealth which acknowledge the sovereign as head of state. The sovereign exercises two important prerogatives with respect to these countries: the appointment and dismissal of their governor-generals. It is suggested in Chapter 10 that the sovereign enjoys a genuine discretion with regard to appointment and dismissal, and that he or she need not be bound by the request of the prime ministers of the countries concerned. But, whether this is the case or not, there can be no doubt that the sovereign can seek information concerning appointment and dismissal, and can put arguments against the course of action which the prime minister concerned is proposing.

If that is so, the sovereign does not act as a rubber stamp in the case of appointment and dismissal of a governor-general. Who, then, undertakes the sovereign's functions if he or she is a minor or incapable? The Regent cannot exercise the functions of the sovereign in an overseas Commonwealth country, while the Council of State is a rubber stamp, with no authority to question a prime minister. According to Harold Laski, the question, 'What is to happen to the royal prerogative in a Dominion if the King goes mad?' was raised at the 1930 Imperial Conference.[7] It is a question which has not yet been answered.

III

The royal consort and the heir to the throne enjoy, with certain exceptions, the legal status of ordinary subjects, but with various special privileges. Since the débâcle in 1821, the queen consort has been crowned and anointed after her husband at the coronation service. The precedent of 1821, when the doors of Westminster Abbey were barred and bolted to Queen Caroline, wife of George IV, shows, however, that it is the king's choice whether or not the queen should be crowned.

While, however, the wife of the king automatically becomes the queen, the husband of the queen has not, since the reign of William III, 1689–1702, been the king, and he is not crowned and anointed with the queen. There are no rules defining the position of the husband of the sovereign and it has varied with each incumbent. Queen Victoria complained on marrying Albert in 1840 that 'It is a strange omission in the Constitution that while the wife of a King has the highest rank and dignity in the Realm assigned to her by law, the husband of a Queen regnant is entirely ignored,'[8] while Albert himself declared that

A very considerable section of the nation had never given itself the trouble to consider what really is the position of the husband of the Queen Regnant. When I first came over here, I was met by this want of knowledge and unwillingness to give a thought to the position of this luckless personage.[9]

The husbands of Mary I, 1553–8, and Mary II, 1689–94, were both kings, and Philip, husband of Mary I, was King both of England and of Spain. William III ruled jointly with Mary II. The husband of Anne, 1702–14, was entitled Prince George, Duke of Cumberland. The husband of Victoria retained his title, Prince Albert of Saxe-Coburg-Gotha, but was created, in 1857, Prince Consort. Unlike

[7] See Geoffrey Marshall, *Constitutional Theory* (Oxford University Press, 1971), 20 n. 2.

[8] Cited in Graham and Heather Fisher, *Consort: The Life and Times of Prince Philip* (W. H. Allen, 1980), 92.

[9] Robert Rhodes James, *Albert, Prince Consort* (Hamish Hamilton, 1983), 224.

Prince George, the Duke of Cumberland, or Prince Philip, Duke of Edinburgh, Prince Albert never became a peer.

The Duke of Edinburgh, apparently, has never wished to be created 'Prince Consort', a title which he believes 'would emphasise his official status without correspondingly underlining his human vocation'.[10] Prince Albert, as we have seen, took it upon himself to exercise constitutional functions, attending audiences with Queen Victoria, receiving state papers, and, in general, acting as joint sovereign. But the Duke of Edinburgh has no such constitutional powers. He neither attends audiences nor receives state papers, and holds no formal position in the structure of government.

The eldest son of the sovereign is generally created Prince of Wales by the sovereign, a title first conferred by Edward I on his son, Edward, in 1301. The son of Elizabeth II was created Prince of Wales in 1958 when aged 10, with an investiture being held in 1969 shortly before his 21st birthday. While the title 'Prince of Wales' dates back to the thirteenth century, the ceremonial investiture fell into abeyance and was revived in 1911 by the chancellor of the exchequer, David Lloyd George. The investiture of 1969 was only the second to be held in modern times. Apart from having been, since 1966, when he reached the age of 18, Regent designate, the Prince of Wales has no formal constitutional functions, but he does receive cabinet papers and gives audiences to cabinet ministers.

In the wider sense, however, the heir to the throne does have a constitutional function in that he or she frequently acts as the sovereign's deputy. Yet, there are no prescribed functions to perform. In his autobiography, the Duke of Windsor complained that, as Prince of Wales, there was 'no specific routine job in the sense, for example, that a vice-president has a job . . . Though I was next in line to the Throne, with all that position implied, I actually possessed no prescribed State duties or responsibilities.'[11] 'This constitutional vacuum', Jonathan Dimbleby, biographer of the Prince of Wales, has noted, 'was not an oversight but documentary evidence of the peculiar position that the heir apparent occupies; there is no formal "role" except to wait.'[12]

[10] Elizabeth Longford, *Elizabeth R* (Weidenfeld & Nicolson, 1983), 153.
[11] The Duke of Windsor, *A King's Story: The Memoirs of H.R.H. The Duke of Windsor* (Cassell, 1951), 211–12; ch. XII contains an interesting account of the functions of the Prince of Wales during the first part of the century.
[12] Jonathan Dimbleby, *The Prince of Wales: A Biography* (Little Brown, 1994), 226.

Thus the role of heir to the throne is very much what its holder chooses to make of it. The future Edward VII sat on two House of Lords committees, and on two Royal Commissions, the first on Housing and the Working Classes in 1884, and the second on the Aged Poor, from 1892 to 1895. He declined, however, to sign either the majority report opposing old age pensions, or the minority report favouring them, as this was a party political matter.[13] The first Prince of Wales to strike the imagination of the public was the future Edward VIII, who became, in the 1920s, a spokesman for the 'war generation' and in particular for ex-servicemen. The current Prince of Wales has taken a special interest in such problems as the inner cities, ethnic minorities, the unemployed and the environment.

The title 'Princess of Wales' belongs to the wife of the Prince of Wales. It is not conferred on the eldest daughter of the sovereign. In 1944, on the eighteenth birthday of Princess Elizabeth, George VI issued a statement stating that he did not intend to confer any title upon her. 'How could I create Lilibet [the Princess's nickname] the Princess of Wales,' the king wrote to Queen Mary, 'when it is the recognised title of the wife of the Prince of Wales?'[14] It has, however, become the custom for the eldest daughter of the sovereign when she is not the heir presumptive to be given the style of 'Princess Royal', a title first conferred by Charles I on his eldest daughter, Princess Mary, who married the Prince of Orange in 1641, and became the mother of William III.

Members of the royal family have no formal constitutional functions, in that, unlike the sovereign, they are not required to speak and act on the advice of ministers. On the other hand, they cannot speak and act with the freedom of ordinary citizens, for their comments and actions could, if partisan, reflect upon the political neutrality of the sovereign. If, therefore, a member of the royal family intends to make a speech which could prove controversial, it is, as a matter of courtesy, sent to the minister whose area of government it affects. Convention, however, demands no more than this, and the Prince of Wales has, apparently, on occasion refused to make changes that ministers have suggested.[15] Clashes are thus possible, and it requires tact to avoid them. When, in June 1935, the Prince

---

[13] Sir Sidney Lee, *King Edward VII: A Biography* (Macmillan, 1925), i. 547–54.
[14] John Wheeler-Bennett, *King George VI: His Life and Reign* (Macmillan, 1958), 591–2.
[15] Dimbleby, *The Prince of Wales*, 427.

of Wales, the future Edward VIII, made a speech to the British Legion, of which he was patron, suggesting that a delegation from the Legion should visit Germany in the near future, he was rebuked by George V. The Prince of Wales argued that he had been asked to make such a statement by the Chairman of the British Legion, but the king refused to accept this explanation, and reminded the heir to the throne that he was under a duty to consult the government before making any speech which might prove contentious.[16] 'If you are one day to be a constitutional monarch,' Lloyd George had apparently told the future Edward VIII, 'You must first be a constitutional Prince of Wales.'[17]

In 1927 the foreign secretary, Sir Austen Chamberlain, asked the Prince of Wales not to visit the United States after his projected visit to Canada. The prince objected to Chamberlain's interference. Baldwin, the prime minister, sent for Lascelles, the prince's private secretary, to make a direct request to the prince not to go, and he complied.[18] In February 1963, following de Gaulle's veto of Britain's entry into the European Community, Princess Margaret, at the request of the government, abandoned a planned unofficial visit to Paris. Speaking in the Commons, the prime minister, Harold Macmillan, referred, perhaps inaccurately, to 'the decision to *advise* Her Royal Highness Princess Margaret to cancel her forthcoming visit to Paris', using the excuse that she was required to act as a Counsellor of State.[19] In 1970 the Foreign Office prevented mention of the 'special relationship' with the United States in a speech that the Prince of Wales made to the annual dinner of the Pilgrims.[20]

The royal dukes—at present the Duke of Edinburgh, the Prince of Wales, as Duke of Cornwall, a title automatically accruing to the eldest son of the sovereign, and the Dukes of York, Gloucester, and Kent—are members of the House of Lords, but accept a self-denying ordinance to avoid identifying themselves with any political party.

Members of the royal family are bound by two statutes when contracting marriages. The first, the Act of Settlement, requires, as we have seen, that neither the sovereign nor the sovereign's consort can

[16] The Duke of Windsor, *A King's Story*, 252.
[17] Philip Ziegler, *King Edward VIII: The Official Biography* (Collins, 1990), 124.
[18] Sir Alan Lascelles to Sir John Colville, 31 Mar. 1954, PRO PREM 11/756.
[19] House of Commons, vol. 671, cols. 965–6, 11 Feb. 1963; see also PRO PREM 11/4436.
[20] Dimbleby, *The Prince of Wales*, 149.

be a Roman Catholic. Therefore, any member of the royal family who marries a Catholic becomes ineligible to succeed. Thus, when Prince Michael of Kent, then sixteenth in the line of succession, married a Catholic, Baroness Marie-Christine von Reibnitz, in 1978, and when the Earl of St Andrews, son of the Duke of Kent and then seventeenth in the line of succession, married a Catholic, Sylvana Tomaselli, in 1988, they lost their rights of succession, for themselves, although not necessarily for their children. The two children of Prince and Princess Michael of Kent, being brought up as members of the Church of England, retain their rights of succession.

Secondly, members of the royal family other than the sovereign are bound by the provisions of the Royal Marriages Act, 1772. This archaic and badly drafted piece of legislation was introduced, not for any grave reasons of constitutional necessity, but as a result of a family quarrel. George III, who saw himself as having been forced to marry for purely dynastic reasons rather than for reasons of the heart, was annoyed to discover that one of his brothers, the Duke of Cumberland, had married Mrs Anne Horton, the widow of a commoner. He then learnt that another brother, the Duke of Gloucester, had, in 1766, married the Dowager Countess Waldegrave, an illegitimate daughter of Sir Edward Walpole.

The Royal Marriages Act applies to all descendants of George II, other than princesses marrying into a foreign family. There are only two methods by which those to whom the Act applies can contract a valid marriage. The first is to obtain the approval of the sovereign. The second is, after the age of 25, to give notice of an intention to marry. Unless, within the next twelve months, both Houses of Parliament expressly disapprove, the marriage can then take place. Any 'marriage' contracted in defiance of these rules is void, although the person contracting the 'marriage' retains his or her right to succeed. Thus, when, in 1785, the Prince of Wales 'married' Mrs Fitzherbert secretly and without obtaining permission, the 'marriage' was void. This was fortunate for the Prince of Wales, since, had the 'marriage' not been void, he could not have succeeded to the throne as George IV, Mrs Fitzherbert being a Catholic. The Act does, however, apply to Catholic descendants of George II, as much as to Protestants, even though Catholics are ineligible to succeed to the throne.

This provision seems to have been misunderstood by Winston Churchill during the abdication crisis when he sought to persuade the Duchess of York, now Queen Elizabeth, the Queen Mother, of Edward VIII's right to marry Mrs Simpson by citing the case of Mrs Fitzherbert. 'Well, that was a long time ago,' the duchess replied; and the king himself was apparently engaged in perusing a *Life of Mrs. Fitzherbert*, marking the chapter relating to her 'marriage' with the Prince of Wales.[21] Both Churchill and Edward VIII seem to have been under the misapprehension that the future George IV had contracted a morganatic marriage with Mrs Fitzherbert under which the marriage was valid, but his heirs would lose the right to succeed, and his wife would not bear the title of 'Queen'. That, for example, was the marriage that the Archduke Franz Ferdinand, heir to the throne of Austria-Hungary, had contracted with Countess Sophie Chotek in 1900, fourteen years before both were assassinated at Sarajevo. But a morganatic marriage is unknown to British law, and the effect of a 'marriage' contracted contrary to the Royal Marriages Act of 1772 is not to make the marriage morganatic but to render it void.

The provisions of the Act would seem almost to encourage a clash between the sovereign and parliament. It would seem at first sight as if the sovereign could refuse consent to a marriage, but be, in effect, overruled by parliament refusing to express its disapprobation. In such circumstances, it would seem possible for a member of the royal family to contract a valid marriage although the sovereign was opposed to it. In accordance with the principles of constitutional monarchy, however, the act of consent is no longer personal, but given by the sovereign on advice. The purpose of the Act, after all, is to ensure that the public interest is taken account of in royal marriages. Since the prime minister will normally command the confidence of parliament, there is little likelihood of a marriage being possible through the second route if the first is blocked. In fact, the second route has never been successfully invoked. Thus, when the Earl of Harewood, the queen's first cousin, became, in 1967, the first member of the royal family to remarry following a divorce, Harold Wilson, as prime minister, devised the formula: 'The Cabinet have advised The Queen to give her consent and Her Majesty has signified her intention to do so.'

Consent would not, however, have been given to Princess Margaret in the 1950s to marry a divorced man, Group Captain Peter Townsend. Attitudes to divorce were more rigid in the 1950s

[21] Sarah Bradford, *George VI* (Fontana paperback edn., 1991), 219–20.

than they were to become during the next decade, and, while the Earl of Harewood was eighteenth in the line of succession, Princess Margaret was at the time third in the line of succession. The queen was obliged to subordinate her personal feelings to requirements of state, and to seek the advice of her prime minister, Sir Winston Churchill, who in 1953 indicated informally that, although the matter had not been formally discussed in cabinet, the government would be unwilling to advise in favour of the marriage.

On reaching the age of 25 in 1955, by which time Sir Anthony Eden was prime minister, Princess Margaret became free of the constraints of the Royal Marriages Act. She could then exercise the option of giving notice to the Privy Council of her intention to marry. Then, unless both Houses of Parliament passed resolutions expressly disapproving of the marriage, it could take place. There was, however, some opposition to the marriage in the cabinet, primarily, it appears, from Lord Salisbury, the Lord President of the Council and leader of the House of Lords and a leading High Churchman.[22] In the country, however, survey evidence showed that a large majority favoured allowing Princess Margaret to marry Townsend.[23]

The government, however, was only prepared to recommend the marriage under certain conditions. Princess Margaret would have had to renounce her right of succession, her annual allowance under the Civil List would have had to be terminated, and she might have been required to live abroad. A draft Bill of Renunciation embodying these conditions was apparently being considered. In the event, however, Princess Margaret declined to exercise her right to marry Townsend. On 31 October 1955 she issued a statement declaring,

I have been aware that, subject to my renouncing my rights of succession, it might have been possible for me to contract a civil marriage. But, mindful of the Church's teaching that Christian marriage is indissoluble, and conscious of the Commonwealth, I have resolved to put these considerations before any other.

The Act of Settlement and the Royal Marriages Act are the only statutory rules affecting royal marriage or divorce. The constitutional position of a member of the royal family is unaffected by a

[22] Roland Flamini, *Sovereign: Elizabeth II and the Windsor Dynasty* (Bantam Press, 1991), 157–8.
[23] Ibid. 161.

separation. When the Prince and Princess of Wales decided to separate in December 1992, John Major, as prime minister, announced in the House of Commons on 9 December that 'their constitutional positions are unaffected', and that 'there is no reason why the Princess of Wales should not be crowned Queen in due course'.[24] That was formally a correct statement of the constitutional position, but perhaps rather unrealistic, since it would appear inappropriate to many to crown and anoint as queen consort a woman who was living apart from her husband. Admittedly, the precedent of 1821, when George IV, who was living apart from his queen, Caroline, refused even to admit her to the coronation service, shows that the queen consort need not necessarily be crowned or anointed. That, however, was before the days of modern constitutional monarchy, and today the public might not recognize as queen consort someone who was not undertaking the duties of the position.

The divorce between the Prince and the Princess of Wales, announced in July 1996, means that the Princess of Wales will not become queen, since she will no longer be the wife of the king; but it will have no other constitutional consequence. The sovereign is, admittedly, Supreme Governor of the Church of England (see Chapter 9). But this imposes no statutory requirements further to those already enumerated.[25] In December 1992 the Archbishop of Canterbury declared that 'the monarch is Supreme Governor of the Church by virtue of being the Sovereign: there is no other legal requirement'.[26] In 1714 George I succeeded to the throne, although divorced. In 1821 George IV sought, unsuccessfully, to divorce his wife, and no one suggested that this would render him ineligible for the throne. Today, the Church of England, by contrast with its position at the time of the abdication crisis of 1936, accepts that divorce is sometimes a regrettable necessity. Thus, the divorce of the Prince of Wales has no effect on the succession to the throne.

The remarriage of a divorced heir to the throne poses a more difficult problem, since the heir is subject to the Royal Marriages Act. In 1938, following the abdication, and again in 1957, following Princess Margaret's renunciation of Townsend, the Church of England passed Acts of Convocation declaring remarriage in church

[24] House of Commons, 6th ser., vol. 215, col. 845, 9 Dec. 1992.
[25] See pp. 43–4.
[26] For an excellent concise analysis of the issues involved, see Dimbleby, *The Prince of Wales*, 557–9.

during the lifetime of a previous spouse inadmissible. But public feeling is far more liberal today than it was in 1957, and clergymen, acting as local registrars, now have the discretion to remarry divorced persons in church. An increasing number of clergymen are in fact willing to exercise this discretion. Moreover, section 9 of the Clergy Ordination Measure, 1990, provides that the General Synod can empower an archbishop to allow a remarried person to be ordained. In 1994 the General Synod called for the Church of England's position on divorce to be reviewed. Further liberalization of the rules of the Church must remain a distinct possibility. It would seem unfair if a right granted to many ordinary citizens and to the clergy were to be denied to the heir to the throne.

Were the Prince of Wales to seek to remarry after becoming sovereign, there would be no statutory barrier to his doing so, since the Royal Marriages Act does not apply to a reigning sovereign; but, as the abdication crisis shows, the sovereign cannot, in practice, marry against the wishes of his ministers.

IV

The rules relating to succession, being a product of the religious struggles of the seventeenth century, are now ripe for reform. The statute specifically prohibiting a Roman Catholic or someone married to a Catholic from occupying the throne is deeply offensive to Catholics, not only in Britain, but also in those Commonwealth countries with large Catholic populations such as Canada and Australia. It should be repealed.

In an era of equality of opportunity, moreover, it will appear increasingly anomalous for male heirs still to take precedence over female. There is at the time of writing a male heir apparent with two sons. Therefore, the succession is unlikely to be affected by any alteration in the law allowing for it to be passed to the eldest child of the sovereign irrespective of gender, as in Sweden. The time is ripe, surely, for such a reform.

Most urgent of all, however, is a reform of the Royal Marriages Act. There are, perhaps, few more absurd pieces of legislation on the statute book. The purpose of the Act, as stated in its preamble, that 'marriages in the Royal Family are of the highest importance to the state', can indeed easily be achieved without needing to invoke its complicated paraphernalia.

There is no reason why a marriage made in contravention, perhaps unconscious contravention, of its provisions by someone who was unaware of his or her descent from George II should be void. It would be better simply to deprive the person concerned of the right to succession, as would occur if he or she married a Catholic. Nor is there any reason why the Act should apply to Catholics, who are ineligible for the throne.

The fundamental weakness of the Act, however, is that it applies to many who are quite remote from the throne and who are never likely to succeed. Conversely, someone who may well succeed—for example, an heir presumptive whose mother has married into a foreign family—would fall outside the provisions of the Act. An obvious reform would be to make provision for the sovereign's approval to be required for the marriages, of the descendants not of George II, but of George VI, or, better still, simply for the first five people in the line of succession. Any member of the royal family to whom it applied would still, of course, have the right to renounce his or her rights of succession and contract a civil marriage, as Princess Margaret could have done in 1955. The second route provided for in the Royal Marriages Act, the declaration at the age of 25, is otiose and should be removed.

3

The Basic Constitutional Rules:
Influence and the Prerogative

———■·◆·■———

I

Under a democratic system of government, two offices may be distinguished—that of head of state and that of head of government. These two positions may be held by the same person, as they are in the United States, in France under the Fifth Republic, and in Russia under the 1993 constitution, where the directly elected president fulfils both functions—those of head of state and of head of government. It is more usual, however, for the two offices to be separated. The head of state can then be either a president or a hereditary sovereign.

The functions of a head of state, where that office is separated from that of the head of government, are generally of three main kinds. First, there are constitutional functions, primarily of a formal and residual kind, such as appointing a prime minister and dissolving the legislature. Secondly, the head of state carries out a wide variety of public engagements and ceremonial duties. Thirdly, and perhaps most important, there is the symbolic or representative function, by means of which the head of state represents and symbolizes not just the state but the nation.[1] It is this role of interpreting the nation to itself that is the crucial one; the ceremonial activities—once dismissed by President de Gaulle as opening exhibitions of chrysanthemums—are means through which the head of state can be seen as fulfilling his or her representative functions. That is why the long withdrawal from public duties of Queen Victoria after the death of the Prince Consort in 1861 proved so damaging to the monarchy. To be an effective symbol, a head of state and

[1] See Antony Jay, *Elizabeth R* (BBC Books, 1992).

particularly a sovereign has to be seen. There is a theatrical element to effective representation, and, unless this is recognized, a head of state will lack the authority which comes from public support. Then, in the long run, he or she will find it impossible, lacking that authority, to perform his or her constitutional functions effectively.

In his book *The English Constitution*, first published in 1867, Walter Bagehot drew a famous distinction between the 'efficient' and the 'dignified' elements of the constitution. The 'efficient' elements were those with the power to make and carry out policy, such as the cabinet. The 'dignified' elements, by contrast, such as the monarchy, enjoyed little effective power. This did not mean, however, that they were unimportant or superfluous. On the contrary, they were of fundamental significance in symbolizing and reinforcing national unity. They helped to reconcile the ruled to the rulers. It was the 'dignified' elements in the constitution which created the aura of authority that helped to render government legitimate.

It is easier for a head of state to fulfil this 'dignified' function if the 'efficient' functions are located elsewhere, for any exercise of the efficient functions is almost bound to be controversial. Thus, when he or she exercises the 'efficient' functions, the head of state will cease to be able to represent all of the people; he or she will be representing only the particular cross-section who agree with his or her activities. That is a fundamental problem with countries where the positions of head of state and head of government are combined. There were many Americans who, in the period when, for example, Richard Nixon was president, felt something very near to horror at the thought that he was also the national representative of the United States. When, moreover, Nixon came to be tainted by the Watergate scandal, the taint extended not just to the head of government, but also to the head of state. It affected, therefore, the very symbolism of the state. In an earlier generation, the same revulsion was felt, from the opposite end of the political spectrum, at Harry Truman, a far more controversial figure as president than he became in retrospect. Similarly, many French men and women did not feel themselves represented by François Mitterrand. For this reason, the position of head of state in the United States and France attracts to itself little of the emotional resonance which attaches to the monarchy in Britain. The central symbol of American life is not the president but the constitution, while in France the central symbol—the French Revolution—is a contested one, and has divided French men and women of Left and Right for over two hundred years. It may be that part of the reason for the political instability of France since 1789 is that the revolution put paid to one symbol of French unity— the monarchy—without putting in its place a viable alternative. The volatile history of French constitutionalism since 1789 may be seen in part as a search for such a symbol, which it has yet to find.

In countries where the office of head of state is separated from that of head of government, the head of state has hardly any political functions, and his or her constitutional functions usually resemble those of the sovereign. In republics, the head of state is generally chosen either by popular election, as, for example, in the Irish Republic, or by the legislature, as in Germany and Italy. The position is almost always filled, however, if not by an ex-politician, then by someone selected by a political party. Although in theory it would be possible to discover a figure without a political history who would admirably fulfil the position of president, in practice the choice of a head of state remains in the hands of the political parties and no candidate without the support of a major party would have much chance of being elected.

It is, of course, perfectly possible for someone selected through the mechanism of party in this way to represent the nation as a whole— it might be argued that both Richard von Weizsaecker in Germany and Mary Robinson in the Irish Republic have succeeded conspicuously well in doing so. Nevertheless, the fact that the head of state has a political history must always make it more difficult to fulfil the symbolic and representative role successfully. In a monarchy, by contrast, the head of state has no political history. Provided that a sovereign carries out the constitutional functions in an impartial way, he or she is in a better position to represent the nation as a whole and to be a representative whom everybody can accept.

Britain is perhaps the prototype of modern constitutional monarchies for two fundamental reasons. First, it is by far the oldest of all monarchies (except, perhaps, for that of Denmark); and, secondly, the monarchy has probably played a more central role in the history of the nation than the monarchies of other countries. From the 1870s onwards there has been a powerful emotional identification with the monarchy which has no real counterpart in the surviving monarchies of the Continent, in Scandinavia or the Low Countries. Yet Britain is also quite unique amongst modern constitutional monarchies in that it has a monarchy but not a codified constitution.

This has important consequences. In other European democracies, it is the constitution which logically—even if not historically—creates the office and specifies the powers with which it is invested. In Britain, by contrast, the opposite is true.

The British Constitution, the collection of rules both written and unwritten which regulate our institutions, is, in Dicey's terms, a 'historic' constitution.[2] By this he meant not only that the British Constitution was an ancient constitution but, more importantly, that it was original and spontaneous, the product not of deliberate design but of historical development. The office of the monarchy has its origins in Anglo-Saxon times, before the idea of constitutional rules was at all understood. Whereas, on the Continent, and also in the overseas realms of the Commonwealth which recognize the queen as their head of state, the constitution has specified the powers of the sovereign, in Britain the process of constitutional development has been such, as we have seen, to whittle away the powers of the sovereign and transfer them to other offices, primarily to ministers.

In Britain, then, the symbol of the state and nation is not a constitution as it is in the United States, nor a historical tradition, which may be deeply contested, as in France or the Irish Republic, but a person. It may be suggested that it is better in general for a state to have a person as a focus of allegiance than a constitution or a historical tradition, for it is easier for citizens both to understand and to feel allegiance to a person than to a concept.

For the people as a whole to feel allegiance to a symbol under a democracy, however, it is essential that the symbol does not enjoy decision-making power, which would make it controversial. Under dictatorships, such as those of Hitler and Mussolini, allegiance to a person with massive political power is enforced. In a constitutional democracy, allegiance is to a person who has no political power. In this way it may be suggested that the existence of a symbol of allegiance without decision-making power serves to humanize power by stressing that the forces of political power are themselves subordinate to the symbol of both the state and the nation.

A democracy whose head of state is a sovereign links together two conflicting, some would say contradictory, notions, for a democracy is a form of government in which political positions derive from

[2] Dicey uses this term in his unpublished lectures on the Comparative Study of Constitutions. The manuscript of these lectures may be found in the Codrington Library, All Souls College Oxford.

popular election. This rule, however, does not apply to the office of head of state, which is filled not by any form of election but is instead transmitted by inheritance and is held for life.

The conflict between the two notions is resolved through the idea of a constitutional monarchy, a set of conventions which limit the discretion of the sovereign so that his or her public acts are in reality those of ministers. The fundamental purpose of the constitutional conventions limiting the position of the sovereign is to ensure that he or she acts in accordance with democratic norms. Thus, under modern conditions, a constitutional monarchy serves not to limit democracy but to underpin and indeed to sustain it. It is not a threat to democracy, but can instead be its ultimate safeguard.

Because a constitutional monarchy is a limited monarchy, it may seem that there is no obvious point at which the limitation of the power of the sovereign—a continuous process, as we have seen, since 1689—should stop. That limit is reached, however, at the point at which the constitution itself, which determines the role of the head of state, appears to be under threat. At that point, it may be suggested, the sovereign has the right to exercise his or her discretion, to act as a constitutional guardian, to ensure that the values which lie at the foundation of a constitutional system are preserved. That was the way in which George V understood his position during the Irish Home Rule crisis in 1914 (see Chapter 5). In such circumstances, some would suggest that the sovereign has the right, and perhaps indeed the duty, to act as a guardian of the constitution. The doctrine that the sovereign is required to act on the advice of ministers presupposes that ministers themselves act within the framework and presumptions of constitutional government. What do these presumptions require?

II

The sovereign is not only the head of state but also, formally, the head of the executive, of what is known as the Crown, which, under prerogative powers, can proclaim war or ratify treaties without the consent of parliament. He or she is also a part of the legislature, the king or queen in parliament, and, in theory, could assent to or veto all legislation in accordance with his or her own political predilections. He or she is, finally, the source of justice, in that the courts are the sovereign's courts and dispense his or her justice throughout the realm. These formalisms, however, have little substantive content in the modern world. In a constitutional monarchy, there is a funda-mental distinction between the actions of the sovereign in a personal capacity and his or her actions taken on the advice of ministers. Thus, although the sovereign is the head of the executive, the vast bulk of the prerogative powers of the Crown—probably over 95 per cent of these powers—are exercised not by the sovereign personally but either on the advice of ministers or by ministers themselves. The sovereign's judicial functions too are exercised entirely on the advice of ministers. The sovereign's personal powers arise in general only in those few sit-uations, at the beginning or the conclusion of a ministry, where he or she may or must act without ministerial advice.

The crucial requirement of constitutional monarchy, that the sov-ereign must be politically impartial, is achieved, then, through the principle that almost all the public acts of the sovereign are taken on the advice of his or her ministers. But what is 'advice'? In everyday speech, to offer advice to someone is to offer an opinion or make a suggestion as to how that person should act. The person to whom the advice is given is quite free to accept or to reject it. The term 'advice' used in connection with constitutional monarchy, however, has a quite different meaning. When ministers offer advice to the sovereign, that advice is binding and the sovereign has normally no option but to accept it. The consequence of rejecting advice would normally be the resignation of the government, and, even if the sov-ereign were able to find another government, that government would be in office as the personal choice of the sovereign. The consequence would be to put the sovereign in a position in which he or she was opposed by one of the great parties of the state. No constitutional sovereign can survive for long once he or she comes to be seen as a partisan.

In the past the doctrine that the sovereign acts on the advice of his or her ministers was, as we have seen, designed to protect par-liament and people from the arbitrary use of royal power. Today, it has a quite different function—that of protecting the sovereign from political involvement—for it follows from the doctrine that the sov-ereign speaks and acts on the advice of his or her responsible minis-ters, that it is ministers and not the sovereign who are held responsible by parliament and by the electorate. Were the sover-eign's actions of giving assent to bills really his or her own, and were the King's or Queen's Speech to represent the sovereign's own personal proposals rather than those of the government, they would become matters of controversy and the sovereign would be open to criticism. Thus the principle that the sovereign speaks and acts on the advice of his or her ministers serves to shield the sovereign from responsibility so that criticism of the sovereign's government is directed not at the sovereign but at ministers.

The consequences of this fundamental principle were drawn out by the constitutional lawyer Sir William Anson, in his authoritative work *The Crown*, first published in 1892. They are:

first that she [the sovereign] should not take advice from others, in matters of State, unknown to them; next, that she should not give public expression to opinions on matters of State without consulting them; and lastly, that she should accept their advice when offered by them as a Cabinet, and support them while they remain her servants.[3]

The second principle requires not only that the sovereign's public statements are made on the advice of his or her ministers, but that any private comments are made discreetly and cautiously so that relations with ministers are not compromised. This applies also to other members of the royal family, even though they do not speak on advice. Full acceptance of this principle has been comparatively recent.

In 1908 the future George V, as Prince of Wales, remarked to Winston Churchill after a dinner party that the prime minister of the government in which Churchill was serving, H. H. Asquith, was 'not quite a gentleman', and on another occasion said to the permanent secretary at the Treasury, 'I can't think, Sir George, how you can go on serving that damned fellow Lloyd George.'[4] George V's entirely correct behaviour as sovereign could not quite efface such comments. 'Before he came to the throne', Lloyd George declared upon the king's death in 1936,

he had the reputation of being very Tory in his views. In those days he was frank to the point of indiscretion in his talk, and his sayings were repeated in wide circles. There is no use concealing the fact that they gave offence to Liberals and his succession to the throne for that reason was viewed with some misgivings.[5]

[3] Sir William Anson, *The Law and Custom of the Constitution*, ii. *The Crown*, 4th edn., ed. A Berriedale Keith (Oxford University Press, 1935), pt. I, pp. 139–40.
[4] Cited in Kenneth Rose, *King George V* (Weidenfeld & Nicolson, 1983), 71.
[5] *News Chronicle*, 22 Jan. 1936, cited in Thomas F. Hale, 'The British Labour Party and the Monarchy', Ph.D. thesis, University of Kentucky (1972), 89.

It was perhaps the king's Tory predilections which were responsible for Asquith requiring the king to promise in advance that he would use his prerogative to create peers to ensure the passage of the Parliament Bill. The prime minister, perhaps, did not otherwise trust the king to do his constitutional duty when the time came. In 1914 George V admitted that Asquith might have had a prejudice against him because of his comment six years earlier: 'I ought not to have said it, and it was a damned stupid thing to say.'[6] Jennings claimed that Edward VIII was the first sovereign to come to the throne whose political opinions upon accession were not known.[7] In fact, his sympathy for the dictators was well known to those who had engaged in political conversations with him, and it is probably George VI who was the first sovereign to come to the throne without having made his political views known to leading politicians. He, however, identified himself publicly with his prime minister, Neville Chamberlain, when he invited him to appear on the balcony of Buckingham Palace to celebrate the Munich agreement in 1938. Support for Munich was, admittedly, widely shared in Britain, and there was a near-hysterical sense of relief at the avoidance of war. Nevertheless, the agreement was controversial, being opposed both by the Labour and Liberal opposition parties and by a small section of the Conservative Party, led by Churchill. Perhaps, then, Elizabeth II is the first sovereign never to have allowed any hint of her political views to reach those outside the circle of her ministers, her private secretaries, and her immediate family.

The third principle—that the sovereign must accept the advice of, and support, his or her ministers—ensures that the sovereign cannot have a policy or his or her own independently of ministers. In accepting the advice of ministers, the sovereign is in effect giving expression to the views of the electorate as manifested in parliamentary elections. In this way the conventions relating to ministerial advice serve to reconcile monarchy with the basic principle of democracy, that the will of the people should prevail. Thus these conventions form the basic foundation of constitutional monarchy.

---

[6] Rose, *King George V*, 71.

[7] Ivor Jennings, *Cabinet Government* (3rd edn., Cambridge University Press, 1959), 329.

III

Concentration upon the constitutional powers of the sovereign is liable to give a misleading picture of the contemporary role of a constitutional monarch, for the prime constitutional role of the sovereign occurs, not when a ministry begins or comes to an end, but during the everyday life of a government, and consists in the exercise of influence rather than power.

In the nineteenth century, as it became clear that the sovereign's powers were being limited, there were some who believed that the sovereign had become a cypher. Disraeli saw that this would be unlikely to occur. 'I know it will be said', he declared in a speech at Manchester in 1872,

that the personal influence of the Sovereign is now merged in the responsibility of the Minister. I think you will find a great fallacy in this view. The principles of the English Constitution do not contemplate the absence of personal influence on the part of the Sovereign; and if they did, the principles of human nature would prevent the fulfilment of such a theory.[8]

Even a cursory reading of the biographies of recent monarchs shows that the sovereign is far more than a merely symbolic head of state, a 'mandarin figure' in Stockmar's phrase. The sovereign is an active rather than a passive element in the constitution.[9]

The rights of the sovereign under normal conditions have been summarized in Bagehot's classical trinity of rights: the right to be consulted, the right to advise, and the right to warn. Bagehot's corollary, however, is less frequently noticed. He adds:

And a king of great sense and sagacity would want no others. He would find that his having no others would enable him to use these with singular effect. He would say to his minister: 'The responsibility of these measures is upon you. Whatever you think best must be done. Whatever you think best shall have my full and effectual support—I do not oppose, it is my duty not to oppose, but observe that I warn'. Supposing the king to be right and to have what kings often have, the gift of effectual expression, he could not help moving his minister. He might not always turn his course, but he would always trouble his mind.[10]

[8] T. E. Kebbel (ed.), *Selected Speeches of Lord Beaconsfield* (Longmans, Green & Co, 1881), ii. 493.

[9] See pp. 72–5, and Chapter 5.

[10] Walter Bagehot, *The English Constitution*, in *Collected Works*, ed. Norman St John-Stevas (The Economist, 1974), v. 253.

The essence of Bagehot's argument is that the wise use of influence will obviate the need for the use of the prerogative powers. So, for example, it may be argued that the use by George V of his right to warn during the Home Rule crisis in 1914 obviated the need for him to use the power of veto or the power to dismiss his ministers (see Chapter 5). The prerogative powers are sometimes called reserve powers, and they are certainly powers that ought to be held in reserve until all possibilities of influence have been exhausted. Thus, Sir John Kerr has been criticized, as governor-general of Australia, for dismissing his prime minister, Gough Whitlam, in 1975, before he had sought to use all the powers of influence which, as the queen's representative in Australia, he enjoyed.[11] The implication of Bagehot's remarks that 'He might not always turn his course, but he would always trouble his mind', and that 'A king of great sense and sagacity would want no others' is not in doubt. 'Probably in most cases the greatest wisdom of a constitutional king would show itself in well-considered inaction.'[12] Influence operates best through stealth and suffers from visibility.

A constitutional monarch, however, is only able to exert influence within the framework of the constitutional rules concerning ministerial advice. This requirement was well analysed by Lord Esher, an unofficial adviser to Edward VII and George V, in a memorandum which he wrote for George V in September 1913, when the king was considering whether he had the right to veto the Home Rule Bill.

Every Constitutional Monarch possesses a dual personality. He may hold and express opinions upon the conduct of his Ministers, and their measures. He may endeavour to influence their actions. He may delay decisions in order to give more time for reflection. He may refuse assent to their advice up to the point where he is obliged to choose between accepting it, and losing their services.

If the Sovereign believes advice to him to be wrong, he may refuse to take it, and if his Minister yields, the Sovereign is justified. If the Minister persists, feeling that he has behind him a majority of the people's representatives, a Constitutional Sovereign must give way.

It is precisely at this point that the dual personality of the Monarch becomes clear. Hitherto he has exercised free volition, he has used his prerogatives of criticism and delay, of personal influence and remonstrance. But now the King ceases to be a free agent.

[11] D. A. Low, 'Wearing the Crown: New Reflections on the Dismissal 1975', *Politics* (Australia), 19 (1984), 20–1.
[12] Bagehot, *Collected Works*, v. 250.

Yet, as Esher concludes, 'It is irrational to contend that because under our constitutional rules and practice the Sovereign has now and then to act automatically, he is therefore an automaton without influence or power.'[13]

The constitutional parameters which the sovereign must respect if he or she is to exercise influence constitutionally were laid out by Sir William Heseltine, the queen's private secretary, in a letter to *The Times* on 28 July 1986. Sir William laid down three propositions. The first was that the queen enjoyed the right, and indeed the duty, to express her opinions on government policy to the prime minister. His second proposition was that the queen must act on the advice of her ministers, whatever her own opinions might be. If, therefore, the sovereign were to express reservations about some area of government policy, but was unable to persuade the prime minister, he or she would be bound, in the last resort, to give way. Sir William's third proposition was that communications between the sovereign and the prime minister were entirely confidential. Indeed, at the weekly audiences which the queen grants the prime minister when both are in London, neither the queen's private secretary nor any civil servant, nor indeed any third person, is present, although the queen may discuss points which arise with her private secretary afterwards.

It is important to notice that the sovereign's right to express his or her opinions on government policy, Sir William's first proposition, *entails* his third proposition, that communications between the prime minister and the sovereign remain confidential. The sovereign, therefore, is not entitled to make it known that he or she holds different views on some matter of public policy from those of the government. It is a fundamental condition of royal influence that it remains private. It follows, therefore, that the sovereign must observe a strict neutrality in public, and great discretion in private conversation.

It is, however, because relations between the sovereign and a prime minister must remain confidential that it is impossible ever to form an accurate estimate of the influence of the current sovereign. 'The metaphysics of limited monarchy', declared Harold Laski in 1938, 'do not easily lend themselves to critical discussion. On no

[13] Memorandum of 10 Sept. 1913, cited in *Journals and Letters of Reginald, Viscount Esher*, ed. Maurice V. Brett and Oliver, Viscount Esher (Ivor Nicholson & Watson, 1934-8), iii. 126-8.

element in the Constitution is our knowledge so inexact.'[14] The historian can estimate the influence of Queen Victoria or King George V, but the political scientist is inevitably unable to answer basic questions about the working of the monarchy in the era in which he or she lives. What has been the nature of the relationships between the queen and her nine prime ministers? Has the queen exerted significant influence over her governments? What is the relationship between the queen and her private secretary? On none of these questions is it possible to pronounce with the slightest degree of confidence. A good journalist might, no doubt, penetrate into the inner sanctum of government so as to produce fairly accurate reports of private governmental discussions; but he or she should not be able to penetrate the monarchy; were he or she able to do so, the monarchy would be in danger. It must remain hidden by an efficient veil of discretion. It is for this reason that, as Bagehot noted, 'there is no authentic explicit information as to what the Queen can do, any more than of what she does'.[15]

In modern times, the sovereign gives an audience to the prime minister once a week, usually on Tuesday, when both of them are in London. Margaret Thatcher has declared that 'Anyone who imagines that they are a mere formality or confined to social niceties is quite wrong; they are quietly businesslike and Her Majesty brings to bear a formidable grasp of current issues and breadth of experience.'[16] Edward Heath has declared that the queen exerts significant influence through an 'exchange of views' with her prime ministers, but that she would *never* tell a prime minister what he or she should or should not do.[17] It has been suggested that the queen adopts a similar technique when dealing with ecclesiastical appointments. According to Kenneth Rose,

A Dean of St. Paul's Cathedral once asked the Queen what she could do if a Prime Minister submitted a name for an ecclesiastical appointment with which she was not happy. 'Nothing constitutionally', she replied, 'but I can always say that I should like more information. That is an indication that the Prime Minister will not miss.'

---

[14] Harold Laski, *Parliamentary Government in England* (Allen & Unwin, 1938), 388.
[15] Bagehot, *Collected Works*, v. 243.
[16] Margaret Thatcher, *The Downing Street Years* (HarperCollins, 1993), 18.
[17] In a BBC TV Panorama programme, 'The Monarchy', BBC TV, 22 Feb. 1993.

'On at least two occasions in recent years', Rose adds, 'the Queen has used this tactful technique when controversial names have been put forward for honours.'[18] James Callaghan in his autobiography records how, in early 1976, the queen encouraged him, as foreign secretary, to take an initiative which he already had in mind, to resolve the Rhodesian problem.

Inevitably [he declares], the Queen's opinion was enough to tip the scales, for she is an authority on the Commonwealth and I respected her opinion . . . I have always thought that the Queen's initiative on Rhodesia was a perfect illustration of how and when the Monarch could effectively intervene to advise and encourage her Ministers from her own wide experience and with complete constitutional propriety.[19]

The exercise of influence by the sovereign, however, demands close familiarity with the affairs of government. 'There is no royal road to political affairs,' Bagehot wrote. 'Their detail is vast, disagreeable, complicated and miscellaneous. A king, to be the equal of his ministers in discussion, must work as they work; he must be a man of business as they are men of business.'[20] Edward VIII, on coming to the throne, found that

The ceremonial framework that provides the public with a romantic illusion of the higher satisfaction of kingship actually disguises an occupation of considerable drudgery. This fact was hardly a discovery for me. From long observation of my father's activities, I knew only too well what I was in for. The picture of him 'doing his boxes', to use his own phrase, had long represented for me the relentless grind of the King's daily routine.[21]

These scattered hints apart, one can only speculate on the influence of Elizabeth II. Three speculations can perhaps be ventured. The first is that the influence of a sovereign is likely to increase during his or her reign, for, the longer he or she remains on the throne, the greater the political experience which he or she accumulates. By 1995 the queen had been on the throne for forty-two years, had known nine prime ministers, and enjoyed a longer experience of public life than anyone else who was politically active.

[18] Kenneth Rose, *Kings, Queens and Courtiers: Intimate Portraits of the Royal House of Windsor from its foundation to the Present Day* (Weidenfeld & Nicolson, 1985), 92.
[19] James Callaghan, *Time and Chance* (Collins, 1987), 380–2.
[20] Bagehot, *Collected Works*, v. 259.
[21] The Duke of Windsor, *A King's Story: The Memoirs of H.R.H. The Duke of Windsor* (Cassell, 1951), 278.

In the course of a long reign [Bagehot declared] a sagacious king would acquire an experience with which few ministers could contend. The king could say: 'Have you referred to the transactions which happened during such and such an administration, I think about fourteen years ago? They afford an instructive example of the bad results which are sure to attend the policy which you propose. You did not at that time take so prominent a part in public life as you now do, and it is possible you do not fully remember all the events. I should recommend you to recur to them, and to discuss them with your older colleagues who took part in them. It is unwise to recommend a policy which so lately worked so ill.[22]

More succinctly, George V is supposed to have remarked, 'I am not a clever man, but if I had not picked up something from all the brains I've met, I'd be an idiot.'[23]

One might speculate secondly that the sovereign's influence is likely to be greater on matters that are not fundamental to party ideology; and finally, perhaps, that the influence of the queen will be felt most strongly where Commonwealth affairs are at stake because of her position as Head of the Commonwealth. But these are no more than speculations.

IV

The rules relating to advice apply only during the existence of a ministry. They do not apply when a ministry comes to an end through the death or resignation of the prime minister; nor when a prime minister seeks a dissolution of parliament. On these occasions the sovereign retains personal prerogatives and acts without advice. These prerogatives are those needed to ensure the functioning of parliamentary government.

But it may be that there is another category of personal prerogative also, the power which the head of state has to act as guardian of the constitution. That power, if it exists, would justify the view of King George V that he had the right to refuse assent to the Irish Home Rule Bill of 1914 (see Chapter 5). It is also possible to imagine pathological circumstances in which a sovereign might think it right to dismiss his or her ministers or to compel a dissolution

[22] Bagehot, *Collected Works*, v. 253.
[23] Cited in Kenneth Rose, *King George V* (Weidenfeld & Nicolson, 1983), 109.

against their wishes. For practical purposes, however, these prerogatives may be regarded as having fallen into desuetude.

When exercising the personal prerogatives, the sovereign acts in a personal capacity and not on the advice of ministers. The extent and scope of the personal prerogatives are, however, unclear. It is difficult if not impossible to circumscribe them accurately. It may, indeed, be inherent in the notion of constitutional monarchy that the personal prerogatives remain undefined in extent and scope. This is perhaps particularly the case in the United Kingdom with its uncodified and uncertain constitution. But the introduction of a codified constitution would not necessarily serve to determine the precise scope of the prerogatives, although it might determine what these prerogatives actually were. Most constitutions lay down the powers of the head of state in purely formal terms—as, for example, in the Belgian Constitution, which states in laconic terms 'The King appoints and dismisses Ministers' (article 65), illustrating 'yet again that the Belgian Constitution is primarily a fundamental charter which, in the main, only sets out general principles'.[24] Whether a country has a codified constitution or not, the real powers of the sovereign are generally determined more by convention than by the articles of a constitution.

A monarchist might conceive it to be a positive advantage that, under the uncodified British Constitution, options are not determined in advance, for too rigorous a characterization of precedents may be used in an attempt to bind the sovereign, so limiting his or her freedom of action. Those who seek to limit the sovereign's power might suggest that a sovereign who took a particular course of action in the past is bound to undertake the same course in the future. But the sovereign cannot be *bound* by precedent. He or she will be called upon to do what is best in a specific situation whose precise contours cannot be predicted. Thus, in 1910, Lord Esher held the view that there ought not to be any discussion of the principle of the use of the prerogative, since 'the principle is entirely dependent' upon the circumstances in which the prerogative is used'.[25] In 1923, when George V chose Stanley Baldwin as prime minister rather than Lord Curzon, he made it clear that he was *not* laying down a general doctrine that a peer could never succeed to the

---

[24] Robert Senelle, *The Belgian Constitution: Commentary* (Belgian Government Publications, 1974), 228.
[25] Esher to Knollys, 9 Jan. 1910, Royal Archives (RA) K2552 (1).

premiership;[26] and indeed, in the very different circumstances of 1940, George VI was to favour the claims of Lord Halifax over Winston Churchill, believing that Lord Halifax's peerage was not an obstacle, since it could be laid in abeyance for the time being. The only claim being made by George V in 1923 was specific, not general. He was saying that, in the particular conditions of the time, the prime minister ought to be in the House of Commons and not the Lords, primarily because the official opposition, the Labour Party, was virtually unrepresented in the House of Lords, thus making it impossible for the opposition to question the prime minister.

There are, however, dangers in the argument that the extent and scope of the powers of the sovereign should be uncircumscribed. There is a tension between the basic principle of constitutional government that the sovereign must remain politically neutral and that his or her prerogative powers should not be laid out in advance in the form of a set of rules. The greater the discretion which the sovereign enjoys, the greater the possibility of his or her using that discretion in a manner that might offend one or other of the major parties of the state. Monarchists seek both to preserve the political neutrality of the sovereign but also to maintain the notion that the sovereign is the fundamental source of political authority. This means that the prerogatives must be preserved intact, so that the sovereign can use his or her powers in situations which cannot at present be foreseen, for the sovereign must have the power to safeguard constitutional democracy when it is threatened in unforeseen ways.

In logic, it is difficult to reconcile the two principles that the sovereign must remain neutral and that the extent of his or her prerogatives should remain undetermined. Reconciliation is possible only if the sovereign exercises the prerogatives without partisanship, and does all that is possible to prevent a situation arising in which the prerogatives have to be used. It is because British sovereigns in the twentieth century have observed these precepts that there has been so little conflict with regard to the sovereign's powers. Indeed, the sovereign has rarely been called upon to exercise his or her prerogatives, and when influence has been exercised this has rarely led to serious clashes with ministers.

The sovereign, through much of the twentieth century, has been

[26] See p. 92.

able to adopt a formal role in relation to the appointment of a prime minister and granting a dissolution of parliament. But this has been contingent. It has rested upon two inter-connected factors. The first is the existence of a two-party system, which has meant that there have rarely been occasions when the sovereign has needed to exercise his or her discretion. The consequences of a return to a multi-party system such as characterized the mid-Victorian era, and of the introduction of proportional representation which would entrench a multi-party system, are examined in Chapter 6.

The second reason why the role of the sovereign has been largely formal in the twentieth century is that, since 1914, Britain has been spared emergency situations of the kind which might call for royal intervention.

In the past, such emergency situations led to the sovereign undertaking an additional constitutional role by acting as a facilitator to help secure agreement between the political parties. Queen Victoria undertook this role in 1869 when she helped to resolve the dispute between the Liberal government and the Conservative House of Lords over the disestablishment of the Irish Church; and again in 1884–5 over the Reform and Redistribution Bills. In July 1914, having secured the agreement of his ministers, George V summoned a conference at Buckingham Palace to discuss the Irish question, it having been ascertained from the leader of the Conservative opposition that he would attend such a conference only if summoned by the king. George V's intervention made it easier for political leaders to parley without being accused of weakness by their supporters.

The sovereign's intervention in such situations can only be undertaken with the support of the government. He or she cannot be an arbiter in the sense of being a judge between the claims of the government and the opposition. The sovereign, therefore, would not normally play an active part in the proceedings once the politicians had met together. In 1914, for example, George V withdrew from the conference after making his opening speech. In 1926 the prime minister, Stanley Baldwin, refused to allow the sovereign to act as a conciliator in the General Strike, since the government believed that it could be ended only by the unconditional surrender of the TUC.

Under emergency conditions, the role which the sovereign might adopt could well become controversial. Some would argue that it is in such a situation that the sovereign should be able to exercise his or her prerogative powers as a guarantor of the constitution, a defender of last resort of the conventions of parliamentary government. That was the role adopted by King Juan Carlos of Spain in 1981 when his country was threatened by a military *coup*. The constitutional lawyer Ivor Jennings argued that, under emergency conditions, the sovereign could legitimately refuse his or her assent to a policy

which subverted the democratic basis of the Constitution, by unnecessary or indefinite prolongations of the life of Parliament, by a gerrymandering of the constituencies in the interests of one party, or by fundamental modification of the electoral system to the same end. She would not be justified in other circumstances . . .[27]

Thus, if either of these two conditions—the two-party system and a situation of political stability—was to change, the role of the monarchy might change also. The largely formal role of the sovereign, therefore, is contingent. It is not inherent in constitutional monarchy.

V

It is generally accepted that certain personal prerogatives are an essential prerequisite for the smooth operation of parliamentary government. In Britain, the most important of these prerogatives are the appointment of a prime minister and the granting or refusal of a dissolution of parliament.

In appointing a new prime minister, the sovereign cannot be bound by the outgoing prime minister: if the prime minister has died, he or she will not be available to give advice; if the prime minister is resigning because he or she has been defeated in cabinet, parliament, or the polls, he or she has clearly lost the authority to give advice. It would clearly have been absurd if James Callaghan, defeated at the polls in 1979, had been asked for advice as to his successor. He might indeed have given the mischievous answer that his Conservative successor should be Edward Heath, the deposed leader of the Conservative Party, rather than the party's actual leader, Margaret Thatcher.

Although the sovereign does not act on advice in choosing a prime minister, he or she will, however, normally consult the out-going

[27] Jennings, *Cabinet Government*, 412.

prime minister. The only exceptions in the twentieth century are 1908, when Campbell-Bannerman resigned; 1923, when Bonar Law resigned; and 1955, when Sir Winston Churchill resigned. But, in 1908 and 1955 the succession was obvious—Balfour, Asquith, and Eden respectively—and two of the three resigning prime ministers— Campbell-Bannerman and Bonar Law—suffered from serious ill health. Both died shortly after resigning the premiership.

The situation in 1923, however, was much more controversial, but once more the resigning premier, Bonar Law, was seriously ill and was to die of throat cancer in November of that year, six months after resigning. It was at Bonar Law's request that the king did not consult him, the ailing prime minister having asked to be excused from having to recommend either Baldwin or Curzon as his successor.[28]

If a resigning prime minister is asked for a view, as normally occurs, it would be disrespectful not to offer it. Today, however, when a prime minister resigns in the middle of a parliament, his or her party will normally elect a new leader, and all that the resigning premier need do is to draw the sovereign's attention to the result of a party ballot.

In addition to consulting the prime minister, the sovereign may consult any other privy counsellor he or she pleases. In 1957, for example, following the resignation of Sir Anthony Eden, the queen consulted the leader of the House of Lords, Lord Salisbury, who had conducted a canvass of the cabinet, and two Conservative elder statesmen, Lords Chandos and Waverley, as well as her first prime minister, Sir Winston Churchill.

The second major personal prerogative is the right to refuse a dissolution. Under normal circumstances, clearly, the sovereign has little option. He or she cannot refuse a dissolution to a government with a majority in the Commons, since the government would then resign, and the sovereign would be unable to find any alternative government able to command the confidence of the Commons. The option of refusing a dissolution might, however, arise if the prime minister of a minority government were to seek a dissolution, or if a prime minister, having lost the support of his or her cabinet or party, were to try to forestall being overthrown by seeking a rapid dissolution.

[28] It is sometimes suggested that Sir Anthony Eden was not consulted following his resignation in 1957, but that is not correct; see p. 94.

Some have argued that the sovereign has no right to refuse a request for a dissolution. That was the position taken by a group of Labour MPs in April 1974, when there was some controversy as to whether Harold Wilson's minority government would be able to secure a dissolution at a time of its own choosing.

In our opinion [they declared], the Prime Minister of the day has an absolute right to decide the date of the election following discussion with his Cabinet colleagues. In such circumstances, we believe, the Queen is both morally and constitutionally obliged to accept the advice given.[29]

This position, however, is not supported by any of the leading constitutional authorities.[30]

The argument that the sovereign has no right to refuse a dissolution is based upon the fact that, although there are a number of Commonwealth examples, there is no unequivocal instance of a dissolution being refused in Britain. Therefore, so it is argued, the right to refuse has fallen into desuetude. But this conclusion does not follow. It could be replied that the sovereign has not refused a dissolution precisely because no prime minister has ever improperly sought one. But, suppose that a prime minister were to ask for a dissolution, instead of resigning immediately after an election which he had lost. Suppose that in 1979 James Callaghan, having been defeated in the general election, instead of resigning, had sought a second dissolution. Clearly the sovereign would have had not only the right but the duty to refuse such an illegitimate request. Suppose that Edward Heath, after the general election of February 1974, which produced a hung parliament, had met the House of Commons, been defeated, and then asked for a dissolution. Here, too, the sovereign would almost certainly have refused to grant it, and would instead have invited Harold Wilson, the leader of the opposition, to form a government. Therefore, what might be called the 'automatic' theory of dissolution seems quite untenable. There must be *some* circumstances—even if only highly unusual ones—in which the sovereign would be justified in refusing a dissolution. Therefore, the issue can-

---

[29] *The Times*, 8 Apr. 1974.

[30] See E. C. S. Wade and A. W. Bradley, *Constitutional and Administrative Law*, 11th edn., ed. A. W. Bradley and K. D. Ewing (Longman, 1993), 256–8; S. A. de Smith and Rodney Brazier, *Constitutional and Administrative Law* (6th edn., Penguin, 1989), 117–20; Robert Blake, *The Office of Prime Minister* (Oxford University Press, 1975), 60–2, and Geoffrey Marshall, *Constitutional Conventions* (Oxford University Press, 1984), ch. 2.

not be *whether* the sovereign is entitled to refuse a dissolution, but rather *under what conditions* he or she is entitled to refuse one. It is suggested that there are two such circumstances. The first is when an alternative government is available. That is most likely to arise in a hung parliament, and is considered in Chapter 6.

The second circumstance when a sovereign is entitled to refuse a request for a dissolution is when the prime minister lacks the backing of his or her cabinet and/or party.

In Britain, since 1918, the convention has been that it is the prime minister, and not the cabinet, who decides to seek a dissolution—although, of course, a wise prime minister will consult his or her colleagues before coming to a decision. The prime minister, nevertheless, acts on behalf of his or her cabinet in seeking a dissolution, and the presumption is that he or she in making the request enjoys the support of the cabinet and the party which give him or her the political authority to remain prime minister. Under normal circumstances, a prime minister who cannot secure the support of his or her cabinet for a dissolution can reconstruct the cabinet so that it does support such a request. If a prime minister is unable to do this, it follows that he or she lacks parliamentary support for the request. It is not, under such circumstances, legitimate for a prime minister to seek a dissolution to overcome opposition within his or her own cabinet or party—in effect, to overcome parliament.

The leading precedent here is one from South Africa. In 1939, upon the outbreak of war, the prime minister, General Hertzog, believed that South Africa should remain neutral, while his minister of justice, General Smuts, believed that South Africa should declare war on Germany alongside Britain. Smuts proposed a motion to this effect and it was passed in parliament. The vote showed that Hertzog did not enjoy the confidence of parliament and that he had the support of less than half of his cabinet and only a minority of his party. The prime minister nevertheless sought a dissolution which was refused, and Smuts was appointed prime minister of a government which declared war on Germany.

This precedent seems to show that the prime minister must have the support of his or her cabinet if he or she is to be able to make a legitimate request for a dissolution.

If the presumption that the prime minister enjoys the support of the cabinet is removed, perhaps because ministers indicate their dissent in some public way, then the presumption is also removed that a prime minister will normally be granted a dissolution at a time of his or her choosing.

The Queen [according to Jennings] must not intervene in party politics. She must not, therefore, support a Prime Minister against his colleagues. Accordingly, it would be unconstitutional for the Queen to agree with the Prime Minister for the dissolution of the Government in order to allow the Prime Minister to override his colleagues.[31]

It is suggested that similar reasoning applies if a prime minister has lost the support of his or her party and seeks a dissolution to overcome the opposition of the party. In 1939 Hertzog, even had he been able to reconstruct his cabinet so that it would have supported his request for a dissolution, would not have been able to survive in parliament. Suppose, moreover, to take a hypothetical example, that a political party is preparing for a leadership election at which the prime minister faces opposition, and perhaps a likelihood of being defeated. It ought not, surely, to be constitutionally possible for the prime minister to forestall opposition by seeking a dissolution before the leadership election has occurred. The sovereign, surely, would be entitled to insist upon a delay until the party had decided upon whom it wished to lead it.

Situations of this type could have occurred on a number of occasions in recent British history. In 1969 Harold Wilson appears at one point to have threatened that, if his government's proposals for trade-union reform, 'In Place of Strife', were opposed by the Labour Party, he would go to the Palace and seek a dissolution. John Major, both in 1992, before the 'paving' vote on the Maastricht Treaty, and in 1994, before a vote to implement the 1992 Edinburgh agreement concerning European Union, which the prime minister made a vote of confidence, threatened that, were he to be defeated, he would seek an immediate dissolution. The question arises of whether he would have been entitled to a dissolution if either his cabinet or his party had been opposed to it. It is not absolutely certain. The former Conservative MP and constitutional historian Sir Robert Rhodes James has suggested that, in 1990, Margaret Thatcher, had she stood and been defeated in the second ballot of the contest for the Conservative leadership, might have sought a dissolution, on the ground that the electorate and not the Conservative Party ought to choose the prime minister. Sir Robert claimed that a dissolution

---

[31] Jennings, *Cabinet Government*, 86.

'would certainly not have had the support of a majority of the Cabinet . . . and . . . the Queen was not bound to accept the advice of one member of the Cabinet even the most senior one'.[32]

It is suggested that, in such circumstances, the sovereign has the right, although not, of course, the obligation, to refuse the prime minister's request. Whether it is wise to refuse the request will depend upon a number of other factors, a necessary condition being the availability of an alternative government.

[32] Robert Rhodes James, 'The British Monarchy: Its Changing Constitutional Role', *Royal Society of Arts*, 142 (Apr. 1994), 25.

4

The Appointment of a Prime Minister

I

Under normal circumstances, the sovereign has no choice whom he or she should appoint as prime minister, and it is obvious who should be called to the Palace. When one party wins an overall majority in a general election, the leader of that party will be appointed prime minister. When a prime minister resigns or dies, the electoral machinery of the party concerned will be used to choose a new party leader, and that person will be summoned to the Palace and appointed prime minister.

The constitutional practice is for the sovereign to summon the party leader and ask him or her to form a government. Normally, the party leader will express an assurance that he or she will be able to form a government, and kiss hands immediately. But there is an alternative formula, which might prove useful in the case of a hung parliament (see Chapter 6). A party leader can merely state 'willingness to hold the necessary consultations to find out *whether* a government can be formed'.[1] That was the formula adopted by Lord Home when the queen asked him to form a government in 1963. Lord Home records that

On October 18 I was sent for by her Majesty and invited to form a Government. I expressed my gratitude, but explained to the Queen that I must ask leave to go away and see if I could form an administration. I was by no means sure, after the drama of the recent weeks, what the attitude of some of my colleagues would be.[2]

Harold Macmillan in his memoirs declares that

---

[1] Harold Wilson, *The Governance of Britain* (Weidenfeld & Nicolson/Michael Joseph, 1976), 40–1.
[2] Lord Home, *The Way the Wind Blows: An Autobiography* (Collins, 1976), 185.

I advised the Queen, both verbally, and in the second part of the written memorandum, *not* to appoint Home as P.M. at his first audience, but to use the older formula and entrust him with the task of forming an administration. He could then take his soundings and report to her.[3]

In the case of resignation, the procedure is that the prime minister immediately resigns the party leadership and announces that he or she will resign the premiership once a new leader has been chosen. Thus, in 1976, when Harold Wilson resigned as party leader, James Callaghan was elected leader of the Labour Party. Wilson then resigned as prime minister, and informed the queen that Callaghan was the choice of the Labour Party as leader. The queen accordingly summoned Callaghan to the Palace and appointed him prime minister. Similarly, in the case of the Conservative Party, when Margaret Thatcher in 1990 announced that she intended not to contest the second ballot for the Conservative leadership, having failed to win by a sufficient majority on the first against Michael Heseltine, a contest was held for the leadership between Heseltine, Douglas Hurd, and John Major. John Major having been elected leader, Margaret Thatcher resigned as prime minister and John Major was appointed.

In the case of the death or permanent incapacity of a prime minister in office, there will be an interregnum until a new leader has been chosen by the party in office. The use of an electoral procedure lengthens the period of the interregnum. In 1976, with six candidates contesting the election for the Labour leadership, it took three weeks for a leader to be chosen, although only one week was necessary in the case of the Conservatives in 1990, when three candidates contested the second ballot, which proved conclusive. During this interregnum there will be an acting prime minister, normally the minister who deputizes for the prime minister when he or she is absent.

This practice contrasts with that in Australia, where there is now a formal deputy prime minister and where a prime minister is appointed immediately there is a vacancy. It is accepted that the acting prime minister may well not succeed, and indeed on some occasions has not been a candidate for the succession. In 1939, upon the death of J. A. Lyons, there happened to be a vacancy in the position of deputy leader in Lyons's United Australia Party. The governor-general appointed Earle Page, leader of the junior partner in the

---

[3] Harold Macmillan, *At the End of the Day 1961–1963* (Macmillan, 1973), 518.

coalition, the Country Party, as prime minister until the United Australia Party, the senior party in the coalition, had chosen its new leader. The new leader turned out to be R. G. Menzies, and, once he had been chosen, Page resigned and the governor-general appointed Menzies prime minister.

In 1945, upon the death of the Labor prime minister John Curtin, the governor-general appointed as prime minister F. M. Forde, the deputy prime minister and the Labor Party's deputy leader. Forde was a candidate for the leadership, but the Labor Party elected as its leader Ben Chifley. Forde accordingly resigned, and the governor-general appointed Chifley prime minister.

Finally, in 1967, following the sudden disappearance and presumed death of the Liberal prime minister, Harold Holt, the governor-general appointed the deputy prime minister and leader of the Country Party, the junior partner in the coalition, John McEwen, as a caretaker prime minister. When the Liberal Party chose Senator John Gorton as its new leader, McEwen resigned and the governor-general appointed Gorton as prime minister. The governor-general incurred some criticism in 1967, since McEwen had made it clear that the Country Party was unwilling to continue the coalition with the Liberals if the deputy leader of the Liberal Party, William McMahon, were to be chosen leader. Some believed that the governor-general should, nevertheless, have appointed McMahon, who was, after all, the deputy leader of the largest party in the coalition. Critics argued that the governor-general had allowed McEwen to help determine who the leader of the Liberal Party ought to be, even though he, McEwen, was not himself a member of it. On the other hand, it could be argued that McEwen as deputy prime minister had a right to be asked, for he had stood in for the prime minister in his absence.[4]

In Britain, by contrast with Australia, there is provision neither for a deputy prime minister nor for a caretaker prime minister. On only one recent occasion has a caretaker head of government been considered, in 1953, when Churchill suffered a stroke, and his private secretary, John Colville, believed that he would not survive the weekend. The natural successor, Anthony Eden, was undergoing an operation in the United States and needed some months to recover. There was no obvious constitutional method by which a caretaker

[4] W. J. Hudson, *Casey* (Oxford University Press, Melbourne, 1986), 308–11.

could be appointed. But Colville remembers that 'The only thing the Queen could do . . . would be to send for somebody she knew very well and could trust implicitly to resign when Eden was well.'[5] Colville himself considered suggesting that the queen 'ask Lord Salisbury, although a peer, to form a caretaker Government, on the express understanding that he would retire when Mr. Eden was well enough to form a new Government'.[6] By contrast with Australia, Salisbury would not have taken the title of prime minister. In the event, however, Churchill recovered and the expedient proved unnecessary.

In Britain, by contrast with Australia, the sovereign has always refused to recognize the position of deputy prime minister. George VI specifically refused to create Anthony Eden deputy prime minister in 1951, 'an office which does not exist in the British constitutional hierarchy'.[7] This, however, is a circular argument. The office would have existed if the king had recognized it. In 1962, when R. A. Butler was styled deputy prime minister, the prime minister, Harold Macmillan, told the Commons that 'This is not an appointment submitted to the Sovereign but is a statement of the organisation of Government.'[8] In 1989, when Sir Geoffrey Howe, having been removed from the Foreign Office, was appointed Lord President of the Council and leader of the House of Commons, the move was sweetened by his being offered the position of deputy prime minister. No application to the Palace was made, however, that Howe be formally appointed deputy prime minister. Such an application might well have been refused.

Nevertheless, the office, as the biographer of George VI recognized in 1958, 'had become established by unofficial usage over the preceding eleven years'.[9] In 1942 Churchill, upon the reconstruction of his government, 'styled' Attlee as deputy prime minister, 'though no constitutional change was made'. The change, therefore, was 'in form rather than in fact'. Although no one has officially been appointed 'deputy prime minister', a number of ministers, who

[5] Robert Lacey, *Majesty: Elizabeth II and the House of Windsor* (Hutchinson, 1977), 198.

[6] Martin Gilbert, *Never Surrender: Winston S. Churchill 1945–1965* (Heinemann, 1988), 849–50.

[7] John Wheeler-Bennett, *King George VI: His Life and Reign* (Macmillan, 1958), 797.

[8] House of Commons, vol. 663, col. 633, 19 July 1962.

[9] Wheeler-Bennett, *King George VI*.

include, apart from Butler, Howe, and Attlee, Herbert Morrison, Anthony Eden, George Brown, Michael Stewart, Reginald Maudling, and William Whitelaw, have *acted* as deputy prime minister. This meant that they presided over cabinet meetings in the absence of the prime minister and chaired a number of key cabinet committees.

'It would', declared the biographer of George VI,

seem highly undesirable that the office of 'Deputy Prime Minister' should be officially recognised; since such recognition would certainly imply the establishment of a line of succession and would thereby impose a certain restriction upon one of the unquestioned prerogatives of the Sovereign— namely, the unfettered choice of a successor in the event of the death or resignation of the Prime Minister.[10]

This argument holds little weight today, however, since, under normal circumstances, with the parties electing their leaders, the sovereign has no real discretion. From the point of view of the political parties themselves, however, there may be a case for not recognizing the position of deputy prime minister, since that might imply that the candidate concerned is a favourite for the succession.

In the past, admittedly, the person acting as deputy prime minister has not been seen as having any right to the succession. Of those who have acted as deputy prime minister, only Eden has succeeded to the premiership. Moreover, some of those who have acted as deputy prime minister, such as Michael Stewart, were never perceived as possible contenders for the premiership.

No commitment is thus made in the nomination of a minister to be deputy prime minister, and there is no reason why formal recognition of this title should in any way restrict the sovereign. There is indeed one very good constitutional reason for recognizing an office which many previous prime ministers have found a highly convenient one, while accepting that it carries no right to the succession.[11] It is that the position following the death or incapacity of a prime minister in Britain is somewhat unsatisfactory. The Labour Party formally elects a deputy leader, who, by the party's rules, automatically becomes leader of the party when there is a vacancy. But there is, as we have seen, no provision for appointing a caretaker prime minister, and, were a minister to be designated at that stage as act-

[10] Wheeler-Bennett, *King George VI.*
[11] See Vernon Bogdanor, 'A Cypher with Substance', *The Times*, 29 July 1989.

ing prime minister, this might well seem a mark of favour. There was a rather unseemly wrangle, following the resignation of Harold Macmillan in 1963, on the issue of whether R. A. Butler, one of the leadership contenders, ought to give the final address, traditionally given by the leader of the party, at the Conservative Party Conference. Similar wrangles might be expected after the sudden death or incapacity of a prime minister as to who should act as prime minister. It might be argued that the function of carrying on the government during the interregnum should be divorced as far as possible from the leadership struggle. For this reason alone there is a case for recognizing the title of deputy prime minister.

One alternative, however, which would certainly prevent controversy arising over the succession might be to establish a convention that a cabinet minister who could not possibly be a leadership contender—for example, the Lord Chancellor—ought to preside over the government during the period of interregnum.

The sovereign's role in appointing a prime minister is today normally formal, and is confined to summoning to the Palace the elected leader of the majority party. There are, however, two circumstances under which the sovereign still has a genuine discretion. The first is where there is a hung parliament—that is, a parliament in which no single party enjoys an overall majority. The problems involved in hung parliaments are considered in Chapter 6.

The second circumstance under which the sovereign may have a genuine discretion in the appointment of a prime minister is when, because of war, as in 1916 or 1940, or economic crisis, as in 1931, a coalition has to be constructed. In two of these cases—1916 and 1940—the person appointed prime minister—Lloyd George in 1916 and Winston Churchill in 1940—was not a party leader. In 1931 Ramsay Mac-Donald was the leader of the Labour Party, but the vast majority of his party proved unwilling to follow him into the National Government, and MacDonald's National Labour Party, consisting of those few Labour MPs who were willing to support the National Government, was only thirteen strong after the general election of 1931.

II

Apart from the appointment of Ramsay MacDonald as prime minister of the National Government of 1931, there have been three controversial prime-ministerial appointments in the twentieth century. All of them have been appointments of Conservative prime ministers, the Labour Party having, from the time of its birth in 1900, always elected its leaders. The three occasions when the appointment of Conservative prime ministers have caused controversy were in 1923, when Stanley Baldwin was preferred to Lord Curzon; 1957, when Harold Macmillan was preferred to R. A. Butler; and 1963, when Lord Home was preferred to R. A. Butler, Reginald Maudling, and Lord Hailsham.

In 1923 the prime minister, Bonar Law, was stricken suddenly with cancer of the throat, and compelled to resign. The choice of successor lay between Lord Curzon, the foreign secretary, and Stanley Baldwin, chancellor of the exchequer and leader of the House of Commons. While there seems to have been a widespread expectation that Curzon would succeed, George V appointed Baldwin, primarily on the ground that the prime minister, in the circumstances then existing, had to be a member of the House of Commons, there being no provision at that time for the renunciation of peerages.

The circumstances were particularly difficult for George V, since Bonar Law, a dying man, was unwilling to offer any recommendation to the king, and, in any case, found it difficult to decide between Curzon, a former Viceroy of India, who had been foreign secretary since 1919 and who had acted as prime minister during his illness; and Baldwin, whom he liked but who had only two years' cabinet experience, and had been chancellor for only six months. Bonar Law expected Curzon to be chosen, feared that it might prove a mistaken choice, but hardly saw how it could be avoided.

George V, being unable to consult the outgoing prime minister, decided to consult Lord Balfour, the only living Conservative ex-prime minister, who recommended Baldwin on the grounds that the prime minister must be a member of the Commons. At the suggestion of Bonar Law, the king also consulted Lord Salisbury, a Conservative elder statesman, who recommended Curzon. It seems, however, that George V had favoured Baldwin from the beginning and that Balfour's recommendation merely confirmed his initial instincts. Others consulted by the king's private secretary, Lord Stamfordham, who favoured Curzon,[12] seem to have had little influence on the outcome.

[12] Randolph Churchill, *Lord Derby* (Heinemann, 1960), 503.

Balfour left a memorandum of the arguments which he had put before the king. He declared that

the king should follow the obvious, though not the inevitable course, and in the first instance ask the Leader of the House of Commons [Baldwin] to form a Government. . . . The apparent trouble was that G.N.C. [Curzon] was a man of greater age, greater experience and greater position than Baldwin whose experience of Cabinet work was relatively insignificant, and who, so far as I was aware, had no special capacity as a Parliamentarian. But undoubtedly there were several difficulties at the present time in having a Prime Minister in the Lords:

(1) Because the important Cabinet Offices were already held in a quite unusual proportion by Peers;

(2) Because to put, in addition to the existing Secretaries of State, a Prime Minister in the Upper House would certainly be resented by a large number of people, and might make the position of the Leader of the House of Commons one of great difficulty.

(3) Because (though I did not mention this) the present Opposition were the Labour Party who had no representatives in the House of Lords at all.[13]

Balfour adds that he 'understood from Stamfordham that these views were probably in very close conformity with those already held by His Majesty'.[14] Lord Stamfordham later told Lord Balfour that

It is a matter of satisfaction to the King that you, with your exceptional experience of a long parliamentary career and of the office of Prime Minister, should have confirmed his opinion that, at all events in the present circumstances, the Prime Minister of this country should be in the House of Commons.[15]

There are grounds for thinking that the peerage question was not, however, the only factor involved, and that Curzon's haughty and arrogant personality, something which could not be mentioned in public, was also of some significance in the king's decision.[16] Dermot Morrah, whose book *The Work of the Queen*, published in 1958, was based upon interviews with the queen's private secretaries, claimed that George V was

---

[13] Cited in Cameron Hazlehurst, 'The Baldwinian Conspiracy', *Historical Studies*, 16 (1974), 169. See also Robert Blake, *The Unknown Prime Minister: The Life and Times of Andrew Bonar Law 1858–1923* (Eyre & Spottiswoode, 1955), ch. XXXII, and David Gilmour, *Curzon* (John Murray, 1994), 581–86.

[14] Cited in Hazlehurst, 'The Baldwinian Conspiracy', 170.   [15] Ibid. 171.

[16] See Gilmour, *Curzon*, 583.

probably influenced by the thought that Baldwin was likely to preserve a milder temper in relations between the parties than Curzon, who was detested by most of the Labour Opposition. (The reason given at the time, that it was impossible to have a Prime Minister in the Lords, is thought to have been suggested by Lord Stamfordham to spare Curzon humiliation, although it now tends to be cited as constitutional precedent.)[17]

There was perhaps no inherent reason why the peerage need have proved an insurmountable obstacle. Had it been thought that Curzon was the right choice as prime minister, legislation might well have been passed allowing peers to speak in the House of Commons. Such legislation had, indeed, been suggested on more than one occasion in the immediately preceding years. In 1940, as we shall see, in the admittedly grave circumstances of wartime, George VI believed that Lord Halifax, rather than Winston Churchill, could succeed Chamberlain. As the biographer of George VI remarks,

none of those who had previously expressed a preference for Lord Halifax as Prime Minister, including Mr. Chamberlain, saw any *constitutional* objections to a Prime Minister in the House of Lords and . . . Lord Halifax's own doubts on accepting the premiership did not include this.[18]

One might speculate that, if Baldwin had been in the Lords and Curzon in the Commons, the constitutional objection might not have been pressed quite so strongly.

The king was, in any case, careful not to lay down any new constitutional doctrine, but only to give an answer to the practical question of how government could be carried on in the specific circumstances of 1923. When the king sent for Curzon to commiserate, the disappointed man asked him: 'Am I to understand then, Sir, that you consider that no peer can ever be Prime Minister?' The king replied: 'No, I didn't say that. What I said was that there were circumstances in which it was very undesirable that a peer should be Prime Minister and in my view this was such a case.'[19]

Some years later, Lord Stamfordham told the editor of *The Times*, Geoffrey Dawson (like Stamfordham, a supporter of Curzon), that he remembered how, in 1923, Dawson had been

inclined to minimize the objection to divorcing the Prime Minister from the House of Commons. But I told you that the king considered it almost

---

[17] Dermot Morrah, *The Work of the Queen* (William Kimber, 1958), 160.
[18] Wheeler-Bennett, *King George VI*, 444 n.
[19] Kenneth Rose, *King George V* (Weidenfeld & Nicolson, 1983), 272–3.

imperative to appoint the Prime Minister from the House of Commons, for were he not to do so, and the experiment failed, the country would blame the King for an act which was entirely his own, and which proved that His Majesty was ignorant of and out of touch with public opinion.[20]

Whatever the relative weight of the various factors, there can be little doubt that George V made the right decision. Baldwin undoubtedly had the support of the majority of Conservative MPs. Colonel Jackson, the chairman of the Conservative Party, told Lord Stamfordham, that, were a Conservative meeting to be summoned, 'they would not get 50 Members to vote in favour of Curzon'.[21] Moreover, the Labour Party, incensed at the thought that the prime minister might be in the Lords, immune from questioning by Labour MPs, issued a communiqué on the very day that Baldwin was chosen, declaring that, if a peer became prime minister, the party would employ 'every political device to precipitate a dissolution'.[22] Curzon's arrogant approach, his lack of awareness of the conditions of life of the majority of his countrymen and women, and his pomposity would certainly have exacerbated relations with the whole Labour movement. At a time of industrial strife, Curzon's approach to the labour problems could have led to social upheaval. Curzon's latest biographer admits that

Baldwin represented the post-war national mood very much better than Curzon. . . . The country was glad, as it later demonstrated, to have a man well-attuned to the temper of the age, a rather ordinary pipe-smoking Englishman with an ear for the concerns of ordinary people and a sympathetic approach to the Labour movement.[23]

III

The situation in 1957 was rather easier than that of 1923. The prime minister, Sir Anthony Eden, found himself compelled to resign on health grounds in January 1957. The two contenders for the premiership were R. A. Butler, the leader of the House of Commons and acting prime minister during Eden's absences due to illness; and Harold Macmillan, chancellor of the exchequer. Early accounts of

[20] Letter from Stamfordham of 16 Oct. 1928, Bodleian Library, Dawson Papers, MS 73, fo. 114.
[21] Cited in Hazlehurst, 'The Baldwinian Conspiracy', 187.   [22] Ibid. 191.
[23] Gilmour, *Curzon*, 586.

Eden's resignation, such as the memoirs of Lord Kilmuir and of Harold Macmillan, suggest that Eden was not consulted by the queen as to who his successor might be. Macmillan declared that Eden 'had neither been asked for his advice nor had volunteered it'.[24] Lord Blake in the *Dictionary of National Biography* maintains that Eden was consulted and that 'there is good evidence that he [Eden] did not recommend Butler'.[25] Eden's papers, however, make it clear that he *was* consulted by the queen and did in fact recommend Butler.

'Her Majesty', Eden recorded in a memorandum written for Sir Michael Adeane, the queen's private secretary, in November 1970, 'followed the constitutional procedure and asked me my advice as to her choice of my successor'.[26] The Royal Archives remain closed for the current reign, but in the Avon Papers there is a record of his audience with the queen, dictated on 12 January 1957, three days after his resignation.

Her Majesty spoke of the future and of the difficult choice that lay before Her. I agreed that it was certainly difficult. The Queen made no formal request for my advice [since Eden was resigning as Prime Minister, he was in fact in no position to offer advice], but enabled me to signify that my own debt to Mr. Butler while I have [sic] been Prime Minister was very real and that I thought he had discharged his difficult task during the three weeks while I was away in Jamaica very well.[27]

While the precedents of 1894 and 1923, then, show that the sovereign is not bound to ask a retiring prime minister for a view as to his or her successor, the precedent of 1957 shows that neither is the sovereign bound to accept the views of a retiring prime minister as to his or her successor.

Eden also recommended the procedure which the queen might adopt to assist her in choosing a successor, suggesting that the cabinet be asked for its view. Accordingly, Lord Kilmuir, the Lord Chancellor, and Lord Salisbury, were asked to poll the cabinet, which, with apparently only one or two exceptions, favoured

[24] Harold Macmillan, *Riding the Storm, 1955–1959* (Macmillan, 1971), 184.

[25] *Dictionary of National Biography, 1971–80* (Oxford University Press, 1986), 271.

[26] Birmingham University Library, Avon Papers (AP) 20/33/12 A. The word 'advice' is perhaps inappropriate here. See the next quotation.

[27] Ibid. See also Keith Kyle, *Suez* (Weidenfeld & Nicolson, 1991), 533. Kyle's account in which he declares that Eden favoured Butler has been confirmed by private information.

Macmillan. The queen also consulted Winston Churchill, the only living Conservative ex-prime minister, who was to tell his constituency executive at Woodford in 1959 that 'I recommended Macmillan and was most delighted to see it was acted upon';[28] and Lords Chandos and Waverley, two senior ex-cabinet ministers from Conservative governments. All of these apparently, quite independently of each other, recommended Macmillan. In addition, the Queen's private secretary, Sir Michael Adeane, conducted a canvass amongst Conservative MPs. While there is no suggestion that the queen's appointment of Macmillan was in any way unjustified, the method by which the appointment was made was subject to some criticism, and, in retrospect, it is difficult to understand the particular qualifications enjoyed by Lords Chandos and Waverley which entitled them to be consulted. The process of consultation enabled critics to caricature the process of selection as one in which the premiership was being decided by an unrepresentative aristocratic clique, out of touch with the realities of the second half of the twentieth century.

The leadership selection in October 1963, following the resignation of Harold Macmillan on health grounds, was perhaps the most complex that any sovereign has had to face in modern times, and the controversy surrounding it led to the Conservative Party instituting an electoral procedure for selecting its leader—which was first used in 1965, when Sir Alec Douglas-Home (as Lord Home had become after assuming the premiership in 1963) resigned the leadership of the Conservative Party and Edward Heath was elected in his place.

The contest of 1963 had three novel factors. The first was that there were no less than four contenders for the premiership: R. A. Butler, once more, now First Secretary of State, Lord Hailsham, the Lord President of the Council and Minister for Science, Lord Home, the foreign secretary, and Reginald Maudling, the chancellor of the exchequer. Lords Hailsham and Home were enabled to be candidates as a result of legislation which had received the Royal Assent only a few weeks earlier allowing for the renunciation of peerages.

The second novel feature was that the vacancy occurred in the middle of the annual party conference, so that, inevitably, party activists were drawn into the process of selection. It was no longer

[28] *The Times*, 7 Jan. 1959.

possible, as it had been in 1957, to confine the process of selection primarily to the cabinet. Therefore, thirdly, in place of the rather haphazard arrangements for consultation adopted in 1923 and 1957, there was, in addition to the polling of the cabinet, a far more detailed canvass of MPs, peers, and leading members of the party outside parliament than had ever been undertaken before.

This process of consultation was instituted by Harold Macmillan, who had already indicated that he would resign the premiership as soon as a new leader of the Conservative Party had been selected. Macmillan called the canvass the 'customary processes of consultation', but this implied precedents where none existed. He has been criticized for taking charge of the procedure and maintaining control of it from his hospital bed. Yet he only did so after discovering that the party was unclear about how a successor should be chosen, and the procedure which Macmillan proposed was, so it seems, accepted by the cabinet.[29]

The outcome, the selection of Lord Home, cannot be said seriously to have misrepresented Conservative opinion at the time. It seems clear that Lord Home was the popular choice of Conservative peers, that he had at least a narrow plurality of votes amongst Conservative MPs as their first choice, gaining more support when later preferences were taken into account,[30] and that he was the first choice of the cabinet, enjoying a plurality although probably not an overall majority amongst his ministerial colleagues. R. A. Butler, who was popularly thought to be the favourite for the succession, had in fact been told in June 1963, four months before Macmillan's resignation, by the chairman of the 1922 Committee, representing all Conservative back-bench MPs, that 'the chaps won't have you'. 'It had not been a warning', comments the historian of the 1922 Committee, 'that was meant to be taken lightly—and it was not.'[31]

Macmillan was widely criticized for foisting Lord Home on an unwilling party. Yet it is doubtful if criticism of Macmillan is

[29] According to Randolph Churchill, not perhaps a wholly reliable witness; see *The Fight for the Tory Leadership* (Heinemann, 1964), 126.

[30] See the evidence of Martin Redmayne, the chief whip at the time, in *The Listener*, 19 Dec. 1963, p. 1013.

[31] Philip Goodhart with Ursula Branson, *The 1922* (Macmillan, 1973), 196. This evidence can now be confirmed from the Butler Papers at Trinity College Cambridge. See Vernon Bogdanor, 'The Selection of the Party Leader', in Stuart Ball and Anthony Seldon (eds.), *The Conservative Century* (Oxford University Press, 1994), from which much of the above is taken.

justified. He lacked both the means and the will to secure the premiership for Home against the wishes of the party as a whole. He was unable to impose his first choice, Lord Hailsham, and he could not have ensured the succession of Home had the latter not genuinely enjoyed the confidence of the party.

Macmillan presented the queen with a memorandum from his hospital bed which, apparently, made an unanswerable case for Lord Home.[32] Iain Macleod, who refused to serve under Home in protest at the method by which he had been selected, admitted that the information tendered by Macmillan was so conclusive that 'it was unthinkable even to consider asking for a second opinion'.[33] Macmillan also asked the queen to act quickly in summoning Home to the Palace so as to forestall a revolt by the defeated candidates, who, in his view, were refusing to accept that the verdict of the party had gone against them. Since Macmillan was in the process of resigning when he presented the queen with his memorandum, he was no longer in a position to offer binding advice. Nevertheless, the queen decided to accept Macmillan's recommendation, to seek no recommendations from anyone else, and to ask Home to form a government. Significantly, Home did not accept immediately, but sought leave to see if he could form an administration. It was only after Lord Home had been able to appoint his leading rivals, Butler, Hailsham, and Maudling, to his government that he was able to report success and accept office as prime minister.

The queen has been criticized for acting so rapidly in summoning Home to the Palace. She should, so it has been argued, first have sought recommendations from leading Conservatives other than Macmillan, and, secondly, have waited so as to ensure that Home really did have the support which was claimed for him. The queen was certainly constitutionally entitled to consult more widely, for Macmillan, having already announced his resignation, was in no constitutional position to offer binding advice to the sovereign.

Nevertheless, the criticisms made of the queen with regard to the 1963 succession crisis lack substance. It is implausible to believe that Macmillan was able to misrepresent the opinion of the Conservative Party in the memorandum which he handed to the queen. Faced with the preponderant judgement in favour of Home, based, the memorandum apparently declared, on a canvass of the cabinet, the

[32] This memorandum has not yet been published.
[33] 'The Struggle for the Tory Leadership', *Spectator*, 17 Jan. 1964.

Conservative Party in both Houses of Parliament, and in the country, it was not for the queen to conduct her own separate canvass and involve herself in the internal politics of the Conservative Party. If the Conservative Party was divided, as clearly it was, the queen could only compromise the position of the monarchy if she were to seem to take part in that conflict. The queen took the straightforward course, and it was for the Conservative Party, if it so wished, to make it clear that it would not accept Home as prime minister. In such circumstances, Home would have proved unable to form a government, as Hartington would have been unable to form a government in 1880, and he would have had to report failure. The queen would then have awaited the outcome of whatever procedure the Conservatives thought appropriate to select an alternative leader.

Although the queen acted perfectly constitutionally, nevertheless the choice of Lord Home seemed almost deliberately to flout the prevailing mood of the public, which had become anxious that, economically, Britain was falling behind the countries of the Continent. The remedy for this deficiency was widely felt to be a political leadership more professional in its approach to economic problems, and more attuned to advances in science and technology. This was a mood which Harold Wilson was able skilfully to exploit, but, in their choice of Home, the Conservatives seemed to be turning their back on the needs of the times. Indeed, Macmillan himself came to believe that the choice of Home had been a mistake, and that R. A. Butler might, after all, have proved a wiser choice.[34] The selection procedure in 1963 seemed both undignified and divisive, and the Conservatives appeared, in William Rees-Mogg's words, to have 'ceased to be gentlemen without becoming democrats'.[35]

It was widely accepted after 1963, therefore, that a more explicitly democratic procedure of selection was needed. No consultative process, however fair, would any longer be accepted as legitimate, for the queen was being asked, not who would make the best prime minister, the question facing the sovereign in Queen Victoria's time, but, in effect, who ought to be leader of the Conservative Party. Yet, if the person whom the queen ought to appoint was that person who had the most support in the Conservative Party, why should she be required to use her own judgement as to who that person might be when Conservative MPs were in a better position than the queen to

[34] Alistair Horne, *Macmillan*, ii. *1957–1986* (Macmillan, 1989), 582.
[35] *Sunday Times*, 13 Oct. 1963.

make that judgement. The Conservatives, before they adopted an electoral procedure, were thus in the odd position of being able to select their leader while in opposition, but unable to do so in office, when their leader would become prime minister!

As early as 1947, George VI's private secretary, Sir Alan Lascelles, had written to the cabinet secretary, Sir Edward Bridges, that

a clear advance indication by the members of the party in power as to the man they want to be their leader is, it seems to me, a help to wise ruling by the Sovereign rather than a derogation of the Sovereign's power. It has been obvious for many years that it is no use the Sovereign sending for somebody who cannot command Parliamentary support; therefore, it is better that the Sovereign should have clear proof of who can command it . . . In fact I should say that the definite and public adoption by the party concerned of a new leader is a more satisfactory, and more dignified way of doing business . . .[36]

For this reason, 1963, therefore, has proved to be the last occasion on which the sovereign was required to appoint a prime minister relying upon 'customary processes of consultation'.

IV

In 1916, 1931, and 1940 the sovereign appointed as prime minister the man who could, he believed, best lead a national coalition government. In 1916 and 1931 this was done by means of inter-party conferences at Buckingham Palace. In 1940, by contrast, Neville Chamberlain, the resigning prime minister, took it upon himself to call a meeting of the two alternative candidates for the premiership, Winston Churchill and Lord Halifax, together with David Margesson, the chief whip, in order to be able to present an unequivocal recommendation to the king.

In December 1916 H. H. Asquith, who had been prime minister of a Liberal government between 1908 and 1915, and of a coalition government since 1915, resigned on the grounds that he was losing parliamentary support. By 1916 the Conservatives had become the largest party in the Commons, but they lacked an overall majority. Since, in wartime, a minority government would be unlikely to provide the strength which the country needed, it was apparent that a

[36] Lascelles to Bridges, 11 Sept. 1947, RA GVI 131/80.

new coalition government of some kind had to be formed. George V began by summoning Bonar Law, the Conservative leader, and asked him to form a government. Bonar Law declared that he would consult his friends, but felt it unlikely that he would be successful. His chances might have been improved had he been able to dissolve parliament. The king, however, deprecated a general election in wartime and indicated that he could not *guarantee* to grant a dissolution to Bonar Law, who was, after all, only a potential prime minister.[37]

After consulting with colleagues, Bonar Law returned to the king to confess that he would be unable to form a government. The question then arose, if a general election were not possible, of how the selection of a new prime minister could be given legitimacy, and how a wartime consensus could be created. The device of an inter-party conference was suggested by A. J. Balfour, the only living ex-prime minister apart from Asquith and Rosebery, and by Arthur Henderson, leader of the Labour Party, a partner in the wartime coalition. Lord Stamfordham, the king's private secretary, was initially sceptical but was eventually convinced, and the king summoned a conference at Buckingham Palace. The conference was attended by Asquith, Bonar Law, and Henderson, the three party leaders, together with Lloyd George, a contender for the premiership, and Balfour, a widely respected elder statesman.

The purpose of the conference was to devise an administration that could command the widest possible support. It was hoped that the new administration would include Asquith, who had been prime minister for a longer period than anyone since Lord Liverpool. It was generally agreed that Asquith would be unable to form another broad-based administration, but it was suggested that, if he would be willing to join a government led by Bonar Law, then the latter should be appointed prime minister. If, however, he was unwilling to join a government led by Bonar Law, then the Conservative leader would finally abandon his attempt to form a government, and Lloyd George would seek to do so. In the event, Asquith refused to

---

[37] Robert Blake, *The Unknown Prime Minister* (Eyre & Spottiswoode, 1955), 337. Blake's account is to be preferred to that given by Harold Nicolson in *King George V: His Life and Reign* (Constable, 1952), 289. Nicolson declares that the king told Bonar Law 'that he would refuse, if asked, to accord him a Dissolution'. There seems no reason to believe that the king would make a commitment in advance that he would not, under any circumstances, grant a dissolution to Bonar Law once he had become prime minister.

serve in a subordinate position, and Lloyd George formed a coalition from which Asquith and his supporters stood aside.

In 1916 the conference method, by making possible the investigation of alternative possibilities, allowed a new prime minister to be appointed with the minimum of disruption and upheaval. The king proved to be a valuable facilitator to the formation of the Lloyd George government, which was, in the circumstances, the government most suited to pursuing the war effectively. The 1916 conference thus 'provided a valuable precedent for forming coalitions during times of acute constitutional stress or national crisis'.[38]

The appointment of a prime minister in 1940, which also involved the transition from a party government to a coalition government, was carried out in a different way, however, such as precluded the king from exercising any influence upon the outcome at all. On 8 May 1940 the Conservative government's majority, normally around 240, had fallen to 81, following an adjournment debate on the Norwegian campaign. Neville Chamberlain, the prime minister, appreciated that the war could be continued effectively only under a coalition government. But he also realized that the opposition Labour and Liberal parties might prove unwilling to serve under him. Under those circumstances, an alternative prime minister who could lead a coalition government would be necessary. There were two obvious contenders—Winston Churchill, the First Lord of the Admiralty, and Lord Halifax, the foreign secretary.

In the normal course of events, the prime minister might have been expected to inform the king of his possible resignation, and, if asked, to recommend a successor. He might also, as Eden was to do in 1957, have suggested a procedure by which a successor could be found. Alternatively, the king might have asked his private secretary to make soundings, as Lord Stamfordham had done in 1923, to consider who might be the most acceptable prime minister.

Chamberlain, however, did not visit the Palace until a successor had already been agreed. He summoned Churchill, Lord Halifax, and David Margesson, the Conservative chief whip, to a meeting on 9 May. The general consensus in the Commons seemed to favour Halifax, although there was some movement towards Churchill as MPs came to realize the dangerous situation which Britain was now

---

[38] John D. Fair, *British Interparty Conferences: A Study of the Procedure of Conciliation in British Politics, 1867–1921* (Oxford University Press, 1980), 159; ch. VII contains a detailed account of the 1916 conference.

facing. Nevertheless, Churchill had aroused widespread distrust during the inter-war years through his erratic political judgements, especially his hostility towards Indian self-government, and his support for Edward VIII long after most politicians had appreciated that abdication was inevitable. In addition, he was seen, on account of his belligerent attitudes during the General Strike of 1926, as an enemy of the labour movement. The Labour leaders, Attlee and Dalton, certainly preferred Halifax.[39] According to Margesson, who was himself a supporter of Halifax, the House of Commons also was for Halifax, and Chamberlain too seems to have favoured Halifax.[40] But Halifax declined the office, saying that it could not be held by a peer during such dangerous times. No one else seems to have regarded that as an obstacle, and no other leader raised any constitutional objection to a peer becoming prime minister. Ironically, Halifax, in his former incarnation as an MP, had himself in 1919 moved the rejection of a Bill providing for the renunciation of peerages in 1919.[41]

On 10 May, the day after the crucial meeting, Chamberlain went to the king to tell him that Labour would enter the government but only under another leader. He therefore offered his resignation. The king's own words describe what happened next.

We then had an informal talk over his successor. I, of course, suggested Halifax, but he told me that H. was not enthusiastic, as being in the Lords he could only act as a shadow or a ghost in the Commons, where all the real work took place. I was disappointed over this statement, as I thought H. was the obvious man, & that his peerage could be placed in abeyance for the time being. Then I knew that there was only one person whom I could send for to form a Government who had the confidence of the country, & that was Winston.[42]

The king shared the general view that Churchill's political course had been erratic during the years before 1940, and in addition he had a personal reason for being suspicious of him, since he could not but regard him as a partisan of the former Edward VIII, now the Duke

---

[39] A. J. P. Taylor, *English History, 1914–1945* (Oxford University Press, 1965), 473.

[40] A. J. P. Taylor, *Beaverbrook* (Hamish Hamilton, 1972), 531.

[41] Andrew Roberts, *The Holy Fox: A Biography of Lord Halifax* (Weidenfeld & Nicolson, 1991), 201; this biography provides the best modern account of the appointment of Churchill.

[42] Wheeler-Bennett, *King George VI*, 444.

of Windsor, whom George VI regarded as an ever-present threat to the stability of the throne. But Chamberlain's recommendation, and the method by which it had been reached, left the king no choice. He had no alternative but to send for Churchill.

What justification did Chamberlain have in undertaking an action which had the inevitable result of limiting the discretion of the sovereign? He did not, admittedly, initiate any recommendation as to a successor; indeed he said nothing until the king asked him for his views. He remained, however, leader of the Conservative Party, which had a large overall majority over all other parties, and this perhaps gave him some authority to institute the procedure of consultation. His position was, in this respect, quite different from that of Asquith in 1916, for Asquith's Liberals did not enjoy an overall majority in the Commons, and he was in the process of being repudiated by an important section of his party. Nevertheless, it was the premiership that was vacant, not the leadership of the Conservative Party, for Chamberlain remained party leader until forced to resign through ill health in October 1940.

It has been suggested that, far from favouring Halifax, Chamberlain wanted Churchill to succeed him, but did not want this preference to be publicly known. That, however, is probably too Machiavellian an explanation. Perhaps the best explanation is the simplest one. Chamberlain wished to save a new and inexperienced sovereign difficulty, and also wanted to save time at a period when rapid decisions had to be made, and an interregnum, even of a few days, might have had calamitous results. In the event, Hitler invaded France, Belgium, and Holland on the morning of 10 May, a few hours after the fateful meeting between Chamberlain, Churchill, Halifax, and Margesson, and Churchill's appointment as prime minister thus came on the very day on which the battle in the west had begun.

Churchill well understood to whom he owed the premiership. On 26 July 1940 he told W. P. Crozier, editor of the *Manchester Guardian*, 'I owe something to Chamberlain, you know. When he resigned he could have advised the King to send for Halifax and he didn't.'[43]

---

[43] Roberts, *The Holy Fox*, 243.

V

The process which led to the formation of the National Government of 1931 was the most contentious of the three coalition formations in which the sovereign has been involved, and it deserves more detailed consideration.

The crisis arose out of the split in the Labour cabinet in August 1931 over whether cuts in unemployment benefit ought to form part of the programme of economic retrenchment needed to stem a flight from the pound, and to maintain Britain's position on the gold standard. The Labour government was in a minority in the House of Commons, and so, if it was to secure acceptance of the economic package which it proposed, it needed the support of MPs from either the Liberal or the Conservative party. The vast majority of politicians, together with the general public, believed that, were Britain to be forced off the gold standard, terrible economic consequences would ensue. There was a state of panic, and almost of hysteria, during the days in which the vital decisions were made, and it should not be imagined that the main actors were considering the options in a calm and detached manner.

The Labour prime minister, Ramsay MacDonald, strove hard throughout August 1931 to secure agreement amongst his colleagues to an economy package. By Sunday, 23 August, however, it was becoming clear that agreement was unlikely. The king had returned from Balmoral on the overnight train, and saw MacDonald at 10.30 in the morning. MacDonald told the king, as he recorded in his diary, that

after to-night I might be of no further use, & should resign with the whole Cabinet. He asked if I would advise him to send for Henderson [the second leading figure of the Labour Party, and the leader of those in cabinet who were resisting the proposed cuts in unemployment benefit]. I said 'No', which he said relieved him. I advised him in the meantime to send for the leaders of the other two parties & have them report position from their points of view. He said he would & would advise them strongly to support me. I explained my hopeless Parlty. position if there were any resignations. He said that he believed I was the only person who could carry the country through. I said that did I share his belief I should not contemplate what I do, but that I did not share it.[44]

[44] MacDonald diary, 23 Aug. 1931, cited in David Marquand, *Ramsay MacDonald* (Jonathan Cape, 1977), 630.

The king made it clear during this interview that he would be reluctant for MacDonald to resign. Indeed, he pressed him not to, even though MacDonald indicated by referring to his 'hopeless Parlty. position if there were any resignations' that he might well not be able to carry the whole of his party with him in carrying through the economy cuts.

The king, acting on MacDonald's advice, then consulted the other party leaders. But the Conservative leader, Stanley Baldwin, could not be found, while the Liberal leader, Lloyd George, was incapacitated by illness throughout the crisis. The king, therefore, next saw Sir Herbert Samuel, the acting leader of the Liberal Party. Samuel recommended that, if MacDonald proved unable to carry his cabinet, the best solution to the crisis would be a National Government, 'unless he [i.e. MacDonald] found that he could not carry with him a significant number of his colleagues'.[45]

Following Samuel, Baldwin arrived at the Palace, imagining that, as leader of the opposition, he would be asked to form a government. Instead, the king asked him whether he would be prepared to serve in a national government under MacDonald. To this question, put by his sovereign, there was only one answer which a patriotic Conservative could give, although, the night before his interview with the king, Baldwin had told his chief lieutenant, Neville Chamberlain, that he 'hoped and prayed that he might not have to join a National Government'.[46]

The king, in suggesting a national government, was using his prerogative to offer a solution to the grave economic crisis faced by the nation. Of the three party leaders whom the king had seen, only one, Samuel, had favoured a national government, and only with the qualification that MacDonald could bring most of his supporters with him into the government.

The idea of a national government had been widely discussed in political circles for much of the previous year.[47] It had the support

[45] Memo. of events, 20–3 Aug. 1931, written 23 Sept. 1931, House of Lords Record Office, Samuel Papers, A/77/7, cited in Vernon Bogdanor, '1931 Revisited: The Constitutional Aspects', *Twentieth Century British History*, 4 (1991), 14. The qualification quoted in the text is omitted in Nicolson's account in *George V*, 461.

[46] Neville Chamberlain to Anne Chamberlain, 23 Aug. 1931, Birmingham University Library, 1/26/447, Chamberlain Papers, cited in Bogdanor '1931 Revisited'.

[47] Bogdanor, '1931 Revisited', 7–10, from which the above account is taken. However, my view of the wisdom of the king's action is rather more critical now than it was in 1991 when the article was published.

of Lord Stamfordham, the king's private secretary until his death in March 1931, who wrote, in December 1930, to one of the leading proponents of the idea, 'I wish you every success in your efforts';[48] and of Stamfordham's successor, Sir Clive Wigram, who wrote, at the beginning of August 1931, to Sir Horace Rumbold, the British ambassador to Germany, 'What we require is a National Emergency Government, but no two men I meet can agree how this can be formed.'[49] Three weeks earlier, Wigram had warned the king that

If a crash comes in Germany we shall have a financial situation something like that at the outbreak of war, and there will be a demand for a moratorium all round. A Minority Government will hardly be able to deal with the situation, and it is quite possible that Your Majesty might be asked to approve of a National Government.[50]

Thus the idea of a national government to deal with the economic emergency had already taken hold in Palace circles, and it must have implanted itself into the mind of the king well before events at the end of August seemed to make it necessary.

Although a national government led by MacDonald seemed the preferred choice of at most one of the three party leaders, Samuel, and that with qualifications, the king knew, following his interviews with Baldwin and Samuel, that they would both be prepared to serve in such a government.

MacDonald, however, seemed determined to resign. After a cabinet meeting on the Sunday evening when it became clear that agreement on expenditure cuts could not be reached, MacDonald left Downing Street for the Palace, saying to Sir Ernest Harvey, deputy governor of the Bank of England, 'I am off to the Palace to throw in my hand.'[51] He told the king that 'he had no alternative than to tender the resignation of the cabinet'. The king, however,

impressed on the Prime Minister that he was the only man to lead the country through this crisis and hoped he would reconsider the situation. His Majesty told him that the Conservatives and Liberals would support him in restoring the confidence of foreigners in the financial stability of the country. The Prime Minister asked whether the King would confer with Baldwin, Samuel and himself in the morning. His Majesty willingly acceded to this request.[52]

[48] Bogdanor, '1931 Revisited', 9.

[49] Wigram to Rumbold, 3 Aug. 1931, Bodleian Library, Rumbold Papers, MS Rumbold, dep. 38, fos. 224–5, cited in Bogdanor, '1931 Revisited', 10.

[50] Cited in Nicolson, *George V*, 449.   [51] Ibid. 464.   [52] Ibid.

At the Buckingham Palace Conference, held on the Monday morning, 24 August, the king gave the three party leaders a virtual instruction that they should form a national government under MacDonald's leadership.

At 10 a.m. the King held a Conference at Buckingham Palace at which the Prime Minister, Baldwin and Samuel were present. At the beginning, His Majesty impressed upon them that before they left the Palace some communiqué must be issued which would no longer keep the country and the world in suspense. The Prime Minister said that he had the resignation of his Cabinet in his pocket, but the King replied that he trusted there was no question of the Prime Minister's resignation: the leaders of the three Parties must get together and come to some arrangement. His Majesty hoped that the Prime Minister, with the colleagues who remained faithful to him, would help in the formation of a National Government, which the King was sure would be supported by the Conservatives and the Liberals. The King assured the Prime Minister that, remaining at his post, his position and reputation would be much more enhanced than if he surrendered the government of the country at such a crisis.[53]

The king's role in the formation of the National Government was much greater than is generally thought. He was not merely the facilitator of the new government, as he had been in 1916, but the instigator of it. Three times he had made it clear to MacDonald that he did not wish to accept his resignation: on the morning of Sunday, 23 August, when he told MacDonald that he would 'advise them [the other two party leaders] to support him'; on the evening of the same day, after the cabinet meeting, when the king impressed upon the prime minister that he was the only man to lead the nation through the crisis, and at the Buckingham Palace Conference itself. Had the king simply accepted MacDonald's resignation on any of these three occasions, either there would have been no national government; or, if there had been, it would not have been led by MacDonald.

But the National Government was a coalition of a highly unusual type. It was to be, in the words of Sir Clive Wigram's memorandum,

---

[53] Memo. by the king's private secretary, Sir Clive Wigram, cited in ibid. 465–6. Nicolson in fact held the view that the king had played an important, perhaps a crucial, role in the formation of the National Government, but he did not allow this view to appear in his official biography of the king. In an unpublished section of his diaries he writes of his interview with Queen Mary on 21 March 1949. 'I talked to her about the 1931 crisis and said that I was convinced that the King had been a determinant influence on that occasion' (cited in Bogdanor, '1931 Revisited', 25).

a National Emergency Government until an emergency bill or bills had been passed by Parliament, which would restore once more British credit and the confidence of foreigners. After that they would expect His Majesty to grant a dissolution. To this course the King agreed. During the Election the National Government would remain in being, though of course each Party would fight the Election on its own lines.[54]

Interestingly, the king granted to MacDonald's National Government what he had refused to Bonar Law in wartime, when the latter was attempting to form a government in 1916,[55] namely, the promise of a dissolution. The reason for this, no doubt, was that a national government was seen as a temporary emergency government—'an emergency Committee of Public Safety' in Sir Samuel Hoare's words[55]—and there would be a reversion to party government once the immediate storm was past.

The conditions under which the National Government was formed were rendered more precise in a memorandum written by Sir Herbert Samuel at the Buckingham Palace Conference, after the king had withdrawn. The relevant conditions were:

1. National Government to be formed to deal with the present financial emergency.
2. It will not be a Coalition in the ordinary sense of the term but a co-operation of individuals.
3. When the emergency is dealt with the Government's work will have finished and parties will return to their ordinary positions.
7. The election which may follow the end of the Government will not be fought by the Government but by the parties.[57]

At the final meeting of the Labour government, held at 12 noon on 24 August, shortly after the end of the Buckingham Palace Conference at which MacDonald had agreed to lead a national government, the prime minister declared that

The proposal was that His Majesty would invite certain individuals as individuals to take upon their shoulders the burden of carrying on the Government and Mr. Baldwin and Mr. Samuel [sic] had stated that they were prepared to act accordingly . . . the Administration would not exist for a period longer than was necessary to dispose of the emergency, and when that purpose was achieved the political Parties would resume their

[54] Cited in Nicolson, *George V*, 466.   [55] See p. 100.
[56] Lord Templewood (Sir Samuel Hoare), *Nine Troubled Years* (Collins, 1954), 22–3.
[57] Samuel Papers, A/77, cited in Bogdanor, '1931 Revisited', 16.

respective positions. The Administration would not be a Coalition Government in the usual sense of the term, but a Government of co-operation for this one purpose.[58]

It had been agreed that, at the general election which would follow the end of the emergency period, there would be no 'coupons', pacts, or other party arrangements. In a letter written the same day to junior ministers, MacDonald reiterated that

The Government that has been formed is not a Coalition but a co-operation between individuals who are banded together to avoid the disaster. No parties are involved in it, and as soon as the country gets on an even keel again, the Government will cease to exist.[59]

The government, then, was not a coalition government of the normal type, but a government of 'co-operation of individuals' formed for the specific purpose of dealing with the national emergency, after which it would be dissolved. But was such a government constitutionally appropriate in an era of party government?

Since at least the 1870s, it had become clear that parliamentary government meant party government, and could be carried out only under conditions in which political parties undertook the work of government. The idea of a 'Government of All the Talents', of a government of individuals, seemed to hark back to the eighteenth century, when the sovereign was able to appoint a government of 'King's Friends'. Indeed, one critic of the king's actions in 1931 declared that 'Mr. MacDonald was as much the personal choice of George V as Lord Bute was the personal choice of George III. He is the sole modern prime Minister who has been unencumbered by party support in his period of office.'[60]

MacDonald presumably appreciated that many, perhaps the majority, in the Labour Party would not endorse his action in forming a national government. In the event, only seven ministers and eight back-benchers followed him. Unlike Lloyd George in 1916, who brought with him a substantial number of Liberal MPs,

[58] 24 Aug. 1931, PRO CAB 47 (31), pp. 1–2, cited in Bogdanor, '1931 Revisited', 17.

[59] PRO, MacDonald Papers, 30/69/383, cited in ibid.

[60] Harold Laski, *Parliamentary Government in England* (Allen & Unwin, 1938), 403. Laski's pamphlet, *The Crisis and the Constitution: 1931 and After* (Hogarth Press, 1932), is also worth consulting. See also for a later criticism of George V, Graeme C. Moodie, 'The Monarch and the Selection of a Prime Minister: A Re-Examination of the Crisis of 1931', *Political Studies*, 5 (1957), 1–20.

MacDonald had no political base upon which he could form a coalition government of the normal type. It is difficult to understand, therefore, why he should have been a candidate for the premiership for any reason other than that the king happened to believe that he was the only man to save the country, a political judgement which many may not have shared. The question of whether MacDonald should remain as prime minister if he could not retain the support of his party might also have been asked by Baldwin. Perhaps the reason why he did not ask it was that the king was pressing him to accept a national government under MacDonald.

It can be argued, therefore, that what happened in 1931 was constitutionally questionable because it ignored the crucial role played by political parties in the formation of a modern government in a democracy. The defence of the king's actions is that he acted under what he saw as the compulsion of necessity, a national emergency which he and almost everyone else believed might lead to a rapid collapse of the currency.

The National Government had been formed for a limited period and for a specific object, the defence of the currency. The terms of the agreement establishing the National Government provided that, once the currency had been saved, traditional party warfare would be resumed. Under no circumstances would the National Government fight a general election as a government.

This agreement was, however, soon forgotten. First, the Labour Party expelled all those serving in the National Government, including MacDonald, who thus became a leader without a party. It would not be possible for him to return to the Labour Party. Secondly, the National Government was forced off the gold standard, less than a month after it had been formed. Thirdly, those in the National camp, and especially the Conservatives, by far the dominant element in the National Government, came to regard the Labour Party's opposition to cuts in public expenditure, many of which the party had supported when in office, as unpatriotic. The Conservatives demanded a general election in which the new government could receive a popular mandate.

For the National Government to fight an election as a government rather than on party lines was a clear breach of the undertakings which had been made at the time of its formation. The king, under whose auspices the agreement had been made, might have been thought to have been the guarantor of the agreement. It might have been expected that he would remind the party leaders of it. But, on the contrary, he took the view that a continuation of the National Government was in the best interests of the country. When, on 29 September, MacDonald told the king that he was having difficulty finding a formula which could unite his colleagues, George V

impressed upon the Prime Minister that the country had to be saved and that there should be a combination of all decent minded politicians towards this end. Party differences should be sunk. If a Socialist Government came into power and carried out their extravagant promises to the electorate, this country would be finished. The King was sure that the present Prime Minister was the only man who could save the country and His Majesty himself was prepared to support him. . . . The King throughout was in favour of an Election and the Prime Minister when he left certainly seemed more courageous and more firm in his conviction that a General Election was necessary.[61]

The king also saw Sir Herbert Samuel and pressed him to support an election; but found that 'his attitude was to oppose any National Appeal and to be mischievous'.[62] On 3 October 'the King told the Prime Minister that he must at all costs find the solution himself, and His Majesty would refuse to accept his resignation. He must be more patient and brace himself up to realise that he was the only person who could tackle the present chaotic state of affairs.'[63] This was the fourth time that the king had indicated that he would refuse to accept the resignation of his prime minister.

The king granted a dissolution under conditions which broke both the letter and the spirit of the agreement on which the government had been formed. The king, it may be suggested, had a special responsibility to preserve the agreement, since, in a country such as Britain, without a codified constitution, there is no reference point, no *pouvoir neutre*, over and above the wishes of the government of the day. Only the king, therefore, could defend the agreement. He did not do so.

The ensuing general election saw the National Government returned with the largest majority ever seen in British politics—554 seats and 67 per cent of the vote—while the Labour opposition won only 52 seats with 31 per cent of the vote. It was fought in a highly

[61] RA GV K2331 (1) 20, cited in Bogdanor, '1931 Revisited', 21, and partially in Nicolson, George V, 492.

[62] 2 Oct. 1931, RA GV K2331 (1) 24, cited in Bogdanor, '1931 Revisited', 21.

[63] RA GV K2332 (1) 29, cited in ibid., and partially in Nicolson, *George V*, 493.

emotional atmosphere at which the presumption throughout was that it was 'unpatriotic' to oppose the National Government. To the extent that the election was justified as being necessary to validate the actions of the king in helping to form the National Government in August, it might be argued that a repudiation of the National Government would also have been seen as a repudiation of the king.

It is perhaps futile to ask whether the king's actions were constitutional. In a country without a codified constitution, it is hardly possible to give a definitive answer. But one way of answering the question would be to consider whether the king's actions in 1931 formed a precedent capable of repetition today. The answer, surely, is that they would not be so capable of repetition. The Labour Party would be unlikely to react as passively as it did in 1931, when such disaffection as occurred was concentrated primarily on the intellectual Left, amongst such figures as Sir Stafford Cripps and Harold Laski. The events of 1931 arose out of the circumstances of a hung parliament and a minority government faced with a massive economic crisis. They illustrate the truth of Disraeli's pregnant remark in his novel, *Sybil*: 'when parties are in the present state of equality, the Sovereign is no longer a mere pageant.'[64]

[63] RA GV K2332 (1) 29, cited in ibid., and partially in Nicolson, *George V*, 493.
[64] Disraeli, *Sybil*, bk, IV, ch. 1.

5

Three Constitutional Crises

—■•❖•■—

I

The constitutional crisis caused by the House of Lords' rejection of Lloyd George's 'People's Budget' in 1909 illustrates the role played by the sovereign under circumstances when hitherto agreed constitutional guidelines come no longer to be accepted. Both Edward VII and George V were faced with requests from their governments to create a large number of peers so as to secure the passage of government legislation; and George V was persuaded, against his better judgement, to agree to a hypothetical understanding by which, if the government were to be returned in the second general election of 1910, and the House of Lords did not give way, he would in fact agree to create peers. The crisis posed more difficult problems for the monarchy than any it had faced since the 1832 Reform Act.

In November 1909 the House of Lords, whose powers were at that time unlimited by statute, and which enjoyed a large Conservative majority, rejected the Lloyd George 'People's Budget' on second reading by 350 votes to 75. The budget had previously passed its third reading in the Commons by 379 votes to 149. The Liberal prime minister, H. H. Asquith, immediately sought a dissolution of parliament, moving a resolution in the Commons to the effect that the action of the House of Lords was 'a breach of the Constitution and a usurpation of the rights of the Commons'.[1]

In the ensuing general election, in January 1910, the Liberals lost their overall majority in the Commons, losing 104 seats to the Conservatives. The outcome of the election was as follows:

Liberals   275 seats,   Irish Nationalist 82 seats,
Conservatives 273 seats,   Labour   40 seats.

[1] Bruce K. Murray, *The People's Budget, 1909–10: Lloyd George and Liberal Politics* (Oxford University Press, 1980), 232–3.

The Liberals thus had two more seats than the Conservatives, but relied upon the Irish Nationalists and Labour for their overall majority.

The Conservatives accepted that the general election was a mandate for the budget, and this was duly passed in the House of Lords in April 1910. The Liberals proposed, however, to limit the power of the Lords to do further mischief. During the election campaign, on 10 December 1909, Asquith had declared that 'We shall not assume office, and we shall not hold office, unless we can secure the safeguards which experience tells to be necessary for the legislative utility and honour of the party of progress.'[2]

The only way in which such 'safeguards' could be secured was by passing a measure limiting the absolute veto of the House of Lords. But this measure would require the consent of the Lords themselves, something very unlikely to occur. Moreover, the Lords, unlike the Commons, could not be dissolved. There was only one way in which the House of Lords could be persuaded to pass legislation limiting its powers and that was by swamping it, or threatening to swamp it, with sufficient Liberal peers to overcome the large Conservative majority. In other words, the king would have to be asked to use his prerogative to threaten a mass creation of peers. There was a precedent for this use of the royal prerogative, since in 1832 William IV had agreed, albeit with considerable reluctance, to create peers if that was necessary to ensure the passage of the Reform Bill. In the event, no creation had been necessary, and the only actual creation had been in 1712, when Queen Anne had created twelve peers to ensure parliamentary ratification of the Treaty of Utrecht.

Edward VII had refused to promise to create peers. He had told Asquith through Lord Knollys, his private secretary, on 15 December 1909, that he regarded 'the policy of the Government as tantamount to the destruction of the House of Lords',[3] and that consequently he would not feel justified in creating peers until after a second general election. The king believed that the coming election might provide a mandate for the budget, but that a second election would be needed if there were to be a mandate for swamping the Lords. The king felt, moreover, that he would not be justified in giving any sort of promise in relation to putative legislation which had

[2] Bruce K. Murray, *The People's Budget, 1909–10:* 240.
[3] J. A. Spender and Cyril Asquith, *Life of Herbert Henry Asquith, Lord Oxford and Asquith* (Hutchinson, 1932), i. 261.

not been submitted to, much less approved by, either house of parliament. Asquith, therefore, was forced to confess, shortly after the January 1910 general election, that he did not have the 'safeguards' which he had sought. Speaking in the Commons on 21 February 1910, in words that were to haunt him later on, the prime minister declared that:

To ask in advance for a blank authority for an indefinite exercise of the Royal Prerogative in regard to a measure which has never been submitted to, or approved by, the House of Commons, is a request which, in my judgment, no constitutional statesman can properly make and it is a concession which the Sovereign cannot be expected to grant.[4]

Asquith's Liberal supporters and the Irish Nationalists, upon whom he depended for his majority, were not, however, prepared to leave the question of House of Lords reform in limbo. The Irish Nationalists were even more eager than the Liberals to remove the absolute veto of the Lords, in order to secure the passage of Home Rule, which the Lords had blocked in 1893, and could be expected to block again. In April 1910, therefore, Asquith presented to the Commons the Parliament Bill, under whose provisions the veto of the House of Lords on money bills was entirely removed, while the veto on other bills would be merely suspensive. It was provided that a non-money bill would become law if passed in three successive sessions, even if opposed by the Lords. At the same time the maximum duration of a parliament was reduced from seven to five years. The prime minister declared that, if the Bill were to be defeated by the Lords, he would seek a second dissolution, but that 'In no case shall we recommend Dissolution, except under such conditions as will secure that in the new Parliament the judgment of the People, as expressed in the Election, will be carried into law.'[5]

The implication of this remark was that the sovereign would be asked to give an advance undertaking before the general election that, if the government were to be returned, he would agree to a sufficient creation of peers to ensure the passage of the Parliament Bill.

Just three weeks after Asquith's speech to the Commons, Edward VII died, to be succeeded by George V. In deference to the new king, politicians agreed to suspend their constitutional battle, and to meet in a constitutional conference so as to resolve their differences by

[4] Ibid. 273.   [5] Ibid. 279.

agreement. By November 1910, however, it was clear that agreement could not be reached, and the position reverted to what it had been before the death of Edward VII.

It was at this point that Asquith presented his demand for what the new king called 'contingent guarantees' and what the prime minister regarded as no more than a hypothetical understanding. What Asquith sought was that the king should promise, in the event of the government being returned and the Conservative peers not surrendering, to use his prerogative to ensure that sufficient peers were created to pass the Parliament Bill. The king took the view that he was bound to act on the advice of his ministers, but that, if he gave a hypothetical promise, he would be compromising his neutrality by adding his weight to the Liberal Party's election programme. It was, of course, perfectly possible that the Liberal Party would be defeated in the forthcoming general election. Then, if the Conservatives discovered his pledge, they might feel that the sovereign had thrown his weight in the scales against them. The correct course, surely, was to wait until a situation requiring the exercise of his prerogative would actually arise, and then decide, in the light of circumstances, how he should use his prerogative powers, being guided, in the normal course of events, by the advice of his ministers.

The members of the cabinet were, however, unable to accept this position. This was partly due to the fact that the prime minister's speech in April had committed them to 'safeguards' and ministers felt that they would be losing face if they did not secure them. But, in addition, they did not trust the king to use his prerogative in their interest because of the incautious remarks he had made, as Prince of Wales, about Asquith and Lloyd George.[6]

The king's two private secretaries, Lord Knollys and Sir Arthur Bigge, later Lord Stamfordham, disagreed as to his correct course of action. Knollys, who was a Liberal, believed that the government's advice should be accepted, even though he had told the king's father, Edward VII, that the request for guarantees was 'the greatest outrage which has ever been committed since England became a Constitutional Monarchy', and that it would be better to abdicate than to accept such a request.[7] But Bigge, who was a Conservative, believed that the king should refuse to make any hypothetical promise.

[6] See pp. 67–8.
[7] Giles St Aubyn, *Edward VII: Prince and King* (Collins, 1979), 431.

Knollys backed up his view by declaring that he would have given the same view to Edward VII, who would have accepted it; and that no alternative government was available. This was, perhaps, not wholly correct, as it is by no means certain that Balfour, the Conservative leader, would have refused to accept office had he been asked. He might well have been willing to accept office to prevent the king being pressed by his ministers into giving hypothetical pledges, which Balfour, together with other Conservatives, believed to be unconstitutional. But, whether or not Balfour would have been prepared to form a government, Knollys hid from the king details of a meeting—the so-called Lambeth Palace Conference that had been held in April 1910—at which Balfour had seemed to indicate that he would definitely be prepared to take office were the Liberals to resign.

Faced with Knollys's determination, the king reluctantly gave way and, on 16 November, agreed to the creation of peers, should the Lords refuse to pass the Parliament Bill after the government had won the general election. He did, however, insist that the Parliament Bill be submitted to the Lords before the general election. The king insisted both that his promise should be kept secret, and that the Lords should have the chance of debating the Parliament Bill before parliament was dissolved for a second time.

The outcome of the second general election held in December 1910 was very similar to that of January, the Liberals suffering a net loss of three seats, the Conservatives suffering a net loss of one. The threat of a mass creation of peers, when finally announced in July 1911, proved sufficient to persuade the House of Lords not to reject the Parliament Act, and it was duly passed in August 1911.

George V felt for the rest of his reign that he had not been treated fairly either by Knollys or by his ministers, whom he considered had bullied him, an inexperienced sovereign, into acquiescence. The king felt that, with more experience, he would have asked the government to put the reasons for seeking the contingent guarantees in writing. Then he could have taken time to reflect upon these reasons before giving his answer.

Every historian who has written on the crisis takes the view that George V acted in the only way in which a constitutional sovereign could have been expected to act in giving the guarantees, and that Knollys was justified in withholding details of the Lambeth Palace

Conference from him, to prevent the new sovereign from committing a disastrous mistake. If the king had refused to give the guarantees, the government would have resigned. He would have had to appoint Balfour, the Conservative leader, as prime minister. But the Conservatives were in a minority in the Commons, and so would have been forced to dissolve. The king would thus have been in the invidious position of granting to one party the dissolution which he had implicitly refused to the other. Indeed, he would seem to have been in the position of dismissing a government which enjoyed the favour of the electorate. The king's conduct, therefore, would have become a topic of public debate at the hustings, and the sovereign's reputation for impartiality gravely weakened.

Yet this conclusion, even though it is generally accepted, seems flawed. There was never any doubt that the sovereign would act on the advice of his ministers, nor that he was prepared to accept the recommendation for a second dissolution of parliament for a general election in December 1910. It does not follow from this that the king was constitutionally required to make a promise as to how he would use his prerogative in hypothetical circumstances.

But, could the sovereign not be forced into such a promise through the threat of resignation of his or her ministers? This too is by no means as clear-cut as it seems at first sight. Had the king sought a memorandum from his government that might have justified the advice they were offering him, he could, had he been so minded, have returned a memorandum which he might have published, putting forward his own interpretation of the constitutional position. He could have said that he would always act on the advice of his ministers, but that he could not make hypothetical promises as to how he might act in unspecified conditions in the future. This was especially the case when an election would intervene between the giving of the promise and its realization. The king could not be seen to be committing himself to either side in the election. Yet he was being asked to commit himself in advance of the election results, and with no knowledge of the form in which the Parliament Bill would emerge from the House of Commons, nor the changes which the Lords might make to it. The government's promise of secrecy was hardly sufficient to protect the king, since it would have been clear to most informed people that the government had in fact obtained the guarantees. The leading article in the *Star* on 19 November 1910 was headed 'We have got the guarantees', while the *Daily News* of

21 November reported Lloyd George as saying 'Does any man, in his senses, think that we would provoke another election unless we were certain that if we can get a majority it will be a final one?'[8] Were the government to have been returned (as, in fact, it was), the king would have had no alternative but to follow its advice. The purpose of the promise, moreover, was not so much to ensure that the king would act constitutionally as to vindicate Asquith's promise to his party. Therefore, the whole point of the guarantee was that it should *not* be secret, but made known at least to the back-benchers in the Liberal Party.

The king might have concluded his memorandum by reminding Asquith of his comments in February that it was wrong for a minister to seek, in advance, authority 'for an indefinite exercise of the Royal Prerogative'; and that, if such a demand were made, it was 'a concession which the Sovereign cannot be expected to grant'. George V could then have agreed to a dissolution as requested by his prime minister, but refused to give the guarantees. It would be difficult to imagine the government resigning in the face of so formidable a document. If it had done so, it would have seemed like a reaction of pique, since it was clear that, were the government to be returned at the general election, the king would have had no alternative but to accept its advice.

Lord Knollys seriously misled the king, and, in doing so, could have endangered the king's position far more than it would have been endangered if George V had refused to give a hypothetical promise. For the Conservatives could justifiably have claimed that, had they known about the secret guarantee before it was publicly divulged in July 1911, in the midst of the proceedings in the House of Lords on the Parliament Bill, they would have acted differently in the preceding eight months. It was due more to good fortune perhaps than to the inherent soundness of the decision that he had made that the sovereign's neutrality was not seriously compromised. There would have been less danger of this neutrality being compromised had he refused to give a hypothetical promise.

The prerogative of refusing to create peers may now have fallen into desuetude, for it has always been possible, since 1911, for a government to overcome the opposition of the House of Lords, unless it wishes to extend the life of parliament, on which issue alone the

[8] Cited in G. H. L. LeMay, *The Victorian Constitution: Conventions, Usages and Contingencies* (Duckworth, 1979), 210.

Lords retains an absolute veto. The delaying period of three sessions in 1911 was reduced to one session in the 1949 Parliament Act, and thus there would seem to be no occasion in the future when a government would need to coerce the Lords.

Yet the issue arose again in the early 1980s, when it seemed for a time as if the Labour Party might come to favour abolition of the House of Lords. In 1977 the Labour Party Conference voted for abolition; and, in opposition after 1979, the party swung to the Left, making it conceivable that a future Labour government might be committed to abolition. Under the provisions of the 1949 Parliament Act, opposition by the Lords to its abolition could be overcome in the next session of parliament by a second vote for abolition in the Commons. But some Labour Party members, most prominently Tony Benn, argued that a Labour government ought not to have to wait to ensure that its policy came into effect. Benn therefore proposed at the 1980 Labour Party Conference that a future Labour government should be prepared to create as many as 1,000 peers so that the Lords would vote for its own abolition.

The question then arose as to whether the sovereign could refuse the request of a Labour prime minister to create sufficient peers to vote for abolition. Some argued that the sovereign would be within his or her rights to refuse until a further general election had shown that the government enjoyed a mandate for its proposals. If both Edward VII and George V had required a second general election in 1910 to agree to create peers for the lesser proposal of reducing the powers of the Lords, then, *a fortiori*, the sovereign would be following precedent in requiring a second election before allowing the Lords to be abolished.

Moreover, were the House of Lords to be abolished, it might be argued that, until some alternative mechanism were devised, it would be the sovereign's responsibility to ensure that a majority in the Commons did not prolong its own life. At present, any Bill to extend the life of parliament needs the consent of both Houses, a provision which acts to prevent a government abusing its powers by extending the life of parliament for purely partisan reasons. Thus, were the Lords to be abolished, the sovereign might be required to act as protector of the constitution until some other form of protection were to be implemented. Or, suppose that a government sought to use the Parliament Act to overcome the provision in the Act of Settlement by which judges can be removed only through an address by *both* Houses, with a view to removing politically inconvenient judges. Would the sovereign be bound to assent?[9]

Even if the precedent of 1910 is unlikely to be invoked again in relation to the House of Lords, it does have some wider import in that it shows how dangerous it is for the sovereign to accede to the request to give a hypothetical promise. From this point of view, the precedent of 1910 is one that is unlikely to be repeated.

In December 1916, following the resignation of Asquith, the king asked Bonar Law to form a government. He foresaw that Bonar Law might make it a condition of acceptance that he be granted a dissolution. The king deprecated a general election in wartime, fearing that it would exacerbate party differences. He therefore sought an opinion from Lord Haldane, a former Lord Chancellor, as to whether he could constitutionally refuse to promise to grant a dissolution to a potential prime minister. Haldane's reply was emphatic:

The Sovereign cannot entertain any bargain for a Dissolution merely with a possible Prime Minister before the latter is fully installed. The Sovereign cannot, before the event, properly weigh the general situation and the Parliamentary position of the Ministry as formed.[10]

Haldane's opinion was restricted to the specific question of a potential prime minister seeking a promise that he would be given a dissolution. Yet it is suggested that Haldane's opinion can be generalized, that a sovereign ought never to be asked and is always justified in refusing to give a hypothetical promise—for that would mean that the sovereign was being required to give a decision as to how he or she should use the prerogative before being given the opportunity properly to 'weigh the general situation and the Parliamentary position of the Ministry'. George V, under pressure from Knollys and his ministers, yielded on this point in 1910— unwisely as he later believed.

The crisis of 1910–11 raises the question of what defence the sovereign has against an attempted abuse of the prerogative on the part of a prime minister. In his play *The Apple Cart*, Bernard Shaw suggests that a sovereign, faced with an abuse of the prerogative by the prime minister, can defend democracy by threatening to abdicate and standing for election to the House of Commons. That is a far-fetched

---

[9] See Lord Crowther-Hunt, 'Abolishing the Lords', *Listener*, 4 Dec. 1980.
[10] Harold Nicolson, *King George V: His Life and Reign* (Constable, 1952), 288.

scenario. It is perhaps unlikely that a sovereign will ever again be asked to give a hypothetical promise. It is even more unlikely that any future sovereign will be prepared to give it.

II

No sooner was the crisis of the House of Lords resolved in 1911 than George V was faced with an even graver constitutional crisis, one which raised, for the first time for nearly three hundred years, the spectre of civil war in Britain. The removal of the absolute veto of the House of Lords had brought Irish Home Rule back on to the political agenda. It would now be possible for a Liberal government to secure passage of a Home Rule Bill within a single parliament without making any further appeal to the electorate; and, with the absolute veto of the House of Lords having gone, the Irish Nationalists upon whom Asquith depended for his majority insisted that the government proceed with a Home Rule Bill. So it was that, in 1912, Asquith introduced a Bill which was passed by the Commons but rejected by the Lords. Under the provisions of the Parliament Act, the Bill would be presented twice more to the Lords and would, in the normal course of events, become law in 1914.

The Conservatives were bitterly opposed to the Bill. But they appreciated that they might not be able to resist the application of the Bill in the predominantly nationalist part of Ireland. They demanded, however, that Ulster be excluded. At a meeting with Asquith in October 1913, Bonar Law, the Conservative leader, agreed that, 'if there were not a general outcry . . . in the south and west of Ireland, if Ulster . . . were left out of the Bill, then [he] would not feel bound to prevent the granting of Home Rule to the rest of Ireland'.[11] The Conservative leader was willing in principle to throw the southern Unionists to the wolves. In so far as the Bill applied, however, to the whole of Ireland, including the north-eastern counties of Ulster, where there was a Protestant and Unionist majority, the Conservatives felt a special responsibility. In their view, to insist upon Ulster being included in Home Rule, which they saw as tantamount to separation, against its wishes was to flout the principle of self-determination, to expel from the kingdom citizens who sought

[11] Robert Blake, *The Unknown Prime Minister: The Life and Times of Andrew Bonar Law, 1858–1923* (Eyre & Spottiswoode, 1955), 163.

no special treatment but wished solely to remain as British subjects. Moreover, while the scattered Unionist minority in the rest of Ireland had no prospect of physically resisting Home Rule, the position of the compact Unionist majority in Ulster was quite different. The Unionists were prepared, the moment that Home Rule was placed on the statute book, to set up their own provisional government in Ulster and to resist its application by force. The Liberal government would then be forced to coerce Ulster if it was to realize its programme of giving Home Rule to the whole of Ireland. There were grave doubts, however, as to whether the Liberals could rely upon the army to use force against Ulster, especially as a number of leading army officers themselves came from Ulster and were reluctant to use force against their own kith and kin. Finally, the claim of Ulster, which was, after all, a claim not for special privileges, but one merely to continue membership of the United Kingdom, from which it was being extruded against its will, was bound to meet with a great deal of support from public opinion in the rest of Britain.

The Conservatives, moreover, added a constitutional argument to their opposition to Home Rule. They declared that, following the passage of the Parliament Act, there was a gap in the constitution. This was because the preamble to the Parliament Act had declared that 'it is intended to substitute for the House of Lords as it at present exists a Second Chamber constituted on a popular instead of hereditary basis, but such substitution cannot be immediately brought into operation'. This preamble had no legal force; and it was put in by the Liberal government solely to mollify Sir Edward Grey, the foreign secretary, who had something of an obsession about the creation of a 'popular' second chamber.[12] The Conservatives, nevertheless, argued that, until such a popular chamber was created, the constitution was in suspense, lacking its normal checks and balances, and that it was for the king to fill this vacuum, either by vetoing the Home Rule Bill, or by using his prerogative to dismiss his ministers if they refused to hold a general election before putting Home Rule on the statute book. Arthur Balfour, Conservative leader until 1911, argued in 1913 that Britain was living under an 'interim constitution'.[13] The king shared this view, asking his prime minister, Asquith, in September 1913:

[12] LeMay, *The Victorian Constitution,* 214.
[13] Undated memo. on 'The Constitutional Question, 1913', British Library, Balfour Papers, BL Add. MS 49869, fo. 127.

Does not such an organic change in the Constitutional position of one of the Estates of the Realm also affect the relations of all three to one another; and the failure to replace it on an effective footing deprive the Sovereign of the assistance of the Second Chamber? . . .

Is there any other Country in the world which would carry out such a fundamental change in its Constitution upon the authority of a single chamber?

Is there any precedent in our own Country for such a change to be made without submitting it to the Electorate?[14]

The position of the sovereign, the king believed, had been affected by the Parliament Act, since 'it has destroyed the very foundations of those precedents to which he would naturally look for guidance at the present time'.[15] The Parliament Act, the king feared, placed him 'in a false position and in one never contemplated by the framers of our Constitution. As I regard it, the King alone can now compel a Government to refer to the Country any measure which hitherto would have been so referred by the action of the Lords.'[16]

Because the Conservatives believed the Liberals to be acting in an unconstitutional manner, they felt that they were no longer bound by the normal conventions of parliamentary life. Bonar Law, the Conservative leader, told Sir Henry Craik in March 1914 that 'The government are trying to carry through the measure in an entirely unconstitutional way and they cannot be prevented from succeeding unless action is taken by us which goes much beyond ordinary Parliamentary opposition.'[17] The Conservative aim was to force a general election. If the election returned the Liberals to power, then the Conservatives would confine their opposition to Home Rule to orthodox constitutional channels. This would make 'all the difference', since 'it was really the certainty of British support which made the strength of the Ulster resistance'.[18]

But how could the Conservatives force an election? 'The difficulty', Bonar Law had declared, 'is to find a method of securing it [i.e. a general election] especially in view of the Parliament Act. I

---

[14] Letter from George V to Asquith, 22 Sept. 1913, cited in Nicolson, *King George V*, 227.

[15] Undated memo., but probably late 1913, RA GV K2553 (5) 81.

[16] Undated memo., RA GV K2553 (5) 98a.

[17] Bonar Law to Craik, 16 Mar. 1914, cited in Jeremy Smith, 'Bluff, Bluster and Brinkmanship: Andrew Bonar Law and the Third Home Rule Bill', *Historical Journal*, 36 (1993), 162.

[18] Blake, *The Unknown Prime Minister*, 162.

hold that the position of the sovereign is very important in this respect.'[19] With the absolute veto of the House of Lords having been removed, only the king stood between the Home Rule Bill and the statute book. The only way in which the Conservatives would be able to force an election would be if the king were to refuse to give the Royal Assent to the Bill, or were to insist upon a general election, dismissing his ministers unless they agreed to such a course of action.

The argument that the constitution was in abeyance and that it could be protected only by the king was not used only by active politicians. It also had the support of Sir William Anson, a former Conservative minister but also an eminent constitutional lawyer, author in 1892 of a standard work, *The Law and Custom of the Constitution*, and Warden of All Souls College Oxford. In September 1913 Sir William wrote to *The Times* to give it as his opinion that:

The Government have taken advantage of a combination of groups in the House of Commons to deprive the Second Chamber of its constitutional right to bring about an appeal to the people on measures of high importance which have never been submitted to the consideration of the electorate. While this part of our Constitution is in abeyance they are pressing on legislation which will shortly lead to civil war.

Our only safeguard against such disaster is to be found in the exercise of the prerogatives of the Crown. I am not ready to admit that, under such circumstances, these prerogatives have been atrophied by disuse.[20]

The Liberal position, on the other hand, was that the Parliament Act had definitively settled a major constitutional question by ensuring that only the government of the day, and not the House of Lords, could decide upon a dissolution. This power had not been transferred to any other body, and Liberals had certainly not intended to remove it from the Lords only to pass it on to the king.

The king, then, was faced with a terrible constitutional dilemma. Bonar Law, in an interview with the king in September 1913,

endeavoured to impress upon His Majesty what is my own firm belief that he could not avoid *personal* responsibility, that whether the Bill were allowed to become law, or whether he exercised his right to secure a General Election, in either case his action would be condemned by half his

---

[19] Bonar Law to A. V. Dicey, 16 March 1913, in Smith, 'Bluff, Bluster and Brinkmanship', 168.

[20] Sir William Anson's letter is reprinted in Ivor Jennings, *Cabinet Government*, (3rd edn., Cambridge University Press, 1959), 541.

subjects, and that it was an open question whether greater permanent harm would be done to the Monarchy by an attack from the extreme supporters of the Government, or by the bitter and lasting resentment of the people of Ulster and of those who sympathised with them.[21]

The king had already told his prime minister in August 1913, 'Whatever I do I shall offend half the population. One alternative would certainly result in alienating the Ulster Protestants from me, and whatever happens the result must be detrimental to me personally and to the Crown in general.'[22]

Were the king to act solely on the advice of his ministers and sign the Home Rule Bill without insisting upon a general election, he would be extruding part of the United Kingdom against the wishes of its inhabitants; and, in the view of Conservatives, condoning a breach of the constitution. Were he, on the other hand, to refuse to sign the Bill or to dismiss his ministers, he would be reviving prerogatives which were generally thought to be long dead. No Bill had been vetoed since the time of Queen Anne in 1707, no government had been dismissed since Melbourne's by William IV in 1834, and that hardly formed an encouraging precedent.

The Conservatives, on the other hand, argued that, just because a prerogative was rarely exercised, this did not of itself mean that it had fallen into desuetude. The prerogative to create peers, after all, had last been exercised in 1712, and no doubt might also have been thought before 1910 to have fallen into desuetude. But, if a prerogative involved an unusual use of the sovereign's powers, it follows that it would be rarely used; and the fact that it had been rarely used, therefore, could not be put forward as evidence of desuetude.

Those who looked just at the practice of the constitution, declared Balfour, in his memorandum on 'The Constitutional Question, 1913', were 'apt to interpret the word "practice" as meaning the ordinary routine of government and therefore unduly to *narrow* the prerogative, by ruling out as unconstitutional anything which is exceptional'.

Nevertheless, the sovereign possessed powers which, although they ought to be rarely exercised,

---

[21] Memo. to Lord Stamfordham from Bonar Law on his interview with the king, 16 Sept. 1913, RA GV K2553 (2) 16. (emphasis added).

[22] From the king's memorandum to Asquith, 11 Aug. 1913, quoted in Nicolson, *King George V*, 223.

have not on that account become obsolete or fallen into desuetude. The contrary doctrine seems indeed absurd; since it would deprive the sovereign of every power which he does not habitually exercise. It is surely obvious that if a prerogative *ought* rarely to be used, it cannot become obsolete, *merely because* it is rarely used.[23]

The right to create peers, Balfour added, was one such right. So was the right to veto legislation or dismiss ministers. These rights were dormant, but not extinct. Bonar Law believed that

the King not only had the constitutional right but that it was his duty before acting on the advice of his Ministers to ascertain whether it would not be possible to appoint other Ministers who would advise him differently and allow the question to be decided by the Country at a General Election.[24]

The king, therefore, was placed 'in a most difficult position, such as no Sovereign of this country has experienced for centuries'.[25]

George V's actions were based throughout, as his private secretary, Lord Stamfordham, made clear in a memorandum written after the Bill had been passed in September 1914, on his view 'that it was for the *politicians* to decide whether Ireland should have Home Rule or not. But that he intended to do everything in his power to prevent Civil War.'[26] Accordingly, from August 1913, he 'insisted upon discussing the question with the Prime Minister who up to that time had never alluded to it in his frequent interviews with His Majesty'.[27]

The king's aim, throughout, was to avert civil war and to obtain a settlement by consent. Such a settlement must have as its central element the exclusion of Ulster in exchange for Conservative acquiescence to Home Rule. To this end, he urged moderation on both sides, and pressed the two party leaders to come to an agreement. It was in part due to the king that private conversations took place between Asquith and Bonar Law from October 1913, which, if they did not achieve agreement, at least succeeded in narrowing the issues on which disagreement remained.

The king shared the view of the Conservatives that, as he put it to his prime minister, 'Ulster will never agree to send representatives to

---

[23] Balfour Papers, BL Add. MS 49869, fos. 123, 124.
[24] Memo. by Bonar Law, 27 Sept. 1912, RA GV K2553 (1) 2.
[25] George V to Asquith, 26 Jan. 1914, RA GV K2553 (3) 76.
[26] Memo. by Lord Stamfordham, 17 Sept. 1914, following the enactment of the Home Rule Bill, RA GV K2553 (6) 103.
[27] Ibid.

an Irish Parliament, no matter what safeguards or guarantees you may provide.'[28] The king also believed that the slightest attempt to coerce Ulster could lead to disaffection in the army. On both of these issues, Asquith thought the king to be alarmist. So far as the prime minister was concerned, the army would obey all orders, while Ulster's opposition would be contained within constitutional channels. Thus, for Asquith, the Home Rule Bill could be treated as a straightforward legislative measure, raising no special constitutional difficulties.

It must be admitted, however, that, on these matters, the king's judgement was superior to that of his prime minister. There was no chance whatever of Ulster agreeing to send representatives to an Irish parliament, and, sooner than accept Home Rule, Ulster would resist by force. Asquith was himself to admit this, in March 1914, only two months after the king had told him that Ulster would never agree to send representatives to an Irish parliament. For the prime minister announced that he proposed to provide for the temporary exclusion for six years of Ulster. It may be that the king's insistence on the intransigence of Ulster played some part in persuading Asquith to agree to exclusion.

The king did not share his prime minister's view that the Home Rule Bill could be treated as merely an ordinary legislative measure. He believed, moreover, that, if a settlement by consent could not be reached, then it was his duty to ensure that there should be a general election before Home Rule was enacted. Only in this way could civil war, in his view, be avoided. An alternative to a general election, however, might be found in a referendum; and, once it had been agreed that Ulster could be excluded from the operation of the Bill, the king did suggest a referendum on the Home Rule Bill. Since Asquith had declared that the counties of Ulster would be able to vote in a referendum on whether they wished to be included or excluded from an Irish parliament, why should the principle of the referendum not be applied to the Bill itself. On 19 March 1914, therefore, the king suggested to Asquith 'that the Home Rule Bill should be submitted to a Referendum especially now that the principle of this method was admitted for the Ulster counties to decide for or against exclusion'.[29] But the prime minister refused to consider either a general election or a referendum on the Bill.

[28] George V to Asquith, 26 Jan. 1914, RA GV K2553 (3) 76.
[29] Memo. by Lord Stamfordham, 19 Mar. 1914, RA GV K2553 (4) 33.

The king had two weapons which he could use to secure a general election. The first was a refusal to give the Royal Assent to the Home Rule Bill. The second was to dismiss his ministers and appoint the leader of the opposition, Bonar Law, as prime minister. Lacking a majority in the Commons, Bonar Law would, of course, be compelled to call a general election. This would be a milder exercise of the royal prerogative than refusal of the Royal Assent, since it would not entail disregarding ministerial advice; and it appears that it was this latter option which the king was considering. Esher suggests that 'dismissing his Ministers' was the course being considered, but that the king, being still inexperienced, did not distinguish very clearly between the two courses.[30] What is unclear, however, is how seriously the king contemplated exercising his powers. It may well be, and this seems the most plausible interpretation, that the king was using the threat of employing his prerogative powers in order to persuade his prime minister either to reach a settlement by consent with the opposition, or to agree to a general election.

On 5 February 1914 the king told Asquith that,

although constitutionally he might not be responsible, still he could not allow bloodshed among his loyal subjects in any part of his Dominion without exerting every means in his power to avert it. Although at the present stage of the proceedings he could not rightly intervene he should feel it his duty to do what in his own judgment was best for his people generally.[31]

The implication of this remark, as understood by Asquith, was that the king reserved the right to use his powers.

Although the king, had he been required to use his prerogative, would have preferred to dismiss his ministers rather than refuse assent, he nevertheless did not entirely abandon the idea that he might have to refuse assent. At one time he considered the possibility that 'Assent might be given on the understanding that the will of the people should be consulted, and at once, as to whether he Act should be put into force or not'.[32] He also believed that he would be entitled to refuse assent if Ulster was not excluded from the ambit of the Bill, although whether he would actually have done so remains an open question.

---

[30] *Journals and Letters of Reginald, Viscount Esher*, ed. Maurice V. Brett and Oliver, Viscount Esher (Ivor Nicholson & Watson, 1934–8), iii. 157.

[31] Cited in Nicolson, *King George V*, 233.

[32] Lord Stamfordham to Lord Salisbury, 5 June 1914, RA GV K2553 (5) 44.

In June 1914 Asquith introduced an amending Bill into the House of Lords, providing for the right of six Ulster counties to opt out of Home Rule for six years. The king told Lord Crewe, a senior minister in the government, 'that the Home Rule Bill and Amending Bill depended one upon the other and that the former would not be presented for Royal Assent without the latter'. If the amending Bill was not passed,

The King could not imagine that advantage would be taken of the Parliament Act to induce him to give assent to a measure which the Government themselves had tried to alter . . . Surely . . . a Body of British Statesmen did not contemplate asking the Sovereign to put his name to a Bill which they themselves believed would result in Civil War. His Majesty did not believe Lord Crewe would be a party to such a proposal and he looked to him to prevent it.[33]

The king said the same to Lord Morley, the Lord President, two days later:

Supposing the Amending Bill falls through the House of Commons rejecting the Lords Amendments surely you, Lord Morley, would not be a party to presenting the Home Rule Bill for my Assent. . . . The King said it would be unfair and unstatesmanlike to press such a Bill upon him—He appealed to Lord Morley as one of the oldest statesmen in the country and in the Government.

Morley agreed that it would be unfair to submit the Home Rule Bill to him without the amending Bill. 'The King answered: "I hope when the time comes, you and others of your colleagues will agree that I cannot be asked to give my Assent."' Lord Morley said: '"We must agree. Redmond [the Irish Nationalist leader] must give way."'[34]

In the event, however, the Home Rule Bill *was* presented for the Royal Assent in September 1914, some six weeks after the beginning of the First World War, without the amending Bill. On the eve of war, on 30 July, Asquith postponed discussion of the amending Bill. Instead, the Home Rule Bill became law, accompanied by an Act suspending its operation until the end of the war. This would allow for negotiations over the position of Ulster. In addition, Asquith

[33] Lord Stamfordham's memo. of a conversation between the king and Lord Crewe, 6 June 1914, RA GV K2553 (5) 46.

[34] Lord Stamfordham's memo. of a conversation between the king and Lord Morley, 8 June 1914, RA GV K2553 (5) 54.

promised that there would be no attempt to coerce Ulster. Nevertheless, the Conservatives regarded the actions of the government as a betrayal of the party truce which had been agreed at the outbreak of the war. The king shared this view. On 25 August he had sent a letter to the prime minister appealing for a settlement based on mutual compromise, and the letter had been read to the cabinet.[35] The king felt deceived by his prime minister in being asked to sign the Home Rule Bill without the amending Bill, since, on 9 May, Asquith had told him that he would not be asked to do this. 'The King merely points out these facts. He can do nothing. The Government must defend their position. He can only deplore that the united front apparently can no longer be maintained.'[36]

The king nevertheless decided that he would not be justified in refusing assent to the Home Rule Bill. After all, the Bill would not settle the controversy. Since it would come into effect only after the end of the war and after negotiations on Ulster had been concluded, the Bill merely postponed the issue. The Royal Assent was thus merely a formal act, since there would be an amending Bill and a general election, together with debate, both in parliament and the country, before Home Rule came into effect. This served to shift the onus of judgement from the king's shoulders. Nevertheless, the king wrote to Sir Francis Hopwood, the Civil Lord of the Admiralty and a friend of Lord Stamfordham: 'I do not conceal from you my regret at having to give my Assent to the Home Rule Bill.'[37] He had intended to require from his ministers 'a statement of the full and considered reasons' which impelled his ministers to advise him to sign the Bill 'in a form which can be put on record for the use of his successors, and referred to if any necessity should hereafter arise'. In this letter, written on 31 July 1914, but never sent owing to the imminence of war, the king made clear that he retained the right to veto legislation, but felt that such an 'extreme course should not be adopted unless there is convincing evidence that it would avert a national disaster, or at least have a tranquillizing effect on the distracting conditions of the time. There is no such evidence.'[38]

There is, then, no doubt that the king believed that he could veto legislation, and that he contemplated doing so in the case of Home Rule. In 1946, when Sir Owen Morshead, the Royal Librarian, was

[35] RA GV K2553 (6) 72, 82.　　[36] 13 Sept. 1914, RA GV K2553 (6) 86.
[37] 5 Sept. 1914, RA GV K 2553 (6) 104.
[38] Cited in Nicolson, *King George V*, 234 n.

preparing the biography of George V for the *Dictionary of National Biography*, he found Stamfordham's memorandum of the king's conversation with Asquith on 5 February 1914, at which the king declared that, when the Bill was presented for the Royal Assent, he would be guided by what in his judgement was best for his people generally. The king's private secretary, Sir Alan Lascelles, wrote to the cabinet secretary, Sir Edward Bridges, saying that there was no justification for suppressing a document 'of considerable historical significance' which

makes no historical innovation—so far as I know, the Sovereign's right to say 'Le Roy s'avisera' is as good now as when it was last exercised in 1707, always provided the Sovereign is prepared to face the consequences; some future Sovereign might well find it useful, as an example, if not a precedent.

Sir Edward Bridges replied to Lascelles that he thought that

the ordinary man's reaction to learning that during our lifetime the King had seriously contemplated using the formula 'Le Roy s'avisera' would be that he had always thought that that power had atrophied through disuse, and that the idea of having recourse to this procedure was a trifle odd.

But the first parliamentary counsel, Sir Granville Ram, assured Bridges that Balfour had been correct in 1913, in denying 'that the prerogative power to refuse the Royal Assent has been or could be atrophied by disuse, though no doubt it might be abolished as a consequence of misuse'. He cited Dicey, who had declared of the refusal of assent: 'Its repose may be the preservation of its existence, and its existence may be the means of saving the Constitution itself on an occasion worthy of bringing it forth.'[39] The Home Rule crisis of 1914 proved that the sovereign retained the prerogative of veto, and that this prerogative might come into play on extreme occasions.

The king also considered dismissing his ministers and appointing as prime minister the leader of the opposition, who, being in a minority in the Commons, would be compelled to seek a dissolution. In a conversation with Redmond on 2 February, Asquith spoke of the king's attitude. It must be borne in mind that this conversation occurred before Asquith's interview with the king at which George V made it clear that he reserved to himself the possibility of vetoing the Bill. The king, Asquith declared,

[39] Lascelles to Bridges, 27 May 1946, Bridges to Lascelles, 3 June 1946; Ram to Bridges, 3 June 1946, PRO T 273/237. The quotation from Dicey is from his letter to *The Times*, 15 Sept. 1913, repr. in Jennings, *Cabinet Government*, 545.

argued that before making himself responsible for the passage of Home Rule, he must be assured that he had his people behind him. The King . . . clearly intimated that he considered his power of dismissing his Minister[s], as was done in 1834, as a course open to him, and one which he might feel called upon to adopt.[40]

Of course, in this conversation Asquith was seeking to persuade Redmond to make concessions to the Ulster point of view, and so his account of the king's attitude is not conclusive. Asquith himself believed that dismissal was a lesser evil than the veto, while Lord Knollys believed that action by the king should 'take the form of insisting on a General Election and not by refusing to give the Royal Assent. I feel sure that the former course will be far less resented by the Liberals than the latter.'[41]

In believing that he had the right to change his ministerial advisers so as to secure a dissolution, George V was supported by eminent constitutional authorities. Bagehot, whose works the king had studied in his youth, had held that 'The Sovereign . . . possesses a power according to theory for extreme use on a critical occasion, but which in law he can use on any occasion. He can dissolve . . .'.[42] The great constitutional lawyer A. V. Dicey also believed that dismissal was preferable to the veto, since 'Every advantage by way of appeal to the electors, in consequence of the exercise of the so-called Royal veto, can be far better and more regularly obtained by a dissolution of Parliament.'[43] Asquith himself did not deny that the king could dismiss his ministers. He asked only that, if it were to be done, it be done quickly.[44] Lord Morley, the Liberal minister, agreed that the king would not be exceeding his rights were he to force a dissolution by dismissing his ministers.[45] Were the king to secure a dissolution by this method, the final decision as to whether Home Rule should be enacted would rest with the electors, and the king felt that, whatever the result, he could not be held personally responsible.

[40] Nicholas Mansergh, *The Unresolved Question: The Anglo-Irish Settlement and its Undoing 1912–72* (Yale University Press, 1991), 68–9; chs. 1–3 contain by far the best account of the ramifications of the Irish problem in the years 1912–14.

[41] 5 Feb. 1914, at his audience with the king, cited in Nicolson, *King George V*, 234. Knollys's view is in RA GV K2553 (3) 9.

[42] This passage is cited in RA GV K2553 (2) 26, in a letter from the king to Asquith.

[43] Letter to *The Times*, 15 Sept. 1913, cited in Jennings, *Cabinet Government*, 545.

[44] LeMay, *The Victorian Constitution*, 33.

[45] G. Bell, *Randall Davidson* (3rd edn., Oxford University Press, London, 1952), 721.

After the Royal Assent had been given to the Home Rule Bill, Lord Stamfordham wrote a memorandum summarizing the contribution that George V had made to resolving what was perhaps the most serious domestic crisis faced by the British political system in modern times. It remains an excellent statement of the influence which a constitutional monarch can exercise in such extreme situations.

For over a year, Stamfordham began, 'His Majesty has devoted quiet, patient, unremitting work to help in arriving at a peaceful and honourable settlement. And his efforts have been consistent.'

The king had 'from the first' advocated 'a General Election and also a Conference'. It was partly as a result of the king's initiative that the two major party leaders, Asquith and Bonar Law, began a series of meetings in October 1913, and that the Buckingham Palace Conference was called in July 1914. The king had from the beginning 'urged the adoption of some system of contracting out the Province of Ulster, or portions of it from the operations of the Bill'; and this, of course, was the solution eventually adopted.

Moreover, Stamfordham continued,

The King has kept in close touch with the leaders and principal representatives of the Opposition as well as with persons of independent views e.g. Lord Loreburn [a former Liberal Lord Chancellor], the Archbishop of Canterbury, Lord Rosebery [a former Liberal prime minister], Sir George Murray [a former permanent secretary of the Treasury], and on yet more intimate terms, Sir Francis Hopwood . . . It was during these months that the question was discussed with the leaders of the Opposition and others of a 'State Paper' being written by the King, should the Home Rule Bill be presented for Assent in which His Majesty might state his views and warn the Government of the dangers they would incur in Ulster if Home Rule was forced upon that Province without submitting the Bill to the Electorate. With a view of [sic] explaining to the country the action of the Crown, the 'State Paper' would be published. Various drafts were prepared according as the circumstances changed.

In the middle of writing this memorandum Stamfordham recorded that

a note was handed to me from Mr. Illingworth, the Chief Whip, reporting that the Session had closed with a remarkable demonstration of loyalty and affection to the King, the singing of the National Anthem in the House of Commons having been started by Mr. Will Crooks, the Labour member for Woolwich and heartily joined in by Mr. J. Redmond.[46]

[46] RA GV K2553 (6) 103.

Asquith, who had undergone so many difficult meetings with the king, nevertheless wrote to George V, when the Royal Assent had been given, that

he hopes he may be allowed to express the respectful sympathy with and admiration of the patience and the strict observance of constitutional practice, together with the tact and judgment, which in a time of exceptional difficulty and anxiety, Your Majesty has never for a moment failed to exercise.[47]

III

The abdication was a unique crisis for the monarchy in Britain, for hereditary monarchy has as its consequence that the destiny of the future sovereign is inescapable. Thus abdication, the voluntary renunciation of sovereignty, strikes at the very heart of the institution, whose central tenet must be that normally succession to the throne is not a matter of choice but automatic. Thus, as soon as the question is raised of who might be best fitted to occupy the throne, the hereditary system comes under challenge. Similarly, as soon as a sovereign treats the office as one which he or she may voluntarily renounce, the automatic rule of succession comes to be under threat. In a monarchy, succession to the throne is a matter not of choice but of duty. It is for this reason that the novelist Bulwer-Lytton, in *The Last of the Barons* (1843), declares that 'What suicide is to a man, abdication is to a king' (III. v. 173).

Edward VIII's abdication in 1936 remains the only example of a voluntary abdication in British history, and it is quite without precedent. Although James II was declared in 1689 to have 'abdicated' by the Convention Parliament, he had in fact fled to the Continent and was deposed by parliament. There was no previous case in which the sovereign of his own free choice declared that he would cease to be king.

'Abdication', declared Lord Beaverbrook, one of the 'King's Friends' during the crisis,

is a very grave course. While it may close one set of problems, it opens another. For instance, it is an object lesson in the quick disposal of a monarch, who got at cross purposes with the executive. And later on, other

[47] RA GV K2553 (6) 102.

and different executives may profit by the lesson. For the fact is, that much of the stability of the throne is derived from the fact that it has been stable.

Then the departing King must necessarily carry with him some measure of public sympathy. This may well grow, as time passes. It will be felt by many that he has been a martyr to his principles. That he has made a sacrifice in acting according to his lights.

And the effect of this may well be that the new King will not be able to command to a complete degree the loyalty and devotion of his people.[48]

That is a fair summary of the fears which were generally entertained as to the likely consequences of abdication in 1936.

The abdication arose out of Edward VIII's desire to marry a twice-married American, Mrs Wallis Simpson. In formal terms, the king did not require the consent of his ministers to marry Mrs Simpson, since the Royal Marriages Act of 1772 does not apply to the sovereign. There was thus no statutory restriction on his choice, other than the requirement in the Act of Settlement that he could not marry a Catholic.

Moreover, contrary to what is often suggested, at no stage during the abdication crisis did Edward VIII seek or Baldwin offer formal advice on whether the king could marry Mrs Simpson; nor did the cabinet at any time advise abdication. 'With the exception of the question of morganatic marriage,' Baldwin told the House of Commons on 7 December,

no advice has been tendered by the Government to His Majesty, with whom all my conversations have been strictly personal and informal. These matters were not raised first by the Government but by His Majesty himself in conversation with me some weeks ago, when he first informed me of his intention to marry Mrs. Simpson whenever she should be free.[49]

Indeed, of the eight audiences that the king held with Baldwin on the issue, only one, the first, on 20 October 1936, was initiated by the prime minister. The others were initiated by the king; the king abdicated on his own free will, and not on ministerial advice.

Nevertheless, the abdication crisis showed that the king's choice of a wife was limited not by statute but by convention. It firmly established the principle that the king cannot marry against the

---

[48] Beaverbrook to Howard Robinson, 11 Dec. 1936, cited in A. J. P. Taylor, *Beaverbrook* (Hamish Hamilton, 1972).

[49] House of Commons, vol. 318, col. 1642, 7 Dec. 1936.

wishes of his ministers. The reason for this convention is clear. The king cannot be allowed the same freedom in his choice of a wife as an ordinary citizen, since the wife of the king becomes queen, with all the status, rights, and privileges which attach to that position. The queen becomes, like the king, a representative of the people. If the sovereign seeks to marry someone who might not suitably fill the position of queen, that would damage the monarchy. Therefore, in his choice of a wife, the view of the nation, through its elected ministers, must be heard. In the debate on the Abdication Bill in the House of Commons on 4 December 1936, the prime minister, Stanley Baldwin, quoted, very appositely, from Polonius's speech in *Hamlet*:

> his will is not his own,
> For he himself is subject to his birth;
> He may not, as unvalu'd persons do,
> Carve for himself. For on his choice depends
> The safety and the health of this whole state.

(I. iii. 19 ff.)

At the first interview between the king and his prime minister, initiated by Baldwin on 20 October, the prime minister asked the king whether he could persuade Mrs Simpson not to continue with divorce proceedings against her husband. So long as Mrs Simpson remained married to another, there could clearly be no question of marriage to the king, and so no possibility of a constitutional crisis. The king, however, declared himself unwilling so to persuade Mrs Simpson, saying that he did not have the right to intervene in the affairs of a private citizen just because she was his friend. Mrs Simpson duly obtained a decree nisi on 27 October, allowing her to marry in six months' time.

Baldwin was at all times during the abdication crisis determined, first, that Mrs Simpson could never become queen, and, secondly, that the ultimate decision as to whether the king would marry Mrs Simpson and abdicate, or, alternatively, renounce her, was one that must be taken by the king and not by his ministers. As Baldwin later told his cabinet, 'However great the inconveniences and even risk, the decision when taken must be the spontaneous decision of the King.'[50] It was for these reasons that Baldwin refused to put to the king, as senior civil servants and some of his ministers were urging,

[50] H. Montgomery Hyde, *Baldwin* (Hart-Davis, MacGibbon 1973), 489.

formal advice to renounce Mrs Simpson. He believed that this would arouse a wave of sympathy for the king, obscuring the constitutional issues and dividing opinion. Far from seeking to hustle Edward VIII off the throne, as the king later came to believe, Baldwin strove hard to retain him. Accused of lethargy by his colleagues for not forcing the pace, Baldwin hoped that the king would remain on the throne, but acted so that, even if he did not, damage to the monarchy would be minimized and the succession made smooth.[51] Indeed, not one minister 'wished to force the King to abdicate; even Chamberlain [the king's strongest opponent in the cabinet] accepted the need to give him time'.[52]

Although no formal advice was ever offered to the king on his association with Mrs Simpson, it was made known informally to him, at his second meeting with Baldwin on 16 November, that a marriage would not be acceptable to the government. There had been no formal cabinet discussion of the marriage, 'for no question of Cabinet advice had arisen'.[53] Baldwin, however, said that marriage to Mrs Simpson, who would become queen, would not be approved by the country. The king then declared that, if that was the case, he would abdicate. From this decision he never resiled.

The objections which ministers had to the marriage had nothing to do with Mrs Simpson being a commoner, still less with her American birth, but flowed from the fact that she had been twice divorced. The sovereign was Supreme Governor of the Church of England, a church which at that time would not remarry a person whose former spouse was still alive. This meant that the sovereign could not marry Mrs Simpson in church.[54] Admittedly, the position of Supreme Governor is one for which no qualifications are required other than being sovereign. Nevertheless, it would be anomalous if the sovereign, who is required to be in communion with the Church

[51] The best statement of the conspiracy theory of the abdication, that Baldwin hustled the king off the throne, can be found in Lord Beaverbrook, *The Abdication of King Edward VIII* (Hamish Hamilton, 1966). The theory is also strongly hinted at in HRH the Duke of Windsor, *A King's Story* (Cassell, 1951). But it is not accepted by any serious historian.

[52] Keith Middlemas and John Barnes, *Baldwin* (Weidenfeld & Nicolson, 1969), 1007.

[53] Bodleian Library, Simon Papers, vol. 8, fo. 12.

[54] After renouncing the throne, the Duke of Windsor, as Edward VIII had become, did in fact marry Mrs Simpson in an Anglican ceremony in France, but the priest who conducted the service was not authorized to conduct it, and was repudiated by his bishop.

of England, were to have contracted a marriage contrary to the rules of that church, and it would not have been in accordance with the sovereign's coronation oath to uphold the Established Church.

'The opposition to the King's project of marriage to Mrs. Simpson', Beaverbrook wrote to a correspondent in December 1936,

is essentially religious in character. He is lay head of the Church of England and the chief priests and the Sanhedrin say, in effect, that he may live in sin with her, but must not marry a woman who has been married twice before.

Now of course everybody does not take that view. The divorced and the free thinkers, for example, might be expected to line up on the King's side. But the trouble about these two elements is this—the divorced are all hard at work trying to become respectable. And the free thinkers don't care much about the monarchy anyway. . . . But there is a large body of opinion in the country—respectable opinion—which believes that this King has built up for himself a position with the people, that gives strength and stability to the whole political structure. This sort of opinion does not much like the marriage to Mrs. Simpson, but it is willing to make concessions in order to keep the King.[55]

There is little doubt, however, that, in the state of public and parliamentary feeling in 1936, ministers were correctly interpreting the will of parliament and people in opposing the marriage. Even if Beaverbrook was correct in his belief that there was a substantial body of 'respectable' opinion which was prepared to accept the marriage, the monarchy could not survive successfully if it were to become a source of division. The government's position was at all times supported by the official Labour opposition, Attlee, the Labour leader, believing that support for the king was confined to 'a few of the intelligentsia who could be trusted to take the wrong view on any subject'.[56] It is, moreover, noteworthy that the king's supporters in the crisis—men such as Winston Churchill and Duff Cooper—did not at first take the view that the king would be constitutionally entitled to marry Mrs Simpson. Their view was that, if only the king was given time, his infatuation, as they believed it to be, with Mrs Simpson would come to an end, and he could remain on the throne. 'He falls constantly in and out of love,' Churchill had told Mrs Belloc Lowndes. 'His present attachment will follow the

---

[55] Beaverbrook to Roy Howard, 8 Dec. 1936, cited in Taylor, *Beaverbrook*, 370–1.

[56] C. R. Attlee, *As It Happened* (Heinemann, 1954), 86.

course of all the others.'[57] 'I plead for time,' Churchill begged the House of Commons on 7 December, believing falsely that the prime minister was pressing formal advice on the king to end the association with Mrs Simpson, and that the king was being forced to abdicate on the advice of his ministers. Churchill issued a statement declaring that 'The question is whether the King is to abdicate upon the advice of the Ministry of the day. No such advice has ever before been tendered to a sovereign in Parliamentary time.' 'No Ministry', he argued, 'has the authority to advise the abdication of the sovereign.' The government was not, however, advising abdication, as Churchill appreciated after the crisis was over when he told his friend Robert Boothby that the king had considered 'that it would not be honourable to play for time when his fundamental resolve was unchanged, and as he declared unchangeable. It was certainly this very strict point of honour which cost him his Crown.'[58] In the Commons on 10 December, during the debate on the abdication, Churchill declared that

It was essential that there should be no room for assertions . . . that the King had been hurried in his decision . . . I accept wholeheartedly what the Prime Minister has proved—namely, that the decision taken this week has been taken by His Majesty freely, voluntarily, spontaneously, at his own time and in his own way.[59]

The king's most loyal supporters wanted to prevent him from marrying Mrs Simpson. It was the king who insisted upon the marriage, even if it would have to be a morganatic marriage.

The idea of a morganatic marriage was first suggested to Mrs Simpson by Esmond Harmsworth, editor of the *Daily Mail*, on 21 November 1936, and Mrs Simpson passed on the idea to the king, who told Baldwin on 25 November that he wanted formal advice on whether it would be possible.

A morganatic marriage is one in which the wife of the sovereign and any children who may be born of the marriage are denied royal status and all the claims or privileges that go with it. This would have allowed Mrs Simpson to marry the king without enjoying the title of queen, and without their descendants being in the line of succession.

[57] Philip Ziegler, *King Edward VIII: The Official Biography* (Collins, 1990), 316.
[58] Churchill to Robert Boothby, 12 Dec. 1937, cited in ibid. 317.
[59] House of Commons, vol. 319, col. 2181, 10 Dec. 1936.

Morganatic marriages have been known in foreign royal houses, primarily because, in those houses, sovereigns are required to marry someone from a narrowly specific range of royal families. In Britain, however, there are no such restrictions on the sovereign, and therefore the concept of a morganatic marriage is unknown to the law. In Britain, for example, Countess Sophie Chotek, the morganatic wife of the Archduke Franz Ferdinand, would have been perfectly eligible to be queen (provided that she renounced her Catholicism!). Thus, a morganatic marriage could not be made legitimate without legislation. It was for this reason that the king needed ministerial consent to the idea.

For the king's proposal to have been successful, it would have required the consent, not only of the British government, but of the governments of the other Dominions, as the other members of the Commonwealth were then known—Canada, Australia, New Zealand, South Africa, and the Irish Free State. The government of the Irish Free State was the only one to support the king. Under de Valera's leadership, it sought to utilize the crisis to loosen ties with the monarchy and declared that it had no interest in the matter. The other Dominion governments returned negative replies, while Baldwin declared that the British cabinet could not support the introduction of the necessary legislation and that parliament would never pass it. The proposal was, in the words of Ramsay MacDonald, the former prime minister, now Lord President, one which he found 'degrading to women, offensive to country'.[60]

The king also sought advice on whether he might make a radio broadcast to his people appealing for their support. Baldwin declined to allow this, on the ground that it would place the king in opposition to his ministers. It would be unconstitutional for the king to ask his subjects to make a decision over the heads of his ministers.

The king, then, could marry Mrs Simpson only if he were prepared to reject the wishes of his ministers. This, contrary to what is generally suggested, was certainly a course that he contemplated and it would have caused a serious constitutional crisis.

---

[60] Ramsay MacDonald diaries, 27 Nov. 1936, PRO 30/69/1753/2, fo. 156. The contents of these diaries were in MacDonald's words 'meant as notes to guide and revive memory as regards happenings and must on no account be published as they are'. The diaries are, however, generally accepted by historians as an accurate record of events.

Writing to the Viceroy of India on 27 November 1936, less than two weeks before the abdication, after an emergency cabinet meeting, Lord Zetland, the secretary of state for India, reported that the king had been prepared to abdicate voluntarily but that he

now said that he believed that he would have the sympathy and support of a very large part of the people and that while he realised that they might be unwilling to accept her as Queen, they would accept a morganatic marriage if the Government were willing to introduce legislation authorising it. Stanley Baldwin told him bluntly that if he thought that he was going to get away with it in that way, he was making a huge mistake.

His present intention seemed to be to refuse to withdraw from his position. It was pointed out at the Cabinet that this might involve the resignation of the Government, and that in this case it would give rise to a Constitutional issue of the first magnitude, viz. the King *versus* the Government. It seems that the King has been encouraged to believe that Winston Churchill would in these circumstances be prepared to form an alternative Government. If this were true there would be a grave risk of the country being divided into two camps—for and against the King. This clearly would be fraught with danger of the most formidable kind.

So now . . . we are faced with a problem compared with which even the international issues, grave as they assuredly are, pale into comparative insignificance.[61]

On 5 December Zetland wrote a further letter to Linlithgow in which he said

that a position of great danger is arising. The King is being advised by two different sets of people—first by his constitutional advisers, the Prime Minister and the Cabinet, and secondly by a body of unofficial advisers whose advice is having the effect of stiffening him against the advice of the Prime Minister and the Cabinet. He is being encouraged to believe that the Cabinet do not by any means reflect the united view of the people in their refusal to introduce legislation to legalise a morganatic marriage . . . Among those who are working on these lines is undoubtedly Winston Churchill . . . The danger of this situation will be apparent to you. Supposing that the King refuses to give a decision on either of the only two alternative courses of action which are open to him so long as the present Government remain in office, namely to give up his intention of marrying Mrs. Simpson or to abdicate, what will happen? The Government may be forced to resign. The Labour Party would almost certainly refuse to form a Government; but the King has undoubtedly been encouraged to believe that Winston would. Winston could not survive in the present House of

[61] Marquess of Zetland, *Essayez* (John Murray, 1956), 213–14.

Commons, but it would be open to him to demand a dissolution. And therein lies the supreme danger, for the country would be divided into opposing camps on the question whether or not the King should be permitted to marry . . . you can imagine the sort of things that would be said in the heat of controversy on the platform and on the pavement—without making her Queen. The Dominion Prime Ministers are strongly opposed to a morganatic marriage and legislation would be necessary not only here, but in every Dominion as well and it would not, so far as I can judge, be forthcoming. On this issue it might well be that the Empire would disintegrate, since the throne is the magnet which at present keeps it together, while there might arise a situation in this country which would not be far short of civil strife.[62]

After further consideration, however, the king decided that he would not marry against the wishes of his ministers. This left only two courses of action open to him. The first, renouncing Mrs Simpson, the king felt unable to do. This left abdication as the only alternative. Accordingly, on 10 December 1936, Edward VIII executed an Instrument of Abdication. Legal effect was given to the Instrument of Abdication by His Majesty's Declaration of Abdication Act, according to which Edward VIII and any issue which he might have were excluded from the succession to the throne, and the next in line to the throne, the king's younger brother, the Duke of York, who became George VI, was to succeed in his place. Edward VIII gave the Royal Assent to this Act on 11 December 1936 after a reign of 325 days.

Legislation was required to give effect to the abdication, since the title to the throne had been defined by the Act of Settlement which provided that the Crown descended to the heirs of Sophia, Electress of Hanover, being Protestant. The succession, therefore, cannot be modified merely by a declaration of the king, an Instrument of Abdication, without parliamentary confirmation, legislation to amend the Act of Settlement. Otherwise, any descendants of Edward VIII could have succeeded to the throne. Moreover, since the Statute of Westminster, 1931, had provided that the Dominions enjoyed complete equality of status with the United Kingdom, the consent and approval of every Dominion had to be secured to any law modifying the succession.

Although, in 1936, the abdication was regarded as a constitutional crisis, it did not, in the strict sense, give rise to any constitutional

[62] Zetland to Linlithgow, India Office Library, MSS Eur. D 609/7.

issue, for the king did not in the last resort circumvent or disregard the advice of ministers. Indeed he strongly resisted attempts by some of his supporters to form a 'King's Party', much to their chagrin. 'We were indeed the King's Party,' Lord Beaverbrook confessed in 1949 to Charles Murphy, who ghosted the Duke of Windsor's memoirs. 'But unfortunately the king was not a member of it.'[63] Yet at one point, as we have seen, he did appear to be contemplating resistance to the wishes of his ministers.

The abdication seemed to many of those closely involved with the monarchy to be a threat to its very existence. 'It is idle to believe', the biographer of George VI declares, 'that, because the Abdication crisis was of short duration and because it was skilfully handled, there are no grounds for the assumption that it was not of the utmost gravity, and that in slightly different circumstances the stability of the Monarchy might not have been imperilled'.[64] George VI himself feared that the monarchy could 'crumble under the shock and strain' of the abdication.[65] However, largely because of the skill of the new king, the abdication turned out to be not the end of the monarchy but 'Britain's vote for monarchy', and a republican motion introduced into the House of Commons received only five votes.[66] But it was a vote for a particular style of monarchy, constitutional, limited, and modest, a monarchy of traditional values of the type that had been established by George V.

[63] Beaverbrook to Charles J. V. Murphy, 3 Aug. 1949, House of Lords Record Office, Beaverbrook Papers, G/25.

[64] John Wheeler-Bennett, *King George VI: His Life and Reign* (Macmillan, 1958), 299.

[65] Ibid. 300.

[66] Robert Lacey, *Majesty: Elizabeth II and the House of Windsor* (Hutchinson, 1977), 109.

6

Hung Parliaments and Proportional Representation

———■+◆+■———

In Britain, general elections normally yield single-party majority government. Unlike most continental countries, Britain is accustomed neither to minority government nor to coalition. In wartime, admittedly, or in a period of national emergency such as 1931, coalition may be acceptable, but it has generally been regarded as a regrettable necessity. Where a general election fails to produce a clear-cut result, however, single-party minority government rather than coalition has been the rule. This has occurred more frequently than is sometimes thought. Of the twenty-five general elections in Britain in the twentieth century between 1900 and 1992, no fewer than five have failed to yield a clear result—the elections of January and December 1910, 1923, 1929, and February 1974. In addition, three general elections—all in the post-1945 period—have resulted in the return of governments with single-figure majorities: 1950, 1964, and October 1974. By April 1976 the Labour majority government returned in the general election of October 1974 had become, through by-elections and defections, a minority government, and it remained a minority government until forced to go to the country in May 1979.

The likelihood of a hung parliament—that is, a parliament in which no single party enjoys an overall majority—is far greater today than it was, for example, in the 1950s. This is primarily because there are now more MPs from the minority parties. Between 1951 and 1964, there were never more than nine MPs who did not belong to the Conservative or Labour parties. Since 1983, there have never been less than forty-four. There are three reasons for this increase. The first is the growth in the Liberal vote, which never reached 6 per cent in the 1950s, but since 1979 has never been lower than 18 per cent. The second reason is the divorce of the Northern Ireland party system from that on the mainland, and in particular the ending of the link between the Conservatives and Ulster Unionists, whose MPs until 1974 sat on the Conservative benches. The third reason is the rise of the Scottish and Welsh nationalists, who failed to win a single seat in any general election until 1970, but returned seven MPs to the House of Commons in 1992. Because any general election in the near future appears likely to yield at least forty MPs owing allegiance to neither the Conservative nor the Labour parties, a party probably needs to win at least fifty more seats than its rival if it is to obtain a working majority likely to last for the whole of a parliament. Such an outcome has occurred in eight out of the fourteen general elections since the war: the general elections of 1945, 1955, 1959, 1966, 1979, 1983, 1987, and 1992. It has been suggested that, at the first election to be held following the 1994 boundary changes the Conservatives would need a 4.8 per cent lead over Labour to secure an overall majority, while Labour would require a 2.1 per cent lead. The Conservatives have, in the post-war period, achieved a lead of 4.8 per cent or more in only five general elections: 1959, 1979, 1983, 1987, and 1992. Labour has achieved a lead of 2.1 per cent or more in the post-war period only in 1945, 1950, 1966, and October 1974.[1]

It is clear, then, that the prospect of a hung parliament in the future remains a very real one. This may pose problems for the sovereign, since it may no longer be obvious who should be appointed prime minister, and a number of different political combinations may be possible. Consider, for example, the last hung parliament, in February 1974, when the result was as shown in Table 6.1.

This outcome would have allowed, in theory, either a Labour minority government, a Conservative minority government, or a coalition between two or more parties. In many situations, a coalition between a major party and a minor party will be sufficient to secure majority government, but the February 1974 results were remarkable in that *no two parties* (other than Labour and the Conservatives) could have formed a majority coalition. Any major-

---

[1] John Curtice and Michael Steed, 'Appendix 2: The Results Analysed', in David Butler and Dennis Kavanagh, *The British General Election of 1992* (Macmillan, 1992), 352.

TABLE 6.1. *General election results, February 1974*

Party	Seats	% share of total vote
Labour	301	37.1
Conservative	297	37.9
Liberal	14	19.3
SNP	7	2.0
Plaid Cymru	2	0.6
Northern Ireland parties	12	2.3
Other	2	0.8
TOTAL	635	100.0

ity government, therefore, would have had to comprise at least three parties.

How, then, is a government to be formed in such circumstances; and, more particularly, how out of the various possible combinations is the sovereign to decide who should be given the first opportunity to form a government? Is it possible to reconcile the part which the sovereign might have to play in a highly complex government-formation process with the prime duty of a constitutional monarch, to remain politically impartial?

In a hung parliament, two major constitutional questions arise: what conventions govern whom the sovereign should send for to form a government; and what conventions govern the sovereign's use of the prerogative of dissolution?

II

Under some constitutions where multi-party politics is an accepted feature of political life and hung parliaments are frequent—Denmark, for example—there is a convention that the prime minister resigns after an election if it is at all unclear whether he or she can carry on; or he or she may retain office as a caretaker with only limited powers until a new government is formed. In Britain, however, there is no such convention. The British system of government does not require the prime minister to resign immediately after an election. Rather, an incumbent prime minister is entitled to remain in office if he or she so wishes until he or she loses the confidence of the Commons.

In the first half of the nineteenth century, when party lines were more fluid, it was the custom for prime ministers to meet parliament following a general election to test whether they could secure sufficient support to continue governing. Disraeli was the first prime minister to break with this practice in 1868, by resigning immediately it was clear that Gladstone's Liberal Party had achieved an overall majority in the general election. Since then prime ministers have invariably resigned without meeting parliament as soon as it has become obvious that a rival party has secured an overall majority. The rationale of this is that there is no point in hanging on and waiting to meet parliament when it is clear that one will inevitably be defeated on the first major vote.

But, the corollary must be that, when the outcome is not obvious, a government is not obliged to resign before the Commons has given its verdict; and where the outcome of the election yields a hung parliament, a prime minister may well wish to test the opinion of the Commons. That was the course adopted by Stanley Baldwin, the Conservative prime minister, after the general election of December 1923 left him fifty short of an overall majority. As leader of the largest party and because he sought to prove to the electorate that the Liberals were prepared to put a Labour government in power, Baldwin decided to meet parliament in January 1924, but was immediately defeated on a no-confidence amendment to the Address and resigned.

There is, however, no twentieth-century example of a prime minister meeting parliament as leader of the *second* largest party, for both Baldwin in 1929 and Edward Heath in 1974 resigned without meeting parliament. To find an example of a prime minister meeting parliament as leader of the second largest party, one has to go back to 1885, when Lord Salisbury, the Conservative prime minister, having won eighty-six fewer seats than the Liberals in the general election, decided nevertheless to test the opinion of parliament. His purpose in doing so was to exhibit the fact that the Liberals could form a government only with the support of the Irish Nationalists, the third party in the system. Salisbury was defeated, on an amendment to the Address, as soon as parliament met in January 1886, and immediately resigned.

Thus in the two twentieth-century examples of a prime minister finding himself leader of the second largest party in a hung parliament, there was a change of government before parliament met. In 1929, with Labour the largest party, Stanley Baldwin decided, by contrast with 1923, to resign without meeting parliament. After the February 1974 general election, however, Edward Heath, the incumbent prime minister, did not resign immediately, but approached the Liberal leader, Jeremy Thorpe, with an offer of coalition involving Liberal participation in government. As can be seen from the statistics in Table 6.1, such a coalition would have made the Conservative–Liberal grouping the largest single grouping in the Commons, although still without an overall majority. Heath therefore also approached Harry West, leader of the Ulster Unionists, and offered the Conservative whip to seven of the eleven Ulster Unionists, excluding the Paisleyites. This would have been sufficient to give him an overall majority.

The Ulster Unionists, however, refused to accept the Conservative whip unless it was offered to all eleven of them, while the Liberals rejected Heath's offer of coalition—although they declared their willingness to support an agreed programme from outside the government. Upon learning of the Liberals' rejection of coalition, however, Heath resigned without meeting parliament.

Heath's negotiations with Thorpe, and his refusal to resign immediately the election result was known, were criticized as 'bordering on the unconstitutional' in a letter to *The Times* on 4 March 1974 by Lord Crowther-Hunt, a constitutional expert, shortly to become a minister in Harold Wilson's Labour government. Crowther-Hunt's reasoning was based on the fact that there was no twentieth-century example of a prime minister failing to resign immediately following an election which left his party the second largest in the Commons. As the last contrary example had occurred nearly one hundred years previously, the implication, Crowther-Hunt believed, was that a convention had arisen to the effect that it is only if a prime minister remains leader of the largest party that he is entitled to meet parliament.

But this reasoning cannot be sustained. It would still have been perfectly possible for a prime minister in Heath's position to construct sufficient parliamentary support for the continuation of his government, and, if that possibility exists, it cannot be unconstitutional for a prime minister to test it. Indeed, having incurred some criticism as a 'bad loser' for not resigning immediately the election results were known, Heath would probably not have incurred much greater odium had he met parliament, despite not having constructed a majority. Indeed, he might well have been better advised to take this course, since he could have gained a tactical advantage by displaying to the country that the Liberals were installing a Labour government in office.

Interestingly enough, Harold Wilson, who became prime minister of a Labour minority government on Heath's resignation, did not share the view that Heath had acted unconstitutionally. In 1976, he wrote:

There were suggestions that, as the Conservatives had fewer seats than Labour, and were having difficulty in securing allies, the Labour leader should have been invited to try. This would have been contrary to precedent. A Prime Minister was there—at Downing Street. If and when he resigned that would create a new situation. Alternatively, were he to face Parliament without allies, and be defeated, then he would resign. As things were, there was no vacancy to fill.[2]

Constitutional authorities, such as Bradley and Ewing, and Blake, support the view that a prime minister can meet parliament whether or not his or her party remains the largest after a general election.[3]

If, however, Heath *had* been successful in creating a coalition, perhaps with the Liberals, then the character of his government would have changed. It would no longer have been a single-party government but a coalition. Would he have had to resign and be reappointed prime minister to mark this change in the character of his government, as MacDonald had done in 1931 and Churchill in 1945 (though not Asquith in 1915)? And, if he had resigned, would the queen have necessarily had to reappoint him, given that he was not leader of the largest party in the Commons and that, even with the Liberals, he could not command a majority? Might the queen not instead have called for Harold Wilson as leader of Labour, the largest party in the Commons? These are constitutional dilemmas which, fortunately, the monarchy did not have to face.

Moreover, the fact that Heath resigned before meeting parliament

[2] Harold Wilson, *The Governance of Britain* (Weidenfeld & Nicolson/Michael Joseph, 1976), 25–6. There is a similar comment in Harold Wilson's account of his last government, *Final Term* (Weidenfeld & Nicolson/Michael Joseph, 1979), 11.

[3] E. C. S. Wade and A. W. Bradley, *Constitutional and Administrative Law*, 11th edn., ed. A. W. Bradley and K. D. Ewing (Longman, 1993), 253; Robert Blake, *The Office of Prime Minister* (Oxford University Press, 1975), 38–9.

means that there is no twentieth-century example of a party without the largest number of seats meeting parliament. It would, therefore, perhaps appear unusual were a party with the second largest number of seats to insist upon meeting parliament, and the public might regard it as somehow unsporting in terms of the cricketing analogy that the party with the most seats has 'won' the election even in a hung parliament. But, whether that is so or not, there is no way in which an incumbent government can be forced out of office until it has been defeated in the Commons, and the sovereign is in no position to take action until that has happened. Until a government has resigned, the question of whom to appoint as prime minister does not arise, for there is no vacancy. Thus it is not until the incumbent has actually resigned that the sovereign faces a problem. There are two particular difficulties which might arise. They are:

1. Whether the sovereign should appoint as prime minister the leader of the largest party, or the party leader best fitted to secure the support of the majority in the Commons—the two criteria may well not yield the same outcome.
2. Whether the right of the incumbent prime minister to remain in office after a general election until defeated in the Commons also extends to an alternative leader from the prime minister's party who might prove to be in a better position to form a government.

The first issue is whether it is right for a prime minister to be given a commission to form a single-party minority government rather than a majority coalition or a minority government with outside support and operating on an agreed programme (as with the Lib.–Lab. pact of 1977–8).

The second issue is whether incumbency lies with the person of the prime minister or with the prime minister's party. These two issues will be discussed in turn.

III

The principle that a government must enjoy the confidence of the Commons—a basic principle of parliamentary government—is, unfortunately, not free from ambiguity. It can mean either that a government commands the *positive* support of a majority in the Commons; or that there is no majority in the Commons *against* it.

In a hung parliament, the first interpretation of the principle that a government must enjoy the confidence of the Commons entails a majority coalition or a minority government with outside support and operating on an agreed programme; the second would allow for a single-party minority government, perhaps living from day to day and seeking a tactical dissolution to try to secure a majority, as Harold Wilson did in October 1974, having been prime minister for seven months of a minority government.

These two interpretations can easily be confused. They are in fact confused in the well-known constitutional law text by Bradley and Ewing when they state as the basic rule *both* that 'In appointing a Prime Minister the Sovereign must appoint that person who is in the best position to receive the support of the majority in the House of Commons', *and* that, upon the resignation of the prime minister after a general election, 'the Queen will send for the leader of the party with the largest number of seats (as in 1929 and 1974) or with the next largest number of seats (as in January 1924 after Baldwin had been defeated by combined Labour and Liberal votes)'.[4] Normally, of course, these two criteria will coincide, but they will diverge when there is a hung parliament. Which has been preferred in the past—minority government or majority coalition?

On all occasions this century when general elections have failed to produce a single-party majority—the two elections of 1910 and the general elections of 1923, 1929, and February 1974—the outcome has been single-party government and never coalition. The election of 1923, perhaps the only genuine three-party election in the twentieth century, is a very striking example. The result of the general election, called by Baldwin, the Conservative prime minister, is shown in Table 6.2. When Baldwin met the House of Commons in January 1924, he was defeated in an amendment to the Address and resigned. The king then summoned Ramsay MacDonald, the Labour leader, and appointed him prime minister, even though he held only a third of the seats in the Commons, 117 seats short of an overall majority, and his party had won just over 30 per cent of the vote. MacDonald was not asked, as he would have been in some continental political systems, whether he could form a government *supported by a majority in the Commons*. That would have required him to obtain pledges of support from the Liberals. He might have had to offer the

[4] Wade and Bradley, *Constitutional and Administrative Law*, 252–3.

TABLE 6.2. *General election results, 1923*

Party	Seats	% share of total vote
Conservative	258	38.1
Labour	191	30.5
Liberal	159	29.6
Others	7	1.8
TOTAL	615	100.0

Liberals places in his cabinet and perhaps an agreed programme in order to obtain this support. In 1931, by contrast, the king was determined to secure a majority government, believing that only a government with a majority in the Commons could confront the economic emergency.

It is clear, however, that there is normally no requirement for a prime minister to seek majority support in a hung parliament. This has profound effects on the fortunes of the political parties, and perhaps also on the future of the party system. The Conservative and Labour parties would probably prefer, in a hung parliament, single-party minority government without any formal agreement with other parties to a majority coalition with the Liberal Democrats, which would have the effect of bringing the Liberal Democrats back as a governing party. For that very reason, the Liberal Democrats would prefer to be in a position whereby one of the major parties was compelled to negotiate with them before being allowed to form a government.

Were he or she to act on the basis of precedent, therefore, the sovereign would not require a government in a hung parliament to command majority support. Were he or she to depart from precedent, the sovereign would be open to criticism from the major parties of acting partially towards the Liberal Democrats, since he or she would not be allowing a prime minister to form a minority government without negotiating its terms with them. On the other hand, the Liberal Democrats can reasonably claim that the working of the system is biased against them.

The truth is that the existing conventions are not—and perhaps cannot be—politically neutral. They favour the two major parties

and handicap the Liberal Democrats. The conventions at the base of
our parliamentary system are dualistic in nature, and it is not easy
for a third party to take advantage of what at first sight may seem
a strong balancing position in a hung parliament. Indeed, it is
noticeable that, in the three hung parliaments since 1918 (those of
1923, 1929, and February 1974), the Liberals on each occasion have
been unable to take advantage of their pivotal position. Moreover,
they lost both seats and votes in the ensuing general elections, since
on each occasion they were associated with an unpopular government, without, however, being able to exert very much influence
upon it. But our existing conventions, which are dualist in nature,
could come under severe pressure were the two-party system again
to come under challenge, as it did in the 1980s, or if proportional
representation were to be introduced.

IV

The second contentious situation would occur if the incumbent party
sought to change its leader immediately after the election in order to
facilitate a coalition or pact with another party. That almost happened after the general election of 1923. Having failed to win an
overall majority, a number of leading Conservatives felt that
Baldwin had made a serious error of judgement in having dissolved
the previous parliament after it had been in existence for only a year,
and that, in consequence, he ought to be deposed. Moreover, many
Conservatives believed that an alternative leader might have been
able to secure a coalition or pact with the Liberals, which would
have commanded an overall majority in the Commons, and could
have kept Labour out of office.

In the event, the plot against Baldwin failed, but, if it had succeeded, it would have posed a serious dilemma for George V. Let us
suppose that some other Conservative had become leader and let us
further suppose that this new Conservative leader had been one with
whom the Liberals would have co-operated. Then, when Baldwin
resigned, should George V have called this new Conservative leader
to the Palace, or should he have called the leader of the Labour
opposition, even though Labour might have had no chance of securing an overall majority in the Commons. This scenario once again
poses the conflict between a government which can command the

support of a majority in the Commons—a Conservative–Liberal government in the example—and a minority government.

The argument for calling the new Conservative leader to the Palace to form a government as soon as Baldwin had resigned would have been that, if the incumbent prime minister has a right to test the verdict of the electorate in the Commons, that right belongs to him or her in virtue of his or her leadership of the cabinet and the party. The Conservatives, it may be suggested, should not have been deprived of an option which they would otherwise have enjoyed simply because their current leader happened to be unacceptable to the Liberals. Suppose, to use a *reductio ad absurdum* argument, Baldwin had died or been assassinated immediately after the general election. Should an event of this sort have deprived the Conservatives of their chance of testing the opinion of the Commons?

Further, Britain is a parliamentary and not a plebiscitary democracy. The constitutional responsibility of the electorate, it may be argued, is to vote in an election. If, as in this situation, it speaks with an uncertain voice and fails to give any party an overall majority, the responsibility passes to MPs. In the situation that is being postulated, a majority of MPs have agreed to support a government of a particular political colour—a Conservative–Liberal coalition—and it would be wrong to allow the wishes of a minority of MPs—those supporting Labour—to prevail over those of the majority.

If this argument is accepted, incumbency lies not with the prime minister but with the party. The realities of contemporary politics dictate that the prime minister holds his or her position not by virtue of any personal qualities he or she may have but because he or she leads a party which enjoys the confidence of the Commons. This reasoning would dictate that, as soon as Baldwin had resigned, in our hypothetical example, the sovereign should have called for the new Conservative leader.

But there are also powerful arguments on the other side. It must be remembered that, in the 1923 election, the Conservatives had lost their overall majority, winning only 258 seats as compared with 345 in the election previous to that, in 1922. It could, therefore, be argued that the Conservatives had been repudiated by the electorate. Labour had gained 49 seats over and above the 142 which it had won in 1922, to give it 191 seats. The argument would, of course, have been even stronger if Labour had won the most seats rather than the second largest number.

Moreover, suppose that the sovereign had called the new Conservative leader and the Conservative–Liberal coalition had proved unstable. It would have been perfectly possible for a coalition entered into in good faith by both Conservative and Liberal MPs to collapse very quickly. There might, for example, have been a grass-roots revolt by Liberal constituency associations objecting to their party forming a coalition with the Conservatives. They might have insisted that they had not supported the Liberals only to see them propping up a discredited Conservative government. Something similar to this happened in 1926 in Canada, when the Conservative leader, Arthur Meighen, was given a written assurance from a third party—the Agricultural Party—that it would support his government. Unfortunately, however, the leader of the Agricultural Party could not fully deliver his party's support, and Meighen's government collapsed after only five days. Were that to have occurred in the circumstances of our hypothetical example, the sovereign could have been gravely embarrassed, just as the governor-general of Canada, Lord Byng, was embarrassed by the events of 1926. If the coalition arrangement of the Conservative prime minister in our hypothetical example had collapsed, he or she would have been forced either to seek a dissolution or to resign. In either case, the sovereign would have had a difficult decision to make. If the prime minister had asked for a dissolution, the sovereign would have had to decide whether to grant a dissolution to a party which had just called a general election; or whether to allow Labour to take office as a minority government. If the prime minister had resigned, the sovereign would, presumably, have been compelled to call for Labour. Whichever course the prime minister took, the sovereign might have been criticized by Labour supporters for ignoring their party, and allowing the construction of an artificial coalition designed to keep Labour out of office.

Moreover, the argument that it is for parliament rather than the electorate to choose a government is by no means an invulnerable one. From the formal point of view, no doubt, it is parliament which determines the colour of the government, but in modern times it is generally the electorate which chooses the government. The electorate might feel cheated if two parties which had fought against each other in the election campaign decided after the election to come together in a coalition or pact. Coalitions, it may be argued, should be formed before the election, not after the votes have been counted.

The arguments as to whether incumbency lies with the person or the party are finely balanced. Perhaps the following may be accepted as a reasonable resolution of the issue.

If the incumbent party is the largest party, as in the 1923 example, then there is a strong case for arguing that it should have the first opportunity to test the opinion of the Commons, so that, in our hypothetical scenario, when Baldwin resigned, the sovereign ought to have called for the new Conservative leader rather than the Labour leader.

In other circumstances, however, when the incumbent party is not the largest party in terms of seats, as in 1929 and February 1974, it may be suggested that incumbency belongs to the *person* and not to the party. Otherwise, were the sovereign to act as if incumbency lay with the party, and the hypothetical Conservative–Liberal coalition collapsed, the sovereign might be blamed, perhaps unjustly. If, on the other hand, the sovereign were to call Labour to office, and Labour were defeated, the sovereign would have a good defence in that he or she would have been acting in accordance with the outcome of the election by appointing the leader of the largest party to office.

These circumstances are perhaps highly unlikely to arise. In general, an incumbent prime minister, finding that he or she was no longer the leader of the largest party in the Commons, would resign immediately, as Baldwin did in 1929. But the example, outlandish though it might seem, is of some interest for our understanding of the role of the sovereign in the complex situations that can arise following a hung parliament. The sovereign must always adopt a worse-case analysis of the consequences of his or her actions. He or she must be able to protect himself or herself from the most unlikely contingencies and ensure that there is a defence available if things go wrong. The same principle needs to be applied when considering the other main area of royal discretion, the question of when if ever the sovereign can refuse a dissolution.

V

Under normal circumstances, the sovereign dissolves parliament at the request of the prime minister. Were he or she to refuse a dissolution to a government with a majority in the Commons, the government might well resign and the sovereign would be unable to find an alternative government capable of securing the confidence of parliament. In a hung parliament, however, there will sometimes be a viable alternative government. Under what circumstances, then, can the sovereign refuse a dissolution?

An authoritative answer to this question was given in 1950 by King George VI's private secretary, Sir Alan Lascelles. Sir Alan's statement was given in a letter published in *The Times* on 2 May under the pseudonym 'Senex'. Sir Alan wrote:

It is surely indisputable (and commonsense) that a Prime Minister may ask—not demand—that his Sovereign will grant him a dissolution of Parliament; and that the Sovereign, if he so chooses, may refuse to grant this request. The problem of such a choice is entirely personal to the Sovereign, though he is, of course, free to ask informal advice from anybody whom he thinks fit to consult. Insofar as this matter can be publicly discussed, it can be properly assumed that no wise Sovereign—that is, one who has at heart the true interest of the country, the constitution, and the Monarchy—would deny a dissolution to his Prime Minister unless he was satisfied that; (1) the existing Parliament was still vital, viable and capable of doing its job; (2) a General Election would be detrimental to the national economy; (3) he could rely on finding another Prime Minister who could carry on his Government, for a reasonable period, with a working majority in the House of Commons.

This statement, coming as it does by the sovereign's private secretary, has naturally proved extremely influential. Nevertheless, it is perhaps in need of qualification. Lascelles's third requirement—that the sovereign can rely on finding another prime minister who could carry on the government for a reasonable period with a working majority in the House of Commons—is the most important. It constitutes a necessary if not a sufficient condition for refusing a dissolution. The sovereign must at all costs avoid the embarrassment of refusing a dissolution to one prime minister in the belief that another person can secure a working majority, only to find that this expectation is frustrated, and that he has to grant a dissolution to the second prime minister having refused it to a rival. That was the embarrassing situation in which the governor-general, Lord Byng, found himself in Canada in 1926. He had refused a dissolution to Mackenzie King, after being given a guarantee by the leader of the opposition, Arthur Meighen, that he could form a government which could survive in the legislature. Meighen, however, was soon beaten in the House and Byng agreed to his request for a dissolution. As Sir Alan put it in his letter, the conditions he laid down seemed to be satisfied, 'but in the event the third proved illusory', since, contrary to what might have been predicted, Meighen's government did not prove viable. In the words of Sir Alan Lascelles to a leading politician of the immediate post-war period:

Meighen gave this guarantee in good faith, having got an assurance from an old rascal called Forke that he & his Agricultural Party would vote for Meighen. The guarantee proved completely illusory. Within a few days Forke & Co. ratted. Meighen was beat & Byng (most inadvisably) gave him a dissolution.

And the consequences were that M. King came back with a thumping majority. Byng was left in a most unhappy position and Mr. Forke was made a Senator.[5]

In the circumstances in which he found himself in 1926, Lord Byng might perhaps have minimized his embarrassment had he, instead of giving a dissolution to Meighen, refused it. Meighen would have been compelled to resign and Byng could then have called for King again, granting him a dissolution, it having been established that the utility of that particular parliament was at an end since no alternative government was possible. That was, apparently, the view of Meighen at the time. He had told Winston Churchill 'that, when he found himself unable to carry on he did actually recommend the Governor-General to send again for King, believing this to be the correct constitutional procedure'. Mackenzie King also apparently agreed with this interpretation of the constitution.[6]

If the third condition in Sir Alan's letter is the vital one, it may be argued that the other two are rather more problematic. Whether a general election would or would not be detrimental to the national economy is not primarily a matter for the sovereign to decide. Politicians will often disagree on this, and the sovereign cannot put himself or herself in the position of an umpire able to determine what might or might not be 'prejudicial to the national interest'. There are, however, extreme circumstances, such as war, national emergency, or very severe economic crisis, when it would hardly be possible to hold a general election. George V was, for this reason,

[5] Lascelles to Oliver Lyttleton, 24 Apr. 1950, RA GVI 320/023.
[6] Copy of a memo. written by Lord Bessborough of a conversation with Mr Winston Churchill, Mar. 1932, RA GVI 320/019.

unwilling to grant a dissolution in 1916. He was 'opposed to a General Election in war time fearing it might have a disintegrating effect'.[7] In August 1931 George V took the view that a dissolution would not be possible in the midst of a currency crisis, and therefore a government had to be formed which could carry the necessary economy measures through the existing House of Commons.

Sir Alan's first condition, that 'the existing Parliament was still vital, viable, and capable of doing its job', also requires some qualification. This too involves value judgements of a political kind which it is hardly for the sovereign to make. Nevertheless, the sovereign may legitimately give some weight to the question of whether parliament is near the end of its term so that a dissolution would in any event be inevitable in the near future; or whether the parliament is newly elected.

Sir Alan's third condition, which is the most important, states the conditions under which the sovereign is *entitled* to refuse a dissolution. In fact, in Britain, whenever a dissolution has been granted to a minority government—as in 1905 to Campbell-Bannerman, November 1910 to Asquith, October 1924 to MacDonald, and September 1974 to Wilson—an alternative government was clearly impossible and the sovereign had no alternative. It does not, however, follow that the sovereign would automatically grant a dissolution to a minority government if an alternative government were possible. George V, before granting MacDonald a dissolution in 1924, made enquiries, through his private secretary, of the two opposition parties as to whether they might be prepared to form a government. Thus the sovereign cannot refuse a dissolution *unless* an alternative government is available. It does not of course follow that the sovereign is *obliged* to refuse a dissolution in such circumstances. Whether he or she could use discretion to refuse must depend upon other factors. These factors, it is suggested, are as follows:

1. War or national emergency. George V told Bonar Law in 1916 that he would not agree to a dissolution if asked.[8] In 1931 he would have refused a dissolution had it been sought before the budget had been balanced.

2. How long the existing parliament has been in existence.

3. Whether the prime minister seeking a dissolution has, within a

---

[7] Harold Nicolson, *King George V: His Life and Reign* (Constable, 1952) 288.
[8] Ibid. 289.

short distance of time, been granted a previous dissolution. To take an extreme example, an incumbent prime minister, following a general election which produces a hung parliament, who is defeated on the Address, as Baldwin was in 1924, is certainly *not* entitled to a second dissolution; although, if no alternative government is available, it must, nevertheless, be granted. It is, of course, not possible to state with any precision how long a government needs to survive to be entitled to a second dissolution, but it must at least survive this first parliamentary test. Otherwise, a prime minister who had called an election and failed to win it would be able to secure a series of dissolutions, and that would be 'a triumph over, and not a triumph of, the electorate'.[9]

4. Whether the alternative government—which might be a coalition—would have any prospect of surviving for some reasonable period of time. The sovereign would have to exercise fine political judgement as to whether pledges made by a second party were likely to prove effective—they did not prove so in Canada in 1926; and also whether an arrangement made in parliament would be supported by leading members of the parties concerned in the country. If it was not, then the chances of the agreement surviving would be considerably lessened. In 1939 Sir Patrick Duncan, the governor-general of South Africa, first assured himself that Smuts could form an alternative government before refusing the dissolution requested by Hertzog. Byng, by contrast, did not so assure himself. He could not have been unaware that the survival of Meighen's government was uncertain, and he took a gamble. But sovereigns and governor-generals cannot afford to gamble.

These are, of course, highly complex issues and, in seeking to resolve them, the sovereign must not only remain impartial, but be seen to be so. In general, the sovereign will best preserve his or her impartiality by following precedent and granting a dissolution wherever there is a real doubt. Were the sovereign to fail to act according to precedent, and refuse a dissolution, it might then be found that an alternative government could not survive—as in Canada in 1926—or that it was repudiated in the country, and the sovereign would be blamed. If, on the other hand, the sovereign agreed to a dissolution, he or she would be merely inviting the electorate to

[9] H. V. Evatt, *The King and his Dominion Governors* (Oxford University Press, 1936), 109.

resolve the conflict. It would be much more difficult to blame the sovereign for the outcome. The sovereign's approach is likely to be dictated by prudence, and one may suspect that he or she would be unlikely ever to refuse a dissolution unless the arguments for such a course were quite incontrovertible.

In general, the sovereign has the right to refuse a dissolution only where the grant of a dissolution would be an affront to, rather than an expression of, democratic rights. In refusing a dissolution, for example, sought by an incumbent prime minister after a defeat on the Address, where an alternative government would clearly be viable, or where the prime minister had lost the support of his or her cabinet or party,[10] the sovereign would not be undermining constitutional government but defending it. Only under circumstances of such a kind can the refusal of a dissolution be justified.

Two conclusions may be drawn from this survey of the sovereign's position in a hung parliament. The first is that the sovereign does not require a potential prime minister to prove that he or she can obtain majority support in the Commons. A party leader is normally asked to form a government without any provision that he or she is able to command a majority.

Secondly, although in theory the sovereign retains the right to refuse a dissolution, in practice he or she is likely to exercise it only in exceptional circumstances. Normally, the prime minister of a minority government will be able to obtain a dissolution at a time of his or her own choosing, as Ramsay MacDonald did in 1924, and Harold Wilson did in September 1974.

The conventions of the constitution thus provide for a minority government, rather than a majority coalition, to be formed in a hung parliament. It is arguable, however, that these conventions do not necessarily make for good government. In the past, minority governments have been short lived and ineffectual. Moreover, minority governments tend also to frustrate the canons of democracy, since they represent only between 30 and 38 per cent of the voters—a far cry from majority rule (see Table 6.3). For these reasons, one commentator has suggested that 'A future in which minority governments become the norm is horrible to contemplate.'[11]

---

[10] See pp. 81–3.
[11] A. H. Birch, 'Britain's Impending Constitutional Dilemmas', *Parliamentary Affairs*, 37 (1984), 98.

TABLE 6.3. *Minority governments*

Governing party	% share of total vote
Labour (Jan.–Oct. 1924)	30.5
Labour (May 1929–Aug. 1931)	37.1
Labour (Mar.–Oct. 1974)	37.1

VI

The constitutional rules which have so far been analysed emphasize the dualistic assumptions of the British political system. They offer an advantage to the incumbent prime minister by yielding him or her a strong tactical position in the confused aftermath of an indecisive general election. Since the rules encourage the formation of single-party minority governments, they strengthen the position of the major parties at the expense of the minor ones, freeing a prime minister from the need to consult with other parties or to negotiate the formation of a government which can command a majority in the House of Commons.

Constitutional conventions do not, however, exist in a vacuum. Rather they reflect the facts of political power. The conventions described above help to preserve the impartiality of the sovereign in a period of two-party politics. They assume that hung parliaments are but a rare interlude in an era of alternating majority governments. The two-party system, defined in this way, has been a reality of British politics since the time of the Second Reform Act in 1867. It has frequently come under challenge—from Irish Nationalists in the nineteenth century, from Liberals in the 1920s, and from the Liberal–SDP Alliance in the 1980s. Although each of these challenges was formidable, the two-party system survived. There is no guarantee, however, that the two-party system will survive permanently.

Suppose, to begin with, that one hung parliament were to be succeeded by a second. This nearly occurred in 1974, when the second general election of that year, in October, gave Labour an overall majority of only three. Had there been a second hung parliament, current conventions might well have come under strain. The queen might reasonably have taken the view that a third general election held soon after the second would not appreciably have changed the political situation. Therefore, in the future, a sovereign might well consider that it would be necessary to be more stringent in considering requests for a dissolution. At this juncture it would no longer be possible to maintain the assumption that a hung parliament was merely an unfortunate interregnum between periods of single-party majority government. In such a situation, new conventions might have to be developed.

New conventions would certainly have to be developed were Britain to adopt a proportional-representation electoral system. Under a proportional system, a party would be able to secure a majority of the seats in the Commons only if it gained the support of 50 per cent of the voters. But the last time that a government secured the support of 50 per cent of the voters was in 1935. In practice, then, most parliaments under proportional representation would be hung parliaments, as they are in those continental countries adopting proportional representation, where single-party majority government has become very rare.

During the immediate post-war years, proportional representation was seen as an eccentric nostrum which could never be adopted in Britain. It is, however, no longer inconceivable that Britain might adopt it. The Liberals, predecessors of the Liberal Democrats, first supported it in 1922. But, until recently, they were alone amongst the main British parties in favouring it. Labour, however, chastened by over sixteen years in opposition, has in recent years become more sympathetic to electoral reform. In 1992 John Smith pledged as Labour leader that a Labour government would hold a referendum on the electoral system. This pledge has been renewed by Tony Blair, who was elected leader of the Labour Party following Smith's death in 1994.

Proportional representation would serve to entrench multi-party politics. New rules would need to be developed to reflect the new realities of political power and to ensure that the impartiality of the sovereign was preserved. What these new conventions might be is obviously highly speculative, but the essence of the new situation produced by proportional representation would be that governments would frequently be formed through a process of inter-party negotiation. Dissolution would cease to be so powerful a weapon in the hands of a prime minister since a general election would be unlikely to give any party a majority, while there might well be, with a hung parliament, an alternative government in the House of Commons.

But, if a government might no longer be automatically entitled to a dissolution, then, if it is to survive, it would need majority support. This could be obtained through negotiating either a coalition, or some arrangement by which another party or parties would support it on an agreed programme, after the model of the Lib.–Lab. pact in 1977–8. Without a dissolution in his pocket, the prime minister would no longer be in a position to put pressure on his or her coalition partners for support. The pressure, by contrast, would be on the prime minister to negotiate. The onus for proving the need for a dissolution would have shifted. Instead of the opposition parties having to prove conclusively that they could form an alternative government—the current situation—the government would have to prove that there was no alternative majority. Instead of the prime minister, in effect, deciding upon when to dissolve, the Commons would decide by making it clear that it would not sustain any alternative majority.

Thus, under proportional representation, a candidate for the premiership might be required to show to the sovereign that he or she could command the support of a majority in the Commons before being appointed prime minister. He or she might then be granted a dissolution only when no alternative government were available. Under these circumstances, the role of the sovereign might become more active both in the formation of governments and in the granting of dissolutions, as it was during the middle years of Queen Victoria's reign, and as it is in the continental monarchies, all of which have proportional systems.

Of course, no alteration in the conventions is likely until the existing ones have been *shown* to be no longer applicable, and therefore exhausted. This would require a succession of hung parliaments and/or the introduction of proportional representation, forcing the political parties to accept that single-party majority government would rarely recur.

What can probably be expected is an extremely messy intervening period in which different conceptions of political reality jostle for acceptance. These conceptions would reflect a conflict between a party system that is dying and one that is struggling to be born.

The future constitutional role of the sovereign will be highly dependent upon the evolution of the British party and electoral systems. Were the configuration of political power to change, then the conventions of the constitution affecting the role of the sovereign would also change, for these conventions do not exist in a world of their own isolated from the realities of political power. Indeed, the isolation of the sovereign from party politics has been easy to achieve only because British politics has been marked for much of the last 130 years by a stable two-party system. It is only when that system seems to be breaking down—1885–6, 1910–14, 1923–4, and 1931—that the sovereign comes to be called upon to play a more active role in the constitution. Under proportional representation, that possibility of a more active role might always be present, for the role which the sovereign has been able to adopt in the exercise of prerogatives for most of the twentieth century is not inherent in the office of sovereign, but contingent upon the continued existence of a two-party system.

VII

Could the position of the sovereign be protected were proportional representation to be introduced into Britain and hung parliaments became a normal occurrence?

The continental monarchies—Belgium, Denmark, Luxembourg, Netherlands, Norway, Sweden, and Spain—all of which use proportional representation to elect their legislatures, have had to grapple with this problem for many years. The problem has two aspects. The first is that of whom to appoint as prime minister. The second is whether to specify that a majority government is to be formed, as George V did in 1931, although not in 1924 or 1929. This second principle arises because the basic principle of parliamentary government—that a government must enjoy the support of parliament—is ambiguous.[12] The principle can either be interpreted to mean that a government must receive the positive support of parliament through a vote of confidence or it can be interpreted negatively to mean that there is not a majority willing to bring the government down in a

[12] This ambiguity has been discussed by Henrik Hermerén, *Regerinsgbildningen i flerpartisystem* (Studentlitteratur, Lund, 1975); there is a summary in English of Hermerén's ideas at the end of the book. He has also written an article in English entitled 'Government Formation in Multi-Party Systems', *Scandinavian Political Studies*, 11 (1976), 131–46.

vote of censure. The principle can mean either that there is a majority *for* the government, or that there is no majority *against* it. These two interpretations of course coincide under a two-party system, but they can easily diverge under a multi-party system. In the continental monarchies, they are interpreted in different ways. In the Netherlands, majority governments are generally formed, but in Scandinavia, and especially in Denmark, minority governments are frequent. Indeed, under article 16[2] of the Danish Constitution, the government enjoys a juridical existence simply in virtue of a prime minister having been nominated by the sovereign. No formal vote of investiture or vote of confidence is needed, the government being presumed to enjoy the confidence of parliament until it is defeated. Thus a minority government can continue for as long as there is not a positive majority against it in the legislature.

The ambiguities in the basic principle of parliamentary government could easily embroil a sovereign in political controversy. The problem is not so much that the sovereign would use his or her powers in the formation of a government in a deliberately biased manner, but rather that, even if the sovereign were to act in a way which he or she genuinely believed to be in accordance with the constitutional proprieties, the supporters of one (or more) of the parties might come to feel that their party had been unfairly treated.

The continental monarchies, unlike Britain, all have codified constitutions. Yet these constitutions offer little guidance to the government-formation process. They play, in general, a purely formal role, confined to laying down certain general principles. For example, article 24 of the Danish Constitution declares that the sovereign appoints and dismisses the prime minister and all other ministers. But it does not discuss what principles the sovereign should adopt when making his or her choice. Similarly, article 65 of the Belgian Constitution declares simply that 'The King appoints and dismisses his Ministers', while article 86.2 of the Dutch Constitution declares that 'The King appoints ministers and dismisses them at will'. Thus the significance of a constitution, in so far as the government formation process is concerned, is almost wholly emblematic. Constitutions say little about the conventions that have arisen during the actual process of forming a government.

Continental monarchies, therefore, have developed methods to protect the sovereign from political involvement. There are, broadly, four ways of achieving this objective. The first, which is almost certainly the method that would be adopted in Britain were proportional representation to be introduced, would be to develop a series of conventions which politicians would be prepared to observe and respect. Such an approach is characteristic of the government-formation process in Denmark and Norway, and it would harmonize with the spirit of British constitutional development.

There are, however, two other methods of protecting the sovereign adopted on the Continent which involve more formalized procedures. The first of these is, as in Belgium and the Netherlands, for the sovereign to appoint *informateurs* to assist in the government-formation process. The task of the *informateur* is to negotiate with party leaders to determine what political combinations are possible. *Informateurs* have also been appointed on occasion in Denmark and Norway, but on an experimental basis rather than as a regular policy, and the experiments have not been particularly successful.

The second alternative method of protecting the sovereign from political involvement in the government-formation process is more drastic, for it involves stripping the sovereign of his or her role in the government-formation process entirely. This method has been adopted in Sweden, where the 1974 constitution known as the Instrument of Government strips the sovereign of his or her prerogative powers, transferring them to the speaker of the single-chamber parliament, the Riksdag. This method was at one time proposed for Britain by Tony Benn, now a republican.[13]

A fourth method has been suggested, in Britain, by the Institute of Public Policy Research, a left-leaning think-tank, which has published a proposed constitution in which the discretion of the sovereign in appointing a prime minister and dissolving parliament is entirely eliminated.[14]

These four methods are considered in turn.

VIII

In both Denmark and Norway, conventions have been developed to protect the sovereign from political involvement. The problem is more difficult to resolve in Denmark than in Norway, since

[13] Tony Benn, 'Power and the People', *New Socialist* (Sept.–Oct. 1982), 9–15.
[14] Institute of Public Policy Research, *The Constitution of the United Kingdom* (IPPR, 1991).

Norwegian politics has generally been characterized by a two-bloc system and the sovereign has rarely been called upon to exercise his or her discretion. In Denmark, by contrast, there is not only a multiplicity of parties but an absence of clearly defined blocs.

In the absence of specific provisions in the Danish Constitution regulating the government-formation process, a series of conventional rules has come to be observed. The first convention is that, after a general election, by contrast with Britain, the prime minister and cabinet immediately resign. The sovereign then consults the party leaders, one at a time, in an order determined by their relative strength in the single-chamber legislature, the Folketing. The party leaders offer their recommendations as to which governmental combinations are feasible and desirable.

If party leaders representing a majority in the Folketing recommend that a particular person be asked to form a government, then the sovereign will ask that person to attempt the task, but if the first round does not yield such a majority, further consultations are arranged until the majority of the parties can finally agree upon a particular candidate for the premiership. So far, the discussions have never led to deadlock, a tribute perhaps to the eagerness to reach agreement in a consensual democracy such as Denmark. While the complex negotiations that ensue would seem to provide ample scope for the Danish sovereign to use his or her discretion to influence the outcome, there has been no major controversy about the role of the sovereign since 1920, some time before the modern conventional rules were developed. Denmark, of course, is a small country without major territorial or regional conflicts, and with a powerful sense of national identity. It does not follow that the conventions which have proved so successful in Denmark would necessarily work equally well in Britain, a country in which political differences are more intense and social conflicts less easy to resolve.

IX

In Belgium and the Netherlands, by contrast both with the Scandinavian countries and with Britain, the sovereign is not only allowed, but expected, to play a more active role in the government-formation process. In both countries, indeed, but especially in Belgium, the sovereign is regarded as a guarantor of national unity.

In Belgium, the sovereign is sometimes seen as the only figure who is above the inter-communal conflict, the only real Belgian in a country in which everyone else is a Fleming or a Walloon.

In Belgium and the Netherlands, the government-formation process is marked by the highly active role played by the *informateur*. The *informateur* is not restricted, as he or she is when employed in the Scandinavian countries, merely to registering the point of view of the parties, but also initiates an active search for agreement on the composition of a coalition government, the distribution of posts, and the programme of the government. Moreover, in Belgium, in particular, the government-formation process is itself a vital part of the attempt to achieve consensus; and the sovereign has on occasion—as for example in 1972–3—pressed for a government comprising all three of the main political groupings—Socialists, Social Christians, and Liberals—so that the government commands the two-thirds majority needed for constitutional change.

In the Netherlands, where the formation of a government can be a long process—it took 207 days in 1977 and 164 days in 1973—the resolution of conflicts between coalition partners occurs during the coalition negotiations rather than after the government has been formed.

In both Belgium and the Netherlands, the sovereign begins the government-formation process by consulting various national leaders. These consultations are of far wider scope than those of their Scandinavian counterparts. They include not only the party leaders, but also other prominent parliamentarians, and, in Belgium, prominent individuals outside parliament, such as leaders of the major trade unions and of the Belgian equivalent of the CBI. In the Netherlands, the sovereign begins by calling the spokesmen of the two chambers of parliament, together with the President of the Council of State, an advisory body with some judicial functions, and the leaders of the main party groups in the lower house. This has become an established practice, and the sovereign in the Netherlands enjoys little discretion until this stage in the negotiations has been completed.

In Belgium, by contrast, the sovereign enjoys some discretion over whom he or she consults, and there are no clearly defined rules regulating this part of the process. It is customary, however, for the sovereign to consult the outgoing prime minister, the speakers of both houses, and the leaders of the main party groups, as well as ministers of state, former ministers, and representative members of the legislature. In addition, the Belgian sovereign will also consult the so-called 'interlocuteurs sociaux', the governor of the national bank, the chairman of the Federation of Belgian Industries, and the leaders of the main trade unions. By contrast with the Netherlands, the process in Belgium is shrouded in some secrecy: government communiqués do not always proclaim the names of those summoned by the sovereign, nor are details of the discussions ever disclosed. In the Netherlands, by contrast, since the late 1960s, all relevant reports on the government-formation process, including the advice of parliamentary leaders to the sovereign, the reports of *informateurs* and *formateurs*, and the drafts of coalition agreements themselves must be published.

In both Belgium and the Netherlands, the sovereign generally appoints an *informateur* after the first round of negotiations has been completed. This office has become more highly formalized in the Netherlands than in Belgium, but it was first used in Belgium in 1935, and not instituted in the Netherlands until 1951. In both countries, the sovereign has discretion as to who the *informateur* should be. It is usually, although not always, someone without political ambitions who is generally acceptable as a negotiator. Often the *informateur* is an elder statesman whose impartiality is respected, although it can on occasion be an active politician. In Belgium, although not in the Netherlands, the *informateur* is always a member of one of the two chambers, often a member of the largest party in the lower house, and on occasion a minister in the outgoing government. In the Netherlands, in recent years, it has become customary to appoint more than one *informateur*.

The *informateur* or *informateurs* report back to the sovereign. If they cannot give any constructive advice, then another *informateur* may be appointed or there may be fresh elections. But, if they have been successful, the sovereign will then appoint a *formateur*, someone who can form a government. The *formateur* will generally consult with party leaders *à deux*, and at this stage the sovereign plays no role at all in the process. The sovereign must under no circumstances engage in parallel discussions with politicians while the *formateur* is at work. However, the *formateur* will call on the sovereign every few days to report on the discussions with the politicians. In Belgium, the sovereign gives the *formateur* a specific mandate to secure agreement between the parties under a named candidate for the premiership. In the Netherlands, however, the sovereign does not specify any particular basis for the government. If the *formateur* succeeds in his or her task, he or she will generally, although not always, become prime minister.

In appointing the *formateur*, the sovereign can always claim to be acting on advice, so protecting his or her constitutional position. But it is in the stages before the appointment of the *formateur* that the sovereign can make his or her influence felt. In both Belgium and the Netherlands, the government-formation process can be so tortuous and complex that there is ample scope for a skilful sovereign to influence its direction. The Belgian sovereign, it has been said, may 'at difficult moments—try to lead the negotiations into a certain direction and to advocate the solution that would coincide with his personal wish'; moreover, 'it is not altogether impossible that the monarch puts aside the personalities who do not enjoy his confidence'.[15]

The procedures adopted in Belgium and the Netherlands to cope with the government-formation process are highly intricate. They have come under strain in both countries, and it might be that they will be unable to serve much longer as consensus-building instruments.

It is, of course, highly unlikely that Britain would come to copy such complex machinery were it to adopt proportional representation. There can be little doubt that existing procedures would be retained until it had become clear that they had broken down. Indeed, in Britain, the sovereign's private secretary, in conjunction with the cabinet secretary and the prime minister's private secretary, would play a role similar to, although far more informal than, that played by *informateurs* in Belgium and the Netherlands. In Britain it is they who can sound out opinion in a hung parliament, and discover which combinations are possible and which are not. There seems no reason to adopt the more cumbrous machinery employed in Belgium and the Netherlands and little to be gained by doing so.

X

The third method of protecting the sovereign from involvement in the government formation process is that adopted in Sweden in the

[15] M. Boeynaems, 'Cabinet Formation', *Res Publica*, 9 (1967), 488 (my translation).

new constitution, the Instrument of Government, of 1974. This method protects the sovereign's impartiality by depriving him or her of any role in the government-formation process at all and transferring the sovereign's personal prerogatives to the Speaker of the Riksdag.

The new procedure is clearly described in chapter 6, articles 2 and 3, of the Instrument of Government.

Article 2

When a Prime Minister is to be designated, the Speaker shall convene representatives of each party group within the Riksdag for consultation. The Speaker shall confer with the Vice Speakers and shall then submit a proposal to the Riksdag. The Riksdag shall proceed to vote on the proposal, not later than on the fourth day thereafter, without preparation within any committee. If more than half of the members of the Riksdag vote against the proposal, it is thereby rejected. In any other case it is approved.

Article 3

If the Riksdag rejects the proposal of the Speaker, the procedure as prescribed in Article 2 shall be resumed. If the Riksdag has rejected the proposal of the Speaker four times, the procedure for designating the Prime Minister shall be discontinued and resumed only after elections for the Riksdag have been held. Unless ordinary elections are, in any case, to be held within three months, extra elections shall be held within the same period of time.

In the twenty years since the Instrument of Government was enacted, two constitutional conventions have already come to be accepted. The first is that, when the Speaker nominates a prime minister, he will at the same time specify the party composition of the government to be formed. The second is that, when one party in a coalition leaves the government, the whole government is obliged to resign, and the Speaker initiates the procedure for the formation of a new government. Thus, for example, in 1981, when the Moderates (Conservatives) left the three-party bourgeois government (Moderates, Peoples Party, Centre) because they could not agree to a proposed tax reform, the whole government was deemed to have resigned, and a new government had to be formed.

One of the aims of the 1974 Instrument of Government was to ensure that a left-wing government in Sweden would not suffer from the supposed prejudices of the sovereign. But the reformers do not seem to have asked themselves whether the Speaker might not be more inclined than the sovereign to manipulate the government-formation process. The effect of the Instrument has in fact been to politicize the speakership.

In Sweden, the Speaker is elected anew in each parliament. Before the Instrument was enacted, there was a tacit understanding that the Speaker should be a member of the majority block. But, after the first election following the promulgation of the Instrument in 1976, the newly victorious government of the Right agreed to support the existing Social Democrat Speaker, Henry Allard. The main reason for this was that Allard was widely respected by all parties, whereas the leading contender from the right bloc, the first vice-speaker, Torsten Bengtson, was not. Thus Allard was re-elected as speaker.

By the time of the next election in 1979, Allard had resigned from parliament, and the right bloc, which enjoyed a majority of one in the Riksdag, decided to put forward its own candidate for the speakership. This turned out to be, not Torsten Bengtson, but Allan Hernelius, a leading Conservative parliamentarian. The Social Democrats, however, refused to support a speaker from the Right and proposed their own candidate, Ingemund Bengtsson. Bengtsson in fact defeated the majority party's candidate, owing to a defection from the right bloc. The defector was assumed to have been Torsten Bengtson, indignant at not being the Right's candidate for the speakership.

These events show how easy it has been for the Speaker's position to become a plaything of the party battle. The danger arises that the parties choose for this position, not a respected politician who remains above the battle, but a skilful political operator who can be relied upon to offer advantage to his or her party in the battle over the appointment of a prime minister. The Speaker, being a former party politician, is more likely than the sovereign to misuse his or her power, whereas the sovereign has no political history and has enjoyed a longer and more continuous political experience. The sovereign has a far greater direct interest in impartiality than the Speaker. For this reason, the method adopted in Sweden does not offer a happy solution to the problem of government formation in a constitutional monarchy.

XI

The final method of protecting the sovereign, which also relies on taking away his or her personal prerogatives, consists in allowing parliament to decide who should be appointed as prime minister and when parliament should be dissolved. This method has been adopted in a draft constitution published by the Institute of Public Policy Research. The IPPR constitution proposes, article 41(2), that 'The Prime Minister shall be elected by the House of Commons from among its members'. The Commons would sit for a fixed four-year term, but could be dissolved earlier if one of two different conditions obtained. Article 60(2) provides that, if, within twenty parliamentary days after the passing of a vote of no confidence in the prime minister, the House of Commons fails to elect a new prime minister, the sovereign shall dissolve the Commons. Article 60(3) provides that, if a vote of no confidence in the government is passed, parliament shall be dissolved.

The purpose of the IPPR's constitution is to make the formation and dissolution of government automatic so that no element of discretion enters into it at all. It seems to make the appointment of a prime minister automatic; but it does not provide for the situation when no candidate has the support of a majority of MPs so that the Commons cannot elect a prime minister, the position in Britain after the general election of February 1974. In the event, the queen was able to appoint Harold Wilson prime minister of a minority government. A minority prime minister might not be approved by a majority of MPs, but, equally, he or she might not be opposed by a majority of MPs. Under the IPPR constitution, however, the device of choosing a minority prime minister would not be available and a general election would be necessary. This, however, might not improve the situation but could merely reproduce the same deadlock. Even worse, a multi-party House of Commons might refuse to endorse any prime minister and yet also refuse a dissolution. There would then be no constitutional method of escaping from the deadlock. Thus, the IPPR's constitution fails to make effective provision for minority government, one possible option in a hung parliament. It evinces a preference for majority government, which would entail coalition in a hung parliament. That is a perfectly reasonable preference, but the constitution offers no guidance as to what should be done when a majority government is not possible.

The effect of the provisions concerning dissolution is, of course, to take away both the prime minister's power to seek a dissolution at any time, and the sovereign's power to refuse one. Dissolution, seemingly, can occur only under two precise and well-defined circumstances, a vote of no confidence in the prime minister when a new prime minister cannot be found, and a vote of no confidence in the government. But, again, this appearance of automaticity is illusory. A prime minister who wanted a dissolution could always circumvent the constitution by engineering a vote of no confidence in his or her government and asking members of his or her party to support it. That is precisely what Willy Brandt did in Germany in 1972, where an analogous convention applies, and Helmut Kohl was to use the same device in 1983. On each occasion, the chancellor sought to dissolve the Bundestag at a favourable moment. He therefore asked his supporters to ensure that a vote of no confidence was passed against his government. Moreover, the constitution offers no solution to the deadlock which could occur when parliament, having selected a particular prime minister, refuses to grant him or her a dissolution and there is no alternative government available. It is difficult to see how such a deadlock can be broken within the assumptions of a constitution wholly controlled by parliament.

Under the British system of government, the sovereign has the right to refuse a dissolution if a prime minister seeks to abuse the constitution by, for example, dissolving a newly elected parliament. Under the constitution presented by the IPPR, however, the sovereign would be unable to prevent the manœuvre of engineering a bogus vote of no confidence even when its employment constituted an abuse of the rights of parliament. One very real defence, therefore, against an abuse of the rights of parliament would have been lost.

For these two reasons—the failure to distinguish the circumstances under which majority and minority governments might be necessary, and the failure to prevent the abuse of provisions for the dissolution of parliament—the constitution produced by the IPPR seems not to achieve the aim it sets itself of removing the role of the sovereign in the formation and dissolution of governments, while ensuring that they remain under constitutional control. It is doubtful, indeed, whether it is possible to achieve the automaticity which the IPPR seeks. The fundamental problem remains that a multiparty parliament may refuse to endorse any prime minister-designate, and yet at the same time refuse a dissolution. Alternatively, it may endorse a prime minister and refuse him or her the right to dissolve.[16]

Were Britain to adopt a codified constitution, therefore, it would still need to preserve the discretionary role of the sovereign if parliamentary deadlock were to be avoided. Moreover, as we have seen from the continental examples, the existence of a codified constitution alters the role and position of the sovereign much less than is commonly thought.

Thus, in a multi-party system such as is likely to be produced by the introduction of proportional representation into Britain, an element of discretion in appointing a prime minister and in dissolving parliament cannot be avoided. Discretion in agreeing to a dissolution can, it is true, be avoided if the term of the legislature is absolutely fixed. But there are only two European countries with fixed-term parliaments, Norway and Switzerland, and in Switzerland the executive is not responsible to the legislature so that different conditions apply. It is, therefore, clear that discretion cannot be conjured away either by institutional reforms or by constitutional rules, whether statutory or conventional.

Were Britain to adopt proportional representation, it would not be possible to lay down by fiat a set of conventions or a code of conduct to which the sovereign should be expected to adhere, although no doubt new conventions regulating the government-formation process would gradually come into play. But it is difficult to predict the nature of these conventions in advance. They would depend upon the extent of agreement between the party leaders, and, more generally, upon social attitudes. Constitutional rules, while they may help to create political stability or consensus, are also to some extent an expression of an underlying social reality. The best safeguard for constitutional monarchy, then, lies not in any specific set of constitutional rules or conventions, but rather in a willingness on the part of both politicians and people to preserve the role of the monarchy by avoiding actions which would have the effect of compromising its neutrality.

---

[16] Norman Gash, 'Power in Suspense', *Times Literary Supplement*, 3 June 1983.

XII

The three constitutional crises considered in the previous chapter—the House of Lords crisis, the Home Rule crisis, and the abdication—all blew up out of a clear sky. None of them could have been predicted in advance. The same is true of most of the constitutional crises in the Commonwealth considered in Chapter 10 and of the hung parliaments considered earlier in this chapter. The last hung parliament after the February 1974 general election took all of the main actors by surprise and they had prepared no contingency plans to deal with it. Moreover, 'hung parliament' is a term of art. No two hung parliaments are the same. A future hung parliament could be like those of 1924 or 1929–31, in which the Liberals held the balance of power; but it would be more likely to be a hung parliament like that of 1974, in which more than one minority party was needed to turn a minority government into a majority government.

Thus, even though there may well be contingency plans to deal with the next hung parliament when it comes, no one can predict its precise contours. Each hung parliament can be quite different from the previous one, and each one poses different problems.

Contingency plans to deal with constitutional crises and hung parliaments could comprise statements of the constitutional conventions such as are contained in Ivor Jennings's classic text, *Cabinet Government*. Yet these conventions would have been of little use in the crises discussed in the previous chapter, or the hung parliaments discussed in this, since the problem in each case was one of a conflict of conventions, and of *which* conventions were the relevant ones to take into account.

In 1910 the question was whether it was constitutional for the prime minister to seek contingent guarantees. One answer was that the sovereign was required to act on advice; another was that the prime minister ought not to seek to bind the sovereign by a hypothetical promise.

In 1914 the question was whether the sovereign had the right to veto the Home Rule Bill or to dismiss his ministers. One answer was that these personal prerogatives had fallen into desuetude; another was that the constitution had been in abeyance since the passage of the Parliament Act, and that Home Rule was far from being an ordinary item of legislation, but was one that would have the effect of extruding from the United Kingdom people who sought to retain their membership of it.

In 1936 the question was whether the sovereign enjoyed the right to marry against the wishes of his ministers. One answer was that, marriage to Mrs Simpson being legal, the sovereign ought not to be bound by any other restriction; another was that, since the king's wife becomes queen, the voice of the people, as represented by the government, must be heard in the king's choice of a wife.

In 1923 the question was asked whether a peer could become prime minister. The answer given was that he could not. In 1940, by contrast, George VI, together with most of the political establishment, took the view that a peer *could* become prime minister. Was this because of the emergency circumstances of the war? Or was the crucial factor in 1923 that Lord Curzon was personally unsuitable to confront a Labour opposition? Would the outcome have been different if Baldwin had been the peer and Curzon the commoner?

In January 1924 the question was whether the king was right to appoint Ramsay MacDonald prime minister even though his party had won just 30 per cent of the votes and held only 30 per cent of the seats in the House of Commons? One answer would suggest that MacDonald, as leader of the opposition, had the right to be called upon to form a government once Baldwin as prime minister had been defeated on a confidence vote in the House of Commons. An alternative answer would suggest that the king ought first to have investigated whether a government commanding a majority in the Commons might not be possible.

In 1931 the question was whether the concept of a government of individuals was known to the constitution. One answer was that it had not been so known since the eighteenth century and that it was an anachronism in an age of party government; another answer was that the quite exceptional economic circumstances of 1931 in which there was widespread fear of a collapse of the currency made traditional shibboleths irrelevant and an emergency government the only way of restoring economic stability.

In the case of a hung parliament, as we have seen, the Conservatives and probably Labour would no doubt urge that the precedent of January 1924 be repeated, and that a prime minister of a minority government be appointed without first considering whether a majority government could be constructed; and they would urge that a prime minister, even of a minority government, should be entitled to a dissolution at a time of his or her own choosing. The Liberal Democrats, no doubt, would disagree; they, together with other supporters of proportional representation, would argue that precedents from the past relate to a political tradition which is no longer relevant in a multi-party constitution. If, as may be the case, we are living in a transitional period, it is the choice of which conventions are relevant that is the crucial issue; and a respectable case can often be made for two quite contradictory alternatives.

The trouble then is that, in each of these examples, the standard conventions are of little use. Constitutional conventions, indeed, are of most use when they are least needed, in the clear-cut cases when no one doubts what needs to be done. In a constitutional crisis, by contrast, the argument is about whether certain conventions, hitherto accepted without question, are still relevant. This is an ostensibly constitutional argument, but in reality it is as much political as it is constitutional, since the political parties will take positions on the issue that suit their own party self-interest.

The question of which conventions are relevant during a constitutional crisis is not primarily a theoretical issue capable of abstract resolution through a process of reasoning.[17] It is fundamentally political, and at bottom an issue of political power. Therefore a constitutional crisis cannot be avoided or resolved simply by laying down constitutional principles. Nor is all-party agreement, perhaps by a committee of privy counsellors, on which principles ought to be employed in, for example, the case of a hung parliament at all likely, since it is these principles themselves which are in contention.[18]

It has been suggested that the queen should herself publish 'during a time of political peace' the principles which should guide her in the case of a hung parliament, and in particular her response to a request for dissolution by the prime minister of a minority government.[19] The queen, however, could only publish such principles upon the advice of her ministers. But her ministers are drawn from

[17] Graeme C. Moodie 'The Monarch and the Selection of a Prime Minister', *Political Studies*, 5 (1957), 1–20.

[18] Peter Hennessy, in his inaugural lecture at Queen Mary and Westfield College in February 1994, 'Searching for the "Great Ghost": The Palace, the Premiership, the Cabinet and the Constitution in the Post-War World' made the suggestion of a committee of senior privy counsellors.

[19] David Butler, *Governing without a Majority* (2nd edn., Macmillan, 1987), 132–3.

the ruling party or parties. There is no reason to believe that leaders of the other parties would concur with the government's view of which particular principles were relevant.

Constitutional crises, then, cannot be resolved through a statement of principles; nor, by the very nature of the constitution, could there be a 'hidden code' with the power of determining how such crises are to be resolved.[20] It is not that the constitution consists of 'instantly invented precedents',[21] but rather that, when the precedents conflict, as they invariably will, there can be no authoritative guidance as to which are relevant in advance of a particular crisis. There is, inevitably, a conflict of principles, and how that conflict is to be resolved cannot be determined until the crisis actually arises. When that happens, the outcome of the crisis is as likely to be determined by the facts of power as it is on the basis of an appeal to principle.

This problem—that of conflicting principles called into play during a constitutional crisis—is not, of course, one peculiar to a constitutional monarchy. It can occur in any state in which political traditions are in flux. A codified constitution, as we have seen, does little to resolve the problem, since constitutions tend to content themselves with laying down the formalities; a codified constitution cannot provide a right answer to a constitutional conflict any more than Britain's uncodified constitution can—as the experience of Australia, for example, demonstrates. Thus, were Britain to adopt a codified constitution, this would make much less difference to the resolution of constitutional crises than is often believed. Perhaps, indeed, constitutional crises are the process through which the 'living constitution', as opposed to the codified constitution, adapts to changing political conditions; such crises may be the means through which the institutions of the state, as opposed to the organization chart delineated in the constitution, can develop to meet new conditions. A constitutional crisis may be the means of bringing the constitutional rules up to date. The question that arises is whether a sovereign is better equipped to guide that process of change than a president.

There can be little doubt, surely, of the answer. Alone in the state, the sovereign enjoys a total freedom from party ties and the

---

[20] The phrase 'hidden code' is Peter Hennessy's ('Searching for the "Great Ghost"').

[21] As Philip Ziegler, biographer of Edward VIII and Mountbatten, has argued.

complete absence of a party history. If an umpire is needed—and no democratic state can operate without one—the sovereign is likely to prove a safer guide than a president who is necessarily the outcome of an electoral process in which political parties will have played a predominant part.

7

The Financing of the Monarchy

I

The financing of the monarchy has always had constitutional implications. In the battles between parliament and the king in the seventeenth century, control of finance was crucial. Indeed, until the seventeenth century, it was difficult to draw any distinction at all between the finances of the sovereign and those of government. The parliamentary opponents of the king during the reign of Charles I insisted, however, that the finances of the monarchy be placed under parliamentary control. This principle was in part conceded at the time of the Restoration in 1660.

Grants for the support of the monarchy were made in 1660, and in 1689 parliament voted an annual sum of £600,000 to William and Mary to finance the civil government. The first Civil List Act was passed in 1697. It granted to the sovereign various hereditary revenues together with customs and excise duties, estimated to yield around £700,000 per annum. This was expected to cover not only the expenses of the sovereign, the sovereign's family, the Royal Household, and annuities to members of the royal family, but also the salaries and pensions of ministers, judges, and other public officials, and the maintenance of the royal palaces and parks, together with various other pensions and salaries. This was a compromise settlement giving the sovereign an independent income, but restricting it to the Civil List, the *only* significant branch of public expenditure not under parliamentary control. This would, it was believed, prevent the sovereign from again becoming a threat to parliament. Similar grants of Civil List revenues were made to succeeding sovereigns at the beginning of each reign.

The constitutional effect of the Civil List Act was to provide parliament with the leverage to limit royal discretion over government revenues so that a distinction could for the first time be made between the revenues of the sovereign and those of the state. Yet, even after this principle had been conceded, the sovereign retained sufficient independent revenues to be able to exert influence—which was sometimes corrupt influence—on ministers and on parliament. The Civil List, indeed, was, in the eighteenth century, 'uniquely the private pasture of the political class'.[1] In 1760 various tax revenues and Crown Lands revenues, hitherto under the independent control of the sovereign, were surrendered to parliament in exchange for Civil List revenues of £800,000. The sovereign still retained, however, certain hereditary revenues, of which the most important were those of the Duchy of Cornwall and the Duchy of Lancaster.

In the eighteenth century, 'Parliament was understandably jealous of the Civil List, for this was the only significant branch of the public expenditure which was not subject to control.' In 1760 the prime minister, the Duke of Newcastle, told the king that the Civil List was 'Your Majesty's own money; you may do with it, what you please.'[2] But the sovereign's control of the Civil List might enable him or her to avoid the constitutional restraints which parliament sought to impose. Burke's Economical Reform Act of 1782 provided for closer—although in the event not very effective—parliamentary supervision of the Civil List, and 'destroyed the conception of the Civil List as an independent financial provision for the Crown'.[3]

During the reign of George III (1760–1820), the Civil List was gradually relieved of government expenditure. But not until 1830 did the finances of the monarchy begin to assume their modern form, for it was in that year that the sovereign's personal expenditure came to be separated from general government expenditure. The Civil List, voted for and scrutinized by parliament, was in future to be employed purely for 'the dignity and state of the Crown and the personal comfort of their Majesties'. That is roughly the modern conception of the Civil List. The sovereign still sought to influence constituency electoral behaviour through financial subventions, but

---

[1] E. A. Reitan, 'The Civil List in Eighteenth Century British Politics: Parliamentary Supremacy versus the Independence of the Crown', *Historical Journal*, 9 (1966), 322. The subtitle of this article summarizes the continuing conflict between the two principles, a conflict which continues to some extent even today. See also Reitan, 'From Revolution to Civil List: The Revolution Settlement and the Mixed and Balanced Constitution', *Historical Journal*, 13 (1970), 571–88.

[2] Reitan, 'The Civil List in Eighteenth Century British Politics', 321, 320.

[3] Ibid. 329.

the last vestiges of the sovereign's independent financial power disappeared as the sovereign ceased to be able to provide such funds from the Privy Purse. By that time, the principle of parliamentary control of royal finances was assured.[4]

This control, however, has never been, and perhaps ought never to be, total. The principle of parliamentary control conflicts with another principle, the independence of the sovereign. Before the nineteenth century, this second principle was used to strengthen the sovereign's *power*. Today, it is invoked to ensure that the sovereign can play his or her constitutional role as a figure of independent *influence*. Were parliamentary control to be total, the monarchy would become a mere department of government and its constitutional independence would be threatened. But the precise balance between these competing principles—parliamentary control and the independence of the sovereign—is a legitimate matter for debate and discussion.

II

The sovereign and the Royal Household are financed from six different sources. They are as follows:

1. The Civil List.
2. Grants-in-aid.
3. The Privy Purse.
4. Direct expenditure from government departments.
5. Net income from visitor admissions to various royal palaces.
6. The sovereign's personal income.

Broadly, the sovereign's public expenditure as sovereign is financed by the Civil List and by direct expenditure from government departments; the sovereign's private expenditure as sovereign is financed from the Privy Purse; while the sovereign's private expenditure as a private individual is financed from his or her own personal income. As will be shown, however, the distinction between these categories is, inevitably, somewhat artificial.

---

[4] See Philip Hall, *Royal Fortune: Tax, Money and the Monarchy* (Bloomsbury, 1992), ch. 1; this book, although written from a standpoint hostile to the monarchy, provides a good deal of new information on the financing of the monarchy.

The Civil List is not, as is sometimes believed, remuneration or 'pay' for the sovereign, but is used to meet official expenditure necessarily incurred through his or her duties as head of state and Head of the Commonwealth. It is paid as an annual sum fixed by parliament, and in 1995 stands at £7.9m. Around 70 per cent of the Civil List is spent on the salaries of those working directly for the sovereign, whose pay and pensions are related to civil-service scales. The Civil List is audited annually by the Treasury. Between 1952 and 1992 the Civil List increased twelvefold, at roughly the same rate as the general price level, during a period in which total government expenditure increased thirty-five fold.[5]

Until the 1970s it was the convention to fix the Civil List at the beginning of a reign, and for it to remain unchanged during the reign. Select Committees were appointed at the beginning of each reign to recommend to parliament what that sum should be. These Select Committees included the prime minister (except in 1952), the chancellor of the exchequer, and senior MPs. There have also been two *ad hoc* Select Committees. The first was appointed in November 1947 to recommend provision for Princess Elizabeth after her marriage to the Duke of Edinburgh. There was no recent precedent for the marriage of an heiress presumptive and no financial provision had been made. The second *ad hoc* Select Committee was appointed in 1971 to deal specifically with the problem of inflation and its effect on the royal finances. The 1971 Select Committee, like the 1952 Select Committee, did not include the prime minister. It was, however, the first Select Committee to publish its minutes of evidence.[6]

The 1971 Select Committee was appointed because inflationary pressures had made the Civil List which had been fixed in 1952, at the time of the queen's accession, unrealistic. The Civil List had, admittedly, been relieved of the burden of rising costs by transferring items of expenditure from it to government departments. Such transfers had in fact occurred since the first Civil List Act was passed in 1697, but transfers had been used with increasing frequency in

---

[5] 'Should One Pay Tax?', *The Economist*, 25 Jan. 1992, p. 36; this article was apparently written with official assistance; it constitutes an important statement of the financial position of the monarchy before the new arrangements of 1992 were introduced (see pp. 191 ff.) and puts forward an opposite point of view from that in Hall, *Royal Fortune*.

[6] The reports of the twentieth-century Select Committees on the Civil List are: 1901, HC 87, HC 110; 1910, HC 211; 1935–6, HC 74; 1936–7, HC 114; 1947–8, HC 18; 1951–2, HC 224; of 1971–2, HC 29.

recent years to meet the problem of inflation. During the reign of Queen Elizabeth II, the transfers had included, in 1952, the wages of industrial staff engaged on the maintenance of the royal palaces, the cost of the Royal Yacht *Britannia*, and various expenses connected with state visits to Britain.

Devices of this kind proved insufficient in the inflationary climate of the 1970s and the Select Committee recommended in 1972 that the Civil List be fixed, not once during the reign, but every ten years. By 1975, however, even this innovation proved insufficient. Inflation, which had been around 8 per cent per annum in 1971, had reached a level of over 20 per cent per annum, so that the 1972 arrangements were already anachronistic and annual supplementary payments had to be made. That was unsatisfactory, since it made for excessive parliamentary interference in the royal finances. But it was not until July 1990 that the prime minister, Margaret Thatcher, was able to announce that, with effect from January 1991, the Civil List would return to the ten-year system. The sum fixed—£7.9m.— assumed an annual inflation rate of 7.5 per cent. The ten-year system proposed in 1971 and in operation since 1991 enjoys 'the great merit . . . that it avoids the need to submit an annual Vote to the House while giving the House a periodic opportunity to review the amount of the provision for the Civil List'.[7]

The Civil List, however, accounts for only a small percentage of government expenditure on the monarchy. In 1990 it amounted to just over £5m., around 10 per cent of total government expenditure on the monarchy.

The second source for the financing of the monarchy is the grant-in-aid voted annually by parliament to the Department of National Heritage. This is used for the upkeep of royal palaces and various other buildings used by the royal family. The grant-in-aid in 1995 was around £25m. Around 75 per cent of it is spent on property maintenance. The grant-in-aid, like other moneys voted by parliament, is subject to the normal procedures of parliamentary control, but is administered by Buckingham Palace.

The third source is the Privy Purse, which meets such of the sovereign's expenditure resulting from his or her responsibilities as head of state as is not covered by the Civil List, together with the

---

[7] Anthony Barber, the then chancellor of the exchequer, commending the report of the 1971 Select Committee on the Civil List to the House of Commons, vol. 828, col. 291, 14 Dec. 1971.

expenditure of other members of the royal family, and various items of private expenditure. Examples are pension funds for past and present employees, part of the cost of Sandringham and Balmoral, together with various charitable subscriptions and donations and moneys spent on the welfare and amenity of staff. The Privy Purse is financed primarily from the net income of the Duchy of Lancaster, which, in 1992, yielded a net surplus of £3.6m. The Duchy is the constitutional responsibility of the Chancellor of the Duchy of Lancaster, who is normally a cabinet minister, and is 'answerable to parliament' for the running of the Duchy.[8] It is the Chancellor of the Duchy of Lancaster who has the final say each year on how much is paid from the Duchy to the Privy Purse to meet royal expenses.[9]

The fourth source comprises the various grants made from government departments for expenditure to support the sovereign's role as head of state on, for example, the Royal Flight and the Royal Train. Such expenditure in 1990–1 amounted to £46.2m., but the figure is likely to be reduced substantially with the forthcoming abolition of the Royal Yacht *Britannia*, which in 1990–1 cost £9,272,000. Moreover, the figure for 1990–1 reflected exceptional expenditure on renovations to Windsor Castle.[10] However, because the cost of the Civil List has been kept down through transferring various charges to government departments, expenditure under this head has increased considerably during the reign of Elizabeth II. In 1952–3, only £343,000 was charged to government departments. The £46.2m. charged in 1992 signifies an increase of 135 times the earlier figure, eleven times the rate of inflation.

Expenditure borne by departmental votes is, of course, scrutinized by the Commons in the same way as other public expenditure; and the permanent secretary of a Whitehall department is, as the accounting officer, held responsible by the Public Accounts Committee, as with any other expenditure for which a Whitehall department is responsible.

Some have argued that closer parliamentary scrutiny is needed. One influential proposal, put forward by Douglas Houghton, then a

---

[8] Kenneth Clarke, Chancellor of the Duchy of Lancaster in *Hansard*, Standing Committee G, col. 11, 17 Nov. 1987.

[9] House of Commons, Select Committee on the Civil List, 1971–2, HC 29, p. xxiv, p. 64.

[10] 'Royal Finances' (Buckingham Palace, 1993), 26–7.

senior Labour MP, to the 1971–2 Select Committee on the Civil List, is that the Royal Household should be recast as a Department of State so as to allow more effective scrutiny of royal expenditure. Under such an arrangement, the financing of the monarchy would become both more visible and also less contentious. It would then be possible to increase the Civil List without this being illegitimately interpreted as a 'pay rise for the Queen'.[11]

It is difficult, however, to understand the constitutional rationale of the Houghton proposal. A department of the Royal Household would be quite unique in that it would lack a ministerial head. Nor would it be staffed by civil servants answerable to ministers. Houghton argued that the Department of State should have a status analogous to that of a department of the House of Commons, as then established. He suggested that the Department of State be controlled by Commissioners of the Crown, of whom a minister would always, by convention, be one. Either the prime minister or the chancellor of the exchequer would then be responsible to the House of Commons for the work of the commission.

The Houghton proposal would have very radical consequences. It would mean that the Royal Household, including the queen's private secretaries, who, as will be shown in Chapter 8, have important constitutional functions, would become dependent upon a government minister and upon the civil service, rather than, as at present, being responsible only to the sovereign. 'The central issue', as Houghton rightly declared, 'appears to be one of control. Who is to be in ultimate control of the Royal Household? Is it to be the Queen or Parliament?'[12] But were the Royal Household to be responsible solely to parliament, normally controlled by the government of the day, the constitutional independence of the sovereign could be compromised: his or her role as sovereign depends precisely on not being entirely beholden to the government of the day.

Moreover, the private secretary's department works for the other countries of which the queen is sovereign as well as for Britain, and these Commonwealth monarchies are completely independent of the British government. It would not, therefore, be constitutionally proper to obtrude the United Kingdom parliament or British ministers into the relationship between the sovereign and other Commonwealth monarchies.

[11] HC 29, pp. xlviii–liii and app. 3.
[12] House of Commons, vol. 828, col. 302, 14 Dec. 1971.

The sixth source of royal finance, the sovereign's personal income, deriving from his or her investment portfolio, is used to meet personal expenditure, including the bulk of the cost of the upkeep of Balmoral and Sandringham. The amount of this income, as with other individuals, is kept private; and the size of the sovereign's personal wealth and investment income is not taken into account when increases are made in the Civil List. In a public statement on 11 February 1993, however, the Lord Chamberlain was authorized to state that one estimate of the size of this wealth—£100m.—was 'grossly overstated'.

On occasion, estimates of the sovereign's private wealth have included such items as the Crown Jewels, Buckingham Palace, and Windsor Castle. But these belong to the Crown rather than to the sovereign; they are inalienable and must be passed on from one sovereign to the next. There is no possibility of realizing their value in the open market. The net income from visitor admissions to the royal palaces is, however, used by the sovereign for the upkeep of the Royal Collection and the restoration of Windsor Castle.

The total cost of the monarchy, therefore, in 1990–1 amounted to £79.1m. (see Table 7.1). This amounts to a minuscule proportion of Britain's total public expenditure of around £250bn. per annum, constituting less than £1.50 for each individual in Britain, and compares very favourably with other items of government expenditure. In 1993, for example, the cost of the Vehicle and Driving Licensing Agency was over twice that of the monarchy, amounting to £187m.[13]

TABLE 7.1. *Cost of the monarchy, 1990–1991* (£m.)

Civil List	7.9
Grant-in-aid	25.0
Expenditure borne on departmental votes	46.2
TOTAL	79.1

Of course, much of the expenditure on the monarchy would also be required under a republican system of government. Under a presidential regime, the cost of maintaining, for example, the royal palaces, and of paying the staff of the president would, presumably,

---

[13] 'Next Steps Review 1993' (HMSO, 1993), 44.

still have to be provided from public funds. Besides, a president has to be elected in some way and that too involves a charge upon public funds!

III

The question of whether the sovereign should be taxed has been a recurrent matter of controversy during the nineteenth and twentieth centuries. In 1842, when Peel reintroduced income tax, Queen Victoria voluntarily agreed to pay it on her private income, and on income from the Duchy of Lancaster and from the Civil List. In June 1901, the chancellor of the exchequer, Sir Michael Hicks-Beach, told the Commons that the government had 'advised' that the new king, Edward VII, should continue to pay tax.[14] In 1910, however, Lloyd George, as chancellor, relieved the sovereign of income tax on the Civil List, the king agreeing in return to pay for the costs of visiting heads of state and for return visits. In 1933 George V was relieved of tax on rental income from the Duchy of Lancaster, and during the reign of George VI between 1936 and 1952 the sovereign was relieved of income tax on his private income. Until 1993, therefore, the sovereign was exempt from income tax. The Prince of Wales, who receives no income from the Civil List, had been exempt since 1921 from income tax on the revenues which he received from the Duchy of Cornwall; the present Prince of Wales, however, voluntarily paid to the Treasury 50 per cent of the revenue he received from the Duchy before his marriage in 1981, and 25 per cent of the revenue after it.[15]

In November 1992, however, John Major, as prime minister, announced in the House of Commons that the queen would, from the 1993/4 tax year, voluntarily pay tax on the Privy Purse and on her personal income.[16] The arrangements are broadly similar to those for other taxpayers, except that the sovereign will be exempt from inheritance tax in relation to bequests left to his or her successor. The reason for this restriction is that

[14] Hall, *Royal Fortune*, 24.

[15] The history of royal exemption from taxation is outlined in Hall, *Royal Fortune*.

[16] House of Commons, 6th ser., vol. 214, cols. 982–3, 26 Nov. 1992. The detailed arrangements and a memorandum of understanding were published on 11 Feb. 1993 as the Report of the Royal Trustees, HC 464.

In order to be constitutionally impartial the Sovereign must have, and be seen to have, an appropriate degree of financial independence. In addition the Sovereign, by virtue of his or her position, cannot generate new wealth in terms of earnings or business activities. At the same time a Sovereign, who does not retire, is unable to mitigate Inheritance Tax by passing on assets at an early stage to his or her successor.[17]

The Prince of Wales, from the 1993/4 tax year, has been paying income tax on a voluntary basis on the revenues which he receives from the Duchy of Cornwall, and continues to pay other taxes. Other members of the royal family continue to be taxed on the same basis as any other taxpayer.

Neither the Civil List, the grant-in-aid, nor income from the vote-borne expenditure of government departments is to be taxed, and indeed there would be no point in doing so. The only effect of taxing these items would be to require an increase in their total amount if they were to meet the monarchy's expenditure needs. As Lloyd George told the Commons in 1910, the Civil List 'is either adequate or it is not adequate for the purpose. If you deduct the sum of the Income Tax, it seems to be giving with one hand and taking away with the other.'[18] It was also agreed in 1992 that the official residences of the queen—Buckingham Palace and Windsor Castle—together with the Crown Jewels and the Royal Collections, should be free of tax, in the light of their status as inalienable.

It was further announced in November 1992 that the queen would reimburse the government for the parliamentary annuities paid from government funds to meet official expenses for all other members of the royal family except for Queen Elizabeth, the Queen Mother, and the Duke of Edinburgh. The costs of this reimbursement amounted to £879,000 per annum in 1993. The queen had already reimbursed the annuities paid to the Duke of Gloucester, the Duke of Kent, and Princess Alexandra since 1975. The costs of this reimbursement amounted to £636,000 per annum. Therefore, the aggregate amount which the Queen reimbursed in 1993 amounted to £1,515,000.[19] By 1995 the Queen Mother and the Duke of Edinburgh were the only members of the royal family other than the queen 'in receipt of money from public funds which is not repaid'.[20]

The introduction of these new arrangements was a response to

---

[17] 'Royal Finances', 22.   [18] Hall, *Royal Fortune*, 35.
[19] HC 464, paras. 21, 22.   [20] Ibid. 17.

widespread public criticism of the cost of the monarchy, a good deal of it misinformed. The essence of the new arrangements is to distinguish between the public and the private income of the sovereign, and to tax the sovereign only on his or her private income.

It is, however, not easy to distinguish in the case of the sovereign between income used for public expenditure and income used for private expenditure. Balmoral and Sandringham, for example, are privately owned by the sovereign, but he or she continues to carry out official constitutional duties when staying there.[21] He or she receives government papers, reports from ambassadors, copies of parliamentary papers, minutes of cabinet meetings and of all important conferences. Papers not scrutinized during a 'holiday' period merely pile up to be scrutinized later; and, as we have seen, it is a condition of the sovereign effectively exercising his or her rights to be consulted, to encourage, and to warn that he or she scrutinize official papers carefully. This work, in the early 1970s, took 'up to two or three hours' a day, in addition to the queen's other engagements, 'in order that, as Head of State, she can have a general knowledge of all current problems'.[22] When the sovereign is abroad, some of this work can be delegated to counsellors of state, but the work which emanates from other Commonwealth countries and much of the British work cannot be so delegated. In addition, the sovereign entertains official visitors such as visiting prime ministers and governor-generals at Balmoral.

It is, therefore, hardly possible to mark off a portion of the sovereign's life which is truly private. Wherever he or she is, official papers will be arriving for scrutiny, as much during 'holidays' as during working periods. In modern times, there can never be a 'holiday' from the work of government, and the sovereign can never be completely 'off duty', or on 'holiday', in the normal sense. This position might perhaps best be compared to that of a doctor who is permanently 'on call'. But there are three very significant differences. The first is that a doctor is not on call for every day of the year, but only for specific periods when he or she is at work. The second is that the doctor enjoys an annual holiday during which he or she can rely upon not being troubled with medical business. Finally the

[21] Contrary to what is said by Hall, *Royal Fortune*, 110.
[22] Sir Michael Adeane, 'Some Points about the Life and Activities of the Queen, Para. 3', HC 29, app. 13; Sir Michael was, at the time of presenting his evidence, private secretary to the queen.

doctor, unlike the sovereign, can look forward to a well-earned retirement. In Britain, however, the sovereign never retires. His or her burden ends only with death. 'We serve', Sir Alan Lascelles, George VI's private secretary, told the Select Committee on the Civil List in 1947, 'may I remind you, one of the very few men in this world who never gets a holiday at all and who, unlike the rest of us, can look forward to no period of retirement at the end of his service, for his service never ends'. George V in fact called his work 'a life sentence'.[23] There can, therefore, be no real analogy between the sovereign's income and that of a private individual and no obvious dividing line between the sovereign's private and public expenditure.

It is thus not possible, despite the new arrangements introduced in 1993, to treat the sovereign as if he or she were an ordinary taxpayer. The income received, whether from the public purse or from private resources, cannot be considered as a salary or 'renumeration' for a 'job', for the 'job' must inevitably be quite unlike that of any ordinary citizen. Therefore it is difficult to find any analogy for the position of the sovereign in relation to income and expenditure. Seen in this light, the new arrangements for taxation introduced in 1993 seem in part to be of symbolic significance, designed less perhaps because of their intrinsic justification than to head off public criticism.

There are, however, two main weaknesses with current methods of financing the monarchy. The first is that they are so complex. The outline above is itself a simplification. There are probably few members of the public who understand either the arrangements or their rationale. That cannot be to the advantage of the monarchy in a democratic age. It has, however, been decided, from the summer of 1995, to publish the grant-in-aid accounts and this could help to make the financing of the monarchy more transparent.

The second weakness of current arrangements for financing the monarchy is that the royal finances have, arguably, been sucked too far into the Whitehall machine, and perhaps also into the realm of party politics. This could pose dangers to the impartiality of the monarchy. As has been seen above, that was the reason why it was deemed so inadvisable to have annual debates on the Civil List. But the reversion to the ten-year arrangement has not stifled public criticism.

[23] Quoted in Helen Hardinge, *Loyal to Three Kings* (William Kimber, 1967), 78, 114.

It was to meet these two weaknesses that the Prince of Wales supported in the late 1980s a proposal to reverse the 1760 arrangement by which the sovereign transferred the hereditary revenues, including income from the Crown Estates, to the government in exchange for the Civil List.[24] The proposal was that the Civil List and all departmental expenditure for the monarchy be abandoned, but that the income from the Crown Estates revert to the sovereign rather than the Treasury. This would, by strengthening royal control over finance, make the monarchy more autonomous and therefore more effective, and also remove contentious items such as the Civil List from the political agenda. Like the Houghton proposal discussed above, it would avoid the misunderstanding by which increases in the Civil List were seen as 'pay rises for the Queen'.

One difficulty with the proposal, however, is that the income from the Crown Estates, which stood in the late 1980s at around £60m. per annum, might be insufficient to finance the total public cost of the monarchy. It would still need to be supplemented by either a smaller grant-in-aid; or, alternatively, government assistance with specific items of royal expenditure such as the Royal Train and the Royal Flight.

There might also be a constitutional difficulty, in addition to the practical one. The government might be unwilling to accept this proposal, believing with Sir Frederick Ponsonby, Keeper of the Privy Purse to George V, that 'it is an essential part of the Constitution that the Sovereign should be dependent on Parliament for the Civil List and should not receive money direct from Crown lands'.[25] However, the principle of parliamentary control needs to be balanced with the equally important principle of the independence of the monarchy. In the eighteenth and nineteenth centuries, no doubt, the main danger was of the sovereign seeking to exert improper influence and building an independent power base. Today, perhaps, the danger is more that the independence of the monarchy could be so whittled down that the sovereign would be unable to fulfil his or her constitutional functions effectively. The danger is that the control which the political parties have established over so many facets of British life would serve to limit the monarchy so that it became a mere cipher. It could be argued, therefore, that a greater degree of financial independence for the monarchy would be desirable on

[24] Jonathan Dimbleby, *The Prince of Wales* (Little Brown, 1994), 507.
[25] Cited in Hall, *Royal Fortune*, 95.

8

The Sovereign's Private Secretary

The office of private secretary to the sovereign has become crucial to the working of constitutional monarchy in Britain. Yet it has evolved in an unplanned and unnoticed way, almost indeed by accident.

Until 1805, the home secretary was responsible for most of the tasks that now fall to the sovereign's private secretary, and in particular for the official correspondence of the sovereign. The home secretary, as well as being a departmental minister, was also the sovereign's constitutional adviser. For much of the nineteenth century there was resistance to the appointment of a private secretary to the sovereign for fear that the holder of such an office would become an irresponsible intermediary between the sovereign and his or her ministers. This view rested on a belief that the sovereign was engaged in a struggle with ministers and parliament, a struggle which it was essential that ministers should win. It was only when it was appreciated that the sovereign's role was rather different, and that his or her task was to support his or her ministers and not to struggle against them, that the office of private secretary was seen as necessary, and the fears of those who were opposed to the appointment began to diminish.

If the sovereign was conceived of as competing with his or her ministers, then it was natural for ministers not to wish to reinforce someone who was, in effect, an opponent. But if, on the other hand, the sovereign enjoyed a position in the constitution which was complementary to, but not competitive with, ministers, then these fears were misplaced; and it was in the interests of ministers to ensure that the sovereign was well informed and well briefed in his or her dealings with them.

The first private secretary to the sovereign was Sir Herbert Taylor, who was appointed in 1805 specifically to deal with an emergency, George III's blindness, which was preventing the sovereign from dealing with his correspondence. Taylor was known to be a Tory, and so his appointment met with the approval of the prime minister, Pitt. Nevertheless, it was not intended that the office should become a permanent part of the machinery of government.

In April 1812 there was a debate in the House of Commons on the propriety of the office of private secretary. Some argued that it was unconstitutional to allow cabinet secrets to pass through the hands of a private secretary, or for the sovereign to communicate with his prime minister through a third person. This view was not controverted, but it was explained that the office was intended only for the duration of the emergency. A sovereign in full possession of his or her faculties would not require such assistance.

However, the Prince Regent, later to be George IV, had also appointed his own private secretary—in 1811, Sir John MacMahon, and then, in 1817, Sir Benjamin Bloomfield, who remained his private secretary until 1822. These two were raffish adventurers, quite unlike the stolid Taylor, and in 1822 George IV's prime minister, Lord Liverpool, suggested that the office might as well be done away with, as being 'incompatible' with 'the constitution of the country'. In fact, the office disappeared in name only, its functions being taken over by the Keeper of the Privy Purse, Sir William Knighton, a man called by Creevey, perhaps unfairly 'the greatest villain, as well as the lowest blackguard that lives'.[1]

Upon the death of George IV, the new king, William IV, re-appointed Sir Herbert Taylor as private secretary, and the office came gradually to take on its modern form. Indeed, G. M. Trevelyan believes that it was during the 1830s that the sovereign came to accept a new view of his obligations towards his ministers, and that this 'was fostered in the King's mind by his Private Secretary, Sir Herbert Taylor, a man of no political prejudice and great political instinct to whom the British Constitution owes much of its development along the paths of peace'.[2]

Although himself hostile to the Reform Bill, Sir Herbert believed

---

[1] Cited in Houghland Van Noorden, 'The Origin and Early Development of the Office of Private Secretary to the Sovereign', Columbia Ph.D. thesis (1952), 78; this thesis provides an excellent account of the early history of the office.

[2] G. M. Trevelyan, *Lord Grey and the Reform Bill* (Longmans Green, 1920), 277.

that the king should not go against his ministers, and he did his best to assist ministers in passing it. In May 1832, acting for the king, Taylor wrote to Tory peers asking them to be absent for a critical division in order that the Bill could go through. Nevertheless, upon the death of William IV in 1837, the criticisms that had been made in 1812 were heard once again. The private secretary, it was said, was an irresponsible adviser, who exerted undue influence over the sovereign by intruding his own views at the expense of those of his ministers. Moreover, by the very nature of his office, there was no real check upon the very great influence that he enjoyed. It is said—but perhaps the story is apocryphal—that, on the day following her accession, Queen Victoria summoned Sir Herbert and asked him if she should employ a private secretary. 'Is Your Majesty afraid of work?', asked Taylor. When the queen replied that she was not, 'Then don't have a Secretary', replied Taylor. Yet, Victoria found that she could not do without a private secretary. Until the queen's marriage in 1840, Lord Melbourne, her first prime minister, acted as her private secretary, with an office in Buckingham Palace, while Baroness Lehzen was responsible for the queen's private correspondence.

This arrangement did not work well, however. The Flora Hastings affair in 1838–9, when the queen falsely accused an unmarried member of her household of being pregnant, led many to believe in the existence of a Whig cabal at court, Lady Flora being the sister of a Tory peer. The 'Bedchamber incident' of 1839 reinforced fears that the queen was too partial to the Whigs.

Upon the queen's marriage, Prince Albert became, in effect, the queen's private secretary, and Melbourne was ejected from his room in the Palace. It was Albert who ensured that the transition from a Whig to a Tory government in 1841 was carried through smoothly without any hint of royal partisanship. Between 1840 and 1861 Victoria and Albert began to create the modern system of administration in Buckingham Palace by insisting that the sovereign be kept informed of government policy. After Albert's death in 1861, the queen made use of General Grey, second son of Lord Grey, prime minister at the time of the Reform Act, as a private secretary. The post was not, however, officially recognized and gazetted until 1867. Since that date, the salary of the private secretary has been paid from the Civil List, not, as it had been under George IV and William IV, from the Privy Purse.

General Grey had been a Liberal MP, but he carried out his duties in a scrupulously non-partisan way, winning the admiration of Disraeli as well as Gladstone. Grey's successors also sought to gain the confidence of political leaders from all of the major parties. (A list of the private secretaries since the death of Grey in 1870 can be found in Appendix 3.)

Although, from the time of General Grey, private secretaries have understood their role as being one of assisting the sovereign in his or her relations with ministers in all parties, nevertheless they did not, for some time, cease to proclaim their partisan affiliations. Stamfordham was a staunch Conservative, while Ponsonby and Knollys were known to be Liberals. Knollys went so far indeed as to write to Mrs Asquith, wife of the prime minister, in September 1909; 'I am as you know a liberal and whenever I have been in the House of Lords I have invariably voted for the Government ever since they have been in office,' ending his letter by stating: 'Of course you will understand that I am only stating my own *individual* views.'[3]

Wigram was the first private secretary without a partisan political history, although few who met him could have been in doubt that he was a strong Conservative. Hardinge was a strong opponent of appeasement who did not hide his detestation of the policies of George VI's first two prime ministers, Baldwin and Chamberlain. His views were at variance with those of his royal master, for George VI supported the efforts of Chamberlain to maintain peace in Europe. Hardinge's opposition to appeasement, however, proved of value after Churchill became prime minister, since it enabled him to improve the relationship between George VI and Churchill, a relationship which had been soured by Churchill's support for Edward VIII during the abdication crisis. Today, however, it would be unthinkable for a private secretary to indicate his own political views. Instead his position is that 'he shall have no politics and shall show no bias in his political work; he must not even remember that he has ever belonged to a party, and certainly not to which'.[4]

In the nineteenth century, as we have seen, the office of private secretary came under attack, since it was said that only ministers could advise the sovereign. The task of the private secretary, how-

[3] Knollys to Mrs Asquith, 20 Sept. 1909, Royal Archives, Knollys Paper, RA Add. C29.
[4] Paul H. Emden, *Behind the Throne* (Hodder & Stoughton, 1934), 223; this book is a useful history of the early private secretaries.

ever, is not to advise the sovereign in the formal sense, still less to proffer views which might put the sovereign in conflict with his or her ministers. His central function is rather to guard the constitutional position of the sovereign. This is done by ensuring that the sovereign is properly informed on those matters concerning which responsible ministers may offer advice, and assisting him or her in decisions about the exercise of discretionary powers. If the sovereign enjoys the three rights identified by Bagehot—the right to be consulted, the right to encourage, and the right to warn—then he or she must also have the right to form a personal opinion on the matters brought before him or her by ministers. The sovereign cannot encourage or warn without being informed. It is the private secretary who ensures that the sovereign is informed. But the private secretary is in no sense a constitutional adviser, since the sovereign is under no obligation to follow his suggestions, which do not constitute advice in the technical sense. The key distinction is that between the sovereign 'taking advice', which can come only from ministers, and 'obtaining information', which can come from a wide variety of sources providing only that the sovereign's relations with his or her ministers are not disturbed.

The private secretary is a personal appointment of the sovereign, although he must also be acceptable to the prime minister and to senior civil servants, and in particular to the cabinet secretary, with whom much of his work is done. This duality is generally recognized by granting the private secretary an honour of the Royal Victorian Order, which lies in the gift of the sovereign, to show that he enjoys the sovereign's confidence, and by also granting him a knighthood in the Order of the Bath, such as is given to senior civil servants on the advice of the prime minister, to show that he enjoys the confidence of the prime minister also.

The method of appointment of the sovereign's private secretary contrasts with the method of appointing the governor-general's secretary in Commonwealth countries, the governor-general being the personal representative of the sovereign. In Australia, the office of official secretary of the governor-general was, until 1984, administered as part of the department of the prime minister. This, however, could have led to a conflict of loyalties between the governor-general and the department. In 1984 the post was established on a statutory basis.

In other Commonwealth countries, secretaries to governor-generals are civil servants who on occasion return to the civil service after their period of appointment has ended. In Britain, however, such a method of appointment has never found favour. 'Never', the biographer of George VI has written, 'must he be a civil servant in forced allegiance to the Government of the day. His complete independence of view must inspire confidence.'[5] On some occasions, the staff working for the governor-general seem not to have been able to advise him. 'Neither in its membership nor in its functions', Sir Paul Hasluck, a former governor-general of Australia has noted, 'is the staff at Government House designed to advise the Governor-General on the decisions he should take.' He himself, Hasluck declared, would never 'discuss political questions with any of them'.[6] Under such circumstances a governor-general's role is likely to be a lonely one, especially during times of constitutional crises. It may well be that Sir John Kerr would have been in a better position in 1975 had he enjoyed the services of a private secretary fulfilling the same role as the queen's private secretary. As it was, he was compelled to seek advice from the Chief Justice of the High Court, itself a highly controversial step.

In Britain, by contrast, the private secretary to the sovereign plays a crucial constitutional role. The private secretary and his assistants are the only people who are solely concerned with the interests of the sovereign. The interests of ministers are necessarily different, since they may, unwittingly perhaps, make requests of the sovereign which would create awkward precedents for the future. Only the private secretary can protect the sovereign from the embarrassment of granting such requests. Moreover, a private secretary may have to suggest to the sovereign that he or she exercise prerogatives in a way that the government might not like; he might, for example, have to suggest that the sovereign refuse a dissolution. Therefore, he cannot be a government appointee.

The main qualification for appointment to the office of private secretary must be the confidence of the sovereign, and the private secretary must be free of political partisanship, since the sovereign will expect to have to deal with governments of different political complexions during his or her reign. Moreover, it is the private secretary's

---

[5] John Wheeler-Bennett, *King George VI: His Life and Reign* (Macmillan, 1958), 820.

[6] Paul Hasluck, *The Office of Governor-General* (2nd edn., Melbourne University Press, 1979), 21.

task to provide information not only on the views of those who support the government, but also on the views of opposition parties, and, more generally, of opinion in the country as a whole. The names of those seen by the sovereign on official business are published in the Court Circular, but the private secretary can see opposition representatives on a private and informal basis, and their names are not publicly divulged. Only, then, if the private secretary is politically independent can the opposition have confidence in him. If the private secretary does not enjoy the confidence of the opposition, problems could arise when the opposition becomes the government.

The difficulties caused when a private secretary fails to retain the confidence of the leader of the opposition were starkly illustrated in the case of Lord Knollys, private secretary to Edward VII and to George V, during the struggle over the Parliament Bill in 1910.

In December 1910 Sir Arthur Bigge, later Lord Stamfordham, joint private secretary with Knollys to George V between 1910 and 1913, wrote to Knollys, questioning his attitude towards discussions with the opposition. Bigge had been told that the prime minister, H. H. Asquith, had persuaded Knollys not to see Arthur Balfour, the leader of the opposition. But Bigge said that

> I saw no reason why Asquith should be asked: that the Private Secretaries could always see or talk to anyone & that personally if I could get a chance of seeing Arthur Balfour I certainly would . . . My view is that by asking for Asquith's consent you are making your communications with Arthur Balfour more formal than is necessary at this period of the situation. In old days for instance in 1884 [when Queen Victoria played an important role in mediating between government and opposition over House of Lords opposition to the third Reform Bill] I feel sure that Henry Ponsonby saw and talked informally with both sides when negotiations were going on for a Conference.[7]

Knollys also believed that any conversations held with members of the opposition should be reported to the government. In the words of the then Archbishop of Canterbury, Randall Davidson:

> Anything more widely different from the view taken by Queen Victoria in the days of Sir Henry Ponsonby I never heard . . . Much of the whole difficulty has arisen in my judgment from this overstrained idea that a private talk by one of the King's people to a member of the Opposition is an act of disloyalty to the Government, and that the King should insist on the

---

[7] Bigge to Knollys, 28 Dec. 1910, Knollys Papers, RA Add. C29.

Government's knowing of any such interviews, however informal and private.[8]

Knollys's misunderstanding of the relations which ought to exist between the private secretary, the prime minister, and the leader of the opposition caused a dispute with Balfour in 1911, when Balfour alleged that comments which he had made to Knollys, in what he had thought was a confidential conversation, had been passed on to Asquith. Balfour wrote in August 1911 to Stamfordham, as Bigge had now become, to complain about the aftermath of a dinner in January 1911 which had been given by Knollys for Balfour, Jack Sandars, his private secretary, and Lord Esher. Balfour told Stamfordham:

I learnt to my surprise that the dinner had been held with the knowledge and approval of the Prime Minister, and that presumably, therefore, everything I said in the freedom of friendly conversation was to be repeated to him. . . . Do you think it fair that I should be asked to discuss public affairs, under circumstances which implied freedom and confidence, with an ambassador by whom I was deliberately kept in ignorance of the most essential features of the situation. . . . Lord Knollys seems therefore to have endeavoured to extract from me general statements of policy to be used as the occasion arose, while studiously concealing the most important elements in the actual concrete problem which had to be solved. He did this after the event, when nothing that I said could possibly aid the King, though it might possibly embarrass me. He could only have done it in order to extract in the course of an 'unbuttoned' conversation *obiter dicta* to be used when the occasion arose.[9]

Balfour also wrote to Stamfordham to tell him that

I told Lord Knollys at the time that if these were to be regarded as the only conditions under which His Majesty's Private Secretary could see politicians outside the circle of his Ministers, His Majesty would be parting with a valuable right which all his predecessors had enjoyed.[10]

Stamfordham told Knollys of Balfour's complaint. When Knollys remonstrated with the leader of the opposition, Balfour wrote to him: 'I thought & still think, that . . . you ought to have told me at

[8] Memo. of 24 July 1910, Davidson Papers, Lambeth Palace Library, vol. XII, fo. 195.

[9] Balfour to Stamfordham, 9 Aug. 1911, RA GV K2552 (2) 56.

[10] Balfour to Stamfordham, 9 Aug. 1911, cited in Kenneth Young, *Arthur James Balfour* (G. Bell, 1963), 302.

the *beginning* and not at the *end* of dinner that Asquith had been consulted about our interview.'[11] Knollys did not deny this accusation, but said that he had not repeated the conversation to the prime minister, only to the king. Nevertheless, the damage had been done, and Knollys had clearly lost the confidence of the leader of the opposition. It would have been difficult in any case for Knollys to work happily with a Conservative government, and in fact he resigned as joint private secretary in 1913. There is little doubt that Stamfordham's and Balfour's conception of the duties of a private secretary is the correct one; and it is this conception that is followed today. The private secretary cannot be the prime minister's agent. He works for the sovereign and for no one else. If, therefore, he believes that it is in the sovereign's interest that the views of opposition leaders be conveyed to him or her, then he must see those leaders without asking the permission, much less seeking the consent, of the prime minister—although he will normally inform the prime minister that he has had conversations with leading opposition figures.

The private secretary's office does not resemble a government department, but is more like the private office of a minister, and the private secretary might best be compared not to the permanent head of a Whitehall department but to a cabinet minister's special adviser whose prime loyalty is to a particular minister. The private secretary's office is not an organization, but a personal adjunct to the work of the sovereign; it has an *esprit de corps* quite unlike that found in a government department. However, the comparison with a special adviser to a minister is not quite exact, since the private secretary's allegiance is as much to the institution of monarchy as it is to the particular person who happens to be sovereign at any particular time. Normally, of course, these requirements will coincide, and it is only in pathological circumstances such as the abdication crisis of 1936 that they will conflict.

II

It was the misfortune of Sir Alexander Hardinge, private secretary to Edward VIII, to face the terrible dilemma of the person versus the

---

[11] Balfour to Knollys, 7 Sept. 1911, Knollys Papers, RA Add. C29.

institution. Hardinge wanted Edward VIII to remain on the throne and did all he could to keep him there. When he realized that this would be impossible, he sought to defend the institution, on occasion acting on his own initiative and without telling the king. Such conduct, which would be indefensible in normal circumstances, can be justified by the exceptional circumstances in which Hardinge found himself.

Never before and never since [his widow has written] did he—or any of the other Royal secretaries of history—have to face a similar conflict of loyalties. All Alec's personal sympathy was with His Majesty, but he had also to work to preserve the Monarchy intact. The safety and credit of the Crown were his concern. His master's emotional state, although very important, was not the only point to be considered.[12]

Hardinge first began to fear for the position of Edward VIII when he heard that Mrs Simpson was seeking a divorce. Until that stage, there could have been no question of the king marrying her, Mrs Simpson being already married to another. It was on 15 October 1936, when Hardinge, learning that divorce proceedings would be heard a week or so later, wrote to Baldwin, the prime minister, on his own initiative and without the king's knowledge. In doing so, he put what he conceived to be the interests of the monarchy above those of the individual, something for which he was to be much criticized by Edward VIII when, as Duke of Windsor, he was to write his memoirs, *A King's Story*.[13]

Hardinge asked Baldwin to see the king to discover whether the divorce proceedings could be stopped and whether the king could be persuaded to refrain from flaunting the association with Mrs Simpson in public, and from putting her name in court circulars. Baldwin, contrary to the view of those who saw him as conspiring to remove the king from the throne, was unwilling to act. But Hardinge's comments pushed him into action, and Baldwin had his first interview with the king on 20 October. When the king refused to act to stop the Simpson divorce, Hardinge began to fear that Edward might not be able to remain on the throne. He therefore visited the Duke of York, later George VI, the next in line to the throne, to warn him that abdication was a possibility.[14] Hardinge's

---

[12] Helen Hardinge, *Loyal to Three Kings* (William Kimber, 1967), 77.

[13] HRH the Duke of Windsor, *A King's Story* (Cassell, 1951).

[14] Robert Lacey, *Majesty: Elizabeth II and the House of Windsor* (Hutchinson, 1977), 93.

aim was to ensure that, were abdication to occur, the succession to the throne would be handled smoothly.

On 15 October, the day on which Hardinge had seen Baldwin, he took another action without the king's knowledge. He wrote to Lord Tweedsmuir (formerly the writer John Buchan), governor-general of Canada, concerning the possible reaction in Canada. He said that he hoped his anxiety was unfounded, but that, if it were not, he would welcome a letter drawing attention to the harm being done in Canada by the king's liaison with Mrs Simpson. He asked Tweedsmuir to provide evidence of the harm so that it might, at some strategic moment, be shown to the king either by himself or by others. Tweedsmuir sent a reply saying that Canadian opinion was anxious, and Hardinge showed this reply to Baldwin, hoping, again, to prod the prime minister to action.

It would be easy to criticize Hardinge for acting behind his employer's back in this situation, but it is important to remember that Hardinge, in common with many others, believed that the monarchy would be seriously damaged by an abdication. Moreover, again in common with many others, Hardinge found it difficult to believe that the king would pursue his desire to marry Mrs Simpson when the facts of the situation were put before him. Hardinge believed that he was doing his best for his king by making these facts available, so that there could be no misunderstanding as to the constitutional position.

At the beginning of November the permanent heads of Whitehall departments were drafting papers for ministers recommending that they advise the king to cease all connection with Mrs Simpson forthwith. Hardinge believed this to be a mistake, as the appearance of an ultimatum would arouse sympathy for the king. Hardinge, therefore, helped to persuade the civil service heads to tone down their proposals.

On 12 November Baldwin sent for Hardinge to ask if there was any change in the king's relationship with Mrs Simpson now that she had been granted a decree nisi, which meant that a divorce would in the normal course of events be granted in six months' time. Hardinge replied that there had been no change in the relationship. Baldwin then told him that he had arranged for a meeting of senior ministers to discuss the matter the following day, the first occasion on which it was to be formally discussed by leading ministers.

Further bad news was to come the next day. Geoffrey Dawson,

the editor of *The Times*, told Hardinge that the silence of the press could not be maintained for more than a few days. Hardinge begged him not to publish details of the king's friendship. Stanley Bruce, the Australian High Commissioner in London, invited Hardinge to lunch and said that his prime minister had told him that Australia would not tolerate a marriage between the king and Mrs Simpson. Therefore, if the king persisted in the marriage, he would have to go.

When Hardinge learnt from the prime minister that there was to be a meeting of senior ministers to discuss the king's position, he determined upon a last desperate action to keep the king on the throne. He decided to compose a letter warning the king of what was happening and asking him to suggest to Mrs Simpson that she leave the country temporarily.

It was at this stage that the loneliness and isolation of the private secretary's position were revealed. Hardinge, although he could consult with others, had to take the responsibility for the letter himself. He was, however, determined to ensure that the king should not proceed with his intention of marrying Mrs Simpson without being aware of the consequences, and he sought to warn the king of the inevitable outcome.

The letter was written on Hardinge's sole responsibility. However, he consulted the other private secretaries, who approved of it. Hardinge showed the letter to Geoffrey Dawson and asked Baldwin whether the meeting of ministers was still to take place, and whether he might mention that to the king—for Hardinge had received this information in confidence and needed the prime minister's permission to make use of it.

Hardinge's letter was sent to the king on 13 November. Had his suggestion been adopted, that Mrs Simpson go abroad for an indefinite period, this would have cut the ground from under the king's critics. Possibly a solution might have been found in the calmer atmosphere created by Mrs Simpson's exodus. Paradoxically, the solution proposed by Hardinge was adopted three weeks later, far too late to do any good, at a time when the crisis was reaching its height.

Edward VIII's official biographer records that the king's reaction to the letter was 'to refuse to have anything more to do with Hardinge, whom he assumed to be Baldwin's agent'.[15] That is incor-

---

[15] Philip Ziegler, *King Edward VIII: The Official Biography* (Collins, 1990), 298.

rect. The king admittedly did not reply to the letter and indeed made no mention of it; he continued, however, to use Hardinge for official business, but asked Walter Monckton to act for him in negotiations with the government on the abdication. The king's immediate reaction to the letter was to tell Hardinge that he wished to see the prime minister, together with other senior ministers. Baldwin decided that it would be best if he were to come alone, since the matter had not yet been before the cabinet, and so ministers were not officially apprised of it. It was at this meeting with Baldwin that the king told him that he had definitely decided to marry Mrs Simpson, even if it meant abdication, so precipitating the final phase of the abdication crisis. During that crisis, the king was under the greatest possible emotional strain, and was quite incapable of transacting business. It was Hardinge who ensured that, at this difficult time, government business, involving matters which required the king's signature, was transacted smoothly. Moreover, he had maintained contact with the king's brother, the Duke of York, the future George VI, during the crisis, without the king's knowledge, to ensure that the succession, when it came, would be a smooth one. In the last resort, his loyalty was to the institution of monarchy rather than to the person. It was due in no small part to Hardinge that the monarchy survived the abdication relatively unscathed.

III

The abdication, precisely because of its pathological nature, casts considerable light on the duties of the private secretary in more normal times. The essence of the private secretary's task is constitutional, to ensure that the machinery of constitutional monarchy works effectively. This requires that the sovereign be kept informed of government policies, an aim which is achieved through co-operation between the sovereign's private secretary and the cabinet secretary so that the position of ministers can be explained to the sovereign and the position of the sovereign can be explained to ministers. In this way, the private secretary, together with the cabinet secretary and the prime minister's private secretary, acts as a channel of communication between the sovereign and ministers, especially the prime minister.

But, today, the private secretary's task is not restricted to his role in the machinery of government of the United Kingdom. He is also private secretary to the Queen of Canada, the Queen of Australia, the Queen of New Zealand, and so on. Communications from the governments of the overseas countries of which the queen is head of state come, not to 10 Downing Street, since Britain plays no role in the government of Canada, Australia, New Zealand, and so on, but to Buckingham Palace. Thus the private secretary has to guard the royal prerogative in relation to these other governments as well as in relation to the government of the United Kingdom.

For this reason alone, it would be impossible for the private secretary's office to be transformed into a department of state such as, for example, the cabinet office, a suggestion that was made by a number of Labour and Liberal MPs during debates on the Civil List in 1972. This proposal reveals a misconception of the nature of the private secretary's role. Because he is private secretary to the Queen of Canada, Australia, New Zealand, and so on, he cannot be part of the machinery of British government. Commonwealth governments overseas which recognize the queen as their head of state would not be prepared to report to a department of the British government with which they have no constitutional relationship.

The private secretary to the sovereign, then, plays an essential part in the constitution. Although he is, at present, assisted by a deputy and by an assistant, the constitutional aspect of his work cannot be delegated. His task cannot be shared with others, since there must be no doubt as to the source from which the sovereign obtains his or her personal—as opposed to official—advice. Thus, although Hardinge consulted his assistants in 1936, he rightly did not seek to involve them in his decision to send his fateful letter to Edward VIII. That decision was his and his alone. The private secretary, as Hardinge ruefully commented, 'ploughs a lonely furrow'.[16]

The role of private secretary requires exceptional qualities in its holder. These have been eloquently, although not wholly accurately, defined by Harold Laski, reviewing a memoir of Henry Ponsonby, Queen Victoria's private secretary. The private secretary's position, Laski declared, was one of 'dignified slavery'.

He must be at her [the sovereign's] beck and call; even the claims of family affection must be sacrificed to a mistress who brooks no rival to her

---

[16] Lord Hardinge of Penshurst, 'Before the Abdication', *The Times*, 29 Nov. 1958.

power. He must know all that is going on; he must be ready to advise upon all. But he must never so advise that he seems to influence the decision taken by the Queen in terms of the premises of his own thought. He is the confidant of all Ministers, but he must never leave the impression that he is anybody's man. He must intrude without ever seeming to intrude. He must learn how to deflect the lightning from others. He must be able to carry the burden of her mistakes. He must not know the meaning of fatigue . . . Receiving a thousand secrets, he must discriminate between what may emerge and what shall remain obscure . . . It is a life passed amid circumstances in which the most trifling incident may lead to major disaster. . . . The royal secretary walks on a tightrope below which he is never unaware that an abyss is yawning. . . . If the Monarch is hard-working, like Queen Victoria, all his tact and discretion are required to keep firmly drawn the possible lines of working relations in a constitutional system. . . . Half of him must be in a real sense a statesman, and the other half must be prepared, if the occasion arise, to be something it is not very easy to distinguish from a lacquey.[17]

Laski is right in his insistence that the private secretary must be a person of consummate tact, that he must be self-effacing, anonymous almost, and never obtrude his own views. Indeed, anyone in close proximity to the sovereign must keep his or her political views private lest they appear to be the views of the sovereign. At the beginning of the century, Lord Esher, an unofficial adviser of Edward VII and George V, was accustomed to write to the press on public affairs, and it was assumed that Esher's views reflected those of the sovereign.[18]

The precise share of the private secretary in the sovereign's work cannot be publicly known, for any credit which the private secretary were to receive would be credit detracted from the sovereign. But Laski misunderstands the office when he draws the analogy with a 'lacquey'. A private secretary who adopted such a posture would be serving neither the sovereign nor the constitution. In fact, however, Sir Henry Ponsonby did not hesitate to tell Queen Victoria when he thought she was wrong, and both Knollys and Stamfordham were accustomed to argue their positions forcefully with George V; while Hardinge, as we have seen, was perfectly prepared to recommend a

[17] Harold Laski, 'The King's Secretary', *Fortnightly Review* (1942), 390–1; Henry Ponsonby is so far the only private secretary to have been the subject of a biography.
[18] James Lees-Milne, *The Enigmatic Edwardian: The Life of Reginald 2nd Viscount Esher* (Sidgwick and Jackson, 1986), 250.

course of action to Edward VIII which he knew the king would find distasteful.

The test of the confidence that a Private Secretary ought to have won is his ability to speak his mind without servility, even in those intimate aspects of royal demeanour, when he considers that the Sovereign's relation with or reputation among her subjects is involved.[19]

However, the foundation of the private secretary's position must always be the confidence of the sovereign. Once that is lost, the position of the private secretary becomes untenable. In the twentieth century, two Private Secretaries, Knollys and Hardinge, have found themselves in this position.

In February 1913 George V felt compelled to persuade Lord Knollys to resign. The king had always regretted giving the 'hypothetical understanding' in November 1910, to his prime minister, Asquith, that he would, in the event of the Liberals being returned in the general election, be prepared to create peers if that was necessary to secure the passage of the Parliament Bill. In February 1913 he told the Archbishop of Canterbury: 'I see now what a blunder I made then. I did it entirely on Knollys's advice.'[20]

The king was to discover, later in 1913, that Knollys had not told him of the Lambeth Palace Conference of April 1910. At this conference, Balfour seems to have declared his willingness to form a government and that might have enabled the king to avoid consenting to the creation of peers. In January 1914 the king told the Archbishop of Canterbury that he

practically regards Knollys as having been disloyal to him in the highest degree. He gave me in minute and dramatic detail an account of the day on which he was forced into giving the undertakings in November 1910. He had pressed as to whether any memoranda existed about King Edward's views on such a matter, or the views of King Edward's advisers, and Knollys had repeatedly assured him that there was nothing. . . . The King says that had he seen this [i.e. the record of the Lambeth Palace Conference] or known anything about it it would have changed the whole situation, for he would not have felt so helpless as he did when, against his will, he was forced by Asquith and Crewe to make the secret promise on which so much turned. He thinks that Asquith, Crewe, the Master of Elibank [the Liberal chief whip] and Knollys were practically in a plot to

[19] Dermot Morrah, 'The Private Secretary', *National and English Review*, 149 (1959), 68.
[20] Memo. of 14 Feb. 1913, Davidson Papers, vol. XII, fo. 346.

entrap the King into something which a more experienced man would never have done. [The King] now sees that if he [i.e. Knollys] had on that day done what every Private Secretary ought to have secured his doing, namely asked for the Government's request to be put into writing, the Government would have been non-plussed, for they would not have dared to put on paper what they said by word of mouth.[21]

Knollys had behaved strangely during the Parliament Bill crisis. He had told Edward VII that the proposal to create peers was 'the greatest outrage which has ever been committed since England became a Constitutional Monarchy', and that if he, Knollys, were king, he would 'rather abdicate than agree to it'.[22] Yet he advised George V in quite the contrary direction, telling him that, as a constitutional monarch, he had no alternative but to agree to the creation of peers; and he gave this advice while concealing relevant facts from the king. Knollys's behaviour can be defended on the grounds that he had become convinced that, if George V failed to agree to the creation of peers, the monarchy might be in danger. Nevertheless, he acted in such a way as to forfeit the sovereign's confidence, so that his usefulness came to an end.

Hardinge, in much more difficult circumstances, seems to have lost the confidence of Edward VIII, who used Walter Monckton to handle negotiations over the abdication. Hardinge also lost the confidence of Edward VIII's successor, George VI. Hardinge had learnt his task under George V, whose practice was thoroughly methodical, and he found it difficult to come to terms with the less methodical habits of George V's two sons. George V had made a practice of always sending for his private secretary after meetings with ministers, and sometimes even while ministers were still in audience, so that a written record could be made of the meeting. This record was then submitted to the king for approval and retained in the Royal Archives. George VI, however, did not follow his father's practice, and Hardinge often had to obtain details of meetings from the minister concerned rather than from the sovereign.[23] George VI from the beginning tended to use the queen as his confidante and was perhaps unwilling to give Hardinge his full confidence. In addition, Hardinge failed to hide his hostility to the government's policy of appeasement. In December 1938 George VI suggested to

[21] Memo. of 21 January 1914, ibid., fos. 362–3.
[22] Philip Magnus, *King Edward the Seventh* (John Murray, 1964), 431.
[23] Wheeler-Bennett, *King George VI*, 579.

Hardinge that he might become governor of Madras, but Hardinge failed to take the hint and remained. In July 1943, however, following the king's tour of North Africa, there was a dispute between Hardinge and his assistant, Sir Alan Lascelles. Hardinge asked the king whether he wished him to resign, and the king said that he did. For George VI, Hardinge's offer of resignation came as a surprise, and the king, although he did not initiate the resignation, willingly accepted the offer, since the opportunity might not have arisen again. The king, according to Sir Alexander Cadogan, permanent under-secretary at the Foreign Office, 'was sorry for A. Hardinge, but burst out with complaints, A.H. had always strong & unhelpful views what was the use of suggesting anything to anyone who, one knew, would always say "No"'.[24]

These examples of how the relationship between the sovereign and private secretary can break down illustrate the delicacy of the relationship, but also its importance for the smooth working of constitutional monarchy. The working of the private secretary's office remains necessarily shielded from the public gaze. Nevertheless, it has become one of the most important posts in the British system of government, and it forms a mainstay of the institution of constitutional monarchy.

---

[24] Sarah Bradford, *George VI* (Fontana paperback edn., 1991), 545.

9

The Sovereign and the Church

I

The sovereign enjoys a special relationship with the Church of England and with the Church of Scotland (a presbyterian church), both of which he or she is under a statutory duty under the Union with Scotland Act, 1707, 'to maintain and preserve inviolably'. Both of these churches are national churches in that they regard themselves as having a responsibility to bring religion to people in every parish in England and Scotland. In the sense that both churches are singled out by statute, both are established churches, although in other senses of the term 'established', discussed below, the Church of England is established while the Church of Scotland is not. The Anglican Communion, however, is established only in England. It was disestablished in Ireland in 1869 and in Wales in 1914 by an Act which came into force in 1920. It is not established in any other member state of the Commonwealth.

The sovereign is supreme Governor of the Church of England, but not its Head, which is Christ. Article 37 of the Thirty-nine Articles declares that he or she

hath the chief power in this Realm of England, and other his Dominions, unto whom the chief Government of all Estates of this Realm, whether they be Ecclesiastical or Civil, in all causes doth appertain, and is not, nor ought to be, subject to any foreign jurisdiction.

The Supreme Governorship is a constitutional position and the sovereign occupies it in virtue of his or her position as head of state, from which it cannot be separated. There is no other qualification for the position of Supreme Governor, and the personal behaviour of the sovereign is irrelevant to it. In the past, indeed, some quite dissolute sovereigns have been Supreme Governors, although today sovereigns are expected to act as role models.

As Supreme Governor, the sovereign is required to be in communion with the Church of England, and in the coronation oath swears to maintain it. The coronation itself includes the rite of holy communion, conducted by the Archbishop of Canterbury, who anoints the sovereign and delivers the orb, the symbol of sovereignty, to the new monarch, set under a cross to symbolize the subordination of the world of power to the world of the spirit.

The sovereign appoints, on the advice of the prime minister, archbishops and diocesan bishops, suffragan bishops, and deans of the Church of England, who take an oath of allegiance to the sovereign upon their appointment, and pay homage to him or her after their consecration. Deacons and parish priests, upon admission, also take an oath of allegiance to the sovereign. As Primate of all England, the Archbishop of Canterbury takes a special position of precedence next to that of the royal family and before the Lord Chancellor. Archbishops and bishops may not resign without royal authority.

The Archbishops of Canterbury and York, the Bishops of London, Durham, and Winchester, and twenty-one other diocesan bishops in order of seniority by appointment to an English see sit in the House of Lords. This is because, ordained members of the Church of England being prohibited, under the provisions of the House of Commons (Clergy Disqualification) Act, 1801, from election to the House of Commons, the leaders of the Church require a guaranteed platform in parliament so that the Anglican point of view can be heard.

The sovereign is not the Supreme Governor of the Church of Scotland, which regards Christ as its only sovereign in matters spiritual, but, when he or she is in Scotland, becomes an ordinary member of that church, and, by convention, a presbyterian. The sovereign is required by the 1707 Act of Union to preserve the Church of Scotland and inviolably to 'maintain and preserve the foresaid settlement of the true Protestant religion with the government, worship, discipline, rights and privileges of this Church as above established by the laws of this Kingdom'. The oath to preserve the Church of Scotland is taken at the meeting of the Privy Council immediately following the sovereign's accession. The Church of Scotland is, however, self-governing and, by the provisions of the Church of Scotland Act, 1921, has power to determine for itself all matters concerned with worship, doctrine, and discipline.

Thus, while both the Church of England and the Church of

Scotland are 'established' in the sense of being singled out by statute, there is another sense of 'established', meaning 'governed by the state', according to which the Church of England is established and the Church of Scotland is not. Even in the case of the Church of England, however, the role of the State has come to be severely attenuated in recent years.

The Church of England and the Church of Scotland enjoy very different relationships with the State and with the sovereign. 'Establishment' is not a precise term denoting a single specific relationship between Church and State. But it signifies at the very least that the church in question is given some sort of statutory recognition by the State. The alternative forms of establishment can, however, have very different constitutional implications and consequences, varying from complete subjection of the Church to the State to a mere recognition of a particular church for certain official or ceremonial purposes. Both the Church of England and the Church of Scotland are nearer the latter end of the spectrum than the former. The precise relationships between the two churches and the State are, however, a product of their history, and can be understood only in that light.

II

A church may be defined as a human or divine association composed of those professing a common body of religious doctrine and using common forms of worship. Such an association may be voluntary, and brought into existence by mutual contract between its members, an arrangement in which the State has no part. This does not mean that the association is of no concern to the State. In a liberal society, the State will see itself as responsible for ensuring the toleration of all law-abiding associations; and it may exercise some degree of control or supervision over an association to ensure that it does not encroach upon the rights of others. Thus, associations, even when entirely voluntary, are subject to various legal obligations. But, in spiritual matters, the State will stand entirely aside from a church which is a voluntary association, and in temporal matters it will stand aside except where it has to intervene to secure certain specific public purposes.

The Church of England, however, is not a voluntary association of this sort, and it was not brought into being by mutual contract between its members. Nor, however, is it a state church in the sense of it having been created by an Act of Parliament. It is, rather, a product of historical development, having evolved by a process of gradualism and of compromise between the political and ecclesiastical centres of power. It is thus difficult to point to a precise date at which the Church of England came into existence. Indeed, like the British Constitution itself, it seems never actually to have begun, but to be the product of a process of historical evolution which was both unplanned and undesigned.

The Church of England was not, in the eyes of most of its members, brought into existence by the Reformation. The Reformation, they would argue, had the effect not of creating a new church, but of denying the spiritual jurisdiction of the Pope over an already existing one. The sovereign then became the secular source of authority in the Church. Members of the Church of England regard their church as a continuous body, as the church founded in England when the English were converted to Christianity in the seventh century. In this sense, the Church preceded both the nation and the monarchy.

In 1215, over three centuries before the Reformation, Magna Carta declared that the 'rights' and 'liberties' of the Church in England are to be preserved, and this indicates that, as early as the thirteenth century, the Church in England was seen not merely as a local branch of the universal catholic church, but as a specifically national church. It was from early times, then, specifically territorial. Until the Reformation, however, it was governed by co-operation between the sovereign and the Pope, although the boundaries between their respective spheres of authority were not always very clear. In place of this dual system of control, the Reformation substituted a unitary system under the control of the sovereign.

The effect of the Reformation was to turn the Church *in* England to the Church *of* England.[1] By a series of statutes in the 1530s, Henry VIII, thwarted in his wish to annul his marriage to Katharine of Aragon, deprived the Pope of all jurisdiction over the Church in England.[2] In his temporal functions, the Pope was replaced by the

---

[1] Geoffrey Elton, *England under the Tudors* (3rd edn., Routledge, 1991), 164.

[2] It is a myth that the Church of England was founded on Henry VIII's desire to secure a *divorce*. He sought an annulment of his marriage to Katharine of Aragon on the grounds that she was his deceased brother's wife, which the Pope, for political reasons, was unable to give. Henry VIII also secured annulments of his second and fourth marriages to Anne Boleyn and Anne of Cleves respectively. Indeed divorce, as we now know it, did not exist in medieval common law.

sovereign, while in spiritual matters the Supremacy of the Crown Act, 1534, declared that the sovereign was 'the only supreme head on earth of the Church of England'. This Act was repealed by Mary I, but re-enacted in a different form by Elizabeth I, as the Act of Supremacy, 1559, declaring the sovereign to be not the head but 'the supreme governor' of the Church of England. Henry VIII and Elizabeth thus defined the position of the Church in relation to the State, while parliament came later to endorse the doctrines and ceremonies of the Church and to give them statutory force through the Thirty-nine Articles, and in 1662 the Act of Uniformity made the revised Book of Common Prayer mandatory.

Many of the features, however, which characterized the established Church of England go back beyond Henry VIII's break with Rome. Although it had been the Pope who appointed archbishops and bishops, the sovereign, by convention, enjoyed a veto over who was appointed. Moreover, archbishops and bishops sat in the House of Lords before the Reformation, while canon laws had been made in England since the time of Edward II, and appeals to Rome were possible only with the sovereign's permission. Thus, the 'establishment' of the Church of England, a term which was not used until Canons of 1603, comprises not only the legislation securing the royal supremacy, but a complex tangle of other legislation, together with various traditions and customs, some of which date back to the Middle Ages. The Church of England is thus not the creation of the State, nor of a mutual contract, but rather the product of a long period of evolutionary growth, comprising both statute and precedent.

From a constitutional point of view, however, the main consequence of the Reformation was to *reform* the Church by replacing papal supremacy over it with royal supremacy. This supremacy, unlike the establishment itself, was set up by a specific Act of Parliament and can be precisely dated. The royal supremacy entails that the sovereign is Supreme Governor of the Church of England, 'in all spiritual and ecclesiastical things and causes', as provided in the Act of Supremacy, 1559. It is this feature, the royal supremacy, which serves to distinguish the Church of England from an association based upon mutual contract, and, in particular, from most of the continental Protestant churches, where authority lies in the scriptures, there being no Supreme Governor. The royal supremacy secured the independence of the Church of England 'and the champion and symbol of independence in both spheres was the King'.[3]

From the end of the seventeenth century, however, the relationship between Church and State was fundamentally changed by two powerful forces—the development of responsible government and the growth of religious toleration.

During the eighteenth century, with the development of responsible government, the actions of the sovereign in relation to the Church came, like most of his or her other actions, to be undertaken on advice. The development of religious toleration also altered the position of the Established Church. For during the sixteenth century, no question of *justifying* an established church could have arisen, since, before the age of toleration, it was difficult to conceive of the Church and the State as separate entities at all; nor was any other church permitted to exist. No church other than the Church of England was recognized as being part of the political nation. The nation in its political aspect was represented by parliament; the nation in its spiritual aspect was represented by the Church. 'There is not any man', declared Hooker in his *Laws of Ecclesiastical Polity*, 'of the Church of England but the same man is also a member of the commonwealth; nor any man a member of the commonwealth which is not also of the Church of England.'[4] The Church of England really could be described, until the beginnings of religious toleration in 1689, as the entire nation at prayer. Even in the eighteenth century, Edmund Burke could argue that the nation expressed itself both in a national state and in a national church and that the two were interdependent.

During the seventeenth century the development of religious toleration first for other Christian churches, and then for non-Christian religions and for those of no religion at all, altered the whole nature of the establishment, and it came under increasing attack from radicals. In the nineteenth century, in Ireland and in Wales, many argued that it was unjust that one church should be singled out for privileged treatment, especially when that church was a minority church which did not represent the nation. In Ireland, the Roman Catholic Church rather than the Church of Ireland was the national

[3] E. Garth Moore and Timothy Briden, *Moore's Introduction to English Canon Law*, 3rd edn., ed. Timothy Briden and Brian Hanson (Mowbray, London, 1992), 10–11.
[4] Cited in P. M. H. Bell, *Disestablishment in Ireland and Wales* (SPCK, 1969), 6.

church of the vast majority, while in Wales this position was held by the Free Churches. That was the basic rationale for Irish disestablishment in 1869 and Welsh disestablishment in 1914.

The disestablishment of these churches shows that the sovereign's oath, made upon accession, to preserve the Church has no legal effect, and, parliament being sovereign, could not be brought into play to prevent disestablishment. The same would be true of the disestablishment of the Church of England, but the extent to which it would be true in Scotland is a moot point, in view of provisions of the Treaty of Union as they affect the Church of Scotland and Scots law.

In England, pressure for disestablishment was on social rather than national grounds, from those who saw the Church of England as the preserve of the landed gentry and a source of privilege. These forces gained political power towards the end of the nineteenth century. With the removal of restrictions preventing those who did not belong to the Church of England from entering parliament, the possibility arose of legislation for the Church being enacted by those who did not belong to it. The general election of 1906, won by the Liberals, was the first to produce a House of Commons which was not predominantly Anglican, while in 1916 Lloyd George became the first non-Anglican prime minister. How could a parliament and a government dominated by non-Anglicans justify being able to legislate for an Established Church to which they did not themselves belong?

In the latter part of the nineteenth century, therefore, Liberals and Radicals took up the cause of the disestablishment of the Church of England, something which they thought would be the next step after the disestablishment of the Welsh Church. Queen Victoria objected to proposals to disestablish the Welsh Church precisely because she saw it as '*the first step towards the disestablishment* and *disendowment* of the Church of England'.[5] Gladstone in a speech at Midlothian in September 1885 declared cautiously that 'the severance of the Church of England from the State' was a question as to which 'the foundations of discussion had already been laid'.[6] But the Radical Programme of that year was less cautious, declaring that 'It is certain that the Church of England will, some day or other, cease as

[5] G. I. T. Machin, *Politics and the Churches in Great Britain 1869–1921* (Oxford University Press, 1987), 209.
[6] Cited in Earl of Selborne, *A Defence of the Church of England against Disestablishment* (Macmillan, 1887), p. xi.

an establishment to exist,' while Karl Marx predicted that 'with its overthrow in Ireland the Established Church will collapse in England'.[7]

There had arisen, then, since the Reformation a secular system of government in the hands of ministers responsible to parliament. These ministers might well propose legislation which the Church did not like, and which the sovereign, as Supreme Governor, might not like either. Yet the sovereign would have no alternative but to give the Royal Assent to such legislation. Thus, were the Church and the prime minister to disagree, the Church would have to give way. In place of royal supremacy then, there grew up a system of parliamentary supremacy, a very different phenomenon.

Yet pressure for disestablishment died away after the First World War when religious issues came to disappear from politics to be replaced by socio-economic ones. In 1934 Philip Snowden, the former Labour chancellor of the exchequer and a Methodist, wrote: 'It is curious how a political question excites great interest for a time, and then becomes a dead issue. The present generation has never heard of the Disestablishment of the Church of England.'[8]

Today, however, the Church of England is almost certainly the church of a minority in England as it was in Ireland and Wales in the nineteenth century, with probably no more than around 1.1 million—2.6 per cent of the population—regularly attending Anglican services.[9] Ought the Church of England not then, by analogy with the Irish and Welsh churches, also to be disestablished?

In the nineteenth century, disestablishment was seen by radicals as a logical corollary of democracy, and many regarded religious independence as the spiritual analogy to free trade in politics. But in twentieth-century England, democracy has led, not to the disestablishment of the Church of England, but to a partial distancing between parliament and the Church. The Church has been granted a wide degree of self-government compatible with establishment so that it can retain its spiritual independence. Self-government was achieved through the Church of England Assembly (Powers) Act,

---

[7] Machin, *Politics and the Churches*, 1.

[8] Philip Snowden, *An Autobiography* (Ivor Nicholson & Watson, 1934), i. 41–2.

[9] As compared with 1.3 million attending Roman Catholic services and 1.2 million attending those of the independent Protestant churches (Michael De-La-Noy, *The Church of England: A Portrait* (Simon & Schuster, 1993), 46; and *The Economist*, 26 Dec. 1992).

commonly known as the Enabling Act, of 1919, through which the Church of England Assembly, replaced by the General Synod in 1970, was given delegated powers from parliament to legislate on Church matters.

The Synod enjoys very wide powers. It can propose Measures—statute laws—on any matter concerning the Church of England. These Measures must be laid before both Houses of Parliament, which cannot amend them, but must either accept or reject them. Measures may amend or repeal Acts of Parliament and are introduced into the House of Commons by the Second Church Estates Commissioner, who is appointed by the government although not a member of it. The government's role is confined to helping to pass Church legislation; it does not take responsibility for it. After acceptance by parliament, Measures are submitted for the Royal Assent, and acquire the full force of law.

The Synod can also make ecclesiastical regulations known as Canons, which are submitted directly to the Crown for the Royal Licence to promulgate the Canon, given on advice, provided that they do not offend against the royal prerogative, the common or statute law, or any custom of the realm. Canons, however, have no statutory authority; they bind only the clergy and not the laity, unless confirmed by a Measure or an Act of Parliament, but they can be enforced by ecclesiastical courts. No Canon has ever been vetoed by the sovereign, although apparently there have been occasions when they have been withdrawn before being presented since it has been held that the home secretary would have advised against the Royal Assent being given.[10]

The purpose of delegating such wide powers to the Church of England in 1919 was twofold. The first was to meet the desire of Church leaders to enjoy a greater degree of independence and to be less dependent upon a legislature the majority of whose members might not adhere to the Church of England. This was achieved by recognizing the Church Assembly, already set up by the Church, rather than parliament, as the appropriate machinery for formulating the opinions of the Church.

Secondly, the legislation was a confession by parliament that it was no longer wholly equipped to legislate for the Church, because

[10] Dissenting memo. by Valerie Pitt, in *Church and State: The Report of the Archbishop's Commission* (The Chadwick Report) (Church Information Service, 1970), para. 8.

pressure of time prevented it from giving full attention to Church matters.

The General Synod is a unique body in the British Constitution in the breadth of its legislative powers. A voluntary association may legislate for its own members, but it cannot alter the law of the land, nor bind those who are not members of it. Statutory bodies have conferred on them by statute the power to make regulations, but these regulations only have force if they fall within the powers conferred upon them. The General Synod, by contrast, has the power to *initiate* laws, subject only to a veto by parliament. These laws have the same force as Acts of Parliament and their validity cannot be questioned in any court of law.

The Enabling Act was defended as retaining parliamentary control of Church legislation, while providing for a swifter and more expeditious method of securing parliamentary consent to such legislation. In reality, however, the 1919 Act showed that parliament was no longer the governing body of the Church, and that its functions had been delegated to another body. It was an acknowledgment that parliament could not claim any longer to represent the laity of the Church of England, an acknowledgment that to be English could no longer be equated with active commitment to the Church of England as a religious body. It was for this reason that Dicey regarded the Enabling Act as heralding 'the approaching disestablishment of the Church of England'.[11] The Church seemed in the process of becoming just one association, albeit a privileged one, in an increasingly pluralistic society. Tension increased when, in 1927 and 1928, the House of Commons rejected the revised Prayer Book approved by the Church, although the majority of MPs representing English constituencies were in favour of it. The House was swayed in 1927 by the speech of a Scottish Labour MP, Rosslyn Mitchell, a Presbyterian who had no connection at all with the Church of England.

In 1974 the powers of parliament over the Church of England were further attenuated when parliament delegated powers over matters of worship and doctrine to the Synod through the Church of England (Worship and Doctrine) Measure. This was a decisive change in the Church–State relationship, repealing as it did the bulk of the Act of Uniformity of 1662. Other matters of worship and doc-

[11] Cited in Machin, *Politics and the Church*, 320.

trine, moreover, can be altered by Canons, which do not need parliamentary approval.

The settlement of 1919 has worked on the whole successfully, and seems to have offered a practical resolution of what might otherwise have proved an intractable conflict. The church could not allow a parliament with only a minority of practising Anglicans to determine fundamental doctrines, while parliament could not totally relinquish its powers over a church which remained established. The settlement of 1919 has served to maintain a balance between the spiritual independence of the Church and establishment. The Church is enabled to regulate its own affairs yet without encroaching upon the sovereignty of parliament. The initiative for Church legislation remains with the General Synod, but parliament retains the right of veto.

One consequence, however, has been to establish a certain distance between parliament and the Church. The Church of England, which has always claimed to serve the whole nation, far beyond the limits of active worshippers, now excludes much of the nation from effective influence in its affairs. Parliament remains in theory sovereign, yet in practice it can no longer initiate legislation affecting the Church. When, in 1981, Viscount Cranborne introduced, under the Ten Minute Rule, a Prayer Book Protection Bill, he was rebuked by the Bishop of Durham and by the Lord Chancellor for breaking what seems to have become an unbreakable convention that the initiative in legislative matters concerning the Church of England must come from the Synod and not from parliament.[12] 'Parliament', Lord Hailsham declared, was 'not the best place in which to discuss the doctrine of the Atonement'.[13]

Even parliament's power of veto, moreover, is used very sparingly. It has, in fact, rejected only three Measures since 1970. The first, the Incumbents (Vacation of Benefices) Measure, was rejected in 1975, but passed in revised form, after reconsideration by the General Synod, in 1977. In 1984 a Measure proposing to alter the episcopal appointments procedure was rejected and was not resubmitted;[14] while in 1989, a Measure allowing divorced clergy to remarry was rejected, but passed the following year.

---

[12] House of Commons, 6th ser., vol. ii, cols. 959 ff., 8 Apr. 1981, and House of Lords, vol. 419, cols. 612 ff., 8 Apr. 1981.

[13] House of Lords, ibid., col. 628.

[14] Colin Buchanan, *Cut the Connection: Disestablishment and the Church of England* (Darton, Longman & Todd, 1994), 46.

Most MPs are embarrassed to use their power of veto, as was shown when the House of Commons debated the ordination of women priests in 1993, one year after the General Synod's decision in favour of ordination. Of the nineteen MPs who spoke, six declared that the Commons should not be discussing it at all, while, of the five who spoke against, three were or were about to become Roman Catholics, while the fourth was the Revd Ian Paisley, an Ulster Presbyterian. Had the Commons used its supposed veto power to prevent the ordination of women, it would undoubtedly have caused a constitutional crisis, and the Church of England might well have sought to break its links with the state. Thus even the limited power of veto which parliament retains is subject to serious limitations. In practice, this theoretical power of veto is perhaps more akin to the delaying power of the House of Lords. It gives the General Synod time for second thoughts if parliament makes clear that it is unhappy about a particular Measure. If, however, the Synod is firm in its determination, it is unlikely that parliament would exercise its veto. But the knowledge that Measures are subject to parliamentary scrutiny can have an important influence in shaping the way proposals are framed. Parliament's role in church affairs, one MP has suggested, has become 'the right to be consulted, to encourage and to warn'![15]

Tensions in the relationship between State and Church have arisen not so much on matters of doctrine and worship, but rather over the appointment of bishops and archbishops. These appointments are formally made by the sovereign, but, as with his or her other public acts, they are taken on advice, and the doctrine of ministerial responsibility serves to safeguard the sovereign from political involvement in Church affairs.

Until 1976 the prime minister had an unfettered right to advise on appointments, and the Church had no formal role in the appointing process at all, although it was invariably consulted, as a matter of courtesy. Since 1976, however, appointments have been submitted to the prime minister through the Church of England's Crown Appointments Commission, a body of which a majority are members of the Synod. The Commission draws up a shortlist of two names for the prime minister which it may offer in order of preference. The prime minister is free to choose either of the two names,

[15] John Cope, MP, House of Commons, vol. 882, col. 1604, 4 Dec. 1974.

or indeed to seek other names from the Commission. Once the prime minister has made a decision, he or she submits it to the sovereign, who, although required in the last resort to act on advice, can, nevertheless, through informal discussion at an earlier stage, secure some influence over the final choice. The advice given by the prime minister over Church appointments is personal advice, rather than advice on behalf of the government or the cabinet, and the prime minister cannot be questioned in parliament about the advice which he or she gives.

Although the Church of England was given a much enhanced role in the appointments process in 1976, there are still many in the church who object to the role allotted to the prime minister, who, after all, need not be an Anglican.[16] In practice, few prime ministers have the time or the inclination to involve themselves sufficiently in Church affairs as to be able to make an informed contribution to the process; and most prime ministers appear to rely on the advice given to them by their appointments secretary. According to one critic of the establishment, this has the consequence that 'The royal supremacy, which began as a personal, almost sacerdotal power, has become part of the modern bureaucracy of government.'[17]

There have been occasions in the twentieth century when it has been believed that appointments were being made on political rather than ecclesiastical grounds. In 1942, following the resignation of Lang as Archbishop of Canterbury, William Temple, Archbishop of York, seemed the obvious successor. There were fears, however, that Churchill would refuse to appoint Temple, who was a socialist, and Temple's two rivals, Geoffrey Fisher, Bishop of London, and Cyril Garbett, Bishop of Winchester, agreed that, if Temple were to be passed over for political reasons, they would each refuse to serve. In the event, however, Temple was appointed but died in 1944. The obvious successor seemed to be Bishop Bell of Chichester, but he had offended Churchill by his opposition to the policy of saturation bombing of German cities. It used to be believed that Churchill had vetoed his appointment, but it is now known that the Church did

[16] However, under the Roman Catholic Relief Act of 1829, sect. 17, and the Jews' Relief Act of 1858, sec. 4, no Roman Catholic or Jew may advise the sovereign on ecclesiastical matters. Were the prime minister to be a Roman Catholic or a Jew, advice would presumably be given by the Lord Chancellor.

[17] Peter Hinchliff, *The One-Sided Reciprocity: A Study in the Modification of the Establishment* (Darton, Longman & Todd, 1966), 171.

not in fact recommend him to the prime minister, and Geoffrey Fisher, a safer choice, was appointed instead. The 'subtle currents' of the political establishment, one commentator has remarked, 'cast him [Bell] aside'. Yet the Church, 'must be a source of vision; it is not a civil service'.[18] The casting aside of Bell raised the question whether the establishment was any longer compatible with the spiritual independence of the Church.

Under the new system for Church appointments introduced in 1976, it is widely believed that on three occasions Margaret Thatcher over-rode the wishes of the Church and appointed the name that was second amongst the preferences of the church rather than its first choice—in 1981, when she recommended Graham Leonard rather than John Habgood as Bishop of London, in 1987, when she recommended Mark Santer rather than Jim Thompson as Bishop of Birmingham, and in 1990, when she recommended George Carey rather than John Habgood as Archbishop of Canterbury. In 1987 it was alleged that Conservative MPs had lobbied against Thompson.[19]

The history of the relationship between the Church of England and the State, then, is one of progressive attenuation. From having been a virtual department of state, the Church has become almost, although not quite, one amongst many denominations, lying through the Anglican Communion overseas, at the centre of a federation of self-governing churches. What then remains of the sovereign's association with the Church?

The sovereign promises to protect both the Church of England and the Church of Scotland. Yet the disestablishment of the Church of Ireland in 1869 and of the Church of Wales in 1914 show that the sovereign's oath to preserve the Church is of no legal effect. When, in 1869, Canon Selwyn made an application questioning the validity of the disestablishment of the Church of Ireland on the ground that it was inconsistent with the coronation oath and the Act of Settlement, his application was refused, since no judicial body could question the validity of an Act of Parliament.[20] In 1994 a plaintiff sought to establish that the Church of England had no power to allow the ordination of women, since this was contrary to, *inter alia*, the coro-

---

[18] Andrew Chandler, 'The Church of England and the Obliteration Bombing of Germany in the Second World War' *English Historical Review*, 108 (1993), 946.

[19] Bernard Palmer, *High and Mitred* (SPCK, 1992), 291, 293.

[20] *Ex parte Canon Selwyn*, [1872] 36 JP 54.

nation oath, requiring the sovereign to maintain the Protestant Reformed Religion established by law and the doctrine of the Church of England as by law established in England. In dismissing the case, Mr Justice Lightman ruled that this meant the Church 'not, as established at any particular point in history, but as currently established; the formula is apt to reflect the self evident possibility that in the case of the established church Parliament may enact or authorise change'.[21] Thus, parliament remains sovereign over the Church of England, and the sovereign's oath could not be brought into play to prevent disestablishment of the Church of England. Nor does the oath serve to freeze the relationship between Church and State at any particular point in time. It has not prevented very considerable changes in Church doctrine and worship, the bulk of which, as we have seen, has been delegated to the General Synod. Thus the contemporary significance of the royal supremacy is perhaps as much symbolic and ceremonial as it is constitutional.

III

In part because the relationship between Church and State has become so attenuated, there is much less contemporary hostility to the establishment of the Church on the grounds that it confers privilege. Instead, paradoxically, the case for disestablishment comes more from a minority *within* the Church of England, from those who believe a close relationship with the State to be corrupting.

Establishment, such critics believe, is a barrier to Christian unity. No other church is willing to unite with a Church of England which is linked to the State. Establishment, these critics suggest, degrades the Church of England, since, far from spiritualizing the State, it serves to secularize Christianity. The Church must be the conscience of the nation, which it cannot be so long as the possibility of conflict with the political authorities is there. The essence of religion indeed is voluntary allegiance. The Church of England would, it is suggested, be in a stronger position to secure this allegiance if it broke its connection with the State. Disestablishment would not, in the view of its critics, encourage irreligion. Neither Ireland nor Wales became less religious after disestablishment, while in the United

[21] *Williamson* v. *The Archbishops of Canterbury and York and the Church Commissioners* (1994).

States, a nation in which Church and State are rigorously separated, religion is a far stronger force than it is in Britain. Indeed, in the past, the establishment was sometimes defended by those who suggested that it *protected* the nation from religion and from clericalism. It was, an MP once suggested, 'the one thing which protects us against Christianity!'[22]

If, as these critics suggest, the Church of England can no longer be said to serve the whole nation, and has become just one amongst a number of religious associations in England, then it ought no longer to be put in the position of having to *represent* the whole English nation. The Prince of Wales, although rejecting disestablishment, has raised the question of how, as Supreme Governor, he could still meaningfully represent the multicultural and multi-denominational society that England had become.

I've always felt [the Prince of Wales declared] that the Catholic subjects of the sovereign are equally as important as the Anglican ones, as the Protestant ones. Likewise, I think that the Islamic subjects or the Hindu subjects or the Zoroastrian subjects of the sovereign are of equal and vital importance.

The prince declared that he would prefer to be thought of as a 'Defender of Faith', rather than a 'Defender of *the* Faith'; that is not incompatible with being an Anglican. The Prince of Wales wanted his coronation to be an inter-faith occasion, like, for example, the D-day commemorations of 1994, in which other faiths were able to participate.[23] If the sovereign represents the nation and if the coronation is intended as a religious affirmation of the sovereign's commitment to the whole nation, why should just one denomination be singled out in it?

If criticism of the establishment comes almost wholly from those within the Church of England, its defence, equally paradoxically, has sometimes come primarily from those of other denominations and faiths. As early as 1953, the Free Churches, traditional advocates of disestablishment, declared that disestablishment would jeopardize valuable co-operation between Church and State.[24] In his Reith Lectures in 1991, the Chief Rabbi defended the establishment as pre-

[22] David Nicholls, *Church and State in Britain since 1820* (Routledge & Kegan Paul, 1967), 100.

[23] Jonathan Dimbleby, *The Prince of Wales, A Biography* (Little Brown, 1994), 528.

[24] Machin, *Politics and the Church*, 327–8.

serving some link, however tenuous, between religion, morality, and power. Disestablishment, he argued, would 'have the effect of signalling a further dissociation between religion and public culture and would intensify the dangers of a collapse in our moral ecology'.[25] Another Rabbi has argued that 'Establishment is the way Britain has traditionally embodied the central role of faith in the life of the nation. If that is removed, all faiths will suffer. Judaism, Catholicism and Islam will become equally marginal to a newly secularised state.'[26]

Moreover, although only a small minority of the population attend Church of England services on a regular basis, the Church nevertheless remains perhaps the focus of some residual loyalty even among the non-religious. Parish priests see themselves as responsible for everyone in their parish, all of whom have the right to avail themselves of its services. All citizens enjoys the common-law right to baptize their children in the parish church, to be married in the parish church, and to be buried in the parish churchyard. The Church of England is open to all, whether members or not, for the rites of baptism, marriage, and burial. It is, in the words of the Archbishop of Canterbury, George Carey, 'there for all. Rather like the National Health Service, some opt out but no-one has to opt in. This is built into our national consciousness.'[27]

The Church of England thus remains for the non-religious a repository of what John Habgood, Archbishop of York, has called 'folk religion', that agglomeration of saws and superstitions which makes even those without religious beliefs seek to mark key rites of passage—birth, marriage, and death—with a religious ceremony.[28] Thus the distinctive role of the Church of England, according to Habgood, is as the 'Apostolate of the Indevout'.[29] 'Christianity', Owen Chadwick has argued, 'is for the lukewarm as well as the devout; and not many of us want congregations to become cliques of the holy.'[30] There are, according to this view, many people of

[25] Jonathan Sacks, *The Persistence of Faith: Religion, Morality and Society in a Secular Age* (Weidenfeld & Nicolson, 1991), 97.

[26] Rabbi Dr Julian Jacobs, 'Keep Faith Central to National Life', *The Times*, 9 July 1994.

[27] George Carey, 'The Established Church', *The House Magazine*, 3 Apr. 1993.

[28] John Habgood, *Church and Nation in a Secular Age* (Darton, Longman & Todd, 1983).

[29] In a sermon at King's College, Cambridge, 15 May 1994, entitled 'Religion and the National Church'.

[30] 'Faith, Hope and Clarity', *Guardian*, 9 Dec. 1993.

inarticulate religious belief who remain outside the formal organization of the Church of England but whose inarticulacy should not be equated with lack of religious belief. The essence of the establishment today, Habgood has argued, is 'a sense of responsibility for the nation as a whole, and in particular for those whose religion is mostly inarticulate and submerged'.[31] The Church of England, therefore, should not be dominated by the activists of the Synod, but parliament also, as representing the 'folk religion' of the nation, should be allowed to express its point of view.

IV

Two attempts have been made by those who, without seeking to disestablish the Church, seek to remove what they see as the element of political control over it. The first is to remove the prime minister's power of recommending the appointment of archbishops and bishops; the second is to restructure the relationship of the Church of England and the State along the lines of that between the Church of Scotland and the State.

The first method, that of divesting the prime minister of his role in senior church appointments, was proposed by the van Straubenzee working party set up by the Standing Committee of the General Synod, *Senior Church Appointments*.[32] The report argued that, as the prime minister could not be questioned in parliament about the advice which he gave, the advice could be divested from him. He declared that it might be perfectly proper constitutionally for advice on senior appointments to be given directly to the sovereign by the Archbishops of Canterbury and York, who, as privy counsellors, enjoy a right of audience with the sovereign. Since parliamentary questions cannot be directed to the prime minister on senior appointments, it would not matter that parliament would be unable to question the archbishops. It was pointed out that deans and provosts of cathedral churches used to be appointed by the sovereign personally. Senior appointments in the Church would then not owe their position to the patronage of the prime minister. In this way the advantages of establishment could be preserved and the symbolic role of the sovereign as Supreme Governor maintained,

---

[31] Habgood, *Church and Nation*, 96.	[32] (Church House Publishing, 1992).

while bypassing the political apparatus which many in the Church of England find offensive.[33]

It is difficult, however, to understand the constitutional rationale behind the van Straubenzee proposal. There are, of course, some matters where the sovereign can act without advice, while on legal matters he or she can be advised by the Judicial Committee of the Privy Council. But there are no non-legal matters on which he or she can be advised by anyone other than a responsible minister. The reason for this is clear. It is that the sovereign shall not be embarrassed by appearing to have made decisions based upon his or her own personal preferences. In the case of the appointment of archbishops and bishops, there is an even more powerful reason why the prime minister must be the person to proffer advice. It is that the archbishops and the senior bishops sit as of right in the House of Lords. Therefore, for as long as the Church of England remains established and remains an episcopal church whose archbishops and senior bishops sit in parliament, the State cannot divest itself from its concern with senior appointments. 'The Sovereign', declared James Callaghan in the House of Commons on 8 June 1976, 'must be able to look for advice on a matter of this kind, and that must mean, for a Constitutional Sovereign, advice from Ministers.'[34] The sovereign is the Supreme Governor of the Church of England not in a personal capacity but as head of state and the role as Supreme Governor cannot be separated from the role of a constitutional head of state.

V

The second method by which it has been suggested that political control over the Church of England could be eliminated without disestablishing it is by making the Church entirely self-governing after the model of the Church of Scotland. To appraise this method, it is necessary to analyse the relationship between the Church of Scotland and the State and the historic evolution which it reflects.

The Church of Scotland is a presbyterian and not an episcopal church, and its officers do not sit in parliament. Its supreme

---

[33] Ibid., paras. 5.27 ff.

[34] These points were made when Callaghan was commending the new arrangements which would give the Church 'a greater say in the process of choosing its leaders' (House of Commons, Written Answers, vol. 912, col. 613).

authority is not the sovereign, but its own General Assembly. The Assembly, unlike the General Synod, is not convened by the sovereign and can meet on its own initiative. It is presided over by a Moderator, who is chosen each year by the Assembly. The sovereign is represented at the Assembly, on occasion in person, but more frequently by a Lord High Commissioner, appointed each year by the sovereign on advice from the prime minister after the secretary of state for Scotland has taken soundings from the Church as to who might be suitable. Symbolically, however, the Lord High Commissioner sits, not in the Assembly itself, but in the gallery. He is not a member of the Assembly and exercises no control over its business.

The Assembly, acting within the law of the land, has the power to pass resolutions, known as overtures, which are submitted to the presbyteries, and, after approval, have effect without the Royal Assent. Thus, in 1968, the Church of Scotland was able to admit women to ordination without needing to make any reference to parliament at all. The Church of Scotland is self-governing in all matters of worship, government, and discipline. It has a higher percentage of active members than the Church of England. Around 850,000 out of a population of 5.6 million belong to it; and the Church of Scotland outnumbers the next largest denomination, which is Roman Catholicism, by a ratio of over two to one.

Thus the Church of Scotland is a collegial church, with supreme authority resting in the body of its members. Supreme authority in the Church of England, by contrast, lies largely with the sovereign as Supreme Governor, but in reality with parliament, which has delegated its powers to the General Synod. The Church of Scotland, unlike the Church of England, is in no way subordinate to civil authority. The sovereign, whose role is minimal, operates through the General Assembly and not through parliament.

The Church of Scotland is, however, an established church in the sense that, as early as 1567, the sovereign of Scotland was required to swear to protect it. In 1592 an Act of the Scottish Parliament established the presbyterian form of government in the Church of Scotland. The Stuarts sought to undermine presbyterianism, but failed to establish their sovereignty or to impose episcopacy, and the presbyterian form of government was restored in 1689. Indeed, in Scotland, the Bill of Rights, by contrast with the situation in England, declared not that James II had 'abdicated' but that he had been 'deposed', and William and Mary were recognized only on condition that the principles of 1592 were reaffirmed and accepted. Because the Church of Scotland is established, the civil courts are bound to assist the judicatures of the kirk, which are courts of the realm. Thus the Church of Scotland, although self-governing, is to be distinguished from the assemblies of the free churches, which are merely voluntary bodies given no special statutory protection.

The statutory protection given to the Church of Scotland was reaffirmed and strengthened in the Treaty of Union of 1707 between England and Scotland. Section 5 of the Treaty provided for an accompanying 'Act for securing the Protestant religion and Presbyterian Church government' as a 'fundamental condition of the Union', 'to continue in all times coming'. The accompanying Act, without which the Treaty would not have been agreed, enacted that the Protestant religion and the presbyterian form of church government were to be 'held and observed in all time coming as a fundamental and essential condition of any Treaty of Union to be concluded between the two Kingdoms without any alteration thereof, or derogation thereto in any sort for ever'. 'The solemnity of words', it has been held, 'could go no further.'[35] Even Dicey, who believed that the sovereignty of parliament was the fundamental principle of the British Constitution, and that parliament could not be bound by the Treaty of Union, held nevertheless that the immutable clauses of the Treaty constituted 'a warning that it cannot be changed without grave danger to the Constitution of the country'.[36]

In Scotland, indeed, the principle of the sovereignty of parliament has always been regarded with some scepticism. It is, declared Lord Cooper in 1953, 'a distinctively English principle which has no counterpart in Scottish constitutional law'.[37] It is doubtful, all the same, whether parliament could be legally constrained from disestablishing the Church of Scotland by the terms of the Treaty. In 1869 the Church of Ireland was disestablished, even though the Union with Ireland Act, 1800, also provided that the Church of Ireland should be established 'for ever'.[38] If, however, the Church of Scotland were to be disestablished against the wishes of the Scottish people, this

[35] A. Taylor Innes, *The Law of Creeds in Scotland* (Blackwood, 1902), 58.
[36] A. V. Dicey and R. S. Rait, *Thoughts on the Union between England and Scotland* (Macmillan, 1920), 252–3.
[37] *McCormick* v. *Lord Advocate*, 1953 SC 396 (Scotland).
[38] *Ex parte Canon Selwyn* (1872) 36 JP 54.

would be seen as a breach of an obligation of honour; it might lead Scots to say that parliament could no longer be relied upon to observe its obligations, and so it would give an impetus to devolution, or even to separatism in Scotland. In practice, therefore, the established Church of Scotland is probably as entrenched as is possible within a political system in which parliament remains theoretically sovereign.

Thus, both the Church of England and the Church of Scotland may be said to be established churches in the sense that they are given statutory recognition, and the sovereign is officially associated with them, taking oaths to protect them. Yet, the relationship between the sovereign and the two churches is quite different. In England, parliament has retained its sovereignty, but has *delegated* it to the General Synod. The authority of the Synod is *derived* from that of the State. In Scotland, by contrast, where there is no difficulty in understanding the idea of a sharing of powers, there is a *division* of powers between Church and State by means of which each can be supreme within its own respective sphere. The Church is the spiritual sovereign and the State the temporal sovereign. In Scotland, from the time of the Reformation, the assumption has been that Church and State are distinct; in England the assumption has been that the Church is subordinate to the State.

For this reason, the role of the sovereign is also quite different in the two churches. Andrew Melville, the leader of the Church of Scotland after John Knox, and the man who gave the church its presbyterian character, told James VI of Scotland:

Sirrah, ye are God's sillie vassal; there are two Kings and two Kingdoms in Scotland: there is King James the head of this commonwealth and there is Christ Jesus the King of the Church, whose subject James VI is and of whose Kingdom he is not a King nor a lord nor a head but a member.[39]

That is not the kind of language which an English church leader would have used in addressing his sovereign.

In Scotland, then, there is no royal supremacy, the chief officers of the Church do not sit in the House of Lords, and parliament has no authority in spiritual matters.

These differences result, however, not merely from differences of constitutional interpretation, but also from fundamental differences

[39] Cited in T. M. Taylor, 'Church and State in Scotland', *Juridical Review* (1957), 122.

in historical experience, and in particular from the different impact of the Reformation in the two countries—for the Reformation had much deeper popular roots in Scotland than in England.

In England, as we have seen, the Reformation was carried out by Henry VIII and his ministers for reasons of State. In Scotland, by contrast, it took on the aspect of a popular movement carried out *against* the State, and it neither sought nor was given royal authority. The English Reformation, Anson believed, 'was led and controlled by the King; the Scots Reformation was a popular movement'.[40]

In Scotland, the State ratified and confirmed the Scottish Reformation, but it did not confer it. Thus the autonomy of the Church of Scotland derives from specific historical circumstances which did not apply in England, where the Reformation had the effect of altering the constitutional status of a church whose episcopal polity remained the same rather than creating a new polity.

The current constitutional position of the Church of Scotland is determined by the Church of Scotland Act, 1921, which came into effect in 1926. By this Act, the Church of Scotland is declared to be self-governing and parliament renounces the right to legislate on its behalf. The Act does not purport to lay down the constitution of the church, but it recognizes as lawful certain Declaratory Articles, already approved by the Church of Scotland, as setting forth its constitution in matters spiritual. These Articles state, *inter alia*, that the Church receives from Christ 'the right and power subject to no civil authority to legislate, and to adjudicate finally, in all matters of doctrine, worship, government, and discipline in the Church'. The Articles, in the view of the Church, are given by Christ and not by the State, and so the State cannot take them away. The Articles themselves, other than the first, which is unalterable, can be altered only by the General Assembly. The 1921 Act is in effect a treaty between Church and State by which the freedom of the Church is formally recognized, rather than a unilateral action on the part of the state. One significant feature of the Act is that section 2 provides that 'Nothing in this Act or in any other Act affecting the Church of Scotland shall prejudice the recognition of any other Church as a Christian Church protected by law in the exercise of its spiritual functions.' In this way, the independence of the Church of Scotland,

[40] William Anson, *The Law and Custom of the Constitution*, ii. *The Crown*, 4th edn., ed. A. Berriedale Keith (Oxford University Press, 1935), pt. II, p. 271.

far from creating a privileged position for that church, acts as a guarantee for the religious freedom of other churches.

Because the historical circumstances are so different, however, it would be difficult to imagine the Church of England adopting the same constitutional status as the Church of Scotland. This is so for two interconnected reasons.

The first is that it would not be easy for the Church of England to achieve sufficient agreement on doctrine to be able to agree upon its own Declaratory Articles. It is indeed arguable that it is the current constitutional organization of the Church of England, linking it with the State, which is a fundamental precondition of preserving its unity. In Scotland, it proved comparatively easy for the Church to agree upon the Declaratory Articles. In England, the link with the State serves to contain fairly wide differences of approach within the Church of England. It is not even clear, moreover, who in the Church of England would have the authority to draw up fundamental Articles of belief by analogy with the Scottish Church.

The second difficulty is that there is no clear focus of authority within the Church of England, within which authority is dispersed. In the Church of Scotland, all power has lain with the General Assembly since the sixteenth century, and this authority has not been challenged either by the officers of the church or by the laity. The powers of the Church of England, however, are not vested in any single person or body but shared between a number of authorities. There is no authority in the Church of England corresponding to the General Assembly, a democratic body with considerable prestige and authority, an authority derived from history, representing a more homogeneous nation and one in which religion is a stronger force than it is in England.

In the past, parliament was seen as the nearest English equivalent of the General Assembly. The General Synod, by contrast with the General Assembly, is very recent, dating only from 1970, and it lacks the prestige of the General Assembly. Moreover, there is a conflict between the democratic authority of the Synod and the episcopal basis of the Church of England.

It is difficult, then, to imagine the Church of England remodelling itself along the lines of the Church of Scotland. It seems as if the Church of England faces a stark choice between retaining its current constitutional links with the State and with the sovereign, and disestablishment. That choice is primarily one for the Church itself to make although it could be forced into action as a by-product of reform of the House of Lords. It is not a decision that parliament is at all equipped or likely to make; still less is it one that the sovereign can make.

Were disestablishment to come, the position of the monarchy would be radically affected. There would be no reason any longer to require the sovereign to be in communion with the Church of England; and, no doubt, the statutory prohibition against Catholicism would be repealed. Thus, the sovereign, like all of his or her subjects, would be able to choose his or her own religious faith. Fundamental alterations would have to be made in the coronation service, and parliament would have to alter the coronation oath. There can be no doubt that a secular monarchy would be a very different type of monarchy from that to which we have historically been accustomed, and this would involve a breach with its historic origins. But a secularized monarchy might nevertheless prove to be a monarchy more in tune with the spirit of the age.

10

The Sovereign and the Commonwealth

I

The monarchy's relationship with the Commonwealth derives from Britain's imperial history. Nearly all of the formerly dependent territories of the Empire have become fully independent states, but they have chosen to co-operate voluntarily together on a basis of full constitutional equality as members of the Commonwealth.

An empire is a form of government in which a superior rules subject peoples who are in a dependent relationship to the imperial power. A commonwealth, by contrast, is a voluntary association of free and independent states. An empire is a form of government in which dependent peoples are ruled by a superior; a commonwealth is the government of peoples by themselves. The commonwealth relationship thus replaces a relationship based on domination with one based on equality.

In its modern form, the term 'commonwealth' seems first to have been used by Lord Rosebery, a future Liberal prime minister, in a speech at Adelaide in 1884, when, considering the growth of Australian nationhood, he asked, 'Does the fact of your being a nation . . . imply separation from the Empire? God forbid! There is no need for any nation, however great, leaving the Empire, because the Empire is a commonwealth of nations.'[1]

Locke, in his second treatise, 'Of Government', had defined (para. 133) a commonwealth as an 'independent Community which the Latins signified by the word *Civitas*'. The Commonwealth, however, comprises not a single 'independent Community' but a collection of communities or rather a community of states, and it is made up not of citizens but of nations.

---

[1] Nicholas Mansergh, *The Commonwealth Experience* (Weidenfeld & Nicolson, 1969), 19.

The Commonwealth can be contrasted with other forms of international or supranational organization such as the United Nations, NATO, or the European Union in that its member states are linked, not through contract or treaty, but through history, through once having been part of the British Empire. Without empire, there would have been no commonwealth, but the Commonwealth involves a transcending of the Empire.

The UN, NATO, and the EU seek to bind together independent nations. The Commonwealth, by contrast, replaces one form of association—the Empire—with another whose basis is voluntary co-operation. As a product of historical development, there is no date at which the Commonwealth, by contrast with the UN, NATO, or the EU, can be said to have begun. It was not created at a specific moment of time, and, because of this, it has no formal constitution or rules. It is a novel form of international organization.

The British Empire, unlike other empires, came to be transformed into a commonwealth primarily because large elements of it— Canada, Australia, New Zealand, and parts of South Africa—were based upon settler communities. In the nineteenth century, the historian Seeley had noted 'the simple obvious fact of the extension of the English name into other countries of the globe, the foundation of Greater Britain'.[2] The settler communities of other imperial powers —such as, for example, the Spanish in South America, the French in Canada, and the Dutch in South Africa—were neither extensive nor enthusiastic enough to make commonwealth possible. The British settler communities, however, were able to provide 'the necessary popular foundation for Commonwealth': 'impatient of imperial rule yet cherishing notions of imperial partnership, [they] pioneered a road along which a metropolitan power of itself would assuredly never have travelled.'[3]

But this popular foundation, although necessary, was not sufficient for commonwealth. Other mid-Victorian forces, both constitutional and economic, also helped to promote it. These forces were the triumph of responsible government and the victory of free trade and non-interference in economic affairs.

In the mid-nineteenth century, Britain enjoyed responsible government and liberal institutions, institutions which it was able to transfer to settler communities abroad. Continental empires, by

---

[2] J. R. Seeley, *The Expansion of England* (Macmillan, 1883), 8.
[3] Ibid. 25–6.

contrast, could not grant responsible government to their colonies, even if they had wished to do so, since they were not secure in the enjoyment of it themselves.

The export of liberal institutions began with the Durham Report of 1839, which proposed responsible government for the Canadian provinces in domestic affairs, and may be regarded as the first step towards the creation of the modern Commonwealth.

At the time of the Durham Report, the Canadian provinces enjoyed representative parliaments but their executives were nominated by the governor and by lieutenant-governors, the sovereign's representatives in the provinces, and were responsible, not to their legislatures, but to the government in London. As a result, however, of the recommendations of the Durham Report, responsible government came to be introduced in the Canadian provinces, beginning with Nova Scotia in 1848. Under this system, not only would the colonial government be responsible to the colonial legislature, but the powers vested in the governor or lieutenant-governor of the province in regard to domestic affairs came to be exercised not on a personal basis but in general on the advice of the government of the colony concerned. Imperial affairs, however—that is, matters affecting the Empire as a whole rather than merely the local legislature, such as foreign relations, trade, and the amendment of the local constitution—were to remain with Westminster; and the governor was enabled to withhold his assent from legislation or to reserve it for the government in London if in his view domestic legislation encroached upon 'the honour of the Crown or the faith of Parliament, or the safety of the State'.[4]

The concession of responsible government to the colonies provided an essential foundation for commonwealth, since it eliminated a main cause of friction between the colonies and the 'mother country'—interference by the imperial authority in the local affairs of a colony, which had caused the loss of the American colonies in the eighteenth century. Responsible government, by contrast, was to prove the antidote to separation; it made the colonies of settlement willing to retain a relationship with Britain even after they had gained autonomy, since such a relationship could be sustained without in any way limiting this autonomy.

The model of responsible government was to be followed in the

---

[4] Lord John Russell 1839, cited in K. C. Wheare, *The Statute of Westminster and Dominion Status* (5th edn., Oxford University Press, 1953), 54.

other colonies of British settlement. By 1914 Canada, Australia, New Zealand, and South Africa—by then known as the Dominions—enjoyed, for practical purposes, complete self-government in their domestic affairs. Control of foreign affairs, however, remained with the Imperial Parliament at Westminster. Britain's declaration of war in 1914 was automatically a declaration of war on behalf of the Dominions as well as the colonial territories. The First World War, however, greatly accelerated the progress of the Dominions towards full nationhood, and this served to raise the question of how these nations, composed primarily of communities of British stock, could remain associated with Britain. What form of association could best reconcile the Dominion autonomy with the retention of a link with Britain?

In the late nineteenth century, one school of imperialists, which included Fabians on the Left, as well as men such as Joseph Chamberlain and Lord Milner on the Right, had sought the answer in imperial federation. Federation required that a federal executive and federal parliament, comprising representatives of the Dominions as well as Britain, would be able to make authoritative decisions for the Empire as a whole. Yet such a programme was unrealistic in the light of the centrifugal tendencies which had given rise to responsible government. Imperial federation was never likely to prove a solution acceptable to the Dominions. The British Empire, Lord Salisbury had pointed out, at the first Imperial Conference in 1887, was distinguished from the German by the facts of geography, by 'a want of continuity; it is separated into parts by large stretches of ocean'.[5] Imperial federation went against the tendency of granting responsible government to the self-governing colonies. The Dominions were unlikely to sacrifice their autonomy by agreeing to a form of association within which they could be outvoted. That would seem to reimpose under another guise the ties from which they had struggled so hard to escape. Thus they resisted the proposals of Joseph Chamberlain at the end of the nineteenth century for full-scale federation, and also for more limited forms of imperial union, whether a *Kriegsverein*—a union for the purposes of defence—or a *Zollverein*—a customs union—which they saw as limiting their freedom of action. Moreover, the implications of a *Zollverein* were that Britain would continue to export manufactured

---

[5] Cited in Mansergh, *The Commonwealth Experience*, 128.

goods to the colonies of settlement, but that they in turn would remain exporters of foodstuffs. The colonies, however, sought to develop their own industries and did not wish to sacrifice the opportunity of industrializing in order to remain the bread-basket for the imperial power.

Imperial federation went against the trends which had made for self-government in the Dominions. In the nineteenth century, free trade and policies of non-interference by government in economic affairs had destroyed the mercantile rationale for a centralized empire. Under free trade, the colonies were no longer needed as an exclusive outlet for manufactures or sources of supply, nor were they bound to the mother country by customs duties. The ending of the commercial monopoly made it no longer worthwhile to hold the colonies in dependence for the sake of commanding their trade. Economics, which had made possible a looser form of political association, prevented the construction of an imperial federation.

Thus imperial federation was precluded by the geographical facts of Empire, by the trends making for colonial independence, and by the economic realities. 'The circumstances of the Empire', General Smuts, South Africa's minister of defence, declared at the Imperial War Conference in 1917, 'entirely preclude the federal solution . . . and to attempt to run even the common concerns of that group of nations by means of a central parliament and a central executive is to my mind absolutely to court disaster.'[6]

But if imperial federation was not feasible, how else might the Dominions be linked to Britain? The answer, in the words of the report of the Imperial War Conference in 1917, lay in basing 'the readjustment of the constitutional relations of the component parts of the Empire . . . upon a full recognition of the dominions as autonomous nations of an imperial Commonwealth'.[7] Their autonomy recognized, these nations would, it was hoped, choose to remain associated with Britain in a 'Commonwealth of Nations', an entirely new form of post-imperial relationship.

During the inter-war years, the autonomy of the Dominions came to be augmented in two main ways. The first was through the removal of various restrictions upon their power to legislate over their own domestic affairs, restrictions which had in any case fallen

---

[6] Cited in Mansergh, *The Commonwealth Experience*, 22.
[7] Cited in ibid. 21.

into desuetude. The second was through the growth of Dominion autonomy in foreign affairs.

In 1919 the Dominions formed part of the British Empire delegation at the Paris Peace Conference, and they, together with India, were to become founder members of the League of Nations, with separate representation at Geneva. The Chanak crisis of 1922, which brought down Lloyd George's coalition government, was to show that the consent of the Dominions to British policy could no longer be taken for granted. In response to a British request for the Dominions to reinforce British troops at Chanak against the Turks, only the New Zealanders accepted unequivocally. Australia complained that it had not been consulted, while the Canadian prime minister, Mackenzie King, declared that he could not respond until he had consulted the Canadian parliament. The Dominions took no part in the Treaty of Lausanne signed with Turkey in 1923, and refused to accept the obligations undertaken by Britain in the Treaty of Locarno 1925, which committed it to defend the status quo in Western Europe. The Kellogg pact of 1928 was signed by each Dominion and ratified separately by each of them. The Dominions could no longer be bound in international affairs without their specific consent.

Thus, while in 1914 the Empire had been a single actor in foreign affairs, and remained so, from the standpoint of international law, between the wars, during the 1920s the Dominions were in the process of becoming separate sovereign states and distinct international entities. In 1920 a Dominion was for the first time given permission to establish its own diplomatic representation when Canada and the United States exchanged envoys, and in 1923 a Dominion for the first time signed a treaty in its own right—the Halibut Fisheries Treaty between Canada and the United States; and the Imperial Conference of 1923 recognized the right of the Dominions to make treaties. The implication of these developments was that the Dominions could follow their own independent foreign policy and even declare neutrality in a war in which Britain was involved. But this implication was hardly noticed in the 1920s when the international situation was peaceful, and it seemed for a brief period as if the First World War really had been what H. G. Wells had hoped it would be, 'the War that will end War'.

The relationship between the self-governing communities of the Empire was to be formally defined at the 1926 Imperial Conference in a formula devised by Lord Balfour, the elder statesman of the Conservative Party. The formula declared that the self-governing Dominions were

autonomous communities within the British Empire, equal in status, in no way subordinate to another in any respect of their domestic or internal affairs, though united by a common allegiance to the Crown, and freely associated as members of the British Commonwealth of Nations.[8]

This formula was given effect in the preamble to the Statute of Westminster in 1931 by which the legislative independence of the parliaments of the Commonwealth was recognized, and it was provided that Britain would not in future legislate for any Dominion without its consent.

The members of the British Commonwealth were united by a common allegiance to the Crown, but the functions of the Crown in the Dominions were undertaken not personally by the sovereign but by a governor-general, appointed by the sovereign. Until 1930 the appointment of the governor-general was made on the advice of the British government, and the governor-general had a dual function. He was first the head of the executive in the Dominion and, as such, expected to act on the advice of his Dominion ministers; but he was also the agent of the imperial government in London, and expected to defend imperial interests where they came into conflict with the local interests of the Dominion concerned.

With the growth of Dominion autonomy and the recognition, through the Balfour formula, of the equality of status of the Dominions with the mother-country, this conception of the constitutional position of the governor-general became outdated. The 1926 Imperial Conference declared that 'an essential consequence' of 'the equality of status' of Britain and the Dominions was that

The Governor-General of a Dominion is the representative of the Crown, holding, in all essential respects, the same position in relation to the administration of public affairs in the Dominions as is held by His Majesty the King in Great Britain, and that he is not the representative or agent of His Majesty's Government or of any Department of their Government.

Thus, wherever the sovereign was expected to act on the advice of his ministers, so also the governor-general would be expected to act

[8] Cmd. 2768 (1926). The text of the formula can be found in, *inter alia, Speeches and Documents on the British Dominions, 1918–1931*, ed. A. Berriedale Keith (Oxford University Press, London, 1938), 151 ff.

on the advice of the relevant Dominion government. The Imperial Conference did not, however, lay down any guidance as to the precise circumstances in which the sovereign or the governor-general was expected to act on advice, and the circumstances in which they enjoyed a discretion to use their reserve powers.

Since the governor-general was no longer an agent of the British government, it was logical for him or her to be appointed in future, not on the advice of the British government, but on the advice of the Dominion concerned. This consequence was accepted in 1930, when Sir Isaac Isaacs an Australian, was appointed governor-general of Australia on the advice of the Australian government against the wishes of George V. It was because the governor-general had been appointed on the advice of the Dominion concerned rather than on that of the British government that Lord Stamfordham, the king's private secretary, minuted: 'It seems to me that this morning's incident was one of the most important political and constitutional issues upon which Your Majesty has had to decide during your twenty years of reign.'[9]

A natural corollary of this change was that the governor-general would be a citizen of the country concerned, rather than a British citizen sent out to govern a far-away Dominion. The first such appointment had been that of Tim Healy as first governor-general of the Irish Free State in 1922; and, during its period of membership of the Commonwealth, Irish governments always insisted that the governor-general should be an Irish citizen. Ireland, however, was regarded very much as an exception, and it was the appointment, made in the teeth of protests by George V, of Sir Isaac Isaacs as the first Australian citizen to become governor-general of Australia in 1930 which was seen as creating a genuine precedent. Since 1952 in Canada, and 1965 in Australia, the governor-general has been a citizen of the country concerned, and today it would be highly unlikely for any of the Commonwealth members of which the queen is head of state to appoint anyone other than a citizen of the country concerned as its governor-general.

Under the Balfour formula, then, the Dominions came to be linked together not through being under the legislative supremacy of a single Imperial Parliament at Westminster which legislated for them, nor through a supreme federal parliament superior to their

[9] Harold Nicolson, *King George V: His Life and Reign* (Constable, 1952), 481.

own domestic legislatures, but through allegiance to the Crown. The Crown indeed was now the only formal link between Britain and the self-governing dominions. To preserve that link, the Statute of Westminster recognized in its preamble two voluntary limitations upon the independence of Britain and the Dominions. They were that any alteration either in the succession to, or in the title of, the Crown would only be made by unanimous agreement. So was preserved the *unity* of the sovereign by prescribing that the *succession* could only be changed by the consent of all of the nations which owed him or her allegiance; while the *identity* of the sovereign in the various Dominions was preserved by prescribing that the *title* could be changed only by the consent of all the nations which owed him or her allegiance.

Although the Crown was now the only formal link between the members of the Commonwealth, it was powerfully buttressed by informal links, and in particular by the existence of a common political culture which gave rise to common interests and ideals. This was shown in the abdication crisis of 1936, the first test of the 1926 arrangements, when common political instincts and habits of mind led the Dominions, with the exception of Ireland, to act together. Canada, Australia, New Zealand, and South Africa accepted British leadership and declared that Mrs Simpson would be as unacceptable to them as she was to the British government even though the Church of England was not established in the Dominions and there seemed no constitutional reason in so far as they were concerned why Mrs Simpson should not be queen.

The Balfour formula of 1926 had declared that the Dominions were 'in no way subordinate to another in any respect of their *domestic or internal* affairs' (emphasis added). It left open the question of the precise degree of autonomy of the Dominions in external affairs. In particular, it left open the question of whether the Dominions had the right to remain neutral in a war in which Britain was involved. Suppose that Britain were to be involved in a war as a result of the Locarno Treaty, which the Dominions had not signed. If the Dominions were not bound by the treaty, why should they be bound to go to war in defence of it? On the other hand, if allegiance to the Crown was the link which held the Commonwealth together, how could the sovereign be neutral in one part of his or her realms— for example, South Africa—at the same time as being at war in Britain. Although the king was now governing different parts of the

Commonwealth upon the advice of different ministers, there was still one sovereign and one realm. The Crown remained, in theory at least, indivisible.

On 3 September 1939 Britain declared war with Germany, in fulfilment of its commitments under the Anglo-Polish Treaty, to which the Dominions were not a party. The Dominions, however, with the exception of Eire (as the Irish Free State had become in 1937), rallied to Britain's side. Australia declared that it was automatically at war, since Britain was at war; Australia's prime minister, R. G. Menzies, in his radio broadcast on 3 September 1939, declared that Britain had declared war on Germany 'and that, as a result, Australia is at war'. He found the concept of an Australia not at war while Britain fought 'a metaphysical notion that quite eludes me'.[10] However, in December 1941, both Australia and New Zealand were to make separate declarations of war against Japan.

In Canada, in 1939, the prime minister, Mackenzie King, determined, as he had done in 1922, to put the issue to parliament. The Canadian parliament decided on 9 September, without dissent, to declare war on Germany. This meant that, for a period of six days, the king was at war in Britain, but at peace in Canada. In South Africa, the government broke up on the issue of war; but a new government was formed under General Smuts and declared war on Germany.

The government of Eire determined upon neutrality, but Eire remained a Dominion only in the eyes of the other members of the Commonwealth. In its own eyes it was an independent republic associated with the Commonwealth. In 1936 the abdication crisis had prompted the Irish government to pass the External Relations Act, restricting the powers of the Crown to the signature of treaties and the accreditation of envoys; and in 1937 the Irish Free State, afterwards known as Eire, adopted a constitution republican in form though not in name with a presidential head of state.

It was dubious whether these new provisions were compatible with the doctrine of allegiance to the Crown. Under the External Relations Act, the Irish state no longer declared allegiance to the sovereign. It merely recognized that the other member states of the Commonwealth owed allegiance to the sovereign, and declared that, for as long as they did so, it would recognize the sovereign as head

---

[10] Sir Zelman Cowen, 'Crown and Representative in the Commonwealth', unpublished Smuts Lectures, Cambridge University, 1984, lecture 1, fo. 14.

of the association and authorize him or her to sign treaties and accredit envoys. The sovereign was no longer the head of the Irish executive, but merely an organ or instrument, authorized by the head of the state, the president of Eire, to play a specific role in external relations, a method of procedure. To this, George VI apparently commented that, while he did not so much mind being called an 'organ or instrument', he objected to being regarded as 'a method of procedure'![11] The method of procedure authorizing the sovereign to act could be withdrawn by the Dáil at any time, as indeed it was in 1949, when the Dáil repealed the External Relations Act, and declared Ireland a republic.

When the 1937 Irish Constitution was enacted, the other members of the Commonwealth did not declare that Ireland had left the Commonwealth. The British government instead issued a statement declaring that it was 'prepared to treat the new Constitution as not effecting a fundamental alteration in the position of the Irish Free State, in future to be described under the new Constitution as Eire or 'Ireland' as a member of the British Commonwealth of Nations',[12] and the governments of the other Dominions—Canada, Australia, New Zealand, and South Africa—declared that they were also so prepared to treat the new Irish Constitution. In *Murray* v. *Parkes* [1942], All ER 123, it was held that Eire remained a member of the Commonwealth and that, in consequence, Irish citizens resident in the United Kingdom were liable for conscription on account of their allegiance to the Crown. This was despite the fact that the king clearly did not play the same role in Eire's constitution as he did in the constitutions of the other Dominions. On the basis of the Balfour formula, indeed, it was difficult to understand how Eire could remain in the Commonwealth, but the other members were unwilling to force it out. In fact, the External Relations Act looked forward to India's republican membership of the Commonwealth in 1949 rather than backwards to the formula of 1926.

Thus the experience of Eire could not, in itself, be used to cast much light on the question of whether a Dominion could remain neutral while Britain was at war. The experience of Canada and South Africa did have relevance, however, and it seemed to show unequivocally that the king could remain neutral in one part of his territories while

[11] Joe Garner, *The Commonwealth Office, 1925–1968* (Heinemann, 1978), 118.
[12] Nicholas Mansergh, *Documents and Speeches on British Commonwealth Affairs, 1931–1952* (Oxford University Press, 1953), 366–7.

being at war in another, for the Canadian and South African parliaments clearly had the power to vote against war and to declare their countries neutral. This meant that the doctrine of the indivisibility of the Crown was being undermined. If either Canada or South Africa had remained neutral, it would have been absurd to suppose that it was the *same* king who was at war in one part of his realms and at peace in another. That situation would be better described by saying that, while the King of Britain was at war with Germany, the King of Canada or the King of South Africa was neutral. Here, then, lay the origins of the doctrine of the divisibility of the Crown which was to be given legislative effect in the Royal Titles Act of 1953.

The position of the Crown in the Commonwealth was also to be changed by alterations in citizenship provisions agreed by the Commonwealth Prime Ministers Conference in 1947 and enacted in Britain in the British Nationality Act of 1948.

Until 1948, Commonwealth citizenship had been defined in terms of allegiance to the sovereign. There was a common code of citizenship and it was accepted that no Commonwealth member would alter its nationality laws without the agreement of the others. Admittedly, divergencies had occurred, in 1921, when a separate Canadian Nationals Act had been passed in Ottawa, and in 1935 when the government of the Irish Free State abrogated British citizenship and defined Irish citizenship without making their citizens British subjects. Despite this legislation, however, Britain continued to treat citizens of the Free State as British subjects. In 1946, however, Canada was to diverge further from the common norm with a new Canadian Citizenship Act, and this made it impossible to maintain a common code of nationality law for the whole Commonwealth.

In 1947, therefore, it was agreed that each Commonwealth member would in future be free to determine by its own legislation who were to be its citizens, but every citizen of a Commonwealth country would automatically enjoy the status of a British subject. At the same time, a new concept of 'Commonwealth citizen' was introduced as an alternative to the status of 'British subject'. A Commonwealth citizen would owe allegiance to the Crown only in respect of his or her own country, together with local allegiance in other Commonwealth countries for acts committed therein.

This development weakened the position of the Crown as a link between the constituent members of the Commonwealth by removing from it the conception of personal allegiance. In introducing a number of separate citizenships in place of a single citizenship, it implied that Commonwealth members were united by a *several* rather than a *joint* allegiance to the Crown. Thus, the concept of a single *Crown* uniting the members of the Commonwealth was coming to be replaced by that of several crowns linked by the *person* of the sovereign. This paved the way for explicit recognition of the divisibility of the Crown. Moreover, since in future citizenship would be derived not from allegiance but from nationality, the possibility was opened of being a citizen of a Commonwealth country without owing allegiance to the Crown at all. Therefore, the reform of Commonwealth nationality law made possible the admission of a republic to Commonwealth membership. Without this change, the admission of India as a republic in 1949 would have appeared as a much sharper breach with the practice of the Commonwealth.

The Commonwealth, then, faced in the immediate post-war periods two complementary challenges. The first was that of re-defining the relationship between the monarchies in the Commonwealth so as to take account of the fact of the divisibility of the Crown. The second was to find a way of accommodating the newly independent states of Asia and Africa within a structure originally devised for white settler communities.

II

By 1945 a commonwealth of independent nations had been created out of the colonies of settlement. In the only one of these nations with a majority non-white population, South Africa, non-whites were denied the franchise except in Cape Colony, where it was enjoyed by coloureds. During the post-war period, however, the dependent empire in Asia and Africa would obtain independence just as the colonies of settlement had done. The question facing Britain and the other member states of the Commonwealth was whether they could match their success in creating a white commonwealth from the empire of settlement by creating a multi-racial commonwealth from the empire of conquest.

I think [declared Malcolm MacDonald, a former colonial secretary and now governor of Malaya, in June 1947] that this is one of the great testing moments of British statesmanship. Our genius for political government

enabled our predecessors in the last generation to transform a large inse-
cure part of the Colonial Empire into a Commonwealth '*of free and equal
nations*'. The ruling people in these nations, however, are white men, most
of them of British stock. The test now is whether we can transform the
'coloured' part of the Colonial Empire also into a commonwealth of free
and equal nations. This is obviously a more difficult task.[13]

The first attempt to undertake this task, to transform a part of the
empire of conquest into a dominion, was to end in failure when
Ireland repealed the External Relations Act, becoming a republic
and leaving the Commonwealth in 1949. The Balfour formula of
1926 had spoken of the Dominions as being 'freely associated' as
members of the Commonwealth. Yet Ireland had been forced to
accept dominion status in 1921 under duress, Lloyd George threatening the Irish delegates that, if they refused to sign the treaty, there
would be a renewal of hostilities against them. 'If the British
Commonwealth can only be preserved by such means,' the imperial
journal, the *Round Table*, had commented, 'it would become a nega-
tion of the principle for which it has stood.'[14] The Irish nationalist
leaders, with the exception perhaps of Arthur Griffith, were republicans, and, while they might have been prepared to accept association with the Commonwealth, they were unwilling to pledge
allegiance to the Crown or to swear an oath to George V, whom they
regarded as an alien king. Thus, especially after 1932, when de
Valera became prime minister, the Irish Free State began to whittle
away the links which tied it to the monarchy.

By the 1940s it was no longer possible for Britain to threaten war
if a country did not wish to remain in the Commonwealth. The right
of secession was first recognized by the Cripps draft declaration to
India in 1942. This declaration offered full self-government after the
end of the war, but also stated, in a clause of which George VI disapproved, that Britain would 'not impose any restriction on the
power of the Indian Union to decide in the future its relationship to
the other Member States of the British Commonwealth'.[15]

[13] MacDonald to Creech-Jones, 27 June 1947, cited R. J. Moore, *Making the
New Commonwealth* (Oxford University Press, 1987), 103–4; this book offers an
excellent account, based on primary sources, of how India's republican status came
to be accommodated within the Commonwealth.

[14] Cited in Ronald Hyam and Ged Martin, *Reappraisals in British Imperial
History* (Macmillan, 1975), 204.

[15] John W. Wheeler-Bennett, *King George VI: His Life and Reign* (Macmillan,
1958), 697 and n.

After the war, Burma declared that it wished to secede from the Commonwealth. In the first explicit acknowledgement of the right of secession, Attlee told the House of Commons on 5 November 1947 that

The British Commonwealth of Nations is a free association of peoples, not a collection of subject nations. When, therefore, after due consideration, the elected representatives of the people of Burma chose independence, it was, I believe, the duty of Her Majesty's Government to take the necessary steps to implement this decision'.[16]

Burma duly left the Commonwealth in 1948, and this raised concern lest the other Asian colonies follow suit. If the newly independent countries of Asia and then of Africa were to be encouraged to retain Commonwealth membership, then the Commonwealth would have to make a fundamental alteration in its constitutional structure.

The Commonwealth, as has been seen, had only one formal link, the Crown, but has held together informally by the links of a common political culture and common traditions of thought. These informal links were powerful enough to bind together the colonies of settlement, but were much weaker in the colonies of conquest, where the Crown symbolized not so much voluntary allegiance but domination. The Irish saw themselves, as the Indians were to do, not as children of the mother country, but as themselves a mother country, belonging as they did to a nation as old as, if not older than, Britain itself; and as a mother country which had itself peopled countries overseas with its children. When, in 1948, the Irish prime minister, J. A. Costello, explained why he wished to abolish the final link between the Irish state and the monarchy, he referred to a long history of domination by Britain.

During all that period, the Crown was a symbol of a political and religious ascendancy and became anathema to the vast majority of the Irish people. The harp without the Crown symbolised the ideal of Irish independence and nationhood. The harp beneath the Crown was the symbol of conquest. The bitter facts of history have inevitably prevented our people from having that outlook which the people of the great self-governing Members of the British Commonwealth of Nations may have for the Crown as their traditional link . . . The question had become . . . whether our constitutional arrangements relating to these matters were in a form which the people as a whole could accept as being compatible with national sentiment and

---

[16] House of Commons, vol. 443, col. 1836.

historical tradition . . . Irish national instincts, deep-rooted in history, recoiled from the forms which were to them, not the embodiment of their national pride in the social structure, but the symbol of centuries of civil and religious persecution and confiscation . . .[17]

Similar sentiments would be likely to animate India and the other non-white countries in the Empire in Asia and Africa. When they came to achieve Dominion status, they also would regard the Crown as an alien symbol. Would it be possible for them to remain in the Commonwealth as republics? A precedent seemed available to allow for this possibility if the member states of the Commonwealth wished to avail themselves of it.

When Ireland had passed the External Relations Act in 1936, and a republican constitution in 1937, the Dominions had been prepared to say that it made no difference to Ireland's membership of the Commonwealth. Yet, had not Ireland for most practical purposes become a republic?

One reason [declared Malcolm MacDonald in 1947] why I advised the Cabinet to adopt that line [that the new constitution should not put Eire outside the Commonwealth] was that it seemed likely that when the time came for India, Burma and other non-white countries in the Empire to attain dominion status, some, at least, of them would adopt a similar attitude as the Southern Irish towards the British Crown.[18]

Admittedly, Ireland was to leave the Commonwealth on declaring itself a republic in 1949. But there was an important difference between Ireland and India: Ireland did not wish to remain within the Commonwealth while India did. As the cabinet secretary, Sir Norman Brook, put it: 'India decided to become a republic but desired, despite this, to remain within the Commonwealth. Eire decided to leave the Commonwealth and finally declared herself a republic for that very purpose.'[19]

The Balfour formula, given statutory form in the Statute of Westminster, prescribed allegiance to the Crown as the formal link between the member states of the Commonwealth. Yet the whole ethos of the Commonwealth was based less on formal ties than upon

[17] Cited in K. C. Wheare, *The Constitutional Structure of the Commonwealth* (Oxford University Press, 1960), 155. Costello was speaking to the Canadian Bar Association in September 1948.

[18] MacDonald to Creech Jones, 27 June 1947, cited in Moore, *Making the New Commonwealth*, 104.

[19] Sir Norman Brook to Sir William Murrie, 3 May 1949, PRO CAB 21/1840.

a willingness to co-operate. The Statute of Westminster itself was an *ex post facto* recognition of a constitutional situation that had already been achieved. Most of the leaders of the Commonwealth in the late 1940s believed that the Balfour formula should not be allowed to put the Commonwealth within a formal strait-jacket. An ex-colony which sought to remain within the Commonwealth and was prepared to accept the practical obligations of co-operation ought not to be excluded simply through an obsession with constitutional forms.

The issue arose in concrete form when India, which had achieved independence in 1947, declared that it proposed to enact a republican constitution, but nevertheless wished to remain in the Commonwealth. There were strong practical arguments for accepting India as a member of the Commonwealth. Britain stood to make gains in terms of trade and investment, and the Commonwealth as a whole had an interest in keeping India out of the Communist orbit during the Cold War era. India, for its part, sought the security of membership in what was then an influential international grouping, and it would be difficult for it to remain comfortably outside the Commonwealth while its enemy Pakistan remained a member. Yet these practical arguments were not perhaps fundamental in the decision to allow republican India to remain within the Commonwealth. More important by far was the spirit of the imperial and Commonwealth experience. Had the other members of the Commonwealth declined to accept a republic as a member, they would in effect have been declaring the Commonwealth to be a white man's club. This would have been inconsistent with the principles upon which the Empire and the Commonwealth had been constructed. As early as 1854, the British government, in establishing representative institutions in Cape Colony, had insisted on a 'colour-blind' franchise. There was to be a common roll of voters, subject only to a financial qualification but not to one of colour. The implication of this was that the coloured as well as the white races would eventually achieve self-government and so be eligible to join the Commonwealth. In this decision lay the germ of the multi-racial Commonwealth. In 1897 Joseph Chamberlain, as colonial secretary, had asked the colonial representatives at the Colonial Conference 'to bear in mind the tradition of Empire, which makes no distinction in favour of, or against, race or colour'.[20] Thus, for the Commonwealth to make a

[20] Cited in M. Rajan, *Transformation of the Commonwealth: Reflections on the Asian–African Contribution* (Asia Publishing House, London, 1963).

decision which implied that only white nations could be members would be to go against its whole history.

To regard the Commonwealth as essentially European in race and British in culture and outlook [Sir Norman Brook declared] would, indeed, be wholly inconsistent with our Colonial policy, which contemplated, as an aim of political development, the ultimate attainment by the dependent territories of responsible self-government within the British Commonwealth'.[21]

It had also become a principle of the Commonwealth that its member states, being equal in status and freely associated, had the right to choose their own form of government. How, then, could India and the other Asian and African members be denied the right to choose a republican form of government and yet to remain in the Commonwealth if they wished to do so? The non-white colonies were achieving independence after the white colonies. Why should they be required to accept rules and conventions created for the older white members?

How could a nationally self-conscious people with separate cultural traditions be associated with the Commonwealth? The Irish answer, first put forward by de Valera in 1921 and given legislative form by him in 1936, was external association. India, however, declared that it was unable to accept any constitutional role for the Crown at all, not even external association on the Irish model. The Indian Constitution, India's first prime minister, Pandit Nehru explained, 'categorically declared that all the President's powers flowed from the people. There was strong feeling in India against any powers being derived from outside.'[22] But Nehru's

idea of the Commonwealth was one that must continually grow and change and that the time had come to fit Republics into it. . . . It was friendship and the acceptance of mutual voluntary obligations that really constituted the Commonwealth. Of this the Crown had been the symbol but the reality was the friendship. If friendship went there would be no Commonwealth, even were the Crown to remain.[23]

But, if the Indian answer was to be that republics should be admitted to the Commonwealth, what link would hold it together?

[21] Cited in Moore, *Making the New Commonwealth*, 107.
[22] Cited in ibid. 185.
[23] Report by Patrick Gordon Walker, Under-Secretary of State for Commonwealth Relations, of conversation with Nehru, 30 Mar. 1949, PRO CAB 21/1821, fo. 142, para. 11.

The link was found, not in allegiance to the Crown, but in recognition of the sovereign as Head of the Commonwealth. This was embodied in what has become known as the London Declaration, issued in 1949 by the Commonwealth Conference meeting in London, a declaration that has been called 'as important a document as any in the history of the development of the British Empire; it is to be numbered in importance with the Balfour Formula of 1926 and with the Statute of Westminster itself'.[24]

The Declaration began by noting the existing structure of the Commonwealth, whose members owed 'a common allegiance to the Crown, which is also the symbol of their free association'. It then went on to note the position of the government of India, which intended to become a republic but had 'declared and affirmed India's desire to continue her full membership of the Commonwealth of Nations and her acceptance of The King as the symbol of the free association of its independent member states and as such the Head of the Commonwealth'. The governments of the other member states, the basis of whose membership was not changed, then declared that they accepted and recognized 'India's continuing membership in accordance with the terms of the declaration'. Accordingly, the member states agreed that they all remained 'as free and equal members of the Commonwealth'.[25]

The Declaration was made specific to India, which was thought of at the time as *sui generis*. It said nothing about whether other republican applicants for Commonwealth membership could be similarly accommodated. But, inevitably, the Indian example became a precedent, to be followed by other Asian and African members. In future, Commonwealth membership would depend not upon allegiance to the Crown but upon 'a declared act of will'.[26]

The provision in the Declaration that all the member states remained 'equal' members of the Commonwealth indicated that there would be no second-class members in the Commonwealth and that a republican member would in no way be in an inferior position to the monarchies.

The Declaration altered the constitution of the Commonwealth

---

[24] Wheeler-Bennett, *King George VI*, 730.

[25] The text of the London Declaration can be found, *inter alia*, in Wheeler-Bennett, *King George VI*, 730–1.

[26] Patrick Gordon Walker, diary entry, 10 Feb. 1949, cited in Moore, *Making the New Commonwealth*, 166.

not, as had occurred in 1931, by a statute, but by a declaration which had no statutory or binding force on the member nations. Until 1931, the Imperial Parliament at Westminster was also the legislative organ for the Commonwealth as a whole. After 1931, however, the Imperial Parliament could act as such an organ only at the request and with the assent of the Dominions. The admission of a republican member to the Commonwealth, however, meant that there was no longer any organ or set of organs which could legislate for the Commonwealth as a whole. There was no corpus of Commonwealth law, and, even if all of the Commonwealth monarchies had legislated for the change, that would not have bound India. The whole essence of republican status in so far as India was concerned was that the sovereign, the only essential link between the member states, was not part of the Indian Constitution and had no place in Indian law. Thus it would not have been constitutionally possible in 1949, as it had been in 1931, to pass a statute binding the Commonwealth as a whole.

III

'To evolve a system by which the Commonwealth could include nations of diverse races and traditions would be an achievement far surpassing any in the political history of the British race,' declared *The Economist* on 9 October 1948.[27] That summarized the consensus of the 1940s, and the London Declaration was greeted with approval as a striking example of the flexibility and adaptability of Commonwealth relationships.

The retention of India within the Commonwealth, and subsequently of the Afro-Asian members, led to a new conception of Commonwealth, the multi-racial Commonwealth in which, by the 1990s, non-whites outnumbered whites by around six to one. The Commonwealth became one of the few international organizations in the world to reach across differences of colour and creed and to unite nations at very different stages of economic development. The multi-racial nature of the Commonwealth was confirmed in 1961 when South Africa, about to become a republic, withdrew its application to remain in the Commonwealth. Had South Africa remained

---

[27] 'What is the Commonwealth?', *The Economist*, 9 Oct. 1948, p. 562.

in the Commonwealth, the other African and Asian members would almost certainly have withdrawn, while the newly independent African states would not have sought to remain. The Commonwealth would thus have reverted to being a white man's club, the very outcome which the London Declaration had been instituted to prevent.

A crucial consequence, however, of the development of the multi-racial Commonwealth was that it became, inevitably, a more amorphous body, no longer united by the pursuit of common aims or ideals, except of the most general kind, and without specific obligations attached to membership.

On 9 October 1948, six months before the London Declaration, in an authoritative article entitled 'What is the Commonwealth?', *The Economist* suggested that membership of the Commonwealth imposed six obligations of membership. They were, first, 'an acceptance of the rules of international law and a willingness to settle disputes with other members of the Commonwealth by discussion, conciliation or arbitration'. However, the Commonwealth has no power to arbitrate between member states except with their consent, and so it has often been unable to settle disputes between members.

The second principle was respect for racial minorities, but here, too, because the Commonwealth has no power to interfere in the internal affairs of its members, its influence is confined to persuasion. Nehru in particular did not wish the Commonwealth to consider South Africa's discriminatory treatment of its Indian population, since this would confer the status of a super-state upon it.

The Economist's third principle was 'a readiness to pursue on the world stage, foreign policies that move on parallel or converging lines'. Until the late 1940s, Commonwealth members had consulted on foreign policy and collaborated on defence. When Eire declared its neutrality in 1939, it was, naturally, excluded from such foreign-policy and defence discussions. In 1950 there was a Commonwealth division fighting in Korea, and in 1951 one authority argued: 'It seems clear to me . . . that the Commonwealth would rapidly dissolve if there were not an unwritten sort of Monroe Doctrine pledging us to its defence.'[28] India, however, became a neutral, as did most of the African and Asian members of the Commonwealth. This

[28] H. D. Ziman, 'The Major Purpose of the Commonwealth', *The Times*, 12 Jan. 1951.

made a common foreign policy impossible and it meant that the fourth principle also, 'a willingness to undertake defensive commitments in accordance with a policy worked out by and for the whole Commonwealth', was no longer practicable. Indeed, the Commonwealth has endured wars between its members—India and Pakistan have fought each other four times since independence—and a breach in diplomatic relations between members—Britain itself broke diplomatic relations with Idi Amin's Uganda, following the murder of a British citizen in Entebbe in 1976.

The fifth principle was 'an undertaking not to pursue unilateral economic policies without regard for their effect upon the other nations of the Commonwealth'. The old Commonwealth had been bound together by the Ottawa agreements of 1932 by which its members agreed to grant tariff preferences to each other. But the General Agreement on Tariffs and Trade (GATT) in 1947, promoted by the United States, committed its signatories not to raise tariffs unilaterally and not to introduce new preferences. While it did not commit its members to the abolition of existing preferences, it made the Ottawa agreements more difficult to maintain. At the Sydney Conference of Commonwealth Finance Ministers in 1951, the new members, India and Pakistan, made it clear that they were more interested in American aid than in a common Commonwealth economic policy. Canada also was becoming more aligned with the United States. Thus it became impossible for the Commonwealth to continue to act as a single economic unit.[29]

The Economist's final principle was free movement within the Commonwealth. 'The essence' of the Commonwealth, one authority had declared in 1948, 'is to be sought in the negative proposition "In the Commonwealth we are not foreign to each other".' Yet this principle was already being undermined by the decision of the Commonwealth Conference in 1947 to accept a fundamental alteration in the provisions for Commonwealth citizenship. If each Commonwealth member could determine its citizenship provisions for itself, then each member could also determine to limit freedom of movement for citizens of other Commonwealth countries, as indeed they did.

Of the supposed obligations of Commonwealth membership, only common citizenship had been the object of precise definition and

[29] Julian Amery, *The Life of Joseph Chamberlain*, vi. *Joseph Chamberlain and the Tariff Reform Campaign* (Macmillan, 1969), 1046.

legislation, and this was already being redefined in 1948, before India was admitted as a republic. What then remained of positive content to be attached to Commonwealth membership? In 1926 the Imperial Conference had declared proudly: 'The British Empire is not founded on negatives. It depends essentially if not formally, on positive ideals. Free institutions are its lifeblood. Free co-operation is its instrument. Peace, security and progress are among its objects . . .'. As late as January 1951, Louis St Laurent, the Canadian prime minister, speaking at a Canada Club dinner, declared that the Commonwealth was a free association of independent nations which used to be linked together politically through belonging to the British Empire; and he added 'and now are associated because of a common attachment to certain political ideals'. It would not be possible to add that corollary today, for, although the Commonwealth may proclaim various political ideals, failure by a member to live up to these ideals does not at present entail any action by the Commonwealth, which cannot interfere in the internal affairs of any member state. So it is that, although the vast majority of Commonwealth members are democracies, Commonwealth membership has survived dictatorship and the ill treatment of minorities. However, a demonstrable willingness to abide by certain fundamental political values is becoming a condition of successful entry to the club. The Auckland Heads of Commonwealth Government meeting in 1995 will be considering whether the Commonwealth should move closer towards becoming a rule-governed association. If it does, that would signify an important change in the character and purpose of the commonwealth.

The decision to make republican status compatible with Commonwealth membership was to determine the structure and nature of the modern Commonwealth. Its leaders decided to create a multiracial Commonwealth, even if it were to prove more amorphous and with less unity of purpose than the old white Commonwealth. Critics have complained, since the 1960s, that the links were too feeble to sustain the organization; yet these criticisms have always been muted by a feeling that the creation of a multi-racial Commonwealth was in some elusive and perhaps ultimately unfathomable sense the fulfilment of an imperial destiny—the transformation of the largest empire the world has ever seen into a free and voluntary association comprising one-quarter of the world's population. 'In all history', the queen declared to the City of London during the Silver Jubilee celebrations on 7 June 1977, 'this has no precedent.'

IV

At the London Conference in 1949 the title 'Head of the Commonwealth' was made specific to 'the King'. It was not conferred as a hereditary title and there was no indication in the London Declaration that it would necessarily pass to the successors of George VI. The presumption, no doubt, was that it would so pass, but perhaps, in the euphoria of achieving a formula which kept India within the Commonwealth, little thought was given to the matter.

Our only possible line about this [declared Sir John Rowlatt, the first parliamentary counsel] seems to me to say that this is an academic question to be tackled when it arises. If it is not an academic question, it is an insoluble one . . . If the succession to the Throne has to be changed, the nature of the Commonwealth tie will also have to be changed just as it was by the announcement of the 27th April [i.e. the London Declaration].[30]

George VI died in February 1952, less than three years after the London Declaration and before further thought had been given to whether the position of Head of the Commonwealth was hereditary. Upon the accession of Elizabeth II, however, Nehru, the prime minister of India, at that time the only republican member of the Commonwealth, sent her a message welcoming her as the new Head of the Commonwealth. On 6 December 1952 Elizabeth II was formally proclaimed 'Head of the Commonwealth'. The queen is thus Head of the Commonwealth not by right of succession but by common consent. The presumption must be that the successor to Elizabeth II to the throne will similarly, by common consent, be greeted as the new Head of the Commonwealth, for only the sovereign can fulfil the peculiar requirement of the position. It was established in 1949 as a specific bargain with the Indian government, which was unprepared to accept any place for the sovereign in the Indian Constitution, or to accept any Head of the Commonwealth with specific functions. It was explicitly agreed that the term 'Head of the Commonwealth' did not imply the existence of a 'super-state' which could have authority over individual member states. That is

[30] 4 May 1949, PRO CAB 21/1828, fo. 9.

the significance of the words 'as such' in the formula that the king was 'the symbol of the free association of its independent member nations and *as such* the Head of the Commonwealth'.[31] When Krishna Menon, India's High Commissioner in London, 'produced these words "as such" . . . the King . . . said to me in jest, "what am I now—As Such?"'[32] Menon, however, paid tribute to George VI's role in helping to obtain acceptance of the formula, telling Nehru, upon the king's death, that 'it is part of history that in the last few years he did far more than is known or need be said to help'.[33]

The sovereign thus exercises no constitutional functions in virtue of the role of Head of the Commonwealth, which is a purely symbolic one.

The first secretary-general of the Commonwealth, Arnold Smith, suggested that the secretary-general or the Commonwealth heads of government could collectively advise the queen in her role as Head of the Commonwealth.[34] Were this to be possible, there would be a real danger of conflict between the advice which the queen was receiving from her ministers in the United Kingdom and that from the Commonwealth collectively. In fact, however, there is no such danger. The position of Head of the Commonwealth does not entail any constitutional functions and so the question of who advises the sovereign in that capacity does not arise. Lester Pearson, Canada's External Affairs Minister, recorded that, with regard to the London Declaration, 'There was some suggestion that we [i.e. the Commonwealth prime ministers] should give him [George VI] collective advice on the matter but I demurred as it seemed that constitutionally we could not do so.'[35] Instead, the Commonwealth ministers agreed to call collectively on George VI but to have Attlee, as Britain's prime minister, read the Declaration on their behalf.

At the 1952 Commonwealth Prime Ministers' Meeting it was agreed

that it should be placed on record that the designation of the King as Head of the Commonwealth does not denote any change in the constitutional relations existing between the members of the Commonwealth, and, in par-

[31] Moore, *Making the New Commonwealth*, 190.

[32] Michael Brecher, 'India's Decision to Remain in the Commonwealth', *Journal of Commonwealth and Comparative Politics*, 12 (1975), 77.

[33] Sarvepalli Gopal, *Nehru*, ii. *1947–1956* (Jonathan Cape, 1979), 53 n.

[34] Arnold Smith, *Stitches in Time: The Commonwealth in World Politics* (Andre Deutsch, 1981), 236, 268.

[35] Lester Pearson, *Memoirs, ii. 1948–1957: The International Years* (Gollancz, 1974), 104.

ticular does not imply that the King discharges any constitutional functions by virtue of the Headship.[36]

When the sovereign speaks for the Commonwealth, he or she in general speaks on the advice only of the prime minister of Britain, although the text of the speech is sent in advance to the other members of the Commonwealth. This was the procedure followed in 1957, for example, when the queen spoke to the General Assembly of the United Nations as Head of the Commonwealth. On that occasion, 'The terms of her address had been accepted by all Commonwealth governments, including the Governments of the republics.'[37] Clearly considerable tact is needed in such situations so that the role of Head of the Commonwealth does not appear to be a mere extension of the queen's position as Queen of Britain.

In general, however, it can be said that the position of Head of the Commonwealth is not an office but rather 'an expression of a symbolic character'.[38] It has no separate constitutional standing or capacity. It is difficult to see who could evoke this symbolism other than the sovereign.

There are only two occasions on which the sovereign regularly speaks as Head of the Commonwealth. They are the Commonwealth and Christmas Day messages to the Commonwealth. The messages are not made in the queen's capacity as Queen of the United Kingdom, nor as queen of her other realms. They are unique in that they are delivered on the queen's own responsibility and not on advice. As a matter of courtesy, however, the messages and the speech will be shown before delivery to the prime minister of Britain.

In 1983 the queen's Christmas message aroused some disquiet since some objected to its concentration upon a Commonwealth Heads of Government Meeting in Delhi, which Mrs Gandhi, the controversial prime minister of India, had chaired. When this was raised in the House of Commons, however, Margaret Thatcher rightly disclaimed responsibility, declaring that 'The Queen makes her Christmas broadcasts as Head of the Commonwealth. She does not, therefore, make them on the advice of United Kingdom ministers.'[39] This does not mean, however, that the sovereign can speak

---

[36] Cmd. 8748 (1952).

[37] William Dale, *The Modern Commonwealth* (Butterworths, 1983), 38. Sir William had been a legal adviser to the Commonwealth Office.

[38] Cowen, 'Crown and Representative', lecture 1, fo. 22.

[39] House of Commons, 6th ser., vol. 52, col. 763, 24 Jan. 1984.

as he or she pleases when giving the Christmas message. Even though the message is delivered by the Head of the Commonwealth, the sovereign never ceases to be King or Queen of the United Kingdom and of his or her other realms, and must avoid giving offence to ministers. Thus the sovereign may not, in the role of Head of the Commonwealth, do or say anything which might disturb the constitutional relationship between sovereign and ministers. It is only on this basis that the gap in the convention of ministerial responsibility remains tolerable.

As Head of the Commonwealth, the sovereign is present, although not a participant, at the biennial Commonwealth Heads of Government meetings, and will receive heads of government separately in private audience, and offer them hospitality. The sovereign's attendance at the Heads of Government meetings, however, seems to be undertaken, by contrast with the comments of Arnold Smith, on the advice of the British government. In her memoirs, Margaret Thatcher records that, before the 1979 Meeting at Lusaka, there were

some worries about Her Majesty's safety, on which it was my responsibility to advise. My feeling was that there was no reason why her visit should not go ahead, and I gave that advice shortly before the start of the Queen's African tour, from which she went on direct to Lusaka where she received an enormous welcome.[40]

That seems a correct statement of the constitutional position. In 1973, however, the queen apparently insisted upon attending the Commonwealth Conference in Ottawa against the wishes of the prime minister, Edward Heath.[41] Heath presumably did not formally advise the queen not to attend, when she would have had no option but to accept his advice.

If the position of Head of the Commonwealth is to prove of value, it must be shown to be something more than a mere extension of the sovereign's role as King or Queen of the United Kingdom. Thus, such informal influence as the sovereign seeks to exert should not be merely on behalf of policies favoured by the British government. It is indeed widely believed that Queen Elizabeth II sees herself as very much the guardian of the Commonwealth connection.

Considerable tact and skill, therefore, are needed by the sovereign

[40] Margaret Thatcher, *The Downing Street Years* (Harper Collins, 1993), 74.
[41] John Campbell, *Edward Heath* (Jonathan Cape, 1994), 494.

to avoid both the Scylla of upsetting the constitutional relationship with ministers, and the Charybdis of appearing to treat the Headship of the Commonwealth as merely an extension of the office of King or Queen of the United Kingdom. The issue of sanctions against South Africa which convulsed the Commonwealth in the 1980s posed this problem in an acute form, for there was a period during which Margaret Thatcher stood alone in the Commonwealth in opposing sanctions. In such conditions the sovereign will be required to exercise great tact and forbearance. There is no way theoretically of resolving conflicts which might arise, but they can nevertheless be resolved in practice if there is a spirit of goodwill and co-operation. In the last resort, the ultimate test of any constitutional arrangement can only be that it works.

V

These two developments in the Commonwealth—the divisibility of the Crown and the special position of the sovereign as Head of the Commonwealth—created a new constitutional position which needed to be regularized in legislative form. The result was the Royal Titles Act, passed, not during the reign of George VI, the first 'Head of the Commonwealth', but during that of his successor, Elizabeth II, in 1953, the preamble of this Act declaring that its aim was 'To reflect more clearly the existing constitutional relations of the members of the Commonwealth to one another and their recognition of the Crown as the symbol of their free association and of the Sovereign as Head of the Commonwealth'.[42]

The Royal Titles Act formally recognized the divisibility of the Crown, which was already a reality in practice. In 1936 George VI had been proclaimed king 'of Great Britain, Ireland and the Dominions beyond the Seas'. There was, in theory at least, one Crown, which acted independently in respect of each of its realms. But this title was clearly no longer appropriate. Ireland had left the Commonwealth in 1949, while, for Canada, Australia, New Zealand, South Africa, Pakistan and Ceylon, the sovereign was as much their sovereign as he or she was the sovereign of Britain. Since

---

[42] See *The Title of the Sovereign*, Cmd. 8748 (1953), and, for a contemporary analysis, S. A. de Smith, 'The Royal Style and Titles', *International and Comparative Law Quarterly*, 2 (1953), 263–74.

all of the monarchies owed allegiance to the sovereign, there was no longer any justification for a generic title for the sovereign in which only one member state of the Commonwealth, Britain, was mentioned by name. In theory, a generic title for the sovereign which specified every monarchy in the Commonwealth might have been devised. In practice, however, such a title would have been too cumbrous to be of use. Moreover, the title contained no mention of the Commonwealth nor of the new position of 'Head of the Commonwealth' as proclaimed in the London Declaration.

The solution was found in the adoption of a locally variable title for the sovereign. At the Commonwealth Prime Ministers' Conference in December 1952, it was decided that each of the monarchies in the Commonwealth should be free to adopt its own title in a form suitable to its own local circumstances. Legislation on the royal title would in future be enacted by each of the monarchies separately rather than, as hitherto, by the Parliament of the United Kingdom with, since the Statute of Westminster, the assent of the other members of the Commonwealth. Each nation's title, however, must include a common element, designating the territory in question of which the sovereign was queen, stating that she was also queen 'of Her other Realms and Territories', and including the designation 'Head of the Commonwealth'. Accordingly, the Royal Titles Act, 1953, declared that the queen's title for use in the United Kingdom should be 'Elizabeth the Second, by the Grace of God of the United Kingdom of Great Britain and Northern Ireland and of Her other Realms and Territories, Queen, Head of the Commonwealth, Defender of the Faith'.

Thus the new title comprised a locally variable element with a common element. The locally variable element was designed to recognize the divisibility of the Crown, itself a product of the changed constitutional relationships between the monarchies of the Commonwealth. Without a common element, however, the link between the various monarchies would have appeared a merely fortuitous one. It would have seemed as if the Queen of Canada, for example, was only by chance the same person as the Queen of the United Kingdom, whereas the reality was that she was Queen of Canada *because* she was Queen of the United Kingdom.

The preamble of the Statute of Westminster had declared that

inasmuch as the Crown is the symbol of the free association of the members of the British Commonwealth of Nations, and as they are united by a common allegiance to the Crown, it would be in accord with the established constitutional position of all the members of the Commonwealth in relation to one another that any alteration in the law touching the Succession to the Throne or the Royal Style and Titles shall hereafter require the assent as well of the Parliaments of all the Dominions as of the Parliament of the United Kingdom.

At the time of the abdication in 1936, each Dominion had to consent to the departure in the line of succession for it to be valid. Since, however, the Commonwealth prime ministers had agreed, in 1952, that there should be a locally variable title, consent was no longer needed to changes in the local element of the title. For a short time after the 1952 decision, the custom was to consult before changes were introduced, but that custom seems now to have fallen into desuetude and today there is merely notification of changes after the event.

With regard to the succession, however, it was essential to retain a common rule so that the Commonwealth monarchies should not be a personal union over a fortuitous conglomeration of territories. When George, Elector of Hanover, became George I in 1714, he ruled over two kingdoms with different rules of succession—for Hanover prohibited the succession of a female to the throne. Accordingly, when Victoria became queen in 1837, the link with Hanover was broken, and Victoria's uncle, the Duke of Cumberland, became Elector of Hanover. Clearly it would not be in accordance with the relationship between the monarchies of the Commonwealth that there should be any differences in the rules of succession. It remains, therefore, a convention that any alteration in these rules must be agreed between all of the members of the Commonwealth which recognize the queen as their head of state. While, therefore, the Royal Titles Act had departed from one of the two principles enunciated in the preamble to the Statute of Westminster, that of the unity of the *title* of the sovereign, it would have been constitutionally inappropriate to depart from the second principle, the unity of the *person* of the sovereign. With a common rule of succession, then, in the words of Louis St Laurent, prime minister of Canada in 1953,

Her Majesty is now Queen of Canada, but she is The Queen of Canada because she is Queen of the United Kingdom and because the people of Canada are happy to recognise as their Sovereign the person who is the Sovereign of the United Kingdom. It is not a separate office . . . it is the

Sovereign who is recognised as the Sovereign of the United Kingdom who is our Sovereign.[43]

VI

The modern Commonwealth comprises, following the entry of Cameroon and Mozambique, fifty-three states, nearly one-third of the world's independent states. Its total population is estimated at nearly one and a half billion people, around one-quarter of the world's total.

Of the fifty-three members, sixteen are monarchies ruled by the queen, six are separate indigenous monarchies, while thirty-one are republics. (The members, with the date on which each became independent, and, where appropriate and where it differs from the date of independence, the date on which it became a republic, are given in Appendix 4.)

Membership of the Commonwealth remains open to any independent state which was once ruled by the Crown, or indeed any other independent state, subject to the consent of the existing members. Mozambique was the first country to join the Commonwealth which had never been ruled by the Crown and in which English was not the official language. The Commonwealth has, however, never refused to accept any ex-colony, and it remains unclear how many members would be needed to block entry. But in 1960 South Africa agreed that retention of its membership following the change to republican status required 'all governments . . . to consent', a consent that was not forthcoming.[44] The Commonwealth, however, has no constitution or set of formal rules and the only condition entailed by membership is recognition of the sovereign as Head of the Commonwealth. Otherwise, 'Members decide what they want to do, and then bring the rules up to date'.[45]

Almost all of the nations of the former British Empire have chosen to join the Commonwealth, the only exceptions being Ireland, Burma, the Sudan, which achieved independence in 1956, British Somaliland, which became independent as Somalia in 1960, Southern Cameroons,

---

[43] Wheare, *Constitutional Structure of the Commonwealth*, 167.
[44] Nicholas Mansergh, *Documents and Speeches on Commonwealth Affairs, 1952–1962* (Oxford University Press, 1963), 366.
[45] Wheare, *Constitutional Structure of the Commonwealth*, 119.

which became independent in 1961, and Aden, which became the People's Republic of South Yemen in 1971. Fiji's Commonwealth membership was deemed to have 'lapsed' after it became a republic following a military *coup* in 1987, and did not formally reapply.

Commonwealth Heads of Government hold meetings every two years, successors to the Imperial and Commonwealth Conferences, to consult and consider how they might best co-operate. In addition, Finance Ministers of the Commonwealth meet annually, while there are also frequent meetings of other Commonwealth ministers and officials. The Commonwealth has, however, no power to bind individual members. All decisions are made through a process of consensus, but it remains with the member states concerned as to whether to act upon them. In 1965, a Commonwealth Secretariat was established in London to service Commonwealth meetings, which had previously been serviced by the Cabinet Office. The Secretariat is headed by a secretary-general who enjoys a right of access to Commonwealth Heads of Government and to the sovereign as Head of the Commonwealth. But he or she has no executive powers of his or her own.

So large an agglomeration of nations as comprise the modern Commonwealth cannot hope to agree upon specific aims or policies. Nevertheless, contrary to what is frequently suggested, the vast majority of the member states are democracies. In 1991, forty-six of the fifty member states had elected governments, and four-fifths of the members had Bills of Rights or constitutional clauses protecting fundamental rights. In recent years, the Commonwealth has taken upon itself a larger role in the monitoring of elections and the protection of human rights; and, at the Harare Heads of Government Meeting in 1991, the promotion of democracy was explicitly laid down as one of the aims of the Commonwealth. In 1995, the Nigerian government, which was held to have violated the principles of the Harare Declaration, was suspended at the Commonwealth Heads of Government meeting at Auckland. Moreover, the Heads of Government established, for the first time, a mechanism to address serious and persistent violations of the Harare principles. This mechanism is an eight-member ministerial committee known as the Commonwealth Ministerial Action Group on the Harare Declaration (CMAG), and is currently composed of ministers from Britain, Canada, Ghana, Jamaica, Malaysia, South Africa and Zimbabwe.

To ask 'What does the Commonwealth do, what is its purpose?' is perhaps to ask the wrong question. The Commonwealth is an association which exists, not for any particular *purpose*, but for what it is, a group of countries connected by a common heritage and historical experience, and also by the English language. 'The Commonwealth', Professor David Dilks has said, 'is the only international organisation which has no need of interpreters.'[46]

The Commonwealth is best understood not as a functional international organization, but as a kind of international Rotary Club, an association whose members choose to confer together and in some cases to co-operate. From this point of view, what the Commonwealth *is* must be more important than what it *does*. Indeed, if it were to do more, its nature would change. If the Commonwealth had a specific purpose, and required its members to engage in specific activities, it would have to draw up a constitution and rules binding individual members. Then, when certain members did not fulfil their obligations, or found themselves in a minority, the questions would arise of whether they could remain within the Commonwealth. Under these circumstances, the Commonwealth would rapidly lose members as some states decided that they did not wish to participate in its activities or to be bound by its edicts. Thus, paradoxically, the more the Commonwealth did, the less cohesive it would become.

No member has ever been formally expelled from the Commonwealth, although Nigeria was threatened with expulsion in 1995 if she did not return to compliance with the Harare principles; and South Africa was *de facto* expelled in 1961 when she decided to withdraw her application to remain in the Commonwealth upon becoming a republic. She did so to avoid pressure from the other member states to modify her apartheid policy—pressure which, if it had been ignored, *would* have led to her expulsion. When South Africa withdrew from the Commonwealth, her Prime Minister, Dr Verwoerd, declared that this represented 'the beginning of the disintegration of the Commonwealth',[47] while Australia's prime minister, R. G. Menzies, claimed that 'a vital principle of Commonwealth association had been abandoned',[48] since the Commonwealth Conference

[46] This remark was made at a conference, 'Young Britain in the Commonwealth', held at Cumberland Lodge, Windsor, July 1994.

[47] Rajan, *Transformation of the Commonwealth*, 52.

[48] Cited in 'Crown and Representative', lecture 1, fo. 6.

of 1961 had discussed, albeit with South Africa's consent, the internal policy of a member state. This criticism of the Commonwealth's attitude to South Africa rests, however, on a misunderstanding of the *raison d'être* of the Commonwealth.

Far from disintegrating, the Commonwealth gained members following the withdrawal of South Africa, since the newly independent African states decided to join, which they almost certainly would not have done had South Africa remained a member. It was not possible for the Commonwealth to consider apartheid a purely internal matter, since the explicit announcement that those with a non-white skin would be treated differently from those with white skins offended against the very foundation of the Commonwealth relationship, the assumption of a free, easy, and colour-blind forum within which every member could meet together with the others in an attitude of friendship. It is true that there have been other Commonwealth regimes which may have caused more human suffering than South Africa. Uganda, under Idi Amin, for example, its president from 1971 to 1979, showed far less respect for human rights than South Africa in the worst days of apartheid, and in 1977 James Callaghan, as prime minister of Britain, made it clear to Amin that he would not be welcome at the Heads of Government Meeting of that year. But the activities of the Amin government, appalling though they were, did not threaten the very foundation of the Commonwealth relationship in the way that apartheid did. They did not undermine the club-like relationship between its members, since they did not explicitly claim that some members of the Commonwealth should be treated differently from others. The key issue which apparently turned most of the member states against South Africa in 1961 had been its refusal to accept non-white High Commissioners from fellow-members of the Commonwealth in Pretoria.[49] Such a policy was clearly incompatible with the relationships of friendship upon which the Commonwealth was based.

The sovereign is the only person likely to be acceptable as a permanent Head of the Commonwealth. Without him or her, the Commonwealth would have to agree upon who ought to be the head; if the Commonwealth were to seek an alternative head, it would be faced with almost insuperable problems. How would such an alternative head be chosen? The Commonwealth, not being a

[49] J. D. B. Miller, *Survey of Commonwealth Affairs: Problems of Expansion and Attrition, 1953–1969* (Oxford University Press, 1974), 156.

supranational organization, has no corpus of law which can bind individual members, and so no means by which it can draw up a rule of succession. Any change in the title of the sovereign as Head of the Commonwealth could only be made with the assent of all the parliaments of the Commonwealth.[50]

The only way in which an alternative Head of the Commonwealth could be chosen is by unanimous agreement of the member states at a Commonwealth Heads of Government Meeting, and it would be highly unlikely that they could agree upon an alternative candidate. Even so, the decisions of one Commonwealth Heads of Government Meeting could not bind its successor, and so the position of Head of the Commonwealth would be enveloped in uncertainty.

It is, moreover, highly unlikely that the Commonwealth could agree upon an alternative *permanent* head. Therefore, it would have to draw up a constitution providing for a rule of succession. The most likely alternative would be a rotating headship, comprising heads of Commonwealth governments. Tony Benn, the Labour MP, has proposed that it rotate quadrennially. But, with fifty-three member states, each country would provide a head only once every 200 years.[51] Moreover, a rotating headship would prove embarrassing were it to devolve upon an Idi Amin. Therefore, the Commonwealth would have to draw up certain standards which entitled heads of government to qualify for the position of Head of the Commonwealth. That would involve defining in fairly specific terms the object and aims of the Commonwealth association, and this would inevitably alienate some of the members. It could also involve dismissing some members as second-class members, and this would be incompatible with the basis on which the Commonwealth operates.

Thus the sovereign plays a fundamental role in preserving the club-like nature of the Commonwealth; and while there is no specific warrant for suggesting that the position of Head of the Commonwealth is inherent in the sovereign, it is difficult to imagine it being held by anyone else.

To choose someone other than the sovereign as Head of the Commonwealth would raise all sorts of difficult questions which are best avoided. Where would the new head reside? Clearly he or she could not reside at Buckingham Palace. Should the new head be a

---

[50] Wheare, *Constitutional Structure of the Commonwealth*, 159.

[51] See H. V. Hodson, 'Crown and Commonwealth', *Round Table* (Jan. 1995), 89–95.

peripatetic figure, travelling around all fifty-three Commonwealth countries? How would the budget for the costs of the Head of the Commonwealth be allocated? At present, there is no separate budget for the position and most of the expenses are subsumed under the Civil List voted by parliament to the sovereign.

Moreover, a Head of the Commonwealth chosen in a different way from the sovereign would seek a function, a positive role. He or she might well not be content to occupy a mere symbolic position without substantive powers. Without the sovereign as Head of the Commonwealth, the Commonwealth would probably need a constitution establishing a procedure for choosing a head. If that happened, the whole nature of the Commonwealth relationship would change.

Whoever was chosen, moreover, could not hope to emulate the symbolism evoked by the sovereign. It is, therefore, difficult to imagine the Commonwealth continuing to exist in its present form without the king or queen as head. Just as the position of the sovereign as Supreme Governor of the Church of England enables that church to continue to exist as a broad church eschewing a precise formulation of doctrine, so also the position of the sovereign as Head of the Commonwealth enables the Commonwealth to avoid contentious definitions or the exclusion of members who wish to remain. In a very real sense, therefore, it is the sovereign who holds together a diverse group of fifty-three nations with little in common except the English language and the experience of once having been part of the British Empire. As David Lange, when prime minister of New Zealand, declared, Queen Elizabeth is 'the bit of glue that somehow manages to hold the whole thing together . . . and I suppose it is to some extent a matter of worry that clearly her personality is a major factor to all of us in the Commonwealth. She does the unifying.' For this very reason, the Head of the Commonwealth can have no functional role 'which would be destructive of the bond'.[52]

But if the Commonwealth is held together by the symbolism of its head, the Commonwealth connection also serves to add to the prestige and authority of the sovereign. It has been said that,

As the world's only international monarch, the Queen has a glamour and uniqueness which renders the Crown virtually impregnable at home.

[52] David Adamson, *The Last Empire: Britain and her Commonwealth* (I. B. Tauris, 1989), 108.

Without the Commonwealth, the monarchy would sink into the humdrum homeliness of its Scandinavian brethren and its cost to the taxpayer would be increasingly questioned.[53]

Were the Commonwealth to disintegrate, the nature of the monarchy in Britain would not remain unaffected.

Of the title 'Head of the Commonwealth', a French-speaking newspaper in Quebec declared in 1983 that 'The solution to the problem is in the good British tradition; it is both efficient and devoid of logic.'[54] The same may perhaps still be said of the continued existence of the Commonwealth itself.

VII

Sixteen members of the Commonwealth, including Britain, recognize the sovereign as their head of state. These sixteen countries in order of population size are:

Britain	57,000,000
Canada	27,100,000
Australia	17,682,000
Papua New Guinea	3,800,000
New Zealand	3,400,000
Jamaica	2,550,000
Solomon Islands	319,000
Barbados	260,000
The Bahamas	254,000
Belize	191,000
St Lucia	153,000
St Vincent and Grenadines	108,000
Grenada	98,000
Antigua and Barbuda	78,000
St Christopher and Nevis	44,000
Tuvalu	9,000

It will be seen that the Commonwealth monarchies fall into two fairly well-defined groups. There are, first, the colonies of settlement—Canada, Australia, and New Zealand—and, secondly, a

[53] Ibid. 117.
[54] Cited in Elizabeth Longford, *Elizabeth R* (Weidenfeld & Nicolson, 1983), 127.

group of members of the New Commonwealth from the West Indies and Oceania. Of this latter group, only two—Papua New Guinea and Jamaica—have a population of over one million. Ten of the sixteen, all in the second group, are micro-states with a population smaller than that of Cornwall.

The sovereign is the head of state in all of these countries, but in all of them except Britain executive authority lies in the hands of a governor-general who is the sovereign's representative. In most of the fifteen overseas countries of which the sovereign is head of state, the governor-general is appointed by the sovereign on the advice of the prime minister, but, in the Solomon Islands and Tuvalu, the prime minister is required to consult the legislature 'in confidence', while the constitution of Papua New Guinea requires the sovereign to appoint the person who is elected by a secret ballot in the legislature. The governor-general communicates directly to the sovereign or via his or her private secretary, and not to the prime minister of Britain, with whom, since the time of the Balfour formula of 1926, he or she has no constitutional relationship. The governor-general can also be dismissed by the sovereign on the advice of the prime minister of the country concerned.

Since the powers of the sovereign are exercised by the governor-general in every country of which the sovereign is head of state other than Britain, there can be no danger of the sovereign receiving conflicting advice from the different realms. Although the sovereign is the king or queen of sixteen countries, he or she in general takes advice only from United Kingdom ministers. In Canada, Australia, and so on, it is the governor-general who takes advice. The position of the governor-general is in general regulated by the constitution of the country concerned.

The constitutional role of the queen in relation to those countries overseas which recognized her as head of state needed to be made clear in November 1975, when the governor-general of Australia, Sir John Kerr, in an exercise of his reserve powers, dismissed the prime minister, Gough Whitlam, in consequence of the inability of the latter to obtain Supply. Sir John Kerr, quite rightly, did not consult the Palace in the constitutional crisis which loomed over him, for the Australian Constitution vested the power of dismissal in the governor-general and not the sovereign. The queen had no powers to act, and would not have wished to become embroiled in the crisis.

My view [Sir John has recorded] was that to inform Her Majesty in advance of what I intended to do and when, would be to risk involving her in an Australian political and constitutional crisis in relation to which she had no legal powers, and I must not take such a risk.[55]

'Governor-Generals', he apparently told the queen, 'are expendable. The Queen is not.'[56]

Following the dismissal, the speaker of the House of Represent-atives, in which Whitlam enjoyed a majority, wrote to the queen ask-ing her to intervene in what he regarded as an unconstitutional exercise of power. The queen's private secretary replied to the speaker, however, declaring that

The written constitutional and accepted constitutional conventions [i.e. of Australia] preclude the Queen from intervening personally in those functions [given to the governor-general by the constitution] once the Governor-General has been appointed, and from interfering with His Excellency's tenure of office except upon advice from the Australian Prime Minister.[57]

Similarly, when, in 1983, Sir Paul Scoon, the governor-general of Grenada, acting in the absence of settled government, on his own ini-tiative invited American forces to keep order on the island, he delib-erately did not inform the queen beforehand. Had he done so, the queen would have been put in a peculiarly embarrassing position. For the British government, under Margaret Thatcher, was opposed to American intervention in Grenada, of which it had not been informed beforehand. Thus, the queen as Queen of Grenada would have been in possession of knowledge which she could not, as Queen of the United Kingdom, pass on to her government. That would have compelled the queen either to withhold information from her gov-ernment, or to subordinate the interests of Grenada, as interpreted by her governor-general, to those of the United Kingdom. This does not, however, preclude a governor-general from consulting infor-mally with the queen's private secretary, and such consultations have on occasion saved governor-generals from serious error.

Even when the queen is in residence in one of her overseas realms, she does not necessarily take over the functions of the governor-general. There are occasions, however, when the queen, opening the

[55] Sir John Kerr, *Matters for Judgment* (Macmillan, 1979), 330.
[56] Robert Lacey, *Majesty* (Hutchinson, 1977), 300.
[57] Cited in Kerr, *Matters for Judgment*, 374–5.

parliament of one of the overseas nations recognizing her as its head of state, reads a Queen's Speech, written for her by the government of the nation in question. On such occasions, she speaks as the queen of the nation in question and not as the Queen of the United Kingdom. This can easily lead to misunderstanding. In 1994, for example, the queen opened the parliament of Belize, and, in the Queen's Speech, declared that law enforcement was not in itself sufficient to combat rising crime. Instead, government needed to get to grips with the real roots of crime, which lay in social conditions. This speech was interpreted by some as a criticism of the policies of the British government, whose home secretary, Michael Howard, had stressed the very opposite doctrine, that stiffer punishments were necessary if crime was to be combatted. The queen was, of course, speaking as the Queen of Belize, on the advice of her ministers in Belize and not as Queen of the United Kingdom.

When the queen pays a state visit to a country outside the Commonwealth, she is generally invited as Queen of the United Kingdom. This, too, can give rise to misunderstanding. In 1984, for example, the queen, visiting Jordan, made a speech which opinion in Australia felt was too pro-Arab, and did not reflect the view of the Australian government. The editor of a leading newspaper, the *Australian*, commented that:

There is no . . . formal understanding of her role when she is in a foreign country. And yet there is no compelling reason why, when she is in Jordan, she should be regarded as the Queen of the United Kingdom and not, to take but one example, the Queen of Australia.

It is not absurdly pedantic to suggest that this could lead to difficulties. It is unlikely that most of the world's inhabitants fully appreciate the intricacies of our constitutional monarchy and some of them may assume that, when the Queen of Australia in the course of her travels says something to which they take exception, she is speaking on our behalf.

A constitutional lawyer, Malcolm Pryles of Monash University, added that 'If the British Government continues to use the Queen in this way the conclusion must be that it is intolerable to have the same person as Head of State of two independent states.'[58]

The retention of the sovereign's position as king or queen of sixteen nations requires particular tact and understanding on the part

[58] Cited in George Winterton, *Monarchy to Republic: Australian Republican Government* (Oxford University Press, Melbourne, 1986).

of the British government in order that such misunderstandings should not occur.

By the Balfour formula and the Statute of Westminster, Commonwealth leaders sought to create in each Dominion a replica of the monarchical system in Britain. The main principles of the Westminster Model were transferred to the Dominions: the separation of the role of head of state from that of head of government who was responsible to parliament, and the conferring upon the head of state of reserve powers, generally of an undefined nature.

But the systems of government in these overseas realms were different from that at Westminster in crucial respects. First, the governor-general's powers are exercised under a codified constitution, while the sovereign's are not, although admittedly a number of Commonwealth constitutions do not codify reserve powers. But secondly, and more important, the sovereign is a hereditary monarch who is neither appointed nor dismissed by the government, but the governor-general is both appointed, and can be dismissed, on the advice of the prime minister who advises him or her.

The governor-general is intended to be a personal representative of the sovereign. Since 1930, however, the appointment has been made on the advice of the prime minister in the country concerned rather than the prime minister of the United Kingdom. In 1930, when the Australian prime minister, Scullin, proposed to appoint Sir Isaac Isaacs as the new governor-general, one of George V's objections to the appointment was that 'Sir Isaac Isaacs, who would be more than ever His Majesty's representative, was personally unknown to him'.[59] As late as the 1950s and 1960s, Menzies, as prime minister of Australia, discussed the various candidates for the governor-generalship with the queen and ensured that each of them was personally known to her.[60] He believed that the governor-general 'will stand in the place of the Queen and carry with him as he goes around the country some derivative atmosphere of royalty. In other words, the presence of a Governor-General should evoke some at least of the emotions which we have when we contemplate the Crown.'[61]

[59] Nicolson, *King George V*, 480.
[60] Robert Menzies, *Afternoon Light: Some Memories of Men and Events* (Cassell, Melbourne, 1967), 256–7.
[61] Ibid. 258.

Three of the four governor-generals nominated by Menzies were British. His fourth, Lord Casey, was an Australian citizen who held a British peerage. Since Casey, however, appointed in 1965, none of the governor-generals could have been said to be on terms of close acquaintance with the queen before appointment. The danger of appointing a citizen of the country concerned, however, is that the governor-generalship could become a party appointee, and so partial to the government which had made the appointment. Yet the governor-general, like the sovereign, must remain impartial and aloof from political controversy. But, unlike the sovereign, the governor-general may have a party history. In 1977 Sir Keith Holyoake, a former prime minister of New Zealand, who had left office as recently as 1972, was appointed governor-general. In 1969 John Gorton, prime minister of Australia, advised the appointment of his defeated rival for the Liberal leadership, Paul Hasluck. In 1989 Bob Hawke advised the appointment of his predecessor as Labor leader, Bill Hayden. Holyoake, Hasluck, and Hayden all acted with complete impartiality and yet it is a weakness of the constitutional arrangements that a prime minister could advise the appointment of a governor-general for purely partisan reasons. That, in the view of Sir Fred Phillips, a former governor of St Kitts/Nevis/Anguilla, is what has happened in the West Indies, where heads of government, in appointing governor-generals, 'appear in the main to have been motivated by narrow party political concerns. Thus the successful appointee becomes less capable of symbolising the total unity of the nation.'[62] One reform which would prevent the governor-generalship being used as a partisan appointment would be to require that advice to the sovereign on whom to appoint be accompanied by a statement that the candidate in question is acceptable to the opposition.

It is a paradox, then, that the Balfour formula, which was an attempt to assimilate the position of the sovereign and the governor-general, actually had the effect of making the offices more different than they had been before. The governor-general's task, in the words of Sir Ninian Stephen, a former governor-general of Australia, is not so much to represent the sovereign in Australia, as to represent 'the Australian nation to the people in Australia'.[63]

[62] Fred Phillips, *West Indies Constitutions: Post-Independence Reform* (Oceana, New York, 1985), 319.

[63] Brian Galligan, 'Regularising the Australian Republic', *Australian Journal of Political Science*, 28 (1993), 59.

A governor-general can be dismissed by the sovereign on the advice of the country concerned. The first such dismissal occurred in 1932, when de Valera, the Irish prime minister, advised George V to dismiss James McNeill, the governor-general, for attending an official reception at the French legation as a representative of the Crown, of which he, de Valera, as a republican, disapproved. De Valera then appointed Donal Buckley, an otherwise unknown crony from his Fianna Fáil party, who could be relied upon to act as *locum tenens* until the office was abolished in 1936. Installed in a private house not at the vice-regal lodge, Buckley abstained entirely from the ceremonial and social duties normally associated with the office.[64]

Such drastic action [it has been said] was quite at variance with the tradition of the independence and party neutrality of the King's representative: the removal under the particular circumstances violated one aspect of this tenure, the new and partisan appointment violated another. This unsavoury precedent stands, however, as a menace to the tenure of all future governors.[65]

Unsavoury or not, however, de Valera's actions created a precedent. Between 1945 and 1991 there were no less than eleven occasions when a governor or governor-general was dismissed or retired prematurely. They were as follows:

Ceylon	1962
Grenada	1967
St Christopher and Nevis	1969
Grenada	1974
Australia	1977
Papua New Guinea	1977
Grenada	1978
St Lucia	1980
St Christopher and Nevis	1981
St Lucia	1982
Solomon Islands	1989.[66]

In Ceylon in 1962, the governor-general resigned following suggestions that he had been implicated in an abortive coup. In St

[64] Brendan Sexton, *Ireland and the Commonwealth 1922–1936: The Governor-Generalship of the Irish Free State*, (Irish Academic Press, Dublin, 1989), 138.

[65] R. McGregor Dawson, *The Government of Canada* (5th edn., University of Toronto Press, 1970), 152.

[66] List taken from David Butler and D. A. Low (eds.), *Sovereigns and Surrogates: Constitutional Heads of State in the Commonwealth* (Macmillan, 1991), 352.

Christopher and Nevis the governor-general resigned because he could not accept the advice of his government. In Australia in 1977, Sir John Kerr resigned prematurely, in order to allow the divisions caused by his dismissal of Whitlam in 1975 to be healed. Had Whitlam won the 1975 general election, Kerr would have resigned immediately.[67]

In Papua New Guinea in 1977, the governor-general resigned, following reports in a newspaper of critical remarks he had made to a minister. In St Lucia in 1980, a new government brought pressure on the incumbent governor-general to retire; but when in 1982 the former government returned to power, and tried to press the new governor-general to retire, he refused, and was dismissed, and the former governor-general reappointed. In St Christopher and Nevis, a new prime minister insisted on the dismissal of the governor-general who had been appointed by his predecessor. The 1989 case in the Solomon Islands is probably not a genuine example of dismissal or premature resignation: it was found that the governor-general was disqualified from his office, because he had neither resigned nor sought leave from the public service before assuming the governor-generalship, as the law required. He therefore stepped down, resigned from the public service, and was promptly re-appointed again.

In Grenada, two governor-generals resigned, in 1967 and 1974, following disputes with the prime minister. In the latter case, following demonstrations, the governor-general, Dame Hilda Bynoe, had promised to resign if the people wished it. The prime minister, Sir Eric Gairy, declared, however, that only he could decide when she should go and sought her dismissal. Dame Hilda, however, left the island before her dismissal could be acted upon. In 1978 the new governor-general selected by Gairy, Sir Leo de Gale, also resigned prematurely to go abroad, and Gairy nominated his former cabinet secretary as governor-general.[68]

The possibility of dismissal is bound to influence the governor-general in the exercise of his powers. Indeed, one Canadian scholar, reviewing a book on the reserve powers of the governor-general, has argued:

[67] Kerr, *Matters for Judgment*, 378.
[68] Butler and Low (eds.) *Sovereigns and Surrogates*, 198, 301.

it is not too much to say that in practice no 'reserve powers' can exist in a Dominion, for the simple reason that a Governor-General who persisted in refusing ministerial advice would be at once recalled on the advice of his ministry given direct to the King.[69]

This is to go too far, for there are a number of successful exercises of the reserve powers in the history of the Commonwealth. But, nevertheless, a governor-general may well feel constrained in the exercise of his or her reserve powers by the fear of dismissal.

If the Governor-General can, in effect, be dismissed by a Prime Minister, the Constitution is destabilised at its heart. Any Governor-General is liable to intimidation by a Prime Minister and the two offices of Head of State and Head of Government are apt, in practical terms, to coalesce.[70]

It was for this reason that de Valera in the 1930s believed that the governor-general ought to be elected, rather than appointed on the nomination of the prime minister. That, however, would not insulate him or her against dismissal at a time when the prime minister, supported by the legislature and the people, demanded it. The best solution would be for the various constitutions to provide for a fixed term for the governor-general, with dismissal being possible only on grounds of incapacity. A provision of this kind would do much to provide security for governor-generals, and so enable them more effectively to fulfil their constitutional functions as representatives of the nation, rather than appearing as mere nominees of their prime ministers.

VIII

The question arises whether the sovereign is bound to act on a request to appoint or dismiss a governor-general—that is, whether such a request constitutes advice in the formal sense. George V believed that in the last resort he had no alternative but to accede to Scullin's request to appoint Sir Isaac Isaacs governor-general of Australia in 1930.[71] Sir John Kerr doubts whether there is any such

[69] W. P. M. Kennedy, reviewing H. V. Evatt, *The King and His Dominion Governors,* in *University of Toronto Law Journal* (1938), 408–9; cited in *Evatt and Forsey on the Reserve Powers* (Legal Books, Sydney, 1990), p. ix.

[70] D. P. O'Connell, cited in Cowen, 'Crown and Representative', lecture 3, fo. 19.

[71] Nicolson, *King George V*, 480.

power to refuse a request to appoint or dismiss, and argues that, if it did exist, its exercise would be likely to 'draw a great weight of controversy immediately upon the Queen herself'.[72]

In 1932, however, the attorney-general, Sir Thomas Inskip, believed that George V could 'with complete constitutional propriety' decline to act on the advice of his Irish ministers in appointing a governor-general. Sir Clive Wigram, the king's private secretary, feared that de Valera, following the dismissal of McNeill, might either appoint himself as governor-general, or, alternatively, 'some rebel or murderer'. It was accepted, however, that, were the king to refuse such a nomination, he would have to be protected by his ministers in the United Kingdom; and Ramsay MacDonald declared that he was 'perfectly prepared to take upon myself the responsibility of giving His Majesty advice . . . not only on grounds of strict law but of high imperial policy'. De Valera at first contemplated appointing the Chief Justice to the governor-generalship, but the king indicated that he would not have been prepared to accept this, since he attached 'great importance to his Representative in a Dominion not combining the chief executive and chief judicial functions for any considerable length of time'. He also indicated that a committee of three, as proposed informally by de Valera, would not be acceptable either. Geoffrey Marshall is, therefore, in error in declaring that 'It seems to have been thought in 1932 that there was no choice but to comply with the de Valera government's advice.'[73] There has, in fact, been no occasion when the queen has refused to accept a request to appoint or dismiss a governor-general. That is not conclusive, however. It may be that the queen has always accepted such a request because it has always been legitimately proffered. This leaves open the possibility that a request may be illegitimately proffered, as might have been the case with de Valera in 1932. Suppose that a prime minister, facing defeat in a vote of confidence in the legislature or in a general election, were to request the appointment of a governor-general for the purpose of subverting the constitution. Suppose that, as could have happened in Australia in 1975, a prime minister were to seek to dismiss a governor-general in order to prevent his or her own dismissal.

[72] Kerr, *Matters for Judgment*, 331–2.
[73] Deirdre McMahon, *Republicans and Imperialists: Anglo-Irish Relations in the 1930s* (Yale University Press, 1984), 95, 98; Geoffrey Marshall, *Constitutional Conventions* (Oxford University Press, 1984), 175.

On 16 October, nearly three weeks before he was dismissed by Sir John Kerr, Whitlam told Kerr jocularly, 'It could be a question of whether I get to the Queen first for your recall or you get in first with my dismissal.'[74] When told of his dismissal on 11 November, Whitlam is alleged to have said, 'I must get in touch with the Palace at once', or 'I will contact the Queen'. He was told that he was too late, 'because you are no longer Prime Minister'. Whitlam always denied that he had made these remarks, but, at a press conference some hours after his dismissal, he declared that

The Governor-General prevented me from getting in touch with the Queen by just withdrawing my commission immediately. I was unable to communicate with the Queen, as I should have been entitled to do if I had any warning of the course that he, the Governor-General, intended to take.[75]

If Sir John had given his prime minister, let us assume, an hour in which to seek a dissolution or resign; and had said that, if Whitlam had not taken either of his courses within the hour, he would be dismissed, Whitlam might well have rung Buckingham Palace and asked the queen to dismiss the governor-general. Would the queen have been required to comply?

There is evidence that the queen would not have made a decision to dismiss the governor-general simply on the basis of one telephone call. Speaking as a witness to the Australian Constitutional Commission's Advisory Committee in 1986, Revd Haldane-Stevenson quoted a letter which he had received in 1982 from Sir William Heseltine, the queen's private secretary, in which Heseltine declared,

I can say that, while a telephone call from the Prime Minister might have frozen the situation, Her Majesty certainly could not, and would not, have acted on the basis merely of a telephone conversation to dismiss her Governor-General. Some formal instrument, whether transmitted by mail or cable, would most certainly have been required.[76]

The queen might even have delayed her decision in the hope that the crisis might resolve itself without the need for her intervention.

There is no evidence, however, that the queen believed that she had the right to refuse to dismiss the governor-general in such circumstances.

[74] Sir John Kerr, *Bulletin*, 10 Sept. 1985, p. 78.
[75] Kerr, *Matters for Judgment*, 358–9; *Bulletin*, 10 Sept. 1985, p. 78.
[76] Transcript of evidence given to Advisory Committee, 1 Oct. 1986, p. 333.

Let us, however, depart from the 1975 example, and imagine that a prime minister sought to dismiss a governor-general in order to subvert the constitution. Could the sovereign refuse to act on the request? If he or she did so, then the prime minister might resign. He or she would complain about 'colonialist' intervention from the United Kingdom, and there might well be a threat to the continuation of the monarchy in the country concerned. On the other hand, if the issue was clear and the sovereign was seen to be defending a constitution which enjoyed popular support, his or her action might be applauded.

The question remains open. To refuse a request to appoint or dismiss a governor-general would obviously be an action to be taken only in very extreme circumstances. Yet it seems possible to imagine circumstances in which it could be justified, in which the sovereign by acting independently could prove the means of saving the constitution and preventing the subversion of the democratic system of which he or she is in the last resort the guardian.

The sovereign may have other ill-defined reserve powers with respect to the Commonwealth realms. During the period of the military *coup* in Fiji in 1987, the queen sent two messages to the governor-general, whom she regarded as the guarantor of constitutional government on the island. In the first message, the queen declared that the governor-general remained the 'sole legitimate source of executive authority in Fiji' and expressed the hope that 'the process of restoring Fiji to constitutional normality might be resumed'. In the second, she acknowledged that the governor-general was unable to preserve constitutional government and was compelled to resign. The queen declared that she was 'sad to think that the ending of Fijian allegiance to the Crown should have been brought about without the people of Fiji being given an opportunity to express their opinion on the proposal'. Both of these messages were, of course, delivered in the queen's capacity as Queen of Fiji, and delivered, therefore, without advice, there being no lawfully constituted government in Fiji which could give advice.

It has been argued that the queen could have taken an alternative course, and that the governor-general of Fiji was not as committed to constitutional government as the queen believed. Accordingly, it has been suggested that the queen should have dismissed him so that the prime minister who had been deposed in the *coup* could have been restored to office. In a revolutionary situation, however, the governor-general might well have flouted the queen, and this would have embarrassed the monarchy. It is difficult to make judgements many thousands of miles away from the scene of action. Use of the queen's authority failed to save constitutional government in Fiji, and the episode indicates, perhaps, that, in the absence of local expertise, it is difficult for an absent sovereign to intervene with good effect.

IX

At the time of the Royal Titles Act, it was argued that, the Crown being divisible, the queen was just as much Queen of Australia, Queen of Canada, and so on as she was of Britain. Patrick Gordon Walker, a former Commonwealth secretary, argued in the House of Commons on 3 March 1953: 'We in this country have to abandon . . . any special sense of property in the Crown. The Queen, now, clearly, explicitly and according to title, belongs equally to all her realms and to the Commonwealth as a whole.'[77]

Gordon Walker, after leaving office, believed that, under the new dispensation, as he told the queen's private secretary in November 1954,

The Queen will have to spend considerable periods outside the United Kingdom which is but one of her Realms. It will become as natural that she should reside, say, in Canberra or Ottawa as at Balmoral or Windsor. It would be appropriate for the Queen during these absences to be represented by a Governor General (doubtless a senior member of the Royal Family) in the United Kingdom, as she is now represented by a Governor General in her absence from her other Realms.[78]

The *legal* reality of a sovereign of the United Kingdom who was equally sovereign of her overseas realms never, however, became a *practical* reality. The Gordon Walker suggestion of a peripatetic queen involved a misunderstanding of the constitutional role of the sovereign. The sovereign, as we have seen, is not merely a ceremonial or passive element in the constitution. He or she is able to exert an active influence through exercising his or her rights to be con-

[77] House of Commons, vol. 512, col. 199.
[78] Patrick Gordon Walker, 'Crown Divisible', *Twentieth Century* (1953), 428. See also *Patrick Gordon Walker, Political Diaries 1932–1971*, ed. Robert Pearce (The Historians' Press, London, 1991), 215. Interview with Sir Michael Adeane, 24 Nov. 1954.

sulted, to encourage, and to warn. A peripatetic sovereign could not possibly exercise these rights in sixteen different political realms. They require continuous involvement in the government of a country if the sovereign is to master the details and intricacies of political problems without which the rights to be consulted, to encourage, and to warn are worth little in practice.

Therefore, the sovereign is bound to spend the greater part of his or her reign in the United Kingdom. Visits to other realms can never be frequent enough to allow the continuous involvement necessary for political influence. Moreover, the costs of the monarchy—the Civil List and the departmental votes—are borne entirely by Westminster, by the British taxpayer. Therefore, the British people are bound to see the monarchy in a different light from that of the peoples of overseas realms.

Gordon Walker's suggestion of a British governor-general involves also a misunderstanding of the constitutional position. In the overseas realms, the governor-general, as we have seen, is appointed and dismissed at the request of the prime minister of the realm concerned, and has constitutional and statutory functions specifically delegated to him or her which the sovereign cannot exercise except by specific statutory authorization. The governor-general is not a figure who exercises certain statutory duties only at certain times when the sovereign is absent. A British governor-general, therefore, as proposed by Gordon Walker, would be a very different figure from his or her Commonwealth counterparts, so different indeed that the very title of 'governor-general' might perhaps be less appropriate than the title of 'regent'. The analogy which Gordon Walker sought to draw is, therefore, deeply flawed.

For these reasons, the hopes of Gordon Walker and of others that the sovereign was likely to be as much the sovereign of realms overseas as he or she was sovereign of the United Kingdom were never likely to be realized. The sovereign is bound to remain primarily the King or Queen of the United Kingdom. Residing mainly in Britain, it is only in Britain that he or she can perform the constitutional and ceremonial duties in person. In Britain, the sovereign is a working part of the constitution in a way that he or she cannot possibly be in an overseas realm.

That the sovereign would be primarily sovereign of the United Kingdom should have been already clear at the time of the abdication crisis. The eight interviews on the constitutional question were held between the king and Stanley Baldwin, not between the king and his Dominion prime ministers, who could play no role in the crisis other than by responding to telegrams sent to them by Baldwin. The Dominion prime ministers could advise the king only through their governor-generals, and they could make their views known only informally through their High Commissioners in London. But in any case the abdication crisis arose so rapidly, as constitutional crises have a habit of doing, that it would have been impossible for the Dominion prime ministers to have obtained the necessary information upon which realistic advice would have had to be based. There was no time for detailed consultation between prime ministers and indeed no machinery whereby the Dominions could advise the Crown on matters concerning them all. Indeed there is still no such machinery.

So it is that, despite the Royal Titles Act and the recognition of the divisibility of the Crown, the sovereign's primary role remains that of King or Queen of the United Kingdom. When the sovereign visits a non-Commonwealth country or even a republic within the Commonwealth, he or she generally speaks as King or Queen of the United Kingdom and not of any other country. This, as we have seen, can lead to misunderstanding, as it did when the queen spoke in Jordan in 1984 along lines which did not reflect the policy of her government in Australia.

It may be said, then, that, far from being equally the sovereign of his or her various realms, the king or queen is primarily sovereign of the United Kingdom. The United Kingdom is the country in which he or she resides and in which he or she is a working element of the constitution in a way that would be impossible elsewhere.

The Gordon Walker view of the constitutional presuppositions of the Royal Titles Act rests upon a misunderstanding of the political background which gave reality to the settlement made between 1949 and 1953. The Act presupposed, not that the queen would become as much a Canadian queen, an Australian queen, a New Zealand queen, and so on, as a British queen, but that Canada, Australia, New Zealand, etc. would, despite being independent and sovereign nations, remain 'British' in feeling. If they were to continue to feel themselves British, they would be perfectly prepared to accept a British sovereign who could visit their countries but rarely and who would remain an absentee head of state. These difficulties would be compensated for by the strength of the attachment to Britain, the mother country from which the settler nations derived. Thus the Royal Titles Act presupposed feelings of attachment to Britain on the part of those countries overseas which accepted the queen as their head of state.

Such a presupposition did not seem as unrealistic in the 1950s as it has since become. In 1953, introducing the Australian Royal Titles Bill to the Australian House of Representatives, Australia's prime minister, R. G. Menzies, spoke of the sovereign as passing on 'a crown that will always be the sign and proof that, wherever we may be in the world, we are one people'; and, by 'one people', he meant the British people.[79]

Menzies, Australia's prime minister between 1939 and 1941, and 1949 and 1966, was fond of referring to himself as 'British to his bootstraps'; in 1948 he had declared that 'the boundaries of Britain do not lie on the Kentish Coast, they are to be found at Cape York and Invercargill . . . If our great Empire . . . is in reality a living and breathing and everlasting unity, then we will no more question the movement of people from England to Australia than we would question a movement of people from Yorkshire to Scotland or from Melbourne to Perth'.[80] When Sir Edmund Hillary, a New Zealander, was the first, with Sherpa Tenzing, to climb Everest in 1953, New Zealand's prime minister, Sidney Holland, declared how proud he was that an Englishman had been the first to climb the world's highest mountain. Nor was this perception confined to politicians of the Right. In Australia, in 1953, Dr Evatt, the leader of the Labor opposition, endorsed Menzies's remarks. He expressed regret that the word 'British' had been dropped from the Commonwealth, saying that 'In this country . . . the word British means to us as much as it does to the people of the United Kingdom itself and of New Zealand and Canada.'[81]

With the growth of nationhood and multiculturalism in the overseas realms, however, such sentiments were bound to become archaic. Realization of the fact that the sovereign is bound to be an absentee head of state in overseas realms has given rise to questioning of the role of the monarchy, and it is one of the factors fuelling the republi-

---

[79] Cited in the Report of the Republic Advisory Committee in Australia, *An Australian Republic, The Options—The Report* (Canberra, 1993), 33.

[80] Quoted in Malcolm Turnbull, *The Reluctant Republic* (Heinemann, Port Melbourne, 1993), 61–2; Invercargill lies at the southernmost tip of New Zealand.

[81] Ibid. 63.

can debate in Australia. In the 1990s, Australia, which, in the 1950s, together with New Zealand, was the most 'British' of the overseas realms, is the most likely of all of these realms to become a republic.

X

The republican issue has come to the fore in Australia owing to the position of the Australian Labor Party, which has proposed that a republic be established by the year 2001, the centenary of the Australian Constitution.[82] Some have argued that Australian concern with the republican issue stems largely from the actions of Sir John Kerr in 1975 in dismissing Whitlam. But, controversial as that action was, it had no relevance to the issue of monarchy versus republic. The queen, as we have seen, was not involved, and had no constitutional power to act. She did not intervene in the crisis in any way, and it had never been intended that she should have the constitutional authority to do so.

The constitutional crisis of 1975 arose because of the peculiar provision in the Australian Constitution by which the senate enjoys the power to deny supply to a government with a majority in the House of Representatives. The Australian Constitution makes no provision other than a dissolution of parliament for a conflict between two fundamental principles of democratic government. The first, championed by Whitlam, is that a government is responsible only to the lower house and not to the upper. The second, championed by Kerr and by Whitlam's Liberal opponents, is that a government which cannot secure supply must either resign or dissolve. Precisely the same conflict could arise if the governor-general were to be replaced by a president. The 1975 crisis, therefore, could arise in exactly the same form, whether Australia were to remain a monarchy or to become a republic, except that a president would probably enjoy more security of tenure than a governor-general.

The real republican case in Australia is based not on what happened in 1975, but on two quite different arguments. The first is that an absentee head of state is an anomaly. The second, and perhaps more important, argument is that psychological damage is done to

[82] In 1994 Jim Bolger, the National Party prime minister of New Zealand raised the possibility of New Zealand becoming a republic, but this has not become a serious political issue in New Zealand as it has in Australia.

the Australian sense of nationhood through its dependence upon the symbols of another country. Of these two arguments, only the first is a genuinely constitutional one.

In Australia, as we have seen, the governor-general performs nearly all of the functions of a head of state but is not himself or herself a head of state. Therefore, so it is argued, Australia is not in reality an indigenous monarchy at all and the queen is not a genuine Queen of Australia. Australia, so it has been said, is not a monarchy but a 'governor-generalship'. The queen, it has been alleged by Malcolm Turnbull, chairman of the Republic Advisory Committee to the prime minister of Australia, is 'no more an Australian institution than the House of Lords or the College of Heralds. They had created Elizabeth a Queen of Australia, but they had not, and could not, make her an Australian Queen.'[83] The Queen of Australia resides in Britain and is supported by the British taxpayer, and the Australian monarchy depends upon British laws of succession which, in, for example, prohibiting a Roman Catholic coming to the throne, relate purely to British historical experience.

Since the queen's primary role is to be Queen of the United Kingdom, and since she never ceases to be Queen of the United Kingdom, it is primarily the United Kingdom that she represents when she travels abroad, rather than her other realms.

When she travels to the United States [to quote Turnbull again], or to Japan, or to the Middle East she does so only in her capacity as the British Queen. She goes to International Trade Fairs and promotes the sale of British goods, she has travelled to the Middle East and assisted in selling British weapons. She has even been to Strasbourg and praised the further integration of the European Community, a trading bloc of which Great Britain is a member and one which . . . has destroyed the livelihoods of thousands of efficient Australian farmers.[84]

In practice, it is the governor-general and not the queen who performs the functions of the constitutional monarch. But, although the governor-general performs most of the functions of the queen, he or she does not have the status of a head of state. Because the queen is the head of state, the governor-general does not enjoy the standing that is the due of a head of state, and, as a result, enjoys less access and influence than a head of state. In the mid-1980s, the governor-general of Australia, Sir Ninian Stephen, cancelled a visit to

---

[83] Turnbull, *The Reluctant Republic*, 68. [84] Ibid. 86.

Indonesia because Indonesia's President Suharto refused to participate in the welcoming party. In 1993 Stephen's successor, Bill
Hayden, visited France to commemorate the seventy-fifth anniversary of battles on the Western Front in which Australian troops had
fought. The highest French official with whom he came into contact
was the veterans' affairs minister and when he left he was escorted
by a member of a minister's staff.[85] In 1994 similar difficulties arose
when Hayden visited Kazakhstan and Mongolia. The governments
of those two countries approached the British Embassies in Alma-
Ata and Ulan Bator for an explanation of Hayden's status and for
an assurance that the queen and the British government had no
objection to Hayden's visit. As Hayden put it to his prime minister,
'You may find it curious that the Presidents of Kazakhstan, Mr
Nazarbayev, and Mongolia, Mr Ochirbat, had great trouble
comprehending my real status *vis-à-vis* the Queen of Britain (not
Australia).'[86]

Moreover, the governor-general is now appointed in most of the
overseas realms and can be dismissed at the discretion of the prime
minister. Given that the governor-general exercises most of the functions of a head of state, it can be argued that this is not necessarily
the best way to appoint someone exercising these functions. Suppose
the governor-general was in fact the actual head of state. Would it
be acceptable to the electorate in Australia, or indeed in any of the
other realms acknowledging the queen as sovereign, that he or she
should be appointed by the prime minister? Would it even be seriously proposed as a sensible solution to the problem of how to
appoint a head of state?

There is no doubt that, to modern eyes, the system evolved during the years 1949–1953 is an odd one. It cannot, as we have seen,
be understood without understanding the history of British colonial
settlement and the gradual growth of the colonies of settlement to
Dominion status and then full independence. It is not a system that
would have been created *ab initio*. However, the oddness of a constitutional arrangement is not itself an argument against it. There are
many odd constitutional arrangements, especially perhaps in Britain,
which work perfectly well, and are best not tampered with. What has
changed in Australia is not any increase in the oddity of the arrangements but an undermining of the presuppositions which made the

[85] Ibid. 221.   [86] *Sydney Morning Herald*, 13 July 1994.

oddity acceptable. The arrangements established between the years 1949 and 1953 are perfectly workable, provided that the will is there to make them work. The question is whether, in Australia, there *is* still the will to make them work. That is, at bottom, a cultural as much as a constitutional question and indeed the debate on the monarchy in Australia is cultural as well as constitutional.

If Australians no longer see themselves as fundamentally 'British', why should they accept a head of state who is fundamentally British. If they do not feel British any longer, then Australians are increasingly likely to regard the monarchy as an alien institution from which they must part if they wish to assert their independence.

'The republic', Malcolm Turnbull has argued, 'is about nothing more than asserting our national identity.' If that is so, then Australia is not only engaged, as Turnbull suggests, in a 'constitutional debate'.[87] It is engaged also in a cultural debate about what it is to be Australian, and about whether Britain is a country to which Australia any longer wishes to be closely tied. A. J. P. Taylor once asserted that the Empire 'had come into being as the result of British commercial enterprise and industrial success'.[88] So, also, it may be the case that Britain's economic decline, and its decline as even a medium-class power in the world, make the former colonies of settlement less willing to maintain a close connection with it. Subconscious attitudes of this kind probably play as important a part in approaches to nationhood as the more obvious constitutional factors. How a country's nationhood is expressed, after all, is affected just as much by feelings and perceptions as by realities. So it may be with Australia; and, where the link with Britain is a matter of controversy, as it was in Ireland and in South Africa, and is today in Northern Ireland, the symbolism of the monarchy, far from promoting unity and political stability, could prove a cause of disaffection. Ireland would probably have enjoyed a more friendly relationship with Britain had it been allowed to become a republic in 1921, rather than reaching that point by stages in 1949. The generous concession of a republic, politically impracticable though it may have been at the time, would have been a better guarantor of good relations with Britain than insistence upon retention of the Crown. It was a mistake that the British government did not make again in the case of India.

[87] Turnbull, *The Reluctant Republic*, 9, 10.
[88] Cited in Mansergh, *The Commonwealth Experience*, 126.

The progress of Australian nationhood, from the time of the Constitution of 1901, has inevitably involved the distancing of Australia from the British state. This progress has been an evolutionary one, the main landmarks being the Balfour formula of 1926, the adoption by Australia of the Statute of Westminster in 1942, and the Australia Act of 1986. The coming of a republic in Australia may seem but the last stage, therefore, in Australia's evolution towards independence.

In distancing themselves from the British state, Australians did not necessarily believe that they were distancing themselves from the sovereign who became Queen of Australia in 1952. Instead, they sought to assimilate executive leadership in Australia to the status of the monarchy in Britain. Yet, as we have seen, this attempt could hardly be expected to succeed. Therefore, so it is suggested, the only way in which Australia can become fully independent is to distance itself from the sovereign as well as from the British state—for the sovereign is fundamentally the head of the British state, and not of the Australian state.

If Australia decided that it wished to become a republic, it would be entitled to do so in accordance with its constitution. The attitude of the monarchy to such a change was well summed up by the Duke of Edinburgh, speaking in Canada in 1969 in words which are also applicable to Australia.

The monarchy [he declared] exists in Canada for historical reasons, and it exists in the sense that it is a benefit, or was considered to be a benefit, to the country or the nation. If at any stage any nation decides that the system is unacceptable, then it is up to them to change it. . . . I think the important thing about it is that if at any stage people feel that it has no further part to play, then for goodness sake let's end the thing on amicable terms without having a row about it.[89]

Were Australia to become a republic, however, this could have important consequences for the monarchy. Australia would be the first of the British colonies of settlement to become a republic. The example of South Africa in 1961 is hardly a precedent, since South Africa was composed of both British and Boer settlers—and by 1961 it was the descendants of the Boer settlers who were securely in

---

[89] Cited in J. D. B. Miller, *Survey of Commonwealth Affairs* (Oxford University Press, 1974), 421.

control. The Australian example might well prove a signal for Canada and New Zealand. If that happened, then the vast majority of the queen's realms overseas would be small island states. Papua New Guinea and Jamaica would be the only monarchies with populations above 350,000. Under such circumstances, the monarchy overseas might not survive for long except perhaps in those microstates which sought British protection.

And yet, paradoxically, such a distancing from the institution of the monarchy could easily coincide with continuing respect and affection for the person of the sovereign. The sovereign would remain Head of the Commonwealth, and many of the republics within the Commonwealth, especially perhaps in Africa, show, as was illustrated during the queen's visit to South Africa in 1995, at least as much respect and affection for the queen as those overseas countries which acknowledge her as sovereign.[90] So also, were Australia to become a republic, there is no reason to believe that this need coincide with any decline in respect or affection for the sovereign. Indeed, that respect and affection might even increase as the monarchy ceased to be a symbol of political controversy in Australia and instead became a symbol of the linking together of a diverse group of nations in the modern Commonwealth. In ending a constitutional relationship with the sovereign, Australians might strengthen their symbolic relationship with him or her, since that relationship would no longer evoke traces of an imperial connection of which Australians no longer wish to be reminded. For this reason the unravelling of the settlement made between the years 1949 and 1953 need not necessarily mean a total abandonment of the sovereign's international role. As long as he or she remained Head of the Commonwealth, the sovereign would retain an international perspective, and this perspective, extending to every continent, would still serve to distinguish the British monarchy from its counterparts elsewhere.

[90] The *Sunday Times* headline in 1986, alleging differences of opinion between the queen and Margaret Thatcher, read 'The African Queen'.

11

The Future of Constitutional Monarchy

Before 1914 monarchy was the predominant form of government in Europe. Only three European states—France, Portugal, and Switzerland—were republics. In modern Europe, by contrast, there are—excluding such mini-statelets as Lichtenstein—only eight monarchies. They are—besides the United Kingdom—Belgium, Denmark, Luxembourg, the Netherlands, Norway, Spain (where the monarchy was restored in 1975, following the death of Franco), and Sweden. Of these, the British monarchy, dating back to the time of King Egbert in the ninth century, is by far the oldest continuous dynasty, except, perhaps, for that of Denmark, and constitutes a prototype for other constitutional monarchies. The Dutch monarchy dates back to the sixteenth century, but other monarchies have a much shorter continuous existence:

Belgium	1830
Luxembourg	1890
Norway	1905
Spain	1975
Sweden	1810.

Monarchy, then, in Europe is a survival. Is it also an anachronism?

It is noticeable that the countries in Europe in which monarchy has survived are amongst the most stable and the most prosperous in the world. One cannot, of course, draw the conclusion that they are stable *because* they are monarchies. It is, rather, more likely that certain countries have retained their monarchies because, enjoying a stable and continuous evolution towards parliamentary democracy, they found no need to alter the form of the state. The absence of ideological conflict in the progress towards democracy was also, no doubt, an important factor in assisting their economic progress. Thus the same factor in the political cultures of the constitutional monarchies which have made for their stability have also persuaded them to retain their monarchies.

It was after the First World War that monarchy ceased to be the predominant form in European states. During the reign of George V, indeed, 'the world witnessed the disappearance of five Emperors, eight Kings and eighteen more dynasties'.[1] This was due less to the spread of republican doctrines than to the military defeat of the great empires of Austria–Hungary, Germany, and Russia and to the revolutionary upheavals of the period. Republics do not generally come about through adherence to republican doctrines. It is true that, for example, Italy and Greece have, in the post-war years become republics in a peaceful and constitutional manner. But states do not normally change their form of government in this way. In general, where republicanism has triumphed, this has been less as a result of conscious and deliberate choice than because the monarchy has been discredited either by defeat in war or by resistance to constitutional change. Republicanism in practice is adopted less because it seems an ideal system than because it is all that is left after monarchy has been rendered unsustainable. It is, as it were, a form of government *faute de mieux*, a lesser evil rather than a preferred alternative.

Moreover, the upheavals which have led to the establishment of a republic have rarely been conducive to progress or stability. After overthrowing the monarchy in 1789, France, with sixteen constitutions, has found it difficult, for over 200 years, to discover a stable form of constitutional government. The overthrow of the Russian Czar led to a short-lived democratic republic and then the long night of Bolshevism. In Germany, the abdication of the Kaiser caused the Weimar regime to be deprived of that symbolic underpinning which might have prevented Hitler's conquest of power, while none of the component parts of the Austro-Hungarian Empire, with the exception of Czechoslovakia, was able to secure stable or democratic institutions during the years between the wars, when, 'Emperors having been driven out, nonentities were elected'.[2] It is a mistake, therefore, to assume that the transition to a republic is likely to be a painless

---

[1] Harold Nicolson, *King George V: His Life and Reign* (Constable, 1952) 106.
[2] Winston S. Churchill, *The Second World War*, i. *The Gathering Storm* (Cassell, 1948), 9.

affair, mastered by middle-of-the-road constitutional reformers. It may begin in that way, but it also has the potential to unleash political forces whose contours can at present be only dimly discerned. To sacrifice a monarchy for a republic is not merely to substitute one person for another as representative of the nation, but to embark upon a change whose outcome, if history is a guide, is likely to prove highly uncertain.

Precisely because Britain has enjoyed a smooth progress towards democracy and has been a victor in two world wars, republicanism in Britain has remained, in the twentieth century, the concern only of a minority, and usually a very small minority. When, in 1923, the Labour Party Conference last debated republicanism, it was very heavily defeated by 3,694,000 votes to 386,000, while in December 1936, in the aftermath of the abdication, a republican motion in the House of Commons attracted only five votes.

Today in Britain, such republican sentiment as exists relies for its support upon the claim that constitutional monarchy underpins a series of values which hinder the modernization of the country. The monarchy, it is alleged, is a profoundly conservative institution serving to inhibit social change. As an institution whose roots lie firmly in the past, it reminds us too much of our history while failing to help us anticipate the future. Monarchy indeed legitimizes a political system which has long outlived its usefulness, and, because it symbolizes deference and hierarchy, it forms a powerful barrier against those reforms, both constitutional and social, which Britain so desperately needs if it is to be able to take its place as an efficient industrial society.[3]

This argument, however, is hardly possible to sustain in an international context. Of the continental monarchies, Denmark, Norway, and Sweden are markedly more egalitarian and socially progressive than Britain and they provide a higher level of social welfare for their citizens. Nor is it immediately obvious that Italy is more modern than Norway, or Portugal more modern than Spain. There is, therefore, no correlation whatever between republicanism and modernization. In Japan, moreover, a monarchy of a highly traditionalist kind has

---

[3] This argument comprises the leitmotif of Tom Nairn, *The Enchanted Glass: Britain and its Monarchy* (Radius (Century Hutchinson), 1988), a brilliant polemic. The same argument can be found in another republican tract, Stephen Haseler, *The End of the House of Windsor: Birth of a British Republic* (I. B. Tauris & Co. Ltd, 1993).

proved perfectly compatible with the development of an advanced and extraordinarily successful industrial society. It is difficult to argue, then, that the monarchy is a barrier against radical change. Indeed, an efficient industrial society can, as it were, use monarchy so as to sustain its legitimacy. Were they so minded, there is no reason at all why the British people should not take either the Japanese path to industrial success or the Scandinavian path to social democracy. If the Left has failed in Britain over the past three decades, it is the Left which is to blame and not the monarchy.

The monarchy, paradoxically, can be just as much of an aid to a reforming government as to a conservative one, for reform is bound to be, in the short run at least, disorientating. Monarchy, however, offers fixed constitutional landmarks and a degree of institutional continuity in a changing world, so that the costs of change come to appear easier to bear. Thus a government committed to social or constitutional reform might need the monarchy even more than a government wedded to the status quo. That, no doubt, is why in the past, with Lloyd George being the only exception, prime ministers leading governments of the Left—Gladstone, Asquith, Attlee, and Wilson—have proved such staunch royalists. They were aware of the strength which the legitimacy of the monarchy offered to a reforming administration of the Left.

Constitutional monarchy is a form of government that ensures, not conservatism, but legitimacy. A constitutional monarchy settles beyond argument the crucial question of who is to be the head of state, and it places the position of head of state beyond political competition. In doing so, it alone can represent the whole nation in an emotionally satisfying way; it alone is in a position to interpret the nation to itself. That is its central function, its essential justification and rationale; everything else is but embellishment and detail.[4]

Constitutional monarchy, then, yields continuity in the form of the state, and this can serve both to accommodate radical change and also to cushion disappointment. In the 1960s, Lord Hailsham declared of the British: 'We are a people that has lost its way.' During much of the post-war period, British governments have failed to secure the aims which they have set themselves, and yet the prestige of monarchy has remained high, cushioning the political

[4] See the review of Nairn by Ferdinand Mount, 'This Sceptred Isle', *Spectator*, 16 July 1988.

system from the consequences of failure. The stability of the British state during a period of massive decolonization and economic decline is indeed the most striking feature of British politics in the post-war years. It is, of course, impossible to estimate precisely the contribution that monarchy has made to this stability. Yet the symbolism of the monarchy was explicitly used as a form of adjustment to the loss of empire when, in 1949, the king assumed the title 'Head of the Commonwealth' in order to enable India to remain in the Commonwealth as a republic. From the standpoint of the 1990s, it is easy to argue that such an adjustment was too peaceful and cosy, and that the British people needed not so much a warm bath of self-congratulation, as a cold shower of political realism. Yet cold showers, while they often prove bracing, can also cause heart attacks which can be fatal, and peaceful adjustment to loss of empire did at least save Britain from the agonies of Fourth Republic France, where the very symbols of the state were shaken by the process of decolonization and by the ideological conflicts to which that process gave rise.

II

If the crucial function of the monarchy in a democracy is to sustain the legitimacy of the state, how is it best able to fulfil this function at the end of the twentieth century?

The only way to answer this question and to estimate the likely future of the monarchy is to understand its past. The most remarkable feature in the history of the monarchy remains the skill with which it has adapted itself to changing conditions. In Britain, the monarchy has been an institution which, behind unchanging forms, has seemed almost infinitely adaptable, even if at times this adaptation has seemed somewhat unwilling. George Washington would more easily recognize Bill Clinton as performing a similar function in the American Constitution to his own than would George III be able to recognize Elizabeth II.

The monarchy, as we have seen, first took on its modern, constitutional form during the reign of Queen Victoria, in large part against her wishes. It developed as an imperial monarchy, partly through Disraeli, who, in the Royal Titles Act of 1876, consciously sought to harness the monarchy to the growing force of empire and to the interests of the Conservative Party. But more important for the future than the title of Empress of India and the association with the Indian Empire was the association of the monarchy with the colonies of settlement, the self-governing colonies, the Dominions, at the Colonial Conferences in the jubilee years of 1887 and 1897. Then, during the reigns of George V and George VI, a less grandiose period than the Victorian era, the monarchy transformed itself into a family monarchy reflecting the domestic ideals of the British people. These changes are not perhaps surprising. Monarchy, like other political institutions, rests upon a social base. If the nature of that base changes, so also will there be changes in the constitutional conventions and relationships which affect the monarchy. Today, monarchy has to accommodate itself to a society which has ceased to venerate tradition, much less to regard it as a source of legitimacy, and a society in which deference is no longer a significant factor in politics.

It is facile to explain these changing aspects of monarchy through the notion of 'the invention of tradition' as if the institution has *consciously* re-created itself to meet changing social needs. Only rarely can institutions contrive to reinvent themselves in this way; more usually, institutions are the product less of contrivance than of a response to fundamental needs, needs perhaps of an emotional kind, strongly felt but often not clearly articulated. So it is with monarchy.

Both Disraeli and Bagehot had seen in their different ways that, under popular rule, the importance of the monarchy would become greater not less. Popular rule required symbols of legitimacy and these symbols were most acceptable when they were personal; a mass electorate needed the reassurance of a visible presence and a symbolic figure who could embody the authority of the state. Where that symbolism was not provided by a constitutional monarch, it would necessarily come to be embodied in a party politician or a former party politician or a figure who owed his or her eminence to the goodwill of a political party or parties. In certain circumstances, moreover, a hereditary and constitutional monarchy has proved able to hold a democratic society together. That has particularly been the case in multinational entities. The Austro-Hungarian Dual monarchy, for example, was held together largely by the person of the emperor, Franz Josef. From the seventeenth century, the British monarchy held together the union between England and Scotland.

In the late twentieth century in a quite different way, the symbolism of the monarchy forms a personal link, perhaps the only link, binding together the heterogeneous group of countries which comprise the modern Commonwealth.

Does the symbolism of monarchy have any role in the European Union, a grouping which has assumed the same importance in British life as the Commonwealth enjoyed a generation ago? European Union, by contrast with the Commonwealth, is unlikely to alter the constitutional position of the sovereign. In February 1993 Lord Tebbit asked how the constitutional position of the sovereign would be altered by the Maastricht Treaty. Baroness Chalker, a Minister of State at the Foreign and Commonwealth Office, replied:

The treaty in no way alters the Monarch's constitutional position in the United Kingdom. Nor does it impose specific duties on any individuals. Her Majesty would be entitled to exercise the rights set out in Articles 8 to 8*e* of the Maastricht Treaty. But in this, she would act on the advice of Ministers.[5]

The European Union does, it is true, affect the role of the monarchy in a broader sense, since parliament has chosen to transfer its sovereignty in a number of areas to European institutions. This means that the queen, as head of state, presides over a country which, by its own choice, enjoys less sovereignty over its affairs. Thus, while the queen's formal powers and influence remain the same, they are exercised over a smaller sphere.

This need not, however, undermine the position of the monarchy. It is worth remembering that, of the fifteen member states of the European Union, seven—Belgium, Denmark, Luxembourg, Netherlands, Spain, Sweden, and the United Kingdom—are monarchies. There is little evidence that the nature of monarchy has changed in any of the other member states, nor that the monarchy in those countries has ceased to provide a focus for their national identity.

The pace of European integration does, however, raise the issue of the modernization of the style of the monarchy. Since the 1870s, after all, the monarchy has been focused not only on Britain but also on the Empire and the Commonwealth. It has been an international and trans-continental monarchy. With British politics focusing more upon Europe, however, it may seem as if the monarchy ought also

[5] House of Lords, Written Answers, vol. 542, col. 43, 10 Feb. 1993.

to orientate itself towards Europe, to become a continental monarchy. The monarchy may have to develop new forms of symbolism so that the head of the nation can represent Britain as a member of European Union. Monarchy, after all, is essentially an institution of the imagination, as Disraeli and Bagehot so well understood. Perhaps today it needs its modern Disraelis and Bagehots who can help it to identify with Britain's continental commitment, and, in so doing, revivify it.

III

For much of the period between the reign of Victoria and the 1990s, the monarchy attracted to itself an allegiance that is difficult to explain in rationalistic terms. The sovereign seemed to be a magical figure, a human being, yet possessing qualities which set him or her apart from others. In 1956, four years after the queen's accession, an opinion poll showed that 35 per cent of the population believed that the sovereign had been chosen by God.[6] The ceremonial aspect of monarchy, the regalia, and the deference which monarchy attracted, all served to reinforce this sense of its magic.

There are signs in the 1990s that this period of the magical monarchy may be coming to an end. This is only in part due to the personal difficulties faced by some members of the royal family. It is highly probable that the period of the magical monarchy would have come to an end even without these difficulties, for the magical monarchy depended upon social attitudes such as deference and respect for authority, which have been passing away.

The long premiership of Margaret Thatcher between 1979 and 1990 saw a determined assault upon many of Britain's traditional institutions—the civil service, the BBC, the Church of England, and the universities. The monarchy itself did not suffer any such direct assault, but it nevertheless could not remain unaffected by the new forces of competitive individualism which arose from the political phenomenon known as Thatcherism. Margaret Thatcher summed up the spirit of an age, a spirit which declared that an institution could not defend itself simply by asserting that it had existed for a long time. Its defence had to be more utilitarian—what good was it

---

[6] Jonathan Dimbleby, *The Prince of Wales: A Biography* (Little Brown, 1994), 9.

doing. If an institution could not justify itself in practical terms, it had to be, not necessarily abolished, but at the very least radically restructured.

There is evidence that similar attitudes are coming to affect the monarchy. In the reigns of Victoria, of George V and of George VI, and during the first part of the reign of Elizabeth II, it was sufficient justification for monarchy for it to be *seen*. It was not expected to justify itself in practical terms. Indeed the search for justification would have seemed positively harmful, since it would have detracted from the magic of the institution. What we are likely to see in the future, however, is the continued erosion of the magical monarchy and an emphasis upon the more practical aspects of monarchy.

Two of the now largely symbolic roles that have underpinned the monarchy—the sovereign as Supreme Governor of the Church of England and the sovereign as Head of the Commonwealth—may well come to be eroded if not removed entirely. The relationship between the sovereign and the Church of England has, as we have seen, come to be almost wholly symbolic and ceremonial as the notion of establishment has been drained of its content in a society in which formal religious observance and even perhaps folk religion have come to decline in importance. The relationship between the sovereign and the Commonwealth has also become less central to British life, and probably less central also to the life of the other member states. It would not be difficult, therefore, to envisage a slimmed-down and secular monarchy confined to Britain, a monarchy which was no longer associated with religion and no longer international.

Whether these developments occur or not does not, of course, depend primarily upon the monarchy. They are not matters that the monarchy can determine. The monarchy can neither ensure that they occur nor prevent them from occurring. Whether the monarchy becomes a purely secular institution depends, not on the activities of the queen nor on those of other members of the royal family, but on broader social and international trends from which monarchy cannot stay aloof.

If the magical monarchy comes to be replaced by the practical monarchy, many of our standard ideas about monarchy may have to undergo revision. In the past, monarchy has been an institution that has remained at a distance from those over whom it reigns. The distance was needed to preserve the magic. Under a practical monarchy, however, distance may no longer be either possible or desirable. The monarchy will come to be seen as a part of society and it will come to be judged in a more practical and utilitarian manner. Wonderment at the magic of monarchy will come to be replaced by hard-headed questions: 'What good does it do?' 'What is the use of it?' These are not questions which the monarchy need necessarily find it difficult to answer.

In the past, part of the very strength of the monarchy lay in its remoteness. 'Always remember who you are,' George V told his son, the future Edward VIII, warning him against too close a contact with his subjects. The mystique of monarchy would be preserved, so it was thought, only if royalty remained on a pedestal, unapproachable and untouchable. While such a conception of monarchy may have been right for an era marked by deference and respect for the past, the spirit of the modern age has now rendered it inappropriate.

The fundamental case for constitutional monarchy is that, under it, the head of state is free from party ties. This is of particular importance in the twentieth century, when the scope of party politics has widened until it has seemed to embrace almost every aspect of national life, choking all too many activities in its unnatural embrace. That the symbol of the state should remain uncontaminated by political controversy remains, therefore, something of inestimable value.

But the monarchy is not merely a piece of constitutional machinery. The sovereign, as well as being the head of state, is also head of the nation, the representative symbol of the United Kingdom. It is best that this symbolism lies in the hands of someone without political power and without a political history, for any head of state with party ties can all too easily divide rather than unite the nation. Since 1952, it has been the queen who has been able to interpret the nation to itself. It is difficult to imagine who else could have done it so successfully during a period in which, in general, politicians and other public figures have not been held in high repute.

In modern times, fulfilment of the role of head of the nation requires that monarchy, far from relying on its remoteness to sustain its mystique, must, while retaining its political neutrality, involve itself even more with society than it has in the past. In the twentieth century, the monarchy, according to one historian, has

made a genuine contribution to national well-being, but one which is largely ignored or misunderstood . . . It may sound curious to those obsessed by constitutional niceties or royal spectacles, but the humdrum, day-in day-out charitable activity of the monarchy may be far more important than the 'dignified' duties.

The philanthropic and charitable work undertaken by the royal family 'may lack mystery, but . . . serves the country by propping up *civil society*, that commonwealth of citizenship outside the state', and also 'pinpoints social needs otherwise ignored by government and offers a voice to minorities and other deprived groups which are little represented politically'. This kind of work has been associated with the monarchy since the late eighteenth century, but it is only at the end of the twentieth century that it has come to assume fundamental importance. It may be seen as

the most important development in the history of the monarchy over the past 200 years . . . By allying itself to prominent philanthropic causes, the monarchy raised its prestige and reaffirmed its importance in a time when it was retiring from national politics. . . . Nothing has done more to democratise the monarchy or make it more visible in this century than its voluntary work.[7]

In our own times, this 'welfare conception' of monarchy has been well understood and developed by the Prince of Wales, who has involved himself in work for the disadvantaged—the unemployed, the disabled, and members of ethnic minorities—through the various Prince's Trusts which he has established. In seeking to help those regarded by society as outsiders, he has enabled the monarchy to reach out to groups for whom hitherto it might have appeared irrelevant. In his work for race relations, for example, the Prince of Wales has made a powerful statement of the need for tolerance and understanding between different ethnic groups and creeds.[8] This is a striking example of how the influence of the monarchy can be brought into play without in the least compromising its political neutrality.

It is in this direction, in the practical employment of its symbolic influence, that the monarchy will find its future. The two elements—

---

[7] Frank Prochaska, 'But the Greatest of These—Civil Society and the "Welfare Monarchy"', *Times Literary Supplement*, 15 Jan. 1993, p. 15. Dr Prochaska's book *Royal Bounty: The Rise of the Welfare Monarchy*, was published by Yale University Press in 1995.

[8] Edward VII through his friendships did a great deal to encourage toleration towards Jews at the beginning of the century.

the symbolic and the practical—need to be more closely intertwined. The symbolic position of the monarchy, its mystique and its magic, are no longer sufficient, by themselves, to sustain it in the questioning world of today. The practical aspect, however, is only possible because of the monarchy's symbolic role. A politician must inevitably be a spokesperson for only part of the nation, not the whole. A politician's motives will always be suspected. Members of the royal family, by contrast, because of their symbolic position, are able to speak to a much wider constituency than can be commanded by even the most popular political leader. Thus, while, in the past, monarchy could content itself with being seen, today it needs not only to be *seen*; it has also to *do*.

It is perhaps idle to argue in the abstract whether constitutional monarchy is in general a desirable form of government. Whether it is regarded as desirable depends, after all, less on general principles than on popular attitudes, which will differ from nation to nation. In the modern world, constitutional monarchs, deprived of power, rest essentially upon opinion. 'I think it is a complete misconception', the Duke of Edinburgh suggested in Canada in 1969, 'to imagine that the monarchy exists in the interests of the monarch. It doesn't. It exists in the interests of the people.'[9] As the twentieth century draws to a close, constitutional monarchy survives in a small number of favoured nations mainly in Western Europe, in which, far from undermining democracy, it serves to sustain and to strengthen democratic institutions; and, if the conjunction of monarchy and democracy may seem a contradiction, it would be well to bear in mind Freud's aphorism that it is only in logic that contradictions cannot exist.

[9] Cited in J. D. B. Miller, *Survey of Commonwealth Affairs* (Oxford University Press, 1974), 421.

APPENDIX 1
SOVEREIGNS SINCE HENRY VIII

—■◆■—

Henry VIII	1509–47
Edward VI	1547–53
Mary I	1553–8
Elizabeth I	1558–1603
James I (VI of Scotland)	1603–25
Charles I	1625–49
Commonwealth	1649–60
Charles II	1660–85
James II	1685–8
William III	1689–1702,
and Mary II	1689–94
Anne	1702–14
George I	1714–27
George II	1727–60
George III	1760–1820
George IV	1820–30
William IV	1830–7
Victoria	1837–1901
Edward VII	1901–10
George V	1910–36
Edward VIII	January–December 1936
George VI	1936–52
Elizabeth II	1952–

APPENDIX 2
PRIME MINISTERS SINCE 1782

Marquess of Rockingham	March–July 1782
Earl of Shelburne	1782–3
Duke of Portland	April–December 1783
William Pitt	1783–1801
Henry Addington	1801–4
William Pitt	1804–6
Lord Grenville	1806–7
Duke of Portland	1807–9
Spencer Perceval	1809–12
Earl of Liverpool	1812–27
George Canning	April–September 1827
Viscount Goderich	1827–8
Duke of Wellington	1828–30
Earl Grey	1830–4
Viscount Melbourne	July–December 1834
Sir Robert Peel	1834–5
Viscount Melbourne	1835–41
Sir Robert Peel	1841–6
Lord John Russell	1846–52
Earl of Derby	February–December 1852
Earl of Aberdeen	1852–5.
Viscount Palmerston	1855–8.
Earl of Derby	1858–9
Viscount Palmerston	1859–65
Earl Russell	1865–6
Earl of Derby	1866–8
Benjamin Disraeli	February–December 1868
W. E. Gladstone	1868–74
Benjamin Disraeli	1874–80
W. E. Gladstone	1880–5
Marquess of Salisbury	1885–6
W. E. Gladstone	February–August 1886
Marquess of Salisbury	1886–92
W. E. Gladstone	1892–4
Earl of Rosebery	1894–5

Marquess of Salisbury	1895–1902
A. J. Balfour	1902–5
Sir Henry Campbell-Bannerman	1905–8
H. H. Asquith	1908–16
David Lloyd George	1916–22
A. Bonar Law	1922–3
Stanley Baldwin	1923–4
Ramsay MacDonald	January–November 1924
Stanley Baldwin	1924–9
Ramsay MacDonald	1929–35
	(National Government from 1931)
Stanley Baldwin	1935–7
Neville Chamberlain	1937–40
Winston Churchill	1940–5
C. R. Attlee	1945–51
Winston Churchill	1951–5
Sir Anthony Eden	1955–7
Harold Macmillan	1957–63
Sir Alec Douglas-Home	1963–4
Harold Wilson	1964–70
Edward Heath	1970–4
Harold Wilson	1974–6
James Callaghan	1976–9
Margaret Thatcher	1979–90
John Major	1990–

APPENDIX 3
PRIVATE SECRETARIES SINCE 1870

Colonel (later Sir) Henry Ponsonby	1870–1895
Sir Arthur Bigge	1895–1901
Sir Francis (later Viscount) Knollys	1901–1910
Viscount Knollys and Sir Arthur Bigge (later Lord Stamfordham), joint private secretaries	1910–1913
Lord Stamfordham	1913–1931
Sir Clive (later Lord) Wigram	1931–1936
Sir Alexander Hardinge	1936–1943
Sir Alan Lascelles	1943–1953
Sir Michael Adeane	1953–1972
Sir Martin Charteris	1972–1977
Sir Philip Moore	1977–1986
Sir William Heseltine	1986–1990
Sir Robert Fellowes	1990–

APPENDIX 4
MEMBER STATES OF THE COMMONWEALTH, 1995

———◦◆◦———

Monarchies under Queen Elizabeth II	Indigenous Monarchies	Republics
Antigua and Barbuda (1981)	Brunei (Sultanate) (1984)	Bangladesh (1971)
Australia*	Lesotho (1966)	Botswana (1965, 1966)
The Bahamas (1973)	Malaysia (1957)†	Cyprus (1960)
Barbados (1966)	Swaziland (1968)	Dominica (1978)
Belize (1981)	Tonga (1970)	The Gambia (1965, 1970)
Canada*	Western Samoa (Paramount Chief) (1962)	Ghana (1957, 1960)
Grenada (1974)		Guyana (1960, 1970)
Jamaica (1962)		India (1947, 1950)
New Zealand*		Kenya (1963, 1964)
Papua New Guinea (1975)		Kiribati (1979)
St Christopher and Nevis (1983)		Malawi (1964, 1966)
St Lucia (1979)		Maldives (1965)
St Vincent and Grenadines (1979)		Malta (1964, 1974)
Solomon Islands (1978)		Mauritius (1968, 1992)
Tuvalu (1978)		Namibia (1990)

Monarchies under Queen Elizabeth II	Indigenous Monarchies	Republics
United Kingdom		Nauru (1968)
		Nigeria (1960, 1963)
		Pakistan‡ (1947, 1956)
		Seychelles (1961, 1966)
		Sierra Leone (1961, 1971)
		Singapore (1965)
		South Africa‡ (1910, 1961)
		Sri Lanka (1948, 1972)
		Tanzania§ (1964)
		Trinidad and Tobago (1962, 1976)
		Uganda (1962, 1967)
		Zambia (1964)
		Zimbabwe (1980)
		Cameroon (1995)
		Mozambique (1995)

Note: The date of independence is cited, and, where appropriate and where it differs from the date of independence, the date on which the member becomes a republic.

* Opinions differ about the years in which Canada, Australia and New Zealand became independent.

† The Federation of Malaya became an independent country within the Commonwealth in 1957, but adopted the name Malaysia in 1963.

‡ Pakistan left the Commonwealth in 1972, but returned in 1989. South Africa left the Commonwealth on becoming a republic in 1961, but returned in 1994, following the election of a multi-racial government.

§ The state of Tanzania was formed from the union of Tanganyika with Zanzibar in 1964. Tanganyika became independent and a member of the Commonwealth in 1961 and a republic within the Commonwealth in 1962. Zanzibar became independent within the Commonwealth in 1963.

APPENDIX 5
SOME CONSTITUTIONAL EPISODES
INVOLVING THE USE OF ROYAL POWER
SINCE 1900

—•❖•—

1909   December. Edward VII refuses to promise to create peers until after a second general election

1910   November. George V agrees to give a secret pledge to create peers, if necessary, to pass the Parliament Bill

1914   George V implies that he might either veto the Home Rule Bill or dismiss his ministers

1916   Buckingham Palace Conference to select new prime minister following the resignation of H. H. Asquith

1922   First local governor-general, Tim Healy, in the Irish Free State

1924   January. George V asks Ramsay MacDonald to form first minority Labour government

1926   Lord Byng, the governor general of Canada, refuses a dissolution to Mackenzie King. King resigns and is succeeded by Arthur Meighen, the leader of the opposition. Meighen's government is granted a dissolution. Mackenzie King wins the ensuing general election

1926   Balfour formula, by which allegiance to the Crown becomes the constitutional link between the Dominions

1930   First local governor-general of Australia, Sir Isaac Isaacs

1931   August. George V invites Ramsay MacDonald to form a National Government

1931   Statute of Westminster

1932   First dismissal of a governor-general when de Valera, prime minister of the Irish Free State, dismisses James McNeill

1936   Abdication

1939   Sir Patrick Duncan, governor-general of South Africa, after ascertaining that General Smuts would be able to form a government, refuses dissolution to General Hertzog, who had been defeated in parliament, and was in a minority in his cabinet

1949   Declaration of London, by which the king becomes Head of the Commonwealth

1957   Elizabeth II appoints Harold Macmillan as prime minister, rather than R. A. Butler

1963 Elizabeth II appoints Lord Home as prime minister, rather than R. A. Butler, Lord Hailsham, or Reginald Maudling

1975 Sir John Kerr, governor-general of Australia, dismisses the prime minister, Gough Whitlam, for seeking to govern without supply

1983 Sir Paul Scoon, governor-general of Grenada, assumes emergency powers

1987 Elizabeth II issues two messages in her capacity as Queen of Fiji, acting without advice

SELECT BIBLIOGRAPHY

Private Papers

Birmingham University Library
  Avon Papers
  Chamberlain Papers
Bodleian Library
  Dawson Papers
  Rumbold Papers
  Simon Papers
British Library
  Balfour Papers
House of Lords Record Office
  Beaverbrook Papers
  Samuel Papers
India Office Library
  Zetland Papers
Lambeth Palace Library
  Davidson Papers
Public Record Office
  MacDonald papers
Royal Archives
  George V Papers
  George VI Papers
  Knollys Papers

Published Works

Two good introductions to the study of the monarchy are *The Oxford Illustrated History of the British Monarchy*, edited by John Cannon and Ralph Griffiths (Oxford University Press, 1988), and *The Royal Encyclopedia*, edited by Ronald Allison and Sarah Riddell (Macmillan, 1991).

Of historical works, the following are perhaps the most useful: Betty

Kemp, *King and Commons, 1660–1832* (Macmillan, 1957), H. J. Hanham, *The Nineteenth Century Constitution: Documents and Commentary* (Cambridge University Press, 1969), and G. H. L. LeMay, *The Victorian Constitution: Conventions, Usages and Contingencies* (Duckworth, 1979). There is still no perfectly satisfactory life of Queen Victoria; the best of a large number is probably Monica Charlot, *Victoria, The Young Queen* (Blackwell, 1991), the first of two volumes. But Dorothy Thompson, *Queen Victoria: Gender and Power* (Virago, 1990), is also stimulating. *The Letters of Queen Victoria* (1st ser., ed. A. C. Benson and Viscount Esher (3 vols.; John Murray, 1907); 2nd ser., ed. G. E. Buckle (3 vols.; John Murray, 1926–8); 3rd ser., ed. G. E. Buckle (3 vols.; John Murray, 1930–2) are an indispensable source. On the Prince Consort, there is Robert Rhodes James, *Albert, Prince Consort* (Hamish Hamilton, 1983).

Harold Nicolson, *King George V: His Life and Reign* (Constable, 1952), is a fine account of a sovereign who had to face numerous constitutional crises. It can be supplemented by Kenneth Rose, *King George V* (Weidenfeld & Nicolson, 1983). On George VI, Sir John Wheeler-Bennett, *King George VI: His Life and Reign* (Macmillan, 1958), is the official biography. Sarah Bradford, *George VI* (Fontana paperback edn., 1991), yields a good deal more. On Edward VIII, the official biography is by Philip Ziegler (Collins, 1990), but more perceptive—indeed one of the most perceptive books on the monarchy ever written—is *Edward VIII* by Frances Donaldson (Weidenfeld & Nicolson, 1974). Edward VIII's autobiography, written as HRH the Duke of Windsor, *A King's Story* (Cassell, 1951), is the only autobiography written by a modern British sovereign, but it has little on constitutional questions. On Elizabeth II, the best of a large number of biographies are *Elizabeth R.* by Elizabeth Longford (Weidenfeld & Nicolson, 1983), Kenneth Harris, *The Queen* (Weidenfeld & Nicolson, 1994), Sarah Bradford, *Elizabeth* (Heinemann 1996), and Ben Pimlott, *The Queen*, (HarperCollins 1996). Antony Jay, *Elizabeth R* (BBC Books, 1992), a book produced to mark the fortieth anniversary of the accession, is highly perceptive. Jonathan Dimbleby, *The Prince of Wales: A Biography* (Little, Brown, 1994), is an important work and deserves more serious consideration than it has yet received.

Of the vast mass of books on the monarchy, few have much to say on constitutional issues. On the role of the monarchy, chapters II and III of Bagehot's *The English Constitution* are a classical source, while Ivor Jennings, in *Cabinet Government* (3rd edn., Cambridge University Press, 1959), collected the major precedents as they existed up to the time he was writing. These are of less value than they might seem. Frank Hardie, *The Political Influence of the British Monarchy 1868–1952* (Batsford, 1970), is the only book of its kind, but it does not dig very deep. Textbooks of constitutional law such as E. C. S. Wade and A. W. Bradley, *Constitutional and*

Administrative Law, 11th edn., ed. A. W. Bradley and K. D. Ewing (Longman, 1993), and S. A. de Smith and Rodney Brazier, *Constitutional and Administrative Law* (6th edn., Penguin, 1989), reprint the standard ideas without thinking about what lies behind them. More useful are two modern works, Geoffrey Marshall, *Constitutional Conventions* (Oxford University Press, 1984), and Rodney Brazier, *Constitutional Practice* (Oxford University Press, 1988). There are, also, two useful books on the dissolution of parliament: Eugene A. Forsey, *The Royal Power of Dissolution in the British Commonwealth* (Oxford University Press, Toronto, 1943), and B. S. Markesinis, *The Theory and Practice of Dissolution of Parliament* (Cambridge University Press, 1972). Also of value is H. V. Evatt, *The King and His Dominion Governors* (2nd edn., Frank Cass, 1967). Two of these books have been conveniently collected into one edition as *Evatt and Forsey on the Reserve Powers* (Legal Books, Sydney, 1990).

But one of the best ways to study the monarchy is by looking at various constitutional crises. For the years 1909–14, the four volumes of *Journals and Letters of Reginald, Viscount Esher*, edited by Maurice V. Brett and Oliver, Viscount Esher (Ivor Nicholson & Watson, 1934–8), are quite indispensable, as well as being highly enjoyable reading. The last chapter of LeMay, *The Victorian Constitution* (cited above), also contains a valuable account of 'The Crisis of the Constitution'. Reginald Bassett, *1931 Political Crisis* (Macmillan, 1958), is a standard work, but the account in Graeme C. Moodie, 'The Monarch and the Selection of a Prime Minister: A Re-examination of the Crisis of 1931', *Political Studies*, 5 (1957), 1–20, is also worth reading. See also Vernon Bogdanor, '1931 Revisited: The Constitutional Aspects', in *Twentieth Century British History*, 4 (1991), 1–25. John D. Fair, *British Interparty Conferences: A Study of the Procedure of Conciliation in British Politics 1867–1921* (Oxford University Press, 1980), is a valuable account, *inter alia*, of the sovereign's role as a mediator at inter-party conferences.

On hung parliaments, there is Vernon Bogdanor, *Multi-Party Politics and the Constitution* (Cambridge University Press, 1983); and David Butler, *Governing without a Majority* (2nd edn., Macmillan, 1987). Also worth looking at is a highly perceptive article by A. H. Birch entitled 'Britain's Impending Constitutional Dilemmas', *Parliamentary Affairs*, 37 (1984), 97–101.

On the financing of the monarchy, E. A. Reitan, 'The Civil List in Eighteenth Century British Politics: Parliamentary Supremacy versus the Independence of the Crown', *Historical Journal*, 9 (1966), 318–37, is an excellent introduction to the historical background. Philip Hall, *Royal Fortune: Tax, Money and the Monarchy* (Bloomsbury, 1992), is a scholarly, if hostile, account of the history of the royal finances. It was criticized from an informed standpoint in an article 'Should One Pay Tax?', *The*

Economist, 25 Jan. 1992, p. 36. The reports of the various twentieth-century Select Committees on the Civil List are also worth consulting for detailed historical information.

On the queen's private secretary, the basic source is appendix B of Wheeler-Bennett's life of George VI. Paul H. Emden, *Behind the Throne* (Hodder & Stoughton, 1934), is also of interest on the history of the office. Kenneth Rose, *Kings, Queens and Courtiers: Intimate Portraits of the Royal House of Windsor from its Foundation to the Present Day* (Weidenfeld & Nicolson, 1985), offers the gossipy view of an insider; while Arthur Ponsonby's account of his father, *Henry Ponsonby, Queen Victoria's Private Secretary: His Life from his Letters* (Macmillan, 1943), is the only biography so far written of a private secretary; but Helen Hardinge, *Loyal To Three Kings* (William Kimber, 1967), is a highly perceptive account of the life of Edward VIII's private secretary by his wife. There is an interesting review of Ponsonby's biography by Harold Laski in the *Fortnightly Review* (1942). The queen's then private secretary, Sir Michael Adeane, gave evidence to the Select Committee on the Civil List, whose Report, HC 29, 1971–2, contains a good deal of information on the queen's everyday duties.

On the Church of England, the basic sources are E. Garth Moore and Timothy Briden, *Moore's Introduction to English Canon Law*, 3rd edn., ed. Timothy Briden and Brian Hanson (Mowbray, London, 1992), and St John A. Robilliard, *Religion and the Law: Religious Liberty in Modern English Law* (Manchester University Press, 1984). Also of importance is *Church and State: The Report of the Archbishop's Commission* (The Chadwick Report) (Church Information Service, 1970). Two contrasting views on the Church of England are John Habgood, *Church and Nation in a Secular Age* (Darton, Longman, & Todd, 1983), which argues the case for establishment, and Colin Buchanan, *Cut the Connection: Disestablishment and the Church of England* (Darton, Longman, & Todd, 1994), which argues the case against. On the Church of Scotland, there is F. Lyall, *Of Kings and Presbyters* (Aberdeen University Press, 1980), and a useful article by T. M. Taylor, 'Church and State in Scotland', *Juridical Review* (1957), 121–37.

On the Commonwealth, Nicholas Mansergh, *The Commonwealth Experience*, first published by Weidenfeld & Nicolson in 1969 and then in two volumes by Macmillan in 1982, is an indispensable and brilliant historical account. There are two valuable constitutional commentaries by K. C. Wheare, *The Statute of Westminster and Dominion Status* (5th edn., Oxford University Press, 1953), and *The Constitutional Structure of the Commonwealth* (Oxford University Press, 1960). Sir William Dale, *The Modern Commonwealth* (Butterworth, 1983), is a standard legal work. On the role of the governor-general, Sir John Kerr, *Matters for Judgment* (Macmillan, 1979), is valuable even for those who believe that he took the wrong course in 1975.

There are two valuable books on governor-generals and constitutional heads in the Commonwealth: D. A. Low (ed.), *Constitutional Heads and Political Crises: Commonwealth Episodes, 1945–1985* (Macmillan, 1988), and David Butler and D. A. Low (eds.), *Sovereigns and Surrogates: Constitutional Heads of State in the Commonwealth* (Macmillan, 1991). Sir Paul Hasluck's Queale Lecture, *The Office of Governor-General* (2nd edn., Melbourne University Press, 1979), offers his reflections on the office. Also of value for the regions with which they deal are Sir Fred Phillips, *West Indies Constitutions: Post Independence Reform* (Oceana, New York, 1985), and Yash Ghai and Jill Cottrell, *Heads of State in the Pacific: A Constitutional and Legal Analysis* (Institute of Pacific Studies, USP, Suva, 1990). See also Vernon Bogdanor and Geoffrey Marshall, 'Dismissing Governor-Generals', *Public Law*, (1996), 205–213.

On the Australian republican debate, the best introduction is George Winterton, *Monarchy to Republic: Australian Republican Government* (Oxford University Press, Melbourne, 1986). There is also a special issue of the *Australian Journal of Political Science* (1993), devoted to the topic. Malcolm Turnbull, *The Reluctant Republic* (Heinemann, Port Melbourne, 1993), argues the case for the republic, while the Turnbull Report, the Report of the Republican Advisory Committee in Australia, *An Australian Republic* (2 vols.; Canberra, 1993), shows how it might be achieved.

Attacks on the monarchy can be found in William Hamilton, *My Queen and I* (Quartet Books, 1975), Tom Nairn, *The Enchanted Glass: Britain and its Monarchy* (Radius (Century Hutchinson), 1988), and Stephen Haseler, *The End of the House of Windsor: Birth of a British Republic* (I. B. Tauris & Co. Ltd, 1993).

INDEX

Abdication 44, 58–9, 135–44, 179, 200,
   205–9, 248, 249, 269, 289
Aberdeen, Lord 25
Accession Declaration Act (1910) 43
Act of Settlement (1701) 6–8, 43–5, 54, 57,
   120
Act of Supremacy (1559) 219
Act of Uniformity (1662) 219, 224
Acts of Union with Scotland (1707) 44, 47,
   215, 216
Adeane, Sir Michael 94–5
advice 54, 65–8, 71, 74, 78, 136, 138, 142–3,
   200–1, 227, 232–3
Agricultural Party (Canada) 156, 159
Albert, Prince Consort 19–21, 23–8, 36–7,
   46, 51, 52, 61, 199
Allard, Henry 174
Anglo-Saxon monarchy 2
Anne, Queen 7, 51, 114, 126
Anson, Sir William 3, 9, 14, 67, 71, 125,
   237
apartheid 272–3
Apple Cart, The 121–2
Appointment of Ministers 32, 34
Appointment of Prime Minister 11, 12, 16,
   17–18, 22, 31, 32, 33, 35, 76, 78, 79,
   84–113, 151–7, 167–82
Archbishop of Canterbury 46, 58, 134, 203,
   212, 216, 227–8, 231
Asquith, H. H. 67, 68, 79, 99–101, 103,
   113–35, 150, 160, 203–5, 212, 301
Assent, Royal 49, 66–7, 74, 125–6, 129–32,
   223, 234
Attlee, C. R. 8, 87, 102, 139, 254, 264, 301
Australia 59, 70, 85–6, 141, 201, 208,
   247–51, 277–9, 280–2, 285–6, 290–7

Bagehot, Walter 26, 30, 37, 40–1, 62, 69,
   70, 72, 73, 74, 133, 201, 303, 305
Baldwin, Stanley 75, 77, 79, 90–3, 105–12,
   136–44, 148–9, 152, 154–6, 161, 179,
   200, 206–7, 288
Balfour, A. J. (Lord Balfour) 39, 79, 90–1,
   100, 117–18, 123, 126–7, 203–5, 245–6,
   253, 255–6, 279
Balfour Formula (1926) 245–8, 255, 258,
   277, 281, 295

Beaverbrook, Lord 135–6, 139, 144
'Bedchamber incident' (1839) 20, 199
Belgium 75, 167–72
Belize 278
Bell, George 227–8
Bengtson, Torsten 174
Bengtsson, Ingemund 174
Benn, Tony 45, 120, 274
Bentinck, Lord George 23
Bill of Rights (1689) 5–8, 43, 234–5
Blair, Tony 164
Blake, Lord 94, 150
Bloomfield, Sir Benjamin 198
Bonar Law, Andrew 79, 90, 100, 106, 121,
   122, 124, 125, 127, 134, 160
Bradlaugh, Charles 28
Bradley, A. W. 150, 152
Brandt, Willy 176
Bridges, Sir Edward 99, 132
British Nationality Act (1948) 251–2
Brook, Sir Norman 255, 257
Brougham, Lord 21
Brown, George 88
Bruce, Stanley 208
Buckingham Palace Conferences:
   (1914) 77, 134
   (1916) 99, 100–1
   (1931) 99, 107–8
Buckley, Donal 281
Bulwer-Lytton, Edward 135
Burdett, Sir Francis 17
Burke, Edmund 12, 184, 220
Burma 253–4, 270
Butler, R. A. 87–90, 93–9
Byng, Lord 156, 158–9, 161

Callaghan, James 73, 78, 80, 85, 233, 273
Campbell-Bannerman, Sir Henry 36, 79,
   160
Canada 38–9, 54, 59, 141, 156, 158–9, 161,
   207, 242, 245, 248–51, 261, 262
Cannadine, David 37
Canning, George 15
Caretaker Government 86–7, 147
Carey, George 228, 231
Caroline, Queen 51, 58
Casey, Lord 280

Catholic Emancipation 12, 14, 15
Chadwick, Owen 231
Chalker, Lady 304
Chamberlain, Sir Austen 54
Chamberlain, Joseph 28, 29, 34, 243, 256
Chamberlain, Neville 68, 92, 99, 101–3, 105, 138, 200
Chanak crisis 245
Chandos, Lord 79, 95
Charles I 53, 183
Charles II 7
Chartism 30
Chief Rabbi 230–1
Chifley, Ben 86
Chotek, Countess Sophie 56, 141
Church appointments 226–7, 232–3
Church of England 7, 44, 58–9, 138–9, 215–39, 248
    General Synod of 223–6, 232, 234, 236, 238
    see also Supreme Governor; van Straubenzee Report
Church of England Assembly (Powers) Act (1919) (Enabling Act) 222–5
Church of England (Worship and Doctrine) Measure (1974) 224–5
Church of Scotland 7, 44–7, 215–17, 233–9
Church of Scotland Act (1921) 216, 237
    General Assembly of 234, 237–8
Churchill Winston 55, 56, 57, 67, 68, 79, 86–7, 89, 92, 95, 99, 101–3, 139–40, 142–3, 150, 159, 227–8
Civil List 57, 183–8, 190, 192, 194–6, 199, 210, 288
    Select Committees on 186–7
Civil List Act (1697) 7, 183–4
Clarendon, Lord 23
Coalition government 12, 25, 35, 89, 99–112, 145, 150–2, 156, 165
Colonial Conference (1887) 243, 303
Colonial Conference (1897) 303
Colville, Sir John 86–7
Commonwealth 40, 45, 47, 49, 57, 59, 74, 80, 141, 189, 193, 201–2, 210, 240–97, 303–4, 306
    Heads of Government meetings 271, 273
    rules of membership 270
    secession from Commonwealth 254, 270, 272
    Secretariat 271
Commonwealth Prime Ministers Conferences:
    (1947) 251, 261
    (1949) 258–9, 263
    (1952) 268–9
Commune Concilium 3
Conservatives, Conservative Party 17, 18,

19, 22, 23, 29, 30, 31, 32, 35, 68, 82–3, 85, 89, 90–106, 113–24, 146–7, 149, 153–7, 301–2
Conventions, constitutional 13, 14, 64, 81, 136–7, 153–4, 163–9, 178–82
Corn Laws, repeal of 22, 23
Coronoation Oath Act (1689) 6, 43
Costello, J. A. 254
Council of State, Counsellor of State 46–50, 54
Craik, Sir Henry 124
Cranborne, Viscount 225
Crewe, Lord 130, 212
Cripps, Sir Stafford 112, 253
crises, constitutional:
    (1909–11) 113–22, 178–82
    (1914) 77, 178–82
    (1931) 29, 89, 104–12, 160, 178–82
    (1936) 44, 58–9, 135–44, 178–82, 200, 205–9, 248, 249, 269, 289
Crown Appointments Commission 226–7
Crowther-Hunt, Lord 149
Crozier, W. P. 103
Curtin, John 86
Curzon, Lord 75, 79, 90–3, 179

Dalton, Hugh 102
Dawson, Geoffrey 92, 207–8
Declaration of Abdication Act (1936) 44, 143
de Gaulle, Charles 54, 61
Denmark 42, 167–9
deputy prime minister 86–9
de Valera 141, 253, 257, 281–2, 284–5
Dicey, A. V. 64, 132, 133, 224, 235
Dilke, Sir Charles 28–30, 34, 39
Dimbleby, Jonathan 52, 53, 54
disestablishment of the Church 215, 220–1, 222–3, 228–9, 239
dismissal of Prime Minister 13, 17–19, 70, 125–6, 129, 132–3, 202, 277–8, 282, 284–6, 291–2
Disraeli, Benjamin 21, 26, 27, 30, 32, 37, 38, 69, 112, 148, 200, 302, 303, 305
    Coningsby 38
    Sybil 112
dissolution of Parliament 17, 21, 22, 49, 76, 78, 79–83, 100, 106, 111–12, 115, 118–19, 121, 157–66, 168–82, 202
divorce 58, 136–8, 206
Dominion, Dominion Status 40, 243–50, 253, 255, 269, 289, 302
Duchy of Cornwall 186, 191–2
Duchy of Lancaster 186, 188, 191
Duff Cooper 139
Duncan, Sir Patrick 161
Durham Report 242

Eden, Sir Anthony 57, 79, 86–8, 93–4, 101
Edinburgh, Duke of 48, 52, 54, 186, 192, 296, 309
Edward I 4, 52
Edward II 219
Edward VI 45, 6
Edward VII 29, 36, 39, 53, 113–15, 117, 120, 191, 203, 211–13
Edward VIII (later Duke of Windsor) 44–5, 48, 52–4, 56–7, 68, 70, 73, 102–3, 135–44, 200, 205–13, 307
Edward the Confessor 3
Egbert, King of Wessex 2
Elizabeth I 219
Elizabeth II 41, 45, 47, 52, 53, 68, 72, 73, 93–9, 186–8, 263, 265–7, 302, 306, 307
Elizabeth, Queen, the Queen Mother 48, 55, 192
Empire 240–1, 256, 303–4
Empress of India 32, 39, 302
Esher, Lord 70, 71, 75, 129, 204, 211
Established Church 215–17, 210–39, 248
European Union 304–5
Evatt, Dr Herbert 291
Ewing, K. D. 150, 152

Fiji 270, 287
Fisher, Geoffrey 227–8
Fitzherbert, Mrs Maria 55–6
Ford, Sir Edward 49
Forde, F. M. 86
Formateur 171–2
Forster, W. E. 40
Fox, Charles James 12, 23, 46
Fox-North Coalition 12
Franz Ferdinand, Archduke 56, 141

Gandhi, Mrs Indira 265–6
GATT (General Agreement on Tariffs and Trade) (1947) 261
general elections:
(1784) 12
(1835) 17–18
(1841) 20–2, 27
(1868) 27, 148
(1880) 31
(1906) 221
January (1910) 113, 145, 152
December (1910) 115–18, 145, 152
(1923) 145, 148, 152–4
(1929) 145, 152, 155
(1931) 110–12
February (1974) 145–7, 149, 152, 178
October (1974) 145, 163
George I 7, 9, 14, 44, 58, 269
George II 7, 10, 11, 44, 46, 55, 60

George III 7, 9–15, 19, 22, 36, 46, 55, 184, 198, 302
George IV 15, 19, 36–7, 51, 58, 198
George V 19, 41, 46, 47, 54, 65, 67, 68, 70, 72, 74, 76, 77, 90–3, 99–103, 104–12, 113, 115–35, 152, 154, 159–60, 179, 191, 194, 195, 203, 211–14, 247, 253, 280, 281, 284, 299, 303, 306, 308
George VI 41, 44, 46–7, 49, 53, 60, 76, 87, 88, 92, 99, 143, 144, 179, 191, 194, 200, 202, 206, 209, 213–14, 250, 253, 263–4, 267, 303, 306
Gladstone, W. E. 19, 24, 27, 30–4, 148, 200, 221, 301
'Glorious Revolution' (1689) 5, 8, 10
Gordon, General Charles 32
Gordon Walker, Patrick 287–90
Gorton, John 86, 280
governor–general 86, 158–9, 201–2, 207, 246–7, 277–8, 280–7, 291–4
appointment of 50, 246, 280–7
dismissal of 50, 281–7
grant-in-aid 185, 187, 190
Grenada 278, 283
Grenville, Lord 13
Greville, Charles 20, 23, 24
Grey, Earl 16
Grey, Sir Edward 123
Grey, General 19–200

Habgood, John 228, 231
Hailsham, Lord 90, 95, 97, 225, 301
Haldane, Lord 121
Halifax, 1st Viscount 30
Halifax, 3rd Viscount 76, 92, 99, 101–3
Harcourt, Sir William 33
Hardinge, Sir Alexander 200, 205–14
Harewood, Earl of 56
Harmsworth, Esmond 140
Harrison, Frederic 29, 30
Hartington, Lord 31, 33, 98
Harvey, Sir Ernest 106
Hasluck, Sir Paul 202, 280–1
Hastings, Lady Flora 199
Hayden, Bill 280–1, 293–4
Head of the Commonwealth 40, 50, 74, 185, 258, 263–8, 270, 273–5, 296–7, 301, 306
Healy, Tim 247
Heath, Edward 72, 78, 80, 95, 148–50, 266
Henderson, Arthur 100, 104
Henry I 3
Henry VIII 46, 218–19, 237
Hernelius, Allan 174
Hertzog, Gen. J. B. M. 81, 82, 161
Heseltine, Sir William 85, 286
Hitler, Adolf 64, 103, 299

Hoare, Sir Samuel 108
Holland, Sidney 291
Holt, Harold 86
Holyoake, Sir Keith 280–1
Home, Lord 84–5, 90, 95–9
Home Rule 32, 35, 65, 70, 74, 77, 115, 122–35, 178–9
Hopwood, Sir Francis 131, 134
Houghton, Douglas 188–9, 195
Howe, Sir Geoffrey 8, 87
Hurd, Douglas 85

Idi Amin 261, 273, 274
Imperial Conferences:
  (1923) 245
  (1926) 245–7, 262
  (1930) 47, 50–1
Imperial Federation 243–4
Imperial War Conference (1917) 244
imperialism 31, 38–9
India 38, 102, 250, 253–62, 265–6, 301
informateur 168, 170–2
Inskip, Sir Thomas 284
Institute of Public Policy Research 168, 175
'invention of tradition' 37–8, 303
Ireland 250, 253, 254, 255, 257, 260, 270, 295
  External Relations Act (Ireland) (1936) 249–50, 253
  Irish Free State 9, 47, 141, 247, 251, 281–2
  Irish Republic 63, 64
  Irish Nationalists 113, 115, 122–35, 148, 163
Isaacs, Sir Isaac 247, 280, 284

James II 5–7, 135, 234–5
James, Sir Robert Rhodes 82–3
Jennings, Sir Ivor 68, 77, 82, 178
John, King 4
Jordan 279, 290

Kerr, Sir John 70, 202, 277–8, 282, 284, 285–6, 291–2
Kilmuir, Lord 94–5
Knighton, Sir William 198
Knollys, Lord 36, 114, 116–17, 119, 121, 133, 200, 203–5, 211–12
Kohl, Helmut 176

Labor Party (Australia) 86, 291–7
Labour Party 29, 68, 76, 80, 85, 88, 89, 101–2, 104–12, 120, 139, 142, 146–8, 150, 153–7, 164, 210, 300
Labouchere, Henry 34
Lambeth Palace Conference 117, 212
Lange, David 275

Lascelles, Sir Alan 99, 132, 158–60, 194, 214
Laski, Harold 29, 50–1, 71–2, 109, 112, 210–11
League of Nations 245
Lehzen, Baroness 199
Liberals, Liberal Party, Liberal Democrat Party 19, 30, 31, 33, 35, 68, 99–101, 102, 106, 113–24, 145–7, 148–9, 152–7, 163–4, 180, 210
Lib.–Lab. pact (1977–8) 165
Lightman, Mr Justice 229
Liverpool, Lord 198
Lloyd George, David 6, 9, 52, 54, 67, 89, 100–1, 105, 109, 113, 191, 192, 221, 253, 301
London Declaration (1949) 258–60, 263, 268
Lyons, J. A. 85–6

Maastricht Treaty 304
Macaulay, T. B. 1, 8
MacDonald, Malcolm 252–3, 255
MacDonald, Ramsay 89, 104–12, 141, 150, 152, 160, 162, 179, 284
McEwen, John 86
Mackenzie King, W. L. 158–9, 245, 249
Macleod, Iain 97
MacMahon, Sir John 198
Macmahon, William 86
Macmillan Harold 54, 84–5, 87, 89, 90, 93–8
McNeill, James 281, 284
'magical monarchy' 305–9
Magna Carta 3, 4, 8, 218
Major, John 58, 82, 85, 191
Margaret, Princess 48, 54, 56, 58, 60
Margesson, David 99, 101–3
Marshall, Geoffrey 285
Mary I 219
Mary II, *see* William and Mary
Maudling, Reginald 88, 90, 95
Meighen, Arthur 156, 158–9, 161
Melbourne, Lord 10, 17, 19, 20–3, 33, 126, 199
Melville, Andrew 236
Menon, Krishna 264
Menzies, R. G. 86, 249, 272, 280, 290–1
Michael, Prince 55
minority government 79, 99, 106, 145, 146, 150, 151–2, 162–3, 175, 179
Mitchell, Rosslyn 224
Monckton, Sir Walter 209, 213
morganatic marriage 56, 136, 140–4
Morley, Lord 130, 133
Morrah, Dermot 91–2
Morrison, Herbert 88
Morshead, Sir Owen 131–2

multi-party system 76, 164–7, 177, 180–2
Munich Agreement (1938) 68

National Government (1931) 89, 104–12
Nehru, Pandit 257, 260, 263
Netherlands 169–72
New Zealand 141, 248, 249, 275, 280, 291
Newton, Tony 45
Norman monarchy 3
North, Lord 11, 13
Northern Ireland 146, 295
Norway 168–9

ordination of Women 226
Ottawa agreements (1932) 261

Page, Earle 85–6
Palmerston, Lord 14, 23, 25, 26
Parliament Act (1911), Parliament Bill
    115–25, 202, 212–13
Pearson, Lester 264
Peel, Sir Robert 16–23, 25, 33, 36, 191
Peers, creation of 113–22
Phillips, Sir Fred 281
Pitt, William the elder 11
Pitt, William the younger 11, 12, 13, 46
Ponsonby, Sir Frederick 195
Ponsonby, Sir Henry 20, 30, 31, 200, 203,
    210–11
Prince of Wales 41, 45, 48, 52–4, 58–9,
    191–2, 194–5, 230, 307–8
Princess of Wales 53, 58
Privy Purse 185, 187–8, 191, 199
proportional representation 154, 164–82

queen consort 51

Ram, Sir Granville 132
Redmond, John 130, 132–4
Rees-Mogg, William 98
Referendum 128
Reform Act (1832) 10, 16, 17, 23, 113, 114,
    198–9
Reformation 218–20, 222, 236–7
Regency 49, 50
Regency Acts:
    (1811) 46
    (1937) 47, 48
    (1943) 48
    (1953) 48
Regent 46, 48, 52
Republicanism 28–30, 144, 291–7, 300
responsible government 14, 15, 40, 241–3
Rhodesia (now Zimbabwe) 73
Robinson, Mary 63
Rockingham, Marquess of 11, 22

Rose, Kenneth 72–3
Rosebery, Lord 30, 33, 100, 134, 240
Royal Marriages Act (1772) 44–6, 55–60
Royal Titles Acts:
    (1876) 239, 302
    (1953) 51, 267–70, 287, 289–90
Rumbold, Sir Horace 106
Russell, Lord John 17, 22, 23, 24

St Laurent, Louis 262, 269–70
Salic law 42
Salisbury, 3rd Marquess of 30, 33, 37, 79,
    148, 243
Salisbury, 4th Marquess of 90
Salisbury, 5th Marquess of 57, 79, 87, 94
Samuel, Sir Herbert 105–12
Scoon, Sir Paul 278
Scullin, J. H. 280, 284
Seeley, J. R. 241
Shaw, Bernard 121–2
Simpson, Mrs Ernest (later the Duchess of
    Windsor) 55, 136–44, 179, 206–9, 248
Smith, Arnold 264, 266
Smith, John 164
Smuts, General Jan 81, 161, 244, 249
Snowden, Philip 222
Sophia, Princess, Electress of Hanover 7,
    44, 143,
South Africa 81, 141, 161, 248, 249, 259–60,
    267, 270, 272–3, 293, 296–7
Speaker 47, 172–4
Spencer, Lord 33
Stamfordham, Lord 90–3, 100, 101, 105–6,
    116–17, 127, 131, 132, 134, 202–5, 211,
    247
Stanley, Lord 26
Statute of Westminster (1931) 45, 143,
    246–8, 255–6, 258–9, 268–9, 279, 295
Stephen, Sir Ninian 281, 293
Stewart, Michael 88
Stockmar, Baron 24, 34, 36, 69
succession, rules of 5, 7, 8, 42–60, 269–70
Supreme Governor of Church of England
    44, 58, 138–9, 215–16, 219, 222, 230,
    232–3, 275, 306
Sweden 42, 59, 172–4

Tamworth Manifesto (1834) 17, 18
tax arrangements of royal family 191–4
Taylor, A. J. P. 295
Taylor, Sir Henry 198–9
Tebbit, Lord 304
Temple, William 227
Thatcher, Margaret 72, 78, 82–3, 85, 187,
    228, 265–7, 278, 305–6
Thorpe, Jeremy 149
Tories 15, 16, 20, 33, 199

Townsend, Group Captain Peter 56–8
Treaty of Union with Scotland (1707) 7,
235
Trevelyan, G. M. 198
Triennial Act (1694) 6
Turnbull, Malcolm 293–5
Tweedsmuir, Lord 207
two-party system 22, 76, 78, 154, 163, 166,
167

Uganda 261, 273
Ulster 122–35
Ulster Unionists 146–7, 149
uncodified constitution 1, 14, 63–4, 75, 111,
178–82, 279

van Straubenzee Report 232–3
Verwoerd, Hendrik 272
veto of legislation 12–13, 15–16, 70
Victoria, Queen 16, 17, 19–41, 43, 45–6,
51–2, 61, 72, 77, 98, 165, 191, 199, 202,
210–11, 221, 269, 302, 305–6
Vitzthum, Count 26

Waverley, Lord 79, 95
Weizsaecker, Richard von 63
'Welfare Monarchy' 307–9
Wellington, Duke of 1, 6, 20, 22
West, Harry 149
Whigs 14, 17–20, 32–4, 199
Whitelaw, William 88
Whitlam, Gough 70, 277–8, 282, 285–6,
291–2
Wigram, Sir Clive 106–8, 200, 284
William IV 17, 18, 19, 22, 33, 36–7, 46, 114,
126, 198–9
William the Conqueror 3
William and Mary 5, 6, 51, 53, 183, 234–5
Wilson, Harold 56, 80, 82, 85, 98, 150, 160,
162, 175, 301
Windsor, Duchess of, *see* Simpson, Mrs
Ernest
Windsor, Duke of, *see* Edward VIII
Witan 2–3

Zetland 142–3